MENTAL HEALTH AND HUMAN RELATIONS IN EDUCATION

EDUCATION FOR LIVING SERIES

Under the Editorship of

H. H. REMMERS

"... and I urge all parents and young people, and all other individuals, as well as agencies and organizations interested in the well-being of children, to increase their understanding of the emotional, social, and spiritual growth of children, so as to apply this understanding in their day-to-day relations with the rising generation."

—DWIGHT D. EISENHOWER, 1953

Mental Health
and
Human Relations
in
Education

by

LOUIS KAPLAN
University of Southern California

HARPER & BROTHERS · PUBLISHERS

New York

MENTAL HEALTH AND HUMAN RELATIONS IN EDUCATION

Library of Congress catalog card number: 58–11585

To My Wife, SALLY
and Our Sons
PAUL and STEVEN

CONTENTS

THAT mental illness is and has been for some decades our number one health problem is not news to those concerned with it professionally. It requires more than half of all available hospital beds for those who are hospitalized. Moreover, it is safe to say that large numbers of mentally ill persons are not hospitalized who should be. The cost of mental illness to society is staggering, to say nothing of the unhappiness and blighted lives it entails.

Despite this, other much less costly diseases receive much more attention in the mass media of communication and command much more financial support for research than does mental illness. It is almost as if society suffers from a kind of psychic blindness that leads to highly selective perception and gross distortion of reality, a distortion that makes it spend more for research on such animal diseases as hog cholera or Bangs disease in cattle than for research on mental disease in humans.

That maladjustment is learned—except for the minor portion related to organic impairment—just as truly as speech and school subjects are learned, provides the key for the major strategy for attacking it. Here indeed the ounce of prevention can be worth many pounds of cure. And the key agency for prevention then is, and must be, the process of education. Hence, it is in our schools that significant, indeed major, gains in mental health in the oncoming generation can be implemented.

Dr. Kaplan here has written an important book based on this premise. The evidence he has brought together will make clear to the reader the huge dimensions of the problem. The present state of our knowledge he reports with thorough scholarship and admirable lucidity. He not only surveys what is known about environmental and intrapersonal dynamic causal factors but also and, more important for prospective and practicing school personnel, he presents with a minimum of technicality ways and means of attacking the problem. In this the reader will be impressed both by his wisdom and his practicality.

The editor is pleased to see added to the series *Education for Living* another basically important book. The substance of its contents will, he hopes, soon be a part of the intellectual and emotional capital of most if not all school teachers and administrators as well as of more and more parents and their children. This capital invested in mentally healthful education of boys and girls will pay dividends beyond calculation in the form of happy, useful, constructive lives.

H. H. REMMERS

May, 1958

THE BASIC contention of this book is that schools have a function beyond the inculcation of knowledge and skills. They must also educate for mental health so that youngsters will learn to work together in wholesome and satisfying ways, and develop the capacity to live with themselves and with other people as mature and responsible citizens.

The schools of this nation are only beginning to accept the ideal of education for mental health and human relations. A generation ago such concepts were hardly mentioned in educational literature. Today there is an abundance of information regarding these important aspects of living, but relatively limited application of this material to the school experiences of children.

This textbook has sought to synthesize current knowledge and experience regarding mental health and human relations, and stimulate teachers, parents, and school officials to direct their efforts toward building a generation of youth who not only are well informed, but who can use their education for the enrichment of their own lives and the betterment of mankind. This is done in four parts:

Part I presents the problem of mental disorder and maladjustment in the United States, shows how it reaches into the school, and describes some of the efforts that have been made to meet this problem. This is done to identify the issues involved in making decisions regarding what schools should do.

Part II deals with environmental influences on the development of mental health and human relations. The home and the culture have such pervasive effects on personality development that it is quite unrealistic for schools to embark upon a mental hygiene program without comprehending fully the influence of environmental factors which operate outside of the classroom.

Part III describes the psychological forces of growth and the symptoms of behavior deviation in children. Insight into the factors which motivate behavior, the characteristics of normal behavior, and the symptoms of maladjustment is deemed essential for the intelligent management of children in school. An expert knowledge of the human organism and its responses to the environment will enable the teacher to take an increasingly intelligent role in shaping children's lives.

Part IV makes practical application of these principles in the school setting. Here knowledge of psychological, social, and cultural influences on human behavior is interpreted in terms of educational procedures and is applied to the mental health and human relations problems of teachers, parents, children, and school administrators.

This volume is designed as a textbook for courses in mental hygiene and human relations. It also contains sufficient material to make it useful in courses such as child psychology, educational psychology, and integrated courses which deal with the learner as a whole. The four parts of the book are relatively independent so that instructors may adapt the material to their particular needs. Individual teachers, parents, and others who are responsible for the mental health of children will find this arrangement especially useful since it permits concentration on those phases which are of primary concern to them.

The approach in this text is practical and applied, without sacrifice of fundamental concepts and principles. An attempt has been made to merge the various streams of knowledge and focus them on the school. In so doing, useless entanglement in theoretical controversy was avoided. Information from all sources was drawn upon freely and used to illuminate the problems discussed.

As in all texts which cover a broad field of human behavior, the author found it necessary to choose among the available materials. This has been done through careful study of the significant problems, and in terms of the author's 20 years of educational service. Some 700 references are included in this book, making it possible for instructors to encourage further investigation of any areas which may have been treated with less emphasis than they deserve.

LOUIS KAPLAN

Los Angeles, California
May, 1958

PART I

HOW SCHOOLS ARE CONCERNED WITH MENTAL HEALTH AND HUMAN RELATIONS

Since the turn of the century, technological progress has brought a new way of life to this nation. For many people it has improved the quality of living; for many others it has meant tragedy and breakdown. Scientific civilization, racing ahead at terrific speed, has left in its wake millions of human beings who could not adapt to the hectic pace of modern living. These are the disturbed, anxious, broken personalities who fill our mental hospitals and overflow into the communities of America.

In the midst of this scene stand the schools with their great power for shaping the citizens of tomorrow. Whether they take an active part in conserving human resources by contributing to the mental health of the nation's youth is a matter of great consequence.

The significance of the problem of mental health is analyzed in the four chapters that follow. A realistic view of the nature of personality disorders, and the extent to which they affect our people, is a necessary preliminary to defining the function of the school as an agency for the improvement of individual and social well-being.

CHAPTER 1

Nature of Psychological Disorders

MENTAL illness was once considered to be the concern of hospitals and medical scientists solely. The mentally ill were thought of as people who lived behind high walls in "lunatic asylums," and who often had to be kept chained to protect other people. Modern science has shown, however, that mental illness is not confined to people in institutions. It reaches into the home and into the school; it can be found among college students as well as among the human derelicts of America's "Skid Rows." It is reflected daily in newspaper accounts of crime, alcoholism, drug addiction, broken marriages, suicides, and acts of violence.

Mental disorders are today the number one public health problem of the nation. They affect more people and more families than any other single disorder, and evidence indicates that maladjusted individuals are being produced at a faster rate than facilities to take care of them can be provided. The schools of America can aid in combating these dis- orders through helping children build personalities which can adapt to the emotional pressures of a complex society. No other social agency has so many of the nation's people under its jurisdiction at an age when personality is being formed. Mental hygienists believe that the schools have only begun to exert their influence in the struggle against mental disorders, and that they can do a great deal more to prevent the waste of lives and money now resulting from mental illness.

It is in this setting that the educator must view his responsibility toward children and toward society. This chapter and the next will describe the magnitude of the problem of mental illness, so that educators may better understand the role of the school in promoting the nation's mental health.

DISTINGUISHING THE NORMAL FROM THE ABNORMAL

An understanding of mental illness must begin with a description of what this illness is—and how to distinguish normal from abnormal behavior. This understanding is necessary in order to see clearly what it is we are hoping to prevent.

A variety of terms are used to describe abnormal behavior. These include terms such as: *mental illness, emotional illness, mental disorders, emotional disorders, personality disorders, behavior disorders, maladjustment, psychological disorders*—all of which refer to a disturbed state of the individual. These terms are used here interchangeably to denote conditions of tension or nervousness characterized by deviations in thinking, feeling, and acting. The more severe the disorder, the more radical are these disturbances, until a point is reached where the individual becomes almost incapable of adjusting to life.

Many people have nervous and anxious states, or mental conflicts, which cause them serious concern at times. Most normal people, at some time or other, experience headaches, insomnia, fatigue, diarrhea, constipation, or depression. These are symptoms of anxiety and if prolonged might lead to personality disorders which would interfere with an individual's ability to live comfortably with himself and with other people, or his ability to earn a living and be a worthy member of society. Fortunately, the average, normal individual has the capacity to overcome these nervous states when his problems are solved or when he reaches a compromise with them.

Those people who cannot overcome their troubles and who cannot compromise with them develop exaggerated, persistent reactions which tend to incapacitate them and to distort their feelings and behavior. These are the people who cross the borderline of normality and become maladjusted individuals—people who substitute for real life a world, or part of a world, in which they can live more comfortably and in which their problems are solved.

Thus, the difference between normality and abnormality is a qualitative difference. The line between the normal and the maladjusted is a very thin one. Many people pass back and forth over this line several times during their lives. No person is completely well adjusted: he is adjusted only to a degree. A normal person may feel such abnormal emotions as resentment, anger, hate, envy, or jealousy. He may be emotionally hyperactive at times, and at other times he may be so depressed that he can hardly live with himself. He may even engage in fantasy or regress to childhood behavior patterns and still be within the range of normal behavior.

What then are the characteristics of a well-adjusted person? To state it simply and concisely, the well-adjusted person is one who maintains a balanced orientation toward reality. His life is like a sturdy ship riding the waves. He may be swayed this way and that way by the wind and water, but he always returns to an even keel. This even keel is his fundamental balance in life that enables him to withstand the thousands of disturbing stimuli which assail him and still keep his bearings and continue to move toward the goals which he has set for himself (4:373).[1]

VARIETIES OF PSYCHOLOGICAL DISORDERS

Just as normality is a matter of degree, so too are psychological disorders relative and varying in degree and intensity. There is a theoretical scale of maladjustment which ranges from conditions just beyond the level of normality to conditions which are so extreme that they are completely separated from normal behavior.

At one extreme of this scale of maladjustment are the very severe ailments which require that the individual be hospitalized as a protection to himself and to society. These ailments are classified as *psychoses.* At the other extreme of this theoretical scale of maladjustment is a category of *nonpsychotic behavior disorders,* characterized by certain odd or socially disapproved behavior tendencies. People in this category are not entirely abnormal, but they have personality problems which interfere with their happiness, their ability to get along with other people, and their general orientation toward life. Between these two extremes is a type of maladjustment known as *neurosis* or *psychoneurosis.* Neurotic persons have a variety of distressing symptoms which make them unhappy, nervous, hypersensitive, and prone to exaggerated emotional reactions. Neurotics need not be confined to a hospital (although about 10,000 were hospitalized in 1954), but they have an urgent need for professional therapy.

[1] The italic numbers in parentheses pertain to the numbered "Selected References" at the end of each chapter. "Selected References" for this chapter are on p. 21.

These categories of maladjustment are not clearly defined. There is much overlapping of symptoms among the three groups described, and some behavior disorders defy any type of classification. However, for purposes of discussion, it is helpful to establish these three categories so that the major symptoms of each may be more readily described.

THE PSYCHOSES

Contrary to popular belief, the psychotic is not a wild, raving maniac. Psychotic persons may at times be destructive; they may injure themselves, destroy property, and injure other people. But the vast majority of psychotics are withdrawn, fearful, out of contact with reality, and harmless. In fact, there is less chance of seeing physical violence in 99 percent of the wards in a mental hospital than there is on the streets of a city (7).

While there is much fluctuation in the behavior of psychotics, this ailment is characterized by extreme disorganization of the emotional, intellectual, and behavioral aspects of an individual. Psychotics must be hospitalized because they are quite incapable of coping with the pressures of society, and they are almost completely divorced from reality. Unfortunately, as will be shown later, not all psychotic persons are in hospitals. Many maintain their place in society where their behavior is described as queer, funny, or bizarre. Here they may remain undetected, unless they become involved in acts of violence, or commit an offense against public morals and values.

Psychoses do not fit under neat titles as do physical ailments. Indeed, there is little agreement among psychiatrists concerning the classification of psychoses, despite the fact that the American Psychiatric Association has issued a recommended classification. Since the data used in the next chapter to describe the prevalence of mental illness in the United States are derived from the National Institute of Mental Health, a modified form of the classification used by this federal agency will be adopted here. Thus, the psychoses are divided into two types: the *organic* and the *functional*. Approximately 75 percent of the patients admitted to state mental hospitals for the first time are diagnosed as psychotic. The remainder are classified as psychoneurotics, alcoholics, mental defectives, or as having other behavior disorders and diseases of a nonpsychotic type (*10*).

Organic Psychoses

These are disorders which result from some type of damage to the brain or central nervous system. Over half of the persons hospitalized for psychoses fall into this group (*10*). General paresis and other forms of syphilis of the central nervous system, alcoholic degeneration, cerebral arteriosclerosis, and senile brain disease are the physical ailments most commonly found among persons who develop organic psychoses. The emotional symptoms displayed by persons who have organic psychoses are many and varied. These persons may have delusions (false beliefs), or hallucinations (see things which others do not see); they may be apathetic (loss of feeling—withdrawn), hyperactive, depressed, possessed with irrational fears, or otherwise imbalanced in their feelings, thinking, and relation to the world of reality.

The unfortunate thing about organic psychoses is that once certain nerve or brain tissue has been damaged or destroyed, it cannot be repaired. Medical science has found ways to help these people adjust to their ailments, but it cannot offer a cure, or replace the destroyed nerve tissue. The prevention of organic psychoses is primarily a medical problem.

Functional Psychoses

These are mental or nervous disorders for which no organic basis has been found. They are thought to result from years of living under emotional stress. The major forms of functional psychoses are classified as schizophrenia, involutional melancholia, and manic-depressive psychoses. These psychoses are described in succeeding paragraphs. Paranoia, paranoid conditions, and psychopathic personality are mentioned briefly, since together these ailments constitute only a minor percentage of the functional psychoses.

SCHIZOPHRENIA. The youngest group—and the largest group—of patients admitted to mental hospitals suffers from this ailment. Schizophrenia means literally "a cleavage of the mind or heart," hence the synonym, "split personality." Another term for this ailment is dementia praecox, which means an insanity developed early in life. Psychiatrists recognize four types of schizophrenia. These are: (1) the simple schizophrenic type, (2) the catatonic type, (3) the paranoic type, and (4) the hebephrenic type.

1. Simple schizophrenic type. The simple schizophrenic is an immature person who withdrew into himself at an early age. He is usually timid, seclusive, and quietly absorbed in his own world. These characteristics give him the appearance of being mentally defective. However, there may be little or no impairment of intellectual capacity present. Simple schizophrenics are rarely harmful. They simply have no interest in developing their capacities or adjusting to the social world. Many of them are childlike in their behavior, understandings, and interest.

The following is a typical case of simple schizophrenia:

> Molly is 41 years old but looks much younger. She had been in the mental hospital one year, working in the laundry. Although she says she has many friends in the hospital, she never talks to anyone. When asked what she does after work, Molly said, "I think about how nice it would be to be back home." Molly was protected all her life by her mother who took care of all her needs. She grew up a kind, subdued, gentle, and immature creature who found no satisfaction in her sheltered life. Before being committed to the hospital, Molly had tied stockings to the end of the bed in an effort to hang herself. She had so little understanding of reality that she couldn't figure out how to complete the job. (4:359)

2. The catatonic type. The catatonic schizophrenic is almost completely detached from life. He may develop a stupor or mutism and not utter a word for weeks or months, then suddenly burst into a talkative streak which again subsides into mutism. Some catatonics assume a position of muscular rigidity (catalepsy), such as a kneeling position with hands clasped together as in prayer. This position is held for extremely long periods of time. In such immobile states the catatonic does not swallow, saliva dribbles from his mouth; he does not eat, and he may not eliminate until natural peristalsis or urination occur. After a siege of catalepsy, the catatonic may become violent and destructive, or he may appear to be quite normal. These patients are very unpredictable in their behavior and seem to have little contact with reality.

3. The paranoic type. The paranoic schizophrenic lives in a world of sounds, forces, and people which no one else can sense. He has many false beliefs and hallucinations, either grandiose or persecutory in type. In some instances he may feel himself to be the victim of bizarre attacks initiated by imaginary enemies. In other instances he develops exalted hallucinations and considers himself a king or president or a wealthy potentate. There is no limit to the imaginary life of a paranoic schizophrenic, and he takes every opportunity to express his condition, although his words are usually so garbled, disorganized, and confused that he makes no sense. The following interview reports describe the persecution complex of two such schizophrenics:

CASE ONE: A woman of about 50. When asked by the psychiatrist to describe her troubles, she said: "I'm bothered by excess air from television sets. It keeps me awake at night. I wake up and there's too much air in my nose and ears and the mattress. They use those things for S.O.S. calls and its wakes me up with a jump."

CASE TWO: A gray-haired man of mild appearance. "So many people on the ward poke planets through my back and out my stomach. It may not be visible right now because the sun planet cuts it off. There's no reason for people to do this. It's pure mischief. They are unmerciful and of a criminal nature. I'm not feeling well right now. People have been poking fists through me all day." (4:361)

4. The hebephrenic type. The hebephrenic schizophrenic is incongruous, confused, and silly. He laughs and smiles without apparent provocation. He will answer questions, but his answers usually relate to something else. He has pleasant but unrealistic notions of himself and seems to enjoy life in a weird, silly, and childish way. Frequently hebephrenics regress physically to childhood behavior. They may become so undisciplined that they urinate on the floor or smear feces on the wall.

In the following illustration, a hebephrenic woman was brought before a group of students by a psychiatrist. Upon entering the room, the patient looked at the audience, then pointed to the psychiatrist and said:

PATIENT: Take the witch out. She's not worth powder and lead to blow her to hell.
PSYCHIATRIST: Say, do you know some of these people?
PATIENT: Do I know some of these people? Yes, and they know me too. I've taught them all to play the piano. Reverend (*addressing a student*), will you take a seat at the piano or violin?
PSYCHIATRIST: Do you know what day this is? (May 26th)
PATIENT: Why sure I know what day this is. This is Christmas Day. Stand up and pray everyone. I made the dinner and cooked it. (4:361)

These four types of schizophrenia have many symptoms in common. During the course of the illness a patient may behave in a manner characteristic of several of the subgroups. Most schizophrenics are identified by their unconcern with the outside world, the adoption of bizarre roles, and the flight of words and ideas which accompanies their attempts to express what they feel.[2]

INVOLUTIONAL MELANCHOLIA. This is an ailment of middle life, occurring at about the time a man or woman undergoes a "change of life," or reorganization of the sex hormone balance. About 80 percent of these patients are between the ages of 45 and 64 years when the ailment becomes critical. Women develop this form of psychosis almost three times more frequently than men (10).

The involutional melancholics are extremely sad and depressed persons. In some this sadness takes the form of apathy. The individual may sit at a window and, with an expression of extreme dejection, stare at an object for hours at a time. Others are so painfully distressed that they pace the floor, moaning and wailing over their sorrows. At times, these patients feel persecuted and have delusions of being tortured by everyone around them. They may develop such extreme feelings of hopelessness that suicide is attempted.

The following stenographic report of an interview between a psychiatrist and his patient illustrates how melancholics continue to grieve over sorrows which occurred long ago:

PSYCHIATRIST: Mrs. X, what is troubling you?
PATIENT: I feel so sad. I don't know what to do.
PSYCHIATRIST: What are you sad about?
PATIENT: Well, I lost my son and my husband at the same time in an accident.
PSYCHIATRIST: How long ago did this happen?
PATIENT: About twenty years ago.
PSYCHIATRIST: You lost your son and husband twenty years ago and you still feel sad?
PATIENT: Yes, I can't help it. (*Begins to cry.*) (*4:355*)

MANIC-DEPRESSIVE PSYCHOSIS (Cyclothymia). This ailment affects a younger group of people than does involutional melancholia. It is manifested as early as 15 years of age, and reaches a peak between the ages of 35 and 44 years (10). Manic-depressive psychosis takes its name from the two extremes of emotional reaction which characterize it. The manic phase of this disorder is a state of elation, excitement, or

[2] See G. Bateson, *et al.*, "Toward a Theory of Schizophrenia," *Behavioral Science* (October, 1956), *1*:251–264.

euphoria. The depressive state is just the opposite—a condition of extreme dejection.

The manic-depressive may alternate between periods of mania and periods of depression. Or there may be a period of mania, followed by a return to normalcy, then another stage of mania, without any intervening depression. Another form of the ailment is a period of depression, followed by recovery, then another period of depression. At times the normal period between cycles of emotional upheaval extends over several years, making it difficult to distinguish between recovery and the quiescence of symptoms. The mixture of hyperactivity, irrationality and excitement which predominates during the manic phase of this psychosis is illustrated in this case:

> Bill is an arrogant, belligerent man of 45. When the psychiatrist asked him how he was getting along, Bill waved his fist and shouted: "I am not a criminal. I've been harmed and tortured by attendants. I've been tortured, do you hear? My bones were cracked in childhood. I went to three or four doctors to find out what was wrong with me. They couldn't do nothing so they sent me to this hospital. I want to get out of this_____place and go home." (4:357)

The following is an illustration of the agitated type of depression which is seen frequently:

> Tom is a middle-aged man who appears furtive and anxious. He described his feelings as follows: "I was unable to find work and my nerves began to crack. When I see two people walking down the street carrying on a conversation, I know they are talking about me. When I sleep I hear whispers outside of the window." (4:358)

PARANOIA. This disorder consists primarily of a system of delusions of grandeur or of persecution. Aside from these delusions, the patient's personality remains relatively normal with no outstanding symptoms of personality deterioration as occurs in paranoic schizophrenia. Delusions usually are related to a single theme, and the person behaves relatively normally as long as he is not stimulated to think or act on this theme. Some common persecution delusions concern problems of everyday living, such as an unfair employer or an unfaithful spouse. Delusions of grandeur frequently take on a religious emphasis, resulting in missionary or soul-saving activities (1:271). Delusions of racial superiority may also be paranoid in nature.

PARANOID CONDITIONS. While paranoia is a continuing form of delusionary behavior, paranoid conditions or states come and go. They are transient delusions in which an individual takes an excursion into abnormal behavior, then returns to normalcy. Many of the "crackpots" whose strange antics are described by the daily newspapers are suffering from paranoid conditions.

PSYCHOPATHIC PERSONALITY. This category applies to individuals who display a definite lack of ethical or moral development; people who are unable to follow socially approved mores and who have a callous disregard for the welfare of others. Included here are individuals varying from hardened criminals and delinquents, to unprincipled quacks and healers who benefit from the sorrows of others. These people fail to respond to the usual appeals of decency. They seem to have no internal controls, no conscience. They never seem to learn from experience and will repeatedly commit the same antisocial acts.

THE NEUROSES

Neurosis, or psychoneurosis, is a psychological disorder characterized by exaggerated emotional reactions to stimuli which ordinarily call forth only a mild reaction from normal people. The stimuli which set off these exaggerated emotional reactions may be external stimuli, such as high places, crowds, closed rooms, fire, etc.; or they may be inner forces such as memories, thoughts, unconscious conflicts, and general apprehension.

In the case of reactions to external stimuli, the neurotic's response is all out of proportion to the dangers of the situation. For instance, a normal person's reaction to high places might be one of caution, or even fear. The neurotic might react to this same stimulus by breaking out into a cold sweat, accompanied by heart palpitations, shortness of breath, and in some cases, unconsciousness.

Transient neuroticism is common among normal people. Anyone may become temporarily neurotic when overwhelmed by emotional stress. For instance, a student who fears an examination may become restless, irritable, unable to sleep; he may lose weight, develop a tic or tremor, or perspire excessively. These are neurotic symptoms, but they will pass when the problem is met. The true neurotic, however, remains constantly in a state of emotional distress. He may have sufficient control over his reactions to hold a job and even to achieve some success in the world. But he can do nothing about his basic anxiety because its roots often lie in personality distortions which originated in childhood and which can be overcome only through professional assistance.

The neuroses may be classified into three major types which, as in the case of the psychoses, are not mutually exclusive and have overlapping symptoms. These types are (1) psychasthenic neuroses, (2) neurasthenic neuroses, and (3) hysteric neuroses.

Psychasthenic Neuroses

These are ailments characterized by a vast range of troublesome mental and emotional symptoms which the person cannot control. The psychasthenic may be a victim of unreasonable fears or *phobias;* he may have *obsessions* (imperative urges to say or think certain things repeatedly); he may be subject to *compulsions* (uncontrollable urges to repeat certain acts over and over). Unreasonable elation, constant depression, and overinhibition are also common symptoms of psychasthenia.

An illustration of this disorder is the case of Grace, a hyperactive girl who is very easily upset. When she gets wrought up, she goes on a talking spree. She talks too much and too violently. Although she knows what she is doing during these periods of hyperactivity, Grace has no control over herself and continues talking until she achieves some relief from her overwrought state (4:350).

Neurasthenic Neuroses

These are neuroses in which some of the anxiety symptoms described above are transferred to physical outlets. Instead of merely feeling in an exaggerated way, the neurasthenic will also have physical reactions to his tensions. These physical reactions include hypochondria (making a business of being sick even when physical causes are absent), insomnia, constant fatigue, indigestion, nausea, vomiting, constipation, diarrhea, headache, or dizziness. When these physical ailments are caused or aggravated by emotional factors, they are known as *psychosomatic ailments.* Disorders such as chronic ulcerative colitis, asthma, peptic ulcer, high blood pressure, migraine headaches, overweight, backache, palpitation of the heart, and various allergies are a few of the physical disabilities which may be of a psychosomatic nature.

An illustration of how mental and emotional symptoms may be expressed through physical channels is the case of Dora who was admitted to a hospital for treatment for neurasthenia.

When Dora was two, the parents divorced and she was left with her mother. Dora loved her father and eased her pain by dreaming about him. She would stay in bed half the day and had a persistent dream of being a bird, flying gaily through the air. Suddenly, in her dreams, she felt tired, and plummeted to the ground, waking up trembling. When admitted to the hospital for psychiatric treatment, Dora described herself as being confused, anxious, fearful, sick at the stomach, and so uncoördinated that she could not walk a straight line. (4:351)

Hysteric Neuroses

This form of neurosis is characterized by severe physical disability which is nonorganic in nature. These disabilities may include paralysis of the limbs, intense aches and pains, deafness, blindness, loss of voice, continuous vomiting, and tremor of the head or hands. The hysteric may develop an anesthesia in which he becomes insensitive to pain and cannot feel the prick of a needle or a burn. He may develop fits and seizures or faint at the least provocation. This form of behavior is not a pretense, or a form of malingering. Hysterics are convinced that their ailments are real, and they are distressed by their symptoms. However, they cling to these physical disabilities as a protection against their unresolved inner anxieties.

Along with these physical disorders may go exaggerated emotional reactions. Reactions such as hypersensitivity, unreasonable irritability, impulsiveness, and mood swings are commonly evidenced. Such people are highly suggestible and seem to be on the look-out for some new ailment upon which to center their anxiety. The mere mention of an ailment they have not had, or a different physical impairment, might be enough to set them off on a new line of hysteric activity.

THE NONPSYCHOTIC BEHAVIOR DISORDERS

This is a "wastebasket" classification of behavior problems; a middle zone between normality and extreme abnormality. In this classification are included people who have personality aberrations which set them apart from normal people. These aberrations are not so serious as to be classified as neuroses or psychoses, but they are of sufficient magnitude that they affect a person's happiness, his ability to get along with other people, and his general orientation toward life. The individuals in this category have found an outlet for their anxiety through certain behavior patterns which are socially undesirable, but which do not necessarily result in severe personality disorganization.

There are literally hundreds of types of personality aberrations which can be classified as nonpsychotic behavior disorders. Only a few will be selected for mention. These are grouped under the general headings of (1) the eccentric group, (2) the inferior group, (3) the dependent group, (4) the antisocial group, (5) the emotionally unstable group, and (6) the sexual deviate group.

The Eccentric Group

Eccentrics are people whose mannerisms, appearance, or habit patterns become a source of amusement or annoyance to other people. The eccentrics cannot see themselves as others see them, or they have a complete disregard for what others think.

Included here are the incorrigible liar—who has been everywhere and seen everything; the suspicious person who seems to be embittered toward life; the person who is seen on a city street or walking along a railroad wearing heavy clothes in the summertime, dirty, disheveled, talking to himself or to an inanimate object. Such people know they are different from others, but they have ceased to care. Yet, they are not sufficiently detached from reality that they can be classified as neurotic or psychotic.

The Inferior Group

These people have a deep-seated feeling of inferiority which reflects in everything they do. They are constantly apologetic about their inadequacies and tend to annoy people with their whining and self-deprecating tactics. They are unable to converse with others in a social setting, and their evident nervousness and discomfort may chill a social gathering.

Often, inferiority feelings are expressed through withdrawal from social contact. Such people may be seen walking along the street with their eyes glued to the sidewalk so that they do not have to meet the eyes of other people. Occupationally, the inferior group tend toward activities which keep them away from people and which do not require them to make major decisions. Some individuals, on the other hand, develop a forced aggressiveness to cover up their feelings of inferiority. This aggressiveness is expressed through domination of others or autocratic and dictatorial roles which gives the person a sense of power to counteract the inadequacy he feels. This role may be maintained for many years, but the person remains insecure and unhappy despite his blustering superiority.

The Dependent Group

Because of emotional immaturity, some people are passive and dependent. They lack "backbone" and lean upon others for support and protection. They try to submerge their lives in the lives of others so that they are not called upon to accept adult responsibility. They are so dominated by fear and insecurity that they may marry a person who will care for them. Or they may cling to their aging parents and never venture into marriage. When such people have positions or circumstances in which they are protected, they can get along reasonably well in life. However, they are always in danger of losing these protective supports and of slipping into a state of neurotic dependency.

The Antisocial Group

The behavior patterns mentioned above affect primarily the individual. There is a large group of people, however, whose behavior endangers not only their own personality, but the welfare of others. These are the hostile, aggressive, antisocial individuals—people who have a distorted view of life and who pursue their satisfactions without regard for others. Included here are behavior patterns ranging from that of the criminal to that of the person who expresses his aggression through the reckless driving of an automobile. These people are their own worst enemy, for by fighting against the current of social mores they intensify their personal conflicts and develop deeper anxieties and hostilities.

The Emotionally Unstable Group

There are many people whose emotional tension seems to be so weakly controlled that the least obstacle "triggers off" an emotional reaction. Many of them relieve their tensions through physical expressions such as tics, tremors, stuttering, nail biting, ear pulling, and similar nervous mannerisms. *Tics* are reflected as intermittent muscular twitches or spasms, usually around the mouth or eyes. *Tremors* commonly take the form of twitching of the head or hands. *Stuttering* is a repetition of initial syllables or some important words in a phrase; the letters b-d-s-t being the most troublesome (1:374). The nail biting, ear pulling, and nose picking are so continuous and persistent that often there is damage to the tissue.

These emotionally unstable people are also restless and jumpy. They cry easily and become excitable and ineffective under stress. Their state of adjustment is dependent upon a calm, predictable environment. When this is lacking, they may become alcoholics or drug addicts in an attempt to relieve their tensions.

The Sexual Deviate Group

Many people find release for their anxieties through sexual practices. When these practices are contrary to the ethical and moral standards of society, they are called sexual deviations. Most of the practices included under this heading were at one time or another sanctioned by some group in society. Many of them are sanctioned today. However, the individual who violates the sex codes of the society in which he lives is classified as a deviate, even if his behavior may be perfectly normal in another society.

Where society applies social and psychological pressures on a practice which an individual uses to gain satisfaction for his internal stresses, this pressure together with the original stress tends to build up a load of anxiety which may force the individual more and more toward some form of release behavior whether it be approved or not approved.

The types of sexually abnormal behavior which are condemned in the United States include the following:

Homosexuality. Erotic relations between members of the same sex. *Transvestitism* is a special form of homosexuality in which individuals dress in clothes of the opposite sex and adopt their mannerisms.
Satyriasis. Exaggerated or excessive sexual desire and practice in men.
Nymphomania. Exaggerated or excessive sexual desire and practice in women.
Incest. Sexual relations between blood members of a family.
Prostitution. Sexual relations for financial gain.
Pedophilia. Sexual gratification is secured through relations with a child. Most pedophiliacs are men.
Bestiality. Sexual deviation in which animals are used for achieving sexual satisfaction. Said to be fairly common among boys in rural areas.
Exhibitionism. The deriving of sexual pleasure through exposure of the genitals to the opposite sex or to children. Rarely found among women.
Voyeurism (Also called scotophilia and inspectionalism). The deriving of sexual satisfaction through peeping at a person of the opposite sex. Occurs mostly among males—hence the term, "Peeping Tom."
Fetishism. Sexual satisfaction derived from some body part or inanimate object related to a sex partner. A lock of hair, perfume, or article of clothing becomes a sex stimulus.

Sadism. The securing of sexual gratification through infliction of pain on the sexual partner. Practiced most often by men.

Masochism. Deriving sexual pleasure through receiving pain or punishment. Believed to be more common among women than men. (*1*)

Tension Reduction of the Nonpsychotic Behavior Disorders

Outside of the antisocial groups and some of the sexual deviates, alcoholics, and drug addicts, persons with nonpsychotic behavior disorders are seldom institutionalized. Most of these people learn to live with their handicaps and characteristics. While they may not be entirely happy people, they feel relatively little distress compared with the neurotics and psychotics. Because they act out their feelings of anxiety, rather than bottle them up as do neurotics, these individuals may go through life with their patterns of undesirable behavior and never suffer a more serious type of personality disorder.

However, these are the people who can benefit greatly from therapeutic care. Under proper therapy, a great many of these individuals who live in the shadows of abnormality can be brought within the range of normal behavior. The difficulties involved in accomplishing this salvage of human lives will be discussed in the next chapter.

SUMMARY OF THE PSYCHOLOGICAL DISORDERS[3]

Classification	Major Disorders	General Characteristics
Organic psychoses	Paresis and other forms of syphilis of brain and central nervous system Cerebral arteriosclerosis Senility Alcoholic deterioration Traumatic injuries	Damage to brain and spinal cord may result in any of the symptoms described under functional psychoses, together with such physical symptoms as loss of memory, paralysis, and sense organ impairment.
Functional psychoses	Schizophrenia Simple	Hallucinations, delusions, phobias, bizarre

[3] For a more complete discussion of the behavior disorders, the reader is referred to textbooks on this subject, such as Coleman (*1*), Strecker (*8*), Maslow and Mittelman (*5*), Eaton (*2*), O'Kelly and Muckler (*6*), or Taylor (*9*).

Classification	Major Disorders	General Characteristics
	Catatonic Paranoic Hebephrenic	behavior, flight of words and ideas, apathy, catalepsy.
	Involutional melancholia	Extreme depression. Occurs generally after "change of life."
	Manic-depressive psychosis	Alternate periods of mania or hyperactivity, depression, and recovery.
	Paranoia and paranoid condition	Delusions of grandeur or persecution, without extreme personality deterioration seen in paranoic schizophrenia.
	Psychopathic personality	Lack of ethical or moral standards; no internal controls to behavior; fail to profit from experience.
The neuroses	Psychasthenic neuroses	Phobias, obsessions, compulsions, unreasonable elation, constant depression, overinhibition.
	Neurasthenic neuroses	Some of above symptoms expressed through physical outlets such as hypochondria, insomnia, fatigue, indigestion, nausea, vomiting, diarrhea, etc.
	Hysteric neuroses	Severe physical disability of nonorganic origin. Paralysis of limbs, deafness, blindness, loss of voice and anesthesia have been observed.

Summary of the Psychological Disorders—*Continued*

Classification	Major Disorders	General Characteristics
Nonpsychotic behavior disorders	The eccentric group	Disregard for what others think of them. Odd or bizarre mannerisms and habits.
	The inferior group	Deep-seated inferiority which results in social withdrawal or compensating aggression.
	The dependent group	Lack of emotional maturity; passive; lack initiative; seek protection.
	The antisocial group	Hostile, aggressive. Secure personal satisfactions at expense of others.
	The emotionally unstable group	Restless, jumpy, excitable. Have tension-relieving mechanisms such as nose picking, tics, tremors, etc. Blow up under emotional stress.
	The sexual deviate group	Find release for tensions through socially disapproved forms of sexual gratification.

PROBLEMS AND PROJECTS

1. Have you ever had a psychosomatic ailment? If so, describe as well as you can the conditions which brought it on and what happened to you.
2. Some people contend that psychotic patients who are capable of reproducing should be sterilized. Do you consider this practice justified? Has your state any laws pertaining to this matter?
3. How does "insanity" differ from "psychosis"?
4. Give some examples of organizations which seem to attract emotionally disturbed people.
5. Why do many people try to cover up any history of mental illness in their families?

6. Find some examples of newspaper or magazine advertisements which seek to cater to emotionally disturbed people.
7. Why would people rather find physical than emotional causes for their illness?
8. How can "mental fatigue" be explained in psychological terms?
9. Describe some people with an "inferiority complex." How is this complex used as an adjustment device?
10. Describe any irrational fears or phobias which you have seen demonstrated among your friends.
11. Who is better adjusted, an introverted person or an extroverted person?
12. Bring in newspaper clippings which illustrate the actions and behaviorisms of people who might be classified as mentally ill.

SELECTED REFERENCES

1. Coleman, J. C., *Abnormal Psychology and Modern Life,* Scott, Foresman and Co., 1956.
2. Eaton, J., and Weil, R., *Culture and Mental Disorders,* The Free Press, 1955.
3. Federal Security Agency, Public Health Service, National Institute of Mental Health, *Patients in Mental Institutions, 1949,* Public Health Service Publication No. 233, 1952.
4. Kaplan, L., and Baron, D., *Mental Hygiene and Life,* Harper & Brothers, 1952.
5. Maslow, A. H., and Mittelman, B., *Principles of Abnormal Psychology,* Harper & Brothers, 1951.
6. O'Kelly, L. I., and Muckler, F. A., *Introduction to Psychopathology,* Prentice-Hall, Inc., 1955.
7. State of California, Department of Mental Hygiene, *Biennial Report for 1950–52,* State Printing Office (Sacramento), 1953.
8. Strecker, E. A., *Basic Psychiatry,* Random House, Inc., 1952.
9. Taylor, W. S., *Dynamic and Abnormal Psychology,* American Book Company, 1954.
10. U.S. Department of Health, Education and Welfare, Public Health Service, *Patients in Mental Institutions, 1952,* Part II, "Public Hospitals For the Mentally Ill," Public Health Service Publication No. 495, 1956.
11. U.S. Department of Health, Education and Welfare, Public Health Service, *Patients in Mental Institutions, 1952,* Part III, "Private Hospitals and General Hospitals with Psychiatric Facilities," Public Health Service Publication No. 495, 1957.

CHAPTER 2

Prevalence of Psychological Disorders in the United States

THE DEVIATE forms of behavior described in the preceding chapter are more widespread than most people realize. Although no scientifically accurate census of the mentally ill in America has ever been made, a reliable estimate issued by the National Association for Mental Health in 1953 indicates that

At the present rate one out of every 12 children born each year will need to go to a mental hospital sometime during his life because of severe mental illness.

At least 9 million Americans—one in every 16—are suffering from a mental or emotional disorder.

About 250,000 people will go to mental hospitals for the first time, this year.

One out of every two patients going to a medical doctor is suffering from an illness which is tied up with mental or emotional disorder. The same is true for one out of three patients who go to general hospitals.

Mental illness has been costing us over a billion dollars a year in tax funds.

The patients going to mental hospitals just this year for the first time will lose about $1,750,000, that they would have earned during the time they are sick.

For each patient being treated for mental illness we are spending less than $4.00 per year on research to find new ways of prevention and treatment.

Right now there are about 650,000 patients in mental hospitals. This is as many as there are in all other hospitals combined.

Three out of every four state mental hospitals are already caring for many more patients than they were built for—and many have waiting lists.

The Federal Government says at least 330,000 more mental beds are needed.

The average state mental hospital has only about 6 doctors for every 10 it needs—3 registered nurses for every 10 it needs—2 clinical psychologists for every 10 it needs.[1]

As astonishing as these estimates may seem, they are born out by the evidence shown in the succeeding paragraphs.

DATA FROM MENTAL INSTITUTIONS

The National Institute of Mental Health is the most reliable source of data on mental illness in America. Even so, there are many sources of error in the data assembled by this federal agency. The institute must rely upon the voluntary coöperation of state governments and individual hospitals. Most states and hospitals coöperate in the surveys made each year, but many provide data which are not entirely comparable. This is due to the varying definitions of terms used to describe mental illness, and to the lack of standardized administrative procedures relating to the admission, parole, and discharge of patients. Also, there is much variation in the types of data kept by hospitals and in the reporting periods for consolidation of this information.

These factors, coupled with the absence of data on mental illness from hospitals administered by the Veterans Administration, the military services, and the Public Health Service, make it difficult to provide exact information regarding the incidence of mental disorders in the United States. The data which follow are inferences which reveal trends, rather than a true picture of the status of mental disorders in the nation.

Patients in Mental Hospitals

Tables 1 and 2 indicate the number of patients carried on the books of state institutions for the care of psychiatric cases from the year 1940 to 1955. These data are set up in separate tables because the methods of calculation and reporting were changed after 1949.

During the period 1940–1949, there was a 17 percent increase in the total number of patients remaining in these hospitals at the end of the year after accounting for discharges, transfers, and deaths. By 1955 the total number of patients in residence or in some type of extra-

[1] The National Association for Mental Health, *12 Facts About Mental Illness,* Leaflet issued by the Association, New York, 1953.

TABLE 1. Resident Patients at End of Year in Hospitals for the Prolonged Care of Psychiatric Patients, and Rates per 100,000 Population: United States, 1940–1949[a]

Year	Total Resident Patients at End of Year	Rate per 100,000
1949	564,160	382.5
1948	554,454	381.6
1947	540,987	379.2
1946	529,247	382.4
1945	518,018	371.1
1944	506,346	366.7
1943	500,564	366.7
1942	497,938	369.8
1941	490,506	368.2
1940	480,637	364.2

[a] Adapted from Federal Security Agency, Public Health Service, National Institute of Mental Health, *Patients in Mental Institutions, 1949*, Public Health Service Publication No. 233, U.S. Government Printing Office, 1952, Table C, p. 14.

TABLE 2. Patients on Books at End of Year in Public Hospitals for the Prolonged Care of the Mentally Ill, 1950–1955[a]

Year	Total Patients in Residence or in Some Type of Extramural Care
1950	598,026
1951	610,458
1952	622,706
1953	632,042
1954	642,419
1955	652,412

[a] Data from U.S. Department of Health, Education and Welfare, Public Health Service, National Institute of Mental Health, *Mental Health Statistics, Current Reports,* Series IMH-B53 and IMH-B54, December, 1952, to December, 1956.

mural care had increased to 652,512. This figure includes only patients in state and county hospitals. If we added the number of patients in private hospitals, general hospitals with psychiatric facilities, and federal hospitals, the total would easily exceed 700,000.

The steadily increasing patient load in mental hospitals is explained only partially by the general growth of population. As shown in Table 1, the rate of hospitalization during the 10-year period for which data were provided increased regularly. This rate, based on a unit of population, indicates that the increased number of patients in mental hospitals is a true increase and not merely a reflection of population growth. There is evidence that the population of mental hospitals has been increasing at a higher annual rate than the civilian population as a whole (*32:9*).

The United States Public Health Service has offered the following explanations for the mounting numbers of patients confined to mental hospitals during the past two decades:

1. The more adequate provision of facilities for the care and treatment of the mentally ill.
2. A considerable and fairly continuous increase in knowledge concerning the nature of mental illness on the part of the medical profession and of psychiatrists in particular. This has resulted in an increased number of cases formerly not recognized as mentally ill being diagnosed and committed to hospitals.
3. A growing realization on the part of laymen that mental illness is a problem in which the individual patient requires psychiatrically oriented treatment and also an increasing knowledge that the individual patient is susceptible of improvement and recovery if treatment is taken in time.
4. An increasing public confidence in the management of a large number of hospitals for the mentally ill with increased use of these hospitals on a voluntary basis by persons who formerly avoided treatment or remained in seclusion elsewhere. (*17:13*)

Age Factors Related to Mental Illness

In addition to the points mentioned above, the chronic nature of many psychoses may also account for the increased number of patients housed in mental institutions. Table 3 indicates the number of first admissions to state mental hospitals by age and sex during 1953. Although these data are quite incomplete, being based on reports from only 180 of the 205 state hospitals, they show that over one-fourth of all first admissions occurs among people who are 65 years of age or older. The great majority of these older patients are afflicted with cerebral arteriosclerosis or senile brain diseases for which the prognosis of recovery is poor.

The resident population of many mental hospitals consists largely of this older group, together with a slowly accumulated residue of schizophrenic patients who are admitted during youth or early maturity and stay until the end of their life span (*14*). A study made in New York State showed that in 1951 the average duration of hospital life

TABLE 3.   First Admissions to State Hospitals for Mental Disease, by Age and Sex: United States, 1953[a]

Age in Years	Total Male	Total Female	Total Number
Under 15	795	434	1,229
15–24	5,871	4,326	10,197
25–34	10,223	8,357	18,580
35–44	10,569	8,013	18,582
45–54	8,968	6,609	15,577
55–64	7,132	5,101	12,233
65–74	7,489	6,158	13,647
75–84	5,496	5,363	10,859
85 and over	1,461	1,692	3,153
Age unknown	574	284	858
Total, all ages	58,578	46,337	104,915

[a] Adapted from U.S. Department of Health, Education and Welfare, Public Health Service, National Institute of Mental Health, *Patients in Mental Institutions, 1953,* Part II, Public Health Service Publication No. 495, U.S. Government Printing Office, 1956, Table 7, p. 21.

for schizophrenics was 21 years (*22*). Discharges from the hospital and deaths have not kept pace with the accumulating reservoir of patients who spend their lives in mental hospitals.

SELECTIVE SERVICE AND ARMED FORCES DATA

The second widely cited source of data on the incidence of mental illness in the United States is the experience of the selective service system and the armed forces during World War II.

This experience is especially valuable because millions of men were for the first time subjected to psychiatric examinations. Also, the process of personality deterioration was telescoped through imposing severe pressures upon thousands of men in a controlled environment. The results of these studies, together with the fact that the effects of senility are eliminated, makes the data on personality deterioration among selective service registrants and military personnel of vital interest.

Selective Service Experience

Up to August 1, 1945, 4.8 million men were found unfit for service in the military forces. Almost one out of five of these rejectees (18 percent) were found to be unfit because of personality disorders and character defects (*13*). More men were rejected for mental and personality defects than for any other single cause.

During the years 1940–1943, an intensive study was made of mental disorders among a sample of selective service registrants. It was found that 55.8 men per 1000 showed signs of mental illness. (*14*). This rate cannot be applied to the general population because men who did not meet minimum educational qualifications and those with certain obvious physical defects were not examined. Yet, if 55.8 men per 1000 in the age group of 18–44 years were suffering from mental disorders, the incidence of these disorders must be considerably higher among the general population where the effects of senility are felt.

Some additional facts on the mental health of selective service registrants are provided by a mental health study made in Miami County, Ohio, by the Division of Mental Hygiene of the Ohio State Department of Public Welfare (*20*). This county was considered representative in character and had a population of about 52,600. One of the two draft boards serving the county kept detailed records of the causes for which men were rejected. Their findings included these observations:

1. Of each 1000 men examined, age 18–37 years, 62 were rejected for some personality disorder.
2. Of those rejected for personality disorders, 71 percent were classed as psychoneurotic, 13 percent as psychopathic personalities, and 6 percent as psychotics. The highest rate of rejection occurred among unskilled workers and agricultural workers. These two groups made up 60.7 percent of all men rejected because of personality disorders.

These findings may be considered as lending support to the conclusions of the 1940–1943 study that about 6 percent of the male population between ages 18 and 44 years have personality disorders which make them unfit for military service. Among unskilled workers and agricultural workers, as high as 10 percent of the men in this age group may be suffering from personality disorders.

Military Experience

Over three-fourths of a million men were lost to the armed services because of mental and emotional disorders which rendered them unfit to wear a uniform. Mental illness continued to be a major problem after men were in service. About a million men were confined in armed services neuropsychiatric hospitals during World War II. Many more suffered temporary breakdowns which were treated at some local point and not included in hospital records.

It might be supposed that most of the neuropsychiatric disorders among combat personnel are caused by the stress and tension of battle. However, evidence reveals that 60 percent of the mental and emotional breakdowns were not from "battle fatigue," but occurred before the men saw combat (*12*). Moreover, whatever basically was affecting the men seemed to be "contagious"—it spread around and resulted in units which had abnormally high rates of neuropsychiatric disorders.

These behavior disorders are continuing to be a burden to the government. Between December, 1941, and December, 1945, 43 percent of the 980,000 disability discharges were for neuropsychiatric reasons (*14*). The Veterans Administration has been spending about $500 million per year to operate 35 hospitals devoted almost exclusively to psychiatric patients, 75 hospitals with psychiatric services, and 62 mental hygiene clinics. In addition, compensation or pensions are being paid to almost half a million veterans with psychiatric disorders—many of them having illnesses dating back to World War I (*18*).

MENTAL ILLNESS IN THE GENERAL POPULATION

Psychiatrists and mental hygienists have long contended that for every person with a personality disorder on record, there are dozens who are unknown. The toll which mental illness exacts from society cannot be measured fully by the tens of thousands who are under treatment. Much of the human suffering and cost of suicide, crime, divorce, alcoholism, juvenile delinquency, and all the rest of society's pathological conditions is a part of this picture. It is the undetected mentally ill that present our greatest problems, not those who enter and leave our hospitals in such great numbers each year. The extent of mental illness in the total population of the United States is indicated by the studies and research cited below.

The Baltimore Survey

In 1936, a one mile square area in the eastern part of the city of Baltimore was subjected to an intensive mental health survey. At the time, this district had about 55,000 inhabitants. The written records of some 43 institutions and agencies that dealt with mental health problems were studied. It was found that in this population there were 3337 active cases of mental disorder. This is equivalent to a rate of 60.5 disordered persons per 1000 population (*14*).

The Tennessee Study

A more thorough study of a community was conducted in Williamson County, Tennessee, from 1935 to 1938. Some 25,000 people were included in this survey. The staff gathered data by studying institutional records, through clinical examinations, and through house-to-house surveys. They found in this community 69.4 cases of mental illness per 1000 population. Where a house-to-house survey was conducted, the rate of mental illness rose to 123.7 per 1000 population (*14*).

The Salt Lake City Study

Using a personal interview approach, trained workers visited 200 consecutive homes in an eight-block area in Salt Lake City and secured information on the incidence of mental illness or gross emotional disturbance. The raters depended on overt symptomatology or the admission of illness for their data. They found that roughly one-third of the adult population sampled in this survey appeared to have some kind of specific mental illness, and about one-half the families sampled contained at least one mentally ill person. Of this group, less than half were receiving psychiatric care (*8*).

Estimated Prevalence of Personality Disorders in the General Population

While these studies suffer from inadequate sampling and from differences in diagnostic techniques, they may be used as a rough index of what might be found in the total population of the United States if an adequate survey could be made. Table 4 represents a projection of the data derived from the Baltimore and Tennessee studies in an attempt to relate them to mental illness in the general population.

This table shows that if we apply the rate of mental illness found in these studies to a population of 171 million (estimate for June 1957), there would be from *10 to 12 million people in the United States who are suffering from personality or behavior disorders.* Included among these are over one million psychotics, half a million psychoneurotics, many thousands of psychopaths, and several million people with disorders of other types.

As far as can be determined, most of the disordered people in the nation are not in institutions or under professional care. The data on mental institutions show that at its maximum, the population of psychiatric hospitals has never exceeded 800,000 in any one year. Therefore, it is fair to assume that there are millions of disordered persons

TABLE 4.   Estimate of Behavior Disorders in Total Population of United States, 1957

Estimate Based on Baltimore Study[a]			Estimate Based on Tennessee Study[a]		
Classification of Disorder	Rate per 1000	Total in General Population[b]	Classification of Disorder	Rate per 1000	Total in General Population[b]
Psychosis	6.7	1,145,700	Psychosis	6.3	1,077,300
Psychoneurosis	3.1	530,100	Psychoneurosis	4.0	684,000
Psychopathic personality	0.5	85,500	Psychopathic traits	7.5	1,282,500
Personality disorder in adults	4.0	684,000	Special personality traits	13.5	2,308,500
Behavior disorder in children	8.1	1,385,100	Conduct and behavior disorders	16.7	2,855,700
Minor and possible disorder in children and adults	11.8	2,017,800	Organic and miscellaneous cases	13.2	2,257,200
Adult delinquency without other information	10.3	1,761,300			
Total active cases	60.5	10,345,500	Total active cases	69.4	11,867,400

[a] Data from R. H. Felix and M. Kramer, "Research in Epidemiology of Mental Illness," *Public Health Reports* (February, 1952), 67:152–160.
[b] Estimate based on population of 171 million.

outside of institutions who are receiving no professional help, and whose emotional problems are so severe as to constitute a real impairment to their health and happiness.

This interpretation is documented by the following statement contained in the Ohio study mentioned earlier: "On the basis of the findings outlined it may be conservatively estimated that from 5,000 to 10,000 people in this one county need professional counseling services.

This would include only those men, women and children whose mental health is to far below par as to interfere seriously with their ability to live happily and usefully" (20). This "conservative" estimate represents from 10 to 20 percent of the population studied. If this ratio is applied to the nation as a whole, the prevalence of personality disorders would far exceed the estimates made on the basis of the Baltimore and Tennessee studies.

Further documentation on this point comes from the St. Paul study where it was found that ". . . the number of persons who showed some symptomatic evidence of disordered behavior known to the total group of adjustment agencies was nearly ten times as great as the number diagnosed by agencies offering qualified local psychiatric service" (6).

Other Evidence of Maladjustment in the General Population

Further information on the prevalence of personal maladjustment in the United States may be derived from data on alcoholism, drug addiction, suicide, broken marriages, and crime.

ALCOHOLISM. The California State Department of Mental Hygiene stated in 1952: "It is estimated that there are 75,000 people in this state who have used alcohol to such an extent that they have seriously impaired their physical or mental health" (31). Based on a population of 10 million at that time, the rate of alcoholism in California would be 7.5 per 1000. If this rate applied to the nation as a whole, there would be 1,200,000 cases of severe alcoholism in the United States.

That this estimate is probably conservative is indicated by Saul (27:7), who states that there are 3 million alcoholics in the nation, and by Ginsburg (16), who says that there are almost 4 million problem drinkers in this country at any one time.

DRUG ADDICTION. No one knows how many users of narcotics there are in the United States. While Ginsburg (16) states that there are about 50,000 narcotic addicts in the nation, there is some evidence that the actual figure is much higher. For instance, in July, 1951, it was estimated that there were between 45,000 and 90,000 drug addicts in New York City alone. Between 1947 and 1950, the admission of patients under 21 years of age to the two government hospitals at Lexington, Kentucky, and Fort Worth, Texas, increased 2000 percent—a jump of from 22 patients to 440 patients (43). These facts suggest that drug addiction is a far more serious problem than is generally realized.

SUICIDE. Each year 100,000 people in the United States attempt to take their own lives (*11*). In 1955, about 17,000 of them succeeded in doing so. For every woman suicide there were four suicides by men. The age at which this solution to life's problems is most common is between 50 and 59 years (*39*).

BROKEN MARRIAGES.   Broken marriages have great mental hygiene significance because one or both parties commonly have some personality difficulties which interfere with satisfactory adjustment to marriage and family life. Also, breaking up a family has serious implications for the children as well as the parents. In 1954, there was approximately one divorce for every four marriages. A total of 377,000 divorces and annulments were reported that year (*38*). There are no exact data on how many children were affected by the breaking up of homes, but reliable estimates indicate that more than a million men, women, and children are involved in divorce each year (*19*). This is exclusive of desertion and of agreements between parents to live separately without recourse to legal action.

CRIME.   According to Saul (*27*), there are 7 million people in the nation who have criminal records. The Federal Bureau of Investigation estimated that 2,563,150 major crimes were committed in the United States in 1956. Crime was up 13.3 percent across the nation in 1956 as compared with the previous year. Since 1950, crime has increased almost four times as fast as population (*41*).

Crime and delinquency may be considered as significant symptoms of personality disturbance, for, contrary to popular belief, most criminals are not mentally deficient but emotionally maladjusted. A study of the inmates of a major prison showed that the great majority of prisoners were psychoneurotics, alcoholics, psychopathics, or deliberate asocial personalities. Only 13 percent were classified as mental defectives, and 1 percent as psychotics (*21*).

Summary of the Prevalence of Mental Illness in the United States

Despite the fragmentary nature of the data, there can be little doubt that many millions of people in the nation are suffering from personality disorders. The situation as summarized by S. W. Ginsburg, is this: "With all due allowance for the statistical inexactness of these figures, there can be no doubt that they add up to an impressive and ominous picture. . . . If they err, it is, in my opinion, on the conservative side" (*16*).

R. H. Felix and Morton Kramer of the National Mental Health Institute make a more guarded statement. They say: "When all facts are taken into consideration, however, these data suggest that at any one time at least 6 percent of our population suffers from a type of serious mental disorder" (*13*). This estimate of 6 percent coincides very closely with other data cited in this section, and reinforces the statement that some 10 million people in the United States are affected by mental illness.

PROBLEMS IN THE PREVENTION AND TREATMENT OF MENTAL ILLNESS

The significance of mental illness as a public health problem is revealed not only in the number of people affected but also in the facilities and personnel available to care for these people. In 1956, the nation spent more money than ever before for the care and treatment of the mentally ill. Over $662 million were expended for the maintenance of state mental hospitals alone.[2] Despite this financial outlay, hospital facilities were overcrowded and understaffed to the extent that a majority of mental hospitals were omitting or restricting the use of known, successful therapeutic treatments (*2*).

Overcrowding in State Mental Institutions

There is no such thing as privacy in the average state mental hospital, except for solitary confinement. In 1949, state mental hospitals in the United States had room for 402,822 patients. The average daily resident population was 475,540. This means that 118 patients were crowded into spaces designed to accommodate 100 patients (*11*:68). As a result, the spectacle of a score or more psychotic patients thrown together into a single ward, with iron cots set side by side, filling the room and overflowing into the hallway was a common one. The situation at present is not greatly improved, despite the efforts which have been made to provide additional beds for psychiatric patients.

The Shortage of Personnel in Mental Institutions

Few mental hospitals in the United States have enough qualified professional personnel to care for the patients hospitalized. As shown in Table 5, in 1949 state hospitals were handicapped by shortages in trained personnel ranging from a 7 percent shortage among attendants to a 42 percent deficit of pathologists.

[2] See U.S. Department of Health, Education and Welfare, Public Health Service, "Mental Patient Data for Fiscal Year 1956," *Public Health Reports,* Reprint No. 3286, January, 1957, pp. 14–15.

The shortage of psychiatrists was particularly significant since there were only 69 psychiatrists on hand for every 100 needed. The shortages among graduate nurses, therapists, and psychiatric social workers was equally acute. Only 3 percent of all registered nurses employed in hospitals were to be found in institutions for the care of psychiatric patients—where 53.3 percent of all hospital patients are found. Nearly

TABLE 5.   Professional Personnel Needed and Vacancies Reported in State Hospitals for Mental Disease, United States, 1949[a]

Position	Number Needed	Vacancies Reported	Percentage Understaffed
Clinical directors	129	27	21
Pathologists	53	22	42
Medical specialists	34	9	26
Staff physicians	2,211	686	31
Psychologists and psychometrists	284	51	18
Graduate nurses	6,046	1,741	29
Other nurses and attendants	60,352	4,252	7
Therapists and assistants	2,877	661	23
Psychiatric social workers	643	136	21

[a] Adapted from Federal Security Agency, Public Health Service, National Institute of Mental Health, *Patients in Mental Institutions, 1949*, Public Health Service Publication No. 233, U.S. Government Printing Office, 1952, Table 17, p. 64.

six times as many psychiatric social workers are needed to staff adequately the mental hospital programs; only 8 percent of the need for clinical psychologists is now being met, and at least 18,000 more attendants were needed to meet the standard of one attendant to six patients (9).

Effects of Overcrowding of Patients and Shortage of Personnel

It is claimed that 60 percent of all patients admitted to mental hospitals are out at the end of the year (2). Unfortunately, not all of these people are cured. Evidence indicates that only one out of four will be discharged as fully recovered. The other three are discharged as improved or incurable. Of those who are released as improved, two out of every seven will later be recommitted to a mental hospital (17:32). In New York State where facilities and personnel for the care of the mentally ill are well above average, the readmission of discharged patients increased from 25 percent in 1931 to 49 percent in 1951. The ratio of readmissions to first admissions was up 60 percent for schizophrenics, and up 138 percent for manic-depressives during the period beginning in 1949 and ending in 1951 (22). This is only part of the penalty which is being paid for overcrowded facilities and the shortage of professional personnel.

The Stockton Pilot Study

The results which might be attained if hospitals were adequately staffed and equipped and if patients were given the care and attention they require was demonstrated in a study conducted at the Stockton State Hospital in California (30:25). This study was undertaken in an effort to determine the effectiveness of added numbers of personnel and intensive treatment of patients who had failed to respond to therapy and who seemed doomed to remain forever in the rear wards of the hospital.

A group of 400 male schizophrenics were the subjects of this study. The patients were 20 to 60 years old and had been in the hospital more than a year (half of them more than 10 years). Two hundred of these men were moved to a special ward for intensive therapy. They were paired with a control group of similar age and condition which remained scattered through the wards of the hospital where they received the usual hospital treatment. The experimental group of 200 patients had the night and day attention of the following personnel—a vast increase over the staffing available on the usual chronic wards:

Staff[a]	Ratio to Patients
1 Psychiatrist	200:1
1 Physician-surgeon	200:1
1 Psychologist	200:1
1 Social worker	200:1
7 Psychiatric nurses	29:1
15 Rehabilitation therapists	13:1
75 Psychiatric technicians	2.7:1

[a] Not all of these positions were filled at all times.

In November, 1951, the director of the study reported:

There is an unmistakable and factually established foundation for believing that personality deterioration can be retarded and that more patients can be returned to the community under this intensive treatment program than under the customary institutional experience. Among the results secured were these:

1. The rate of separation has been three times that of the control group. At present there are 24 patients released from the hospital from the experimental group, eight from the control group.
2. Patient days out of the hospital show a marked increase. In terms of patient days out of the hospital (therapeutically desirable even if the patient must return), the experimental patients show a 200 percent rise over the controls.
3. Twice as many experimental patients as controls showed a return to their pre-morbid personality level.
4. Only 6 percent of the experimental patients have regressed, as compared to 16 percent of the control group.
5. The number of patients capable of performing hospital industry increased by 34 percent in the experimental group. No such figure could be shown for the control group.

To see patients who formerly led a vegetative existence become more and more aware of their surroundings seems to present the greatest hope for the thousands of forgotten patients on the back wards of mental hospitals throughout the country. (*30*)

This experiment reveals what might be accomplished in mental institutions if sufficient professional personnel were available to provide the care and treatment required by chronic patients.

PROFESSIONAL SERVICES FOR THE GENERAL POPULATION

While the lack of professional personnel in mental institutions presents a serious obstacle to the rehabilitation of psychiatric patients, even more serious is the situation of the psychologically disturbed people who are not in mental hospitals.

On an average day in 1949, there was one staff psychiatrist for each 310 patients in state mental institutions. Outside of these institutions there were about 4192 psychiatrists in private practice who were attempting to serve the general population. If we can assume that there are 10 million people outside of mental hospitals who need professional help, each of the psychiatrists in private practice would have to serve 2500 patients. Since a psychiatrist sees, on an average, 200 patients per year, obviously there are many thousands of people who could not possibly secure psychiatric treatment even if they desired it (*4*).

To complicate this problem, psychiatrists are not evenly distributed over the country. Almost 75 percent of the psychiatrists in private practice are found in cities over 100,000 population. Over 85 percent of the psychoanalysts are located in 11 cities in the United States. This means that psychiatric service is largely unavailable to the people who live in rural areas or in small towns and cities.

Training of Psychiatrists

There appears to be little possibility that the nation will soon have the number of trained psychiatrists it requires. It is estimated that from 15,000 to 20,000 psychiatrists are needed in the United States to provide adequate service for the people. Education in psychiatry generally consists of 5 years of specialized training after the medical internship. The supply of psychiatrists depends upon how many medical students become interested in entering a specialty requiring so long a period of study. At the present time they are not doing so in anywhere near the required numbers.

In 1947, there were approximately 1300 psychiatric residents in training. About 350 complete their training each year, and only 35 percent of these graduates go into private practice (9). At this rate, it would take 25–40 years, depending upon the number of graduates each year, to prepare the 20,000 psychiatrists needed in the nation—disregarding deaths, retirements, and population increase.

MENTAL HYGIENE PROGRAMS AND THE PREVENTION OF MENTAL ILLNESS

Mental hygienists have studied carefully the data on personality disorders among the American people and what it is costing in money and wasted lives. They are agreed that this problem cannot be solved by waiting until mental disorders appear and then attempting to cure them with inadequate facilities and insufficient personnel. The ultimate conquest of mental illness must come through attacking these disorders at their point of origin—by preventing their occurrence if possible, or by instituting early treatment to reduce the severity of the illness. This is the preventive approach to disease which has worked so successfully in eliminating such scourges as typhoid fever, bubonic plague, and smallpox—ailments which once menaced entire populations.

Since about 1900, preventive mental hygiene programs have been conducted by both public and private agencies. These projects range from local radio programs for education of the people, to fully organized preventive health projects which involve an entire state. Many new services have been created to prevent or alleviate mental illness. These include mental hygiene clinics, mental hygiene education, guidance services, the promotion of group interaction, recreational opportunities, and the improvement of community living.

However, while preventive mental hygiene measures gained momentum during the past half-century, mental disorders continued to increase. Crime, divorce, and other symptoms of personal and social maladjustment have in fact become a more serious problem than they were at the beginning of the century. This does not mean that mental hygiene programs are ineffective. It means that these programs must be better organized, better financed and better supported by the public.

Financing Mental Hygiene Activities

The extent to which preventive mental hygiene activities are being supported financially provides an interesting clue to how well the American public recognizes the significance of mental illness and the need for prevention.

It might be thought that a nation which spends over $662 million a year on caring for and curing the mentally ill cannot afford the false economy of neglecting prevention. Yet, the evidence indicates that more and more money is going into the care and treatment of the mentally ill, while financing for prevention, research, and education has been negligible in comparison to the need.

In 1945, the Surgeon General of the United States told Congress: "In proportion to the importance of the mental diseases, importance as measured by any yardstick, very little research is being done. Very few brilliant minds are at work on this huge problem, almost none of the basic and related fundamental sciences are being brought to bear upon this problem with a view to its solution." It was further stated that the United States had spent far less on mental health research than we have on the research which led to the development of high octane gasoline (*12*).

Since 1945, both the federal government and state governments have allocated funds for the training of mental health workers, for research and for preventive mental hygiene activities. But the funds allocated show that we are still a long way from recognizing what needs to be done. For example, in the year 1952–53, a little over $11 million were appropriated by the federal government for mental health activities. In this same year, the National Cancer Institute received $17,887,000; and the National Heart Institute more than $12 million (*42*). While cancer and heart ailments are serious health problems, they affect relatively few people as compared to the number affected by mental disease. For every $1.30 spent for other types of medical research, the nation has been spending only 2 cents for research in the fields of neurology and psychiatry (*31*).

Even more indicative of our scale of values are the funds appropriated for research and prevention in the area of animal disease. In 1952, the Bureau of Animal Industry, Agricultural Research Administration, was allocated over $26 million for investigations concerned with livestock, the domestic raising of fur-bearing animals, and for animal disease control and eradication (*42*:132). The funds allocated for research and prevention of disease in animals were more than double those allocated for the prevention of mental disease in human beings.

At the state and local levels, the financing of research and prevention programs in the various fields of public health likewise give mental illness a low priority for funds. For instance, the Southern California Society for Mental Hygiene compared funds available in Los Angeles for health education agencies in 1952, and found this distribution of money (*28*):

Polio	$839,432
Tuberculosis	408,966
Cancer	301,288
Heart	158,434
Mental illness	36,564

The State of California spent almost $50 million in 1952 for its mental hospitals and clinics. Only 1.1 percent of this sum, approximately $550,000 was spent on all community services, preventive and otherwise (*14*). In this same year, the state spent $1,125,195 for the control of infectious diseases in livestock and poultry. An additional $662,764 was spent for protecting the public from unwholesome and objectionable meat products (*29*).

A similar story is told by the actions of the state legislature in Oregon. Appropriations for the biennium, 1949–1951 included $24,778 for the Mental Hygiene Section of the Oregon State Board of Health, while $42,425 were appropriated for the eradication of predatory animals, and $45,000 went to the agricultural department for the control of Bang's Disease in cattle (23:304).

These facts and many others like them indicate that the nation has no real conception of the public health significance of mental illness. More money is spent for the prevention of physical diseases like cancer, tuberculosis, and infantile paralysis, than for mental illness which hospitalizes more people than these three ailments combined. In fact it appears that the nation is spending more money to protect the public from spoiled meat and to eliminate diseases among animals, than is being spent to protect the public from the effects of mental disorders.

CHEMOTHERAPY AND THE PREVENTION AND CURE OF MENTAL ILLNESS

For many years scientists have been searching for a biochemical application to mental illness. The recent discovery of chemical tranquilizers, or ataractic drugs (from *ataraxia*—a detached serenity) has been heralded as the opening of a new "gateway to the brain." So dramatic are the effects of these drugs that psychiatry has been said to have advanced more in the past decade than in all the decades before it (33).

Therapeutic Use of Tranquilizers

The modification of behavior through medicine has captured scientific interest and has led to widespread experimentation with the use of ataractic drugs. These drugs are said to be so effective in reducing motor activity, anxiety, and hostility that manic patients who formerly required many months of treatment before they could be removed from the disturbed wards of mental hospitals are now brought under control in a few days or weeks (24). Destruction, assault, and aggression in some mental hospitals have been reduced to a point where disturbed wards are no longer needed, and shock therapy has ceased to be the major treatment for hyperactive patients. Not only do tranquilizers quiet upset patients, but many who previously were unreachable become available for psychotherapy (5). Tranquilizers have also been used effectively to modify the behavior of extremely disturbed, defiant, and hostile children who had resisted other types of sedation and therapy (15). They have been used, too, to relieve the distress of nonpsychotic persons who were suffering from anxiety, tension states, alcoholism, insomnia, headaches, and various psychosomatic disorders (*10*).

Limitations of Tranquilizers

There are now on the market over twenty types of tranquilizers, with more to be expected soon. Very few of these drugs have had a thorough scientific test, and there has hardly been time to determine their long-range effects on the human body.

Current indications are that ataractic drugs are potent chemicals which can cause serious reactions and complications. Some of the untoward effects already observed are dermatitis, muscular tremors, hypotension, agranulocytosis and other blood changes, jaundice, seizures, delirium, circulatory insufficiency, edema, cardio-vascular disturbances, and gastro-intestinal disorders (*3, 7*).

Exactly how tranquilizers act on the body is not known. Their effects are not fully predictable. Some tense people are depressed rather than calmed by these drugs, and others experience an extreme state of excitation. Some drugs are less potent than others, but none are sufficiently harmless to be taken indiscriminately by laymen. It is a matter of serious concern to the medical profession that in 1956 doctors issued an estimated 30 million prescriptions for drugs about which so little is known, and that the public spent between $135 and $150 million on them (*25*). The unquestioned acceptance of tranquilizers, or "happy pills," as a panacea for the relief of common anxiety, emotional upsets, and the routine tensions of everyday living may itself be considered a neurotic manifestation (*26*).

Chemotherapy as an Adjunct to Psychotherapy

There is a widespread feeling that the therapeutic advantages of ataractic drugs outweigh the risk involved in using them. However, few informed people look upon these drugs as the answer to the problem of mental illness. Drugs are a valuable adjunct to psychotherapy, but they are not a cure. Without accompanying psychotherapy, a relapse rate as high as 80 percent has been reported after 6 months of withdrawal from treatment with tranquilizers (*44*). Nor are chemicals the answer to the tensions of everyday life. Tranquilizing pills provide a feeling of ease and relaxation, but they do not treat the stress conditions underlying an individual's emotional state. The day has not yet come when lasting peace of mind can be found in a pill or capsule.

SUMMARY

During the past 50 years, mental illness has assumed the significance of a major public health problem. The rate of mental illness has climbed steadily, and today more than half the hospital beds in the United States are occupied by psychiatric patients.

This increase of mental illness has not been paralleled by an increase in professional personnel or facilities. As a result, few patients in mental hospitals are receiving the type of treatment designed to rehabilitate them in the shortest possible time.

Outside the mental hospitals, it is estimated that about 10 million people are suffering from some type of mental or emotional disorder which requires professional care. There is little prospect that sufficient professional services will be made available to these people unless something is done about accelerating the training programs for therapists and equalizing their distribution over the nation.

The solution to the problem of mental illness lies in its prevention. A great deal has been done in the field of preventive mental hygiene during the past half-century. However, the American public does not appear to be fully aware of the significance of this problem as judged by its willingness to finance research and prevention programs for mental illness.

PROBLEMS AND PROJECTS

1. Determine the amount of money allocated in your state for the support of maladjusted individuals. How does this compare with the funds allocated for the prevention of maladjustment?
2. About what percent of the total population of your state is now confined to mental institutions? What is a fair estimate of the number of maladjusted people in your state who are not in institutions?
3. How many psychiatrists are there in your state? How are they distributed over the state? About how many people have no access to psychiatric services?
4. Where are the institutions in your state for the care of (a) the aged, (b) delinquent boys, (c) delinquent girls, (d) psychotic persons, (e) mentally deficient people? What is the procedure whereby people are confined to these institutions?
5. List some of the contemporary pressures which may possibly be contributing to the increase of personality disorders.

6. Interview several people who have used tranquilizer drugs for a period of time. Describe how these drugs affected them physically, mentally, and emotionally. How did the drugs influence the manner in which these people handled their personal problems?

7. List several organizations in your community which are working toward improvement of mental health. What financial support do they receive? What are their activities?

8. Discuss some movies or novels built around mental health themes. Do you think they have any influence on the public's attitude toward mental illness?

9. Is mental illness primarily an American problem? Do similar problems exist in foreign countries? In primitive societies?

10. Do you consider it fair to measure governmental interest in the prevention of mental illness by comparing allocations for research in this field and in the field of animal diseases? Why?

SELECTED REFERENCES

1. Appel, K. E., "Mental Hygiene in the World Today," in W. B. Terhune, *Living Wisely and Well,* E. P. Dutton & Co., 1949.

2. Barton, W. E., "Hospital Services for the Mentally Ill," in *Mental Health in the United States,* The Annals of the American Academy of Political and Social Science (March, 1953), 286:107–115.

3. Bernstein, C., "Allergenicity of Tranquilizing Drugs," *Journal of the American Medical Association* (March, 1957), *163*:930–933.

4. Blain, D., "Private Practice of Psychiatry," in *Mental Health in the United States,* The Annals of the American Academy of Political and Social Science (March, 1953), 286:136–149.

5. Bowes, H. A., "The Ataractic Drugs: The Present Position of Chlorpromazine, Frenquel, Pacatal, and Reserpine in the Psychiatric Hospital," *American Journal of Psychiatry* (December, 1956), *113*:530–539.

6. Buell, B., "Planning Community Wide Attack on Behavior Disorders," in *Mental Health in the United States,* The Annals of the American Academy of Political and Social Science (March, 1953), 286:150–157.

7. Cohen, I. M., "Complications of Chlorpromazine Therapy," *American Journal of Psychiatry* (August, 1956), *113*:115–121.

8. Cole, N. J., *et al.,* "Mental Illness: A Survey Assessment of Community Rates, Attitudes, and Adjustments," *Archives of Neurology and Psychiatry* (April, 1957), 77:393–398.

9. Coleman, J. V., "Workers in the Field of Mental Health," in *Mental Health in the United States,* The Annals of the American Academy of Political and Social Science (March, 1953), 286:81–91.

10. Davies, E. B., "A New Drug to Relieve Anxiety," *British Medical Journal* (March, 1956), *1*:480–484.
11. Federal Security Agency, Public Health Service, National Institute of Mental Health, *Patients in Mental Institutions, 1949,* Public Health Service Publication No. 233, 1952.
12. Federal Security Agency, Public Health Service, National Institute of Mental Health, *The National Mental Health Program, Progress Report,* 1951.
13. Felix, R. H., and Kramer, M., "Extent of the Problem of Mental Disorders," in *Mental Health in the United States,* The Annals of the American Academy of Political and Social Science (March, 1953), *286*:5–14.
14. Felix, R. H., and Kramer, M., "Research in Epidemiology of Mental Illness," *Public Health Reports* (February, 1952), *67*:152–160.
15. Gatski, R. L., "Chlorpromazine in the Treatment of Emotionally Maladjusted Children," *Journal of the American Medical Association* (April, 1955), *157*:1298–1300.
16. Ginsburg, S. W., "The Neuroses," in *Mental Health in the United States,* The Annals of the American Academy of Political and Social Science (March, 1953), *286*:55–64.
17. Kaplan, L., and Baron, D., *Mental Hygiene and Life,* Harper & Brothers, 1952.
18. Lowry, J. V., "Public Mental Health Agencies, State and National," in *Mental Health in the United States,* The Annals of the American Academy of Political and Social Science (March, 1953), *286*:100–106.
19. Mangus, A. R., "Family Goals for the Rearing of Children," *On the Record,* Division of Mental Hygiene, Ohio State Department of Public Welfare (September, 1948), vol. 14, no. 7.
20. Mangus, A. R., and Seeley, J. R., *Mental Health Needs in a Rural and Semi-Rural Area of Ohio,* Division of Mental Hygiene, Ohio State Department of Public Welfare, 1950.
21. "Mental Health in Corrective Institutions," *Proceedings of the Seventy-First Congress of the American Prison Association,* New York, 1941.
22. Metropolitan Life Insurance Company, *Mental Disorders in the United States,* Charts, undated.
23. *Oregon Blue Book, 1951–52,* Office of the Secretary of State, Oregon State Printing Office (Salem, Oregon), 1952.
24. Pennes, H. H., "The Nature of Drugs with Mental Actions and Their Relation to Cerebral Function," *Bulletin of the New York Academy of Medicine,* (February, 1957), *33*:81–88.
25. Rodman, M. J., "Drugs for the Age of Anxiety," *R. N., A Journal for Nurses* (July, 1957), *20*:48–53.

26. Sargant, W., "On Chemical Tranquilizers," *British Medical Journal* (April, 1956), *1*:939–943.
27. Saul, L. J., *Bases of Human Behavior,* J. B. Lippincott Co., 1951.
28. Southern California Society for Mental Hygiene, *Annual Report* (Los Angeles), 1952.
29. State of California, Department of Mental Hygiene, *Biennial Report for 1950–52,* State Printing Office (Sacramento), 1953.
30. State of California, *Budget for Fiscal Year July 1, 1953 to June 30, 1954,* State Printing Office (Sacramento), 1953, pp. 51, 548–550.
31. State of California, Department of Mental Hygiene, *Mental Illness in California,* State Printing Office (Sacramento), 1953.
32. State of California, Department of Mental Hygiene, *Statistical Report for the Year Ending June 30, 1955,* State Printing Office (Sacramento), December, 1956.
33. The Institute of Living, *Annual Report 1955–56* (Hartford, Connecticut, 1956.
34. U.S. Department of Health, Education and Welfare, Public Health Service, National Institute of Mental Health, *Mental Health Statistics, Current Reports,* Series IMH-B53, December, 1952, and April, 1953.
35. U.S. Department of Health, Education and Welfare, Public Health Service, National Institute of Mental Health, "Patients in Public Hospitals for the Prolonged Care of the Mentally Ill, 1955," *Mental Health Statistics, Current Reports,* Series MHB-H-2, December, 1956.
36. U.S. Department of Health, Education and Welfare, Public Health Service, National Institute of Mental Health, *Patients in Mental Institutions, 1953,* Part II, "Public Hospitals for the Mentally Ill," Public Health Service Publication No. 495, 1956.
37. U.S. Department of Health, Education and Welfare, Public Health Service, National Institute of Mental Health, *Patients in Mental Institutions, 1953,* Part III, "Private Hospitals and General Hospitals with Psychiatric Facilities," Public Health Service Publication No. 495, 1957.
38. U.S. Department of Health, Education and Welfare, Public Health Service, National Office of Vital Statistics, *Vital Statistics of the U.S., 1954,* vol. I, 1956.
39. U.S. Department of Health, Education and Welfare, Public Health Service, National Office of Vital Statistics, *Vital Statistics of the U.S., 1955,* vol. II, 1957.
40. U.S. Department of Justice, Federal Bureau of Investigation, *The Crime Problem,* Mimeographed Bulletin, May 20, 1953.
41. U.S. Department of Justice, Federal Bureau of Investigation, *Uniform Crime Reports,* vol. XXVII, no. 2, Annual Bulletin, 1956.

42. U.S. Treasury Department, Fiscal Service, Bureau of Accounts, *Digest of Appropriations For the Support of the Government of the U.S., Fiscal Year Ending June 30, 1953,* 1953, p. 73.
43. Vogel, V. H., and Vogel, V. E., *Facts About Narcotics,* Science Research Associates, 1951.
44. Winkelman, N. W., Jr., "An Appraisal of Chlorpromozine," *American Journal of Psychiatry* (May, 1957), *113*:961–971.

Maladjustment in the Schools

WHETHER the schools of America promote mental health or neglect it has a significant impact on all preventive mental hygiene efforts. Almost every adult, irrespective of his current state of adjustment, was at one time or another under the influence of a school. What the school did, or did not do, to aid his adjustment is reflected in his personality development.

In this chapter our consideration is transferred from the problem of mental illness in society to the problem of actual or incipient mental illness in the schools. As we examine the mental health of school-age children and the mental health of the teachers who affect their development, we shall be able to judge more clearly the magnitude of the task faced by the schools of the nation.

MALADJUSTMENT AMONG SCHOOL-AGE CHILDREN

The mental health problems of adults are seen in miniature today among many children who are reacting to the pressures of growing up in ways which foreshadow serious personality disorders in the future.

The daily newspapers provide a dramatic picture of how some children are solving their problems. Hardly a day goes by that the press does not carry a startling story of children who through a distorted sense of values, or because of disturbed, frightened feelings, strike out blindly against themselves or against society.

In Figure 1 are titles selected from news items appearing in the nation's newspapers. Beneath these titles are stories of youngsters who are well on their way toward becoming the criminals, the neurotics, the psychotics, and the unhappy, ineffective citizens of tomorrow.

There are stories of murder, such as these: An 8-year-old girl killed her 10-month-old brother by holding his head in a tub of water. "I was jealous," the little girl said. She also confessed that she tried to injure another 10-month-old baby and a 3½-year-old cousin. "I hate them," she told the police, "my mother paid too much attention to them."

Boy Hacks Mother, Burns Body Over 'Bawling Out'

Parents Killed By Schoolboy

Convict Who Shot Two First Stole in 5th Grade

TEEN-AGE ARRESTS SOLVE 25 LOOTINGS

Seventh-Grade Pupil Hangs Self in School

11-Year-Old Boy Lives on Streets By Selling Bottles

GIRL OF 16 TELLS OF LIFE AS PROSTITUTE

Boy's Present Shower Ends---Theft Discovered

Child Admits Killing Brother

FATHER SLAYER SAYS HE DID RIGHT

Girl Takes Her Life With Father's Gun

ONE TWIN TO BE BURIED TODAY, OTHER EXAMINED

Boy Admits Starting Fire in School

Boy, 9, Faces Murder Charge on Girl's Death

Boy, 9, Confesses Thefts of $1425

Texas Sex Club Bared

Psychiatrists Probe Young Killer's Mind

Teen-Age Dope Addiction Huge Problem

FIGURE 1. A Newspaper Picture of Juvenile Delinquency.

In another instance, a 9-year-old boy was charged with murder after inflicting 100 stab wounds on a girl playmate. "She pushed me and I got mad," he explained—then added, "When I was hitting her with my knife I had to change blades because this one blade on my knife was too dull."

Cases of homicide among older children are almost commonplace.

A 12-year-old boy shot his father with a rifle because, "My father was always whipping me and I didn't like that kind of punishment." A 14-year-old boy shot his mother and father because his mother was "stingy" and his father "kept punishing me when I didn't have it coming." A 14-year-old girl shot her twin sister. She explained, without remorse, that she had hated her for years and, "I would kill her again." And a 16-year-old boy hacked his mother to death with a hatchet, then ignited her body with kerosene because, "She bawled me out for playing hookey."

All of these stories appeared in the daily newspapers within a period of a few months.

Other stories tell of children who solve their problems by taking what they want or need. For instance, a 10-year-old boy grabbed a bag containing over $300 and calmly walked out of a store. He bought presents for his teachers (who did not accept them), and distributed coins freely to his classmates. When apprehended he explained, "I just thought the teacher would give me better marks."

Another 9-year-old was caught snatching $225 from an unguarded cash register. It was found that his lifetime total of robberies already amounted to $1425. A 15-year-old boy picked up by police after a gang war was found to have five automatic pistols, a bayonet, and two gas guns—loot from previous robberies.

Some stories are of children who seek escape from their problems. Stories such as those of a boy of 13 who was found hanging dead in the school locker room after having been reprimanded for chewing gum and denied the use of the gym; a girl who shot herself with her father's pistol after having been told she was in ill health; and an 11-year-old boy who spent three weeks living in service station rest rooms after having been sent home from school with a note telling of some trouble he had been in.

And there are many stories of teen-agers whose disturbed emotions or warped sense of values lead them to the use of narcotics and sex as forms of expression. Recently a 16-year-old girl was apprehended working as a prostitute. Her record showed two arrests on similar charges, dating back to the age of 14. In one town, two dozen teen-agers were discovered in a sex club where, instead of paying dues, members were required to indulge in sex relations once a week. In another city, 24 high school boys and girls were arrested at a morphine and marijuana party.

These are but a few instances of children whose behavior has reached the attention of the newspaper. It might be said that the cases cited are unusual instances, or that they exaggerate the problem. While it is true that these stories are unusual, dealing as they do with children who murder, rob, steal, and rape, evidence shows that they do not exaggerate the problem. Research data, while less dramatic than newspaper accounts of individual incidents, indicate that maladjustment among children is so prevalent that it is difficult to exaggerate its influence on society.

Juvenile Delinquency

It may be something of a shock to learn that school-age children are capable of the crimes reported in the public press. It is even more shocking to read the national statistics which indicate that children not only commit these crimes, but that they commit them frequently and at an alarmingly increasing rate.

MAGNITUDE OF JUVENILE DELINQUENCY.   In 1956, almost half of all persons arrested were youths under 18 years of age. These youngsters were involved in

24.7 percent of the arrests for robbery

53.9 percent of the arrests for burglary

66.4 percent of the arrests for auto theft

9.5 percent of arrests for crime against the person (*50*).

More than 1,450,000 boys and girls came to the attention of the police in 1955. Most of these youngsters were dealt with directly on an unofficial basis. However, each year police departments find it necessary to refer more and more children to the juvenile courts. Half a million juveniles appeared in court in 1955 and the predictions are that this number will double by 1965 (*17*).

INCREASE OF DELINQUENCY.   The rapid increase of juvenile delinquency in recent years is illustrated in Figure 2. In the 7-year period following 1948, juvenile court cases increased 70 percent, although there was only a 16 percent increase in the population of youngsters 10 to 17 years of age during this same period (*47*). In nonurban areas, the increase in juvenile delinquency was even more marked, showing an average increase from 1948 to 1955 of 78 percent. Thus, juvenile delinquency is not only increasing faster than the juvenile population but it has gone beyond being merely a "big city" problem and has reached the hamlet as well as the metropolis (*17*).

UNDISCOVERED JUVENILE DELINQUENCY.   There exists today a large "underworld" of juvenile delinquents for whom there are no official records. This hidden delinquency makes the true magnitude of juvenile crime in the United States impossible to determine. It is known among persons who work with children that many youngsters whose behavior is just as asocial as those brought into the courts manage to avoid ap-

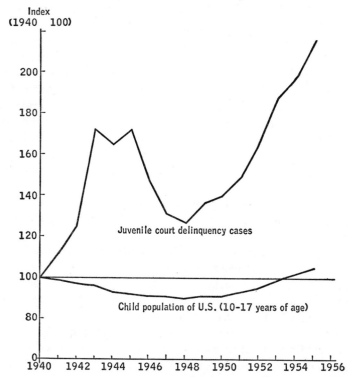

FIGURE 2. Juvenile Court Delinquency Cases and Child Population of the United States (10–17 Years of Age), 1940–1956. (Adapted from U.S. Department of Health, Education and Welfare, Social Security Administration, Children's Bureau, *Juvenile Court Statistics, 1955,* Children's Bureau Statistical Series No. 37, 1956, p. 6.)

prehension. In any large city, it is probable that as many undetected delinquents may be found in the local high schools as there are official delinquents confined to juvenile detention homes.

Evidence on this point is provided in several studies. In one study, 114 boys who had committed 616 serious offenses were observed over a 10-year period. Only 40 of these boys became delinquent officially, and 13 committed no further delinquencies. However, 61 boys, who admitted 174 serious offenses, did not come to the attention of any official agency (23). In other words, about 60 percent of the delinquent juveniles in this study were unknown to the police or to juvenile agencies. In another eastern city, a survey of the case records of social agencies revealed that one-third of the boys and girls who spoke of their delinquent behavior to the case workers were unknown to the police (46).

While this evidence is inconclusive, it suggests vast amounts of hidden delinquency. As mentioned previously, only a small percentage of the juveniles apprehended by police are brought to the attention of the juvenile courts. For instance, in 1949, Los Angeles police made over 50,000 juvenile arrests, but only 10,000 were brought before the court; the others were disposed of without record (56). The United States Children's Bureau estimates that at least three-fourths of the apprehended juvenile offenders in the nation are never entered on any official records (46).

Taken together, these facts indicate the records of official agencies paint a very conservative picture of juvenile delinquency in the United States.

RECIDIVISM AND COST.   Few citizens realize that each year the nation's taxpayers spend more money on criminals and delinquents than for the support of the public schools. In 1953–1954, about $9 billion were spent to operate public elementary and secondary schools, and to put up new school buildings (44). The annual cost of crime in America is almost twice as great—about $15 billion per year (45). The cost to the public of handling each year's crop of delinquent children exceeds $105 million—an average of $300 per child. It is even more expensive to retain boys and girls in corrective institutions, the cost being about $2500 per child. These expenditures make an interesting comparison with the $264.76 per year spent for the education of the average pupil in the public schools (44).

Despite the huge sums of money expended, we haven't been doing a very good job with delinquent children. Recidivism—the repetition of delinquent acts—is so common that many of the children picked up by police are familiar faces. In 1945, the Federal Bureau of Investigation received 49,566 finger-print arrest cards for persons under 18. Of these, 10,734 (21.7 percent) were repeaters. In 1952, more than 23 percent of the arrest cards for persons under 18 years of age were recidivists (14).

The United States Children's Bureau believes that much of the money being spent on juvenile delinquents is wasted. This conclusion is supported by the following facts:

1. More than half the inmates of our prisons were once juvenile delinquents. That is, half of the youngsters who appear before juvenile courts continue with their asocial behavior and end up as adult criminals.
2. Approximately 35 percent of the boys and girls who come before juvenile courts have been there before.
3. Many of the boys and girls released from training schools or detention homes are sent right back to them after a few months of freedom.
4. Hundreds of children just on the verge of trouble are known to police, but the police cannot do anything about them. (*45, 46*)

These facts stress the importance of preventing juvenile delinquency, wherever possible, through alleviating problem behavior as soon as it appears in the life of a child.

DELINQUENCY AND THE SCHOOLS. Children start to develop delinquent tendencies much earlier in life than most people realize. The majority of boys and girls who come before juvenile courts are between 15 and 17 years of age (*45*). The Gluecks' study (*10*) of 500 delinquent boys found that the largest number appeared in court when they were between 11 and 13 years old. However, nine-tenths of these boys showed signs of becoming delinquent before they were 11 years old.

The following case illustrates how far back in life the roots of delinquent behavior may reach:

> At nine years of age, Jerry and five other young boys were picked up by police for stealing about $2.50 worth of small articles from a downtown department store. Jerry had always been an oversensitive and erratic boy, and often had uneasy feelings which he could not control. His father had stomach trouble and was exceedingly nervous. His mother was nervous to the point of becoming hysterical when trouble arose. One day, in a fit of annoyance, his father told him he was an adopted child. Perhaps that was why Jerry had gone downtown with the other boys and let them persuade him to steal from the store. He'd known it was wrong, and he didn't really want the stuff, but he just hadn't cared.[1]

Here was a boy who attempted to overcome his discouragement and anxiety through the satisfaction derived from delinquent companions. He had a real need for frequent contacts with someone who would

---

[1] Condensed from Stone, Castendyck, and Hanson (*41*), p. 30.

show complete acceptance of him and with whom he could discuss the many things that bothered him. Fortunately, he found this sympathetic counselor in the community. Had he not, another life of crime might have been nurtured at the age of 9.

The Director of the Federal Bureau of Investigation described the build-up toward delinquency in this manner: "In the public mind, juvenile delinquency is associated with arrests and juvenile courts. This is the last step. Juvenile delinquency first manifests itself in truancy, in rebellion against orderly home life, and in acts of vandalism" (13).

This brings the problem of delinquency prevention directly into the schools. Delinquency starts early. By the time a juvenile is brought before a court he has spent several years under the influence of the school. The nature of this influence is expressed in the reactions of numerous institutionalized delinquents who blame unfriendly teachers and an uninteresting curriculum for much of their trouble (39).

Unadjusted Children in School

Symptoms of emotional distress and inability to get along in school are often the first danger signals of delinquency in the offing. Among the unhappy, disturbed, rebellious children in school are the potential delinquents and the emotionally maladjusted adults of tomorrow.

The studies reviewed in this section indicate that from kindergarten through college there are many children who need help in adjusting to life: so many, in fact, that schools may be justly criticized for paying too much attention to the development of intellectual prowess and too little to the education of feelings.

STUDIES OF ELEMENTARY SCHOOL CHILDREN. Evidence shows that many youngsters begin school with serious emotional handicaps. For instance, the New York Mental Hygiene Committee study of 277 kindergarten and preschool children found that 10 to 15 percent of these 4- and 5-year-olds were in need of active psychiatric help (19). Similarly, studies of young children in the Ohio schools revealed a large percentage of unadjusted youngsters in the elementary grades. The Ohio State Division of Mental Hygiene analyzed the mental health of 543 first graders in Butler County and found the distribution of nervous traits shown in Figure 3. The reporting of four or more of the nervous traits indicated was considered to be symptomatic of serious maladjustment. Upon this basis, the investigators classified 20 percent of the first graders as seriously maladjusted (55).

Another mental hygiene survey conducted among fourth, fifth, and sixth grade children in the Butler County schools involved 1638 youngsters. Through personality tests, teacher evaluations, and personal data from school records it was determined that 30 percent of the boys and 19 percent of the girls rated low in total adjustment (*21*).

An adjustment survey of third and sixth grade children in the public

Trait	Percentage of children reporting trait
Nail biting	46%
Frequent colds	36%
Undue tiredness	30%
Bad dreams	26%
Insomnia	17%
Frequent eye pain	15%
Frequent illness	12%
Frequent crying	9%

FIGURE 3. Percentage of 543 First Grade Children Reporting Specified Nervous Traits. (Adapted from R. H. Woodward and A. R. Mangus, *Nervous Traits Among First Grade Children in Butler County Schools* (Hamilton, Ohio), Butler County Mental Hygiene Association, July, 1949.)

schools of Miami County, Ohio, found 19.1 percent of the children maladjusted to a serious degree. The prevalence of maladjustment was higher among sixth graders (20.8 percent) than among third graders (17.8 percent). The greatest incidence of maladjustment was found among children with IQ's below 100 (*20*).

Roger's study (*37*) of 1524 pupils in grades one to six of the Columbus, Ohio, elementary schools found that 12 percent of the children were seriously maladjusted, and 30 percent more were poorly adjusted. It was noted also that 23 percent of the children were reading a year below capacity, 22 percent were too bright for their grades, and 23 percent were too dull to be benefited by schooling.

Mental health surveys of children in other sections of the country tend to support the general data on maladjustment found in the Ohio studies. For instance, Snyder's study (*40*) of elementary school children in New Jersey concluded that 44 percent of the 829 children examined were "problem children." In Oregon, the Mental Health Association estimated that 15 percent of the children in the third grade, and 21 percent of the children in the fifth grade were emotionally damaged (*24*). In New York, the State Youth Commission studied 5795 children in grades three through six, using tests of intelligence, school achievement records, a check list of behavior patterns, personality evaluations, and sociometric devices. It was found that 17 percent of the children examined showed some symptoms which suggested the possibility of serious social breakdown or personal unhappiness in adult life (*18:39*).

STUDIES OF SECONDARY SCHOOL STUDENTS. The United States Office of Education reports that only about half of the children now in the fifth grade will stay in school long enough to graduate from high school (*51*). It might be supposed that the maladjusted elementary school children would drop out of school, leaving the better adjusted children to go on through high school. Research shows that this is not the case. Maladjustment among high school students continues to reflect the emotional disorders reported in studies of elementary school children.

Hertzman's study (*11*) of 4213 high school students in Cincinnati, Ohio, reported that 45 percent of the boys and girls had symptoms of mental illness. The symptoms of maladjustment found among these students were as follows:

Symptom	Number of Cases
Fits	25
Stuttering	242
Kidney trouble (nonorganic)	172
Allergies	448
Stomach trouble (nonorganic)	55
Asocial behavior	103
Nightmares	225
Choking sensations	351
Dizziness or fainting	185
Examination excitement	92
Total	1898

One of the most carefully conducted studies of the mental health of high school students was made in Maryland by the Prince Georges County Mental Health Clinic (*43*). Under the guidance of the National Institute of Mental Health, the adjustment of 810 ninth grade pupils of the white public high schools in the county was studied intensively.

The overall findings of the survey follow:[2]

Level of Adjustment	Number of Children	Percent
Well adjusted: A happy child who gets along well and accomplishes reasonably well the things that usually go with his age or level of development.	564	69.6
Moderately maladjusted: A child who is not so happy as he might be, has moderate difficulties in getting on, growing up presents something of a struggle.	182	22.4
Severely maladjusted: A child who at his present rate is likely sooner or later to have serious problems of adjustment and may need special help or care because of such problems.	64	8.0

OTHER STUDIES. The St. Paul Survey (*41*), which involved a detailed study of 1466 children, isolated 727 children who were referred to the Community Service for guidance or therapy. This represented almost half of the children who lived in the area selected for analysis. Their problems ranged from academic difficulties, to conflict with authority, undesirable personality traits, stealing, fighting, and withdrawal into a world of fantasy.

Mental health studies of college students reveal that personality difficulties exist at all educational levels. Typical of these studies are those of Rice (*36*) and Palmer (*32*). Rice used faculty ratings, personal evaluations by roommates, and self-evaluations to assay the mental health of 385 college women. She found that 32 percent of these students had some psychotic tendencies. More than two-thirds of the total group had such delicate emotional balance that a precipitating cause might easily have pushed them into a psychosis. Palmer used a questionnaire to study the physical, emotional, and socioeconomic problems of college students. He found that 65 percent of the men and women students showed evidences of emotional maladjustment. Approximately 16 percent of the groups was considered to be seriously maladjusted.

SUMMARY OF STUDIES OF CHILD MALADJUSTMENT. The studies cited above were made under varying conditions, using different techniques, different populations, and different definitions of maladjustment.

[2] Adapted from Ullman (*43*) Table 12, p. 25.

Therefore, it is not possible to summarize them in terms of exact quantitative standards. However, when viewed as a whole, these studies lead to some tentative interpretations on the extent of maladjustment among school children in America.

The thirteen studies listed in Table 6 indicate that from 10 to 50 percent of the children observed could be classified as either moderately or seriously maladjusted. The median percentage of maladjustment among the studies cited is 25 percent.

TABLE 6. Findings of Thirteen Studies Related to Maladjustment Among School-Age Children

Study[a]	Grade Level Studied	Percent Found To Be Moderately or Seriously Maladjusted
Stone (41)	Elementary and secondary	50
Hertzman (11)	Secondary	45
Snyder (40)	Elementary	44
Rogers (38)	Grades 1–6	42
Ullman (43)	Grade 9	30
Mangus and Woodward (21)	Grades 4, 5, and 6	25
Woodward and Mangus (55)	Grade 1	20
Mangus and Seeley (20)	Grades 3 and 6	19
New York State Youth Commission (18)	Grades 3 to 6	17
Palmer (32)	College men and women	16
Oregon Mental Health Association (24)	Grades 3 and 5	15–21
Lowrey (19)	Preschool	10–15
Median of studies, all ages		25

[a] Italic numbers in parenthesis refer to studies cited at the end of this chapter.

It appears safe to assume, then, that 25 percent of the children and youth in American schools and colleges are sufficiently maladjusted to require professional care or therapy. The Midcentury White House Conference on Children and Youth supported this conclusion in its statement that one-fourth of the nation's 21 million elementary school children were in need of special mental health treatment. However, Rogers (37) considers this estimate of maladjustment too low. His studies indicate that out of a class of 40 children, from 30 to 50 percent will be more or less maladjusted. Among this group, 17 to 26 percent will later on have disturbed feelings ranging from unhappiness to psychoses; 1 to 2 percent will commit major crimes; 8 to 10 percent will become seriously ill mentally; and 3 to 4 percent will be so retarded that self-support will be difficult.

If we use the conservative estimate of 25 percent of maladjustment among children and youth, and apply this rate to the total population of youngsters in the nation's schools, we can obtain some indication of the maladjustment problem. In 1956–57, there were 39.4 million children and youth in the schools and colleges of the United States. If one-fourth of these were maladjusted, it would mean that about 9.85 million youngsters are having a difficult time growing up. This estimate corresponds very closely with the prediction that approximately 10 million people in the general population are psychologically disturbed. It points to the possibility that most of these disturbed individuals are being nurtured in the schools of the nation.

School Drop-Outs

Each year, large numbers of children who are out of harmony with their schools, drop out and disappear into the general population. In numbers alone, the drop-out problem is a serious one. Table 7 shows what happened to the group of children who entered the public schools in 1938. By the time the first graders reached the eighth grade, over a million and a half children had dropped out of school. Only 45 percent of the children who entered the first grade in 1938 remained to enter high school in 1946. More than 2 million children drop out of the public schools between the first and the twelfth grades.

This represents a serious loss in human potential for the nation. Some of these children leave school because their earnings are urgently needed at home. Some do not have the academic ability required, although this factor seems to be less important than commonly supposed. As one study shows (*1*), more than two-thirds of the high school drop-outs are of normal intelligence—yet most of them were failing in their studies at the time they left school.

The reasons most frequently given by the drop-outs themselves tell a story of school failure and school misery. These children had learned that school had nothing to offer them, so they left at the earliest possible opportunity. The Midcentury White House Conference summarized the plight of the drop-outs in this way:

A large percentage come from backgrounds which leave them without the experience in abstract thought required for good showing on intelligence tests; they are not academically minded; their speech, clothing and habits deviate from those of the middle income groups conventionally accepted as standard by the school. Early in their school careers they are segregated in large numbers into opportunity groups, they fail, they don't fit, and they feel it. (54:269)

TABLE 7.   Enrollment by Grade in Full-Time Public Day
Schools, 1938–1949[a]

Grade	Year	Enrollment
First	1938–39	3,167,803
Second	1939–40	2,333,076
Third	1940–41	2,263,315
Fourth	1941–42	2,196,732
Fifth	1942–43	2,101,723
Sixth	1943–44	1,997,806
Seventh	1944–45	1,897,743
Eighth	1945–46	1,653,683
Ninth	1946–47	1,761,020
Tenth	1947–48	1,502,743
Eleventh	1948–49	1,494,477
Twelfth	1949–50	1,122,872

[a] Adapted from U.S. Office of Education, Federal Security Agency, "Statistics of State School Systems, 1949–50," *Biennial Survey of Education in the United States, 1949–50,* U.S. Government Printing Office, 1952, Table 10, p. 46.

In other words, youngsters don't simply drop out of school. They are squeezed out by a curriculum which has nothing to do with their needs, by standards which they cannot measure up to, and by social forces which they cannot comprehend. These millions of embittered, dissatisfied, discouraged drop-outs add to the problem of psychological disorder in the nation.

MALADJUSTMENT AMONG TEACHERS

Mental health studies of teachers reveal that most teachers are well-adjusted men and women who exert a wholesome influence on the personality development of children. However, there are among the public school teachers of the nation a relatively small group whose presence in the classroom is a sore spot in education. There are teachers who in their daily contact with children are doing much damage to the lives of others. These teachers are a serious concern to themselves, to parents, and to school administrators.

The Nature of Teacher Maladjustment

We need not look far for evidence of maladjusted teachers. Almost anyone who has gone through the public schools can relate instances of "queer" teachers. In fact, Townsend's study (42) indicates that it is almost impossible for a child not to encounter such teachers during the years he spends in school. According to this study, the chances are seven to one that a child will be under the influence of at least two unstable, neurotic, or psychopathic teachers during the course of his 12 years in school.

Sometimes these maladjusted teachers are exposed dramatically as in the case of a teacher who was discharged from a school district for brutality. This woman had been punishing children unjustifiably and cruelly for years. She was known to hit children with her baton, slap their faces, choke them, and pull their hair. The final act which led to her dismissal was that of striking a child over the head with a cello! More often, however, maladjusted teachers exert their influence within the classroom in ways which do not reach public attention, but which are nonetheless devastating to children's emotional health. For example, Altman's observations (3) of classroom teachers in New York City found some teachers who indulged in vicious temper tantrums, others who humiliated and antagonized children through the use of sarcasm, nagging, and shouting, and some who were almost sadistic in their disciplinary treatment of children.

Three studies dealing with the classroom behavior of teachers who later became psychotic show how some teachers remain in the classroom for years, while displaying serious symptoms of emotional disorder. Wall's analysis (53) of 50 women teachers who were hospitalized for psychoses disclosed that while they were in the classroom these women were tense, overactive, and unable to relax. They drove themselves and they drove the children. Thirty of these teachers were hypochondriacs, consulting physician after physician and seeking out health cults. Fourteen had shown evidence of increasing sensitiveness, suspiciousness, and withdrawal over a long period of time.

Allen's study (2) of psychotic men teachers showed a classroom pattern of seclusiveness, irritability, overconscientiousness, overactivity, and excessive worrying. Fifteen of these men had previous attacks of mental illness prior to this study.

Mason's investigation (*22*) of 733 men and women teachers confined in mental hospitals found that while they were in the classroom these teachers exhibited the following forms of behavior (listed in rank order of importance):

Men Teachers	*Women Teachers*
Introversion	Overambition
Overambition	Hyperactivity
Hyperactivity	Efficiency
Efficiency	Quiet and retiring disposition
Neuroticism	Irritability
Quiet and retiring disposition	Introversion
Anxiety	Neuroticism
Irritability	Anxiety
Selfishness	Selfishness
Eccentricity	Eccentricity

When Fenton (*9*:318 ff.) studied maladjusted teachers in the California schools, he discovered teachers who had little interest in children, who were mean, sarcastic, moody, and irritable. Others were so dependent upon the principal that they would run to him several times a day for assurance. Some had frequent sick spells in the classroom, some made sexual advances toward children, and a few were so antagonistic toward children and toward their colleagues that no one could approach them. In addition to these cases of serious maladjustment, there are many teachers who must struggle so with their emotional problems that their teaching efficiency is seriously impaired. Thousands of teachers are working under such great emotional strain that it interferes with sleeping, eating, and the ability to relax. Thousands more are in ill health because of worry and nervousness.

The Incidence of Teacher Maladjustment

Few parents would willingly send their children to teachers such as those described above. Fortunately, maladjusted teachers represent only a small minority of the total number of teachers in the nation's classrooms.

As a group, teachers are no more maladjusted than are other professional groups. For example, the studies of Fenton, Wall, and Allen showed that only about 5 percent of all psychiatric patients admitted to mental hospitals are teachers. If teachers were hospitalized for psychoses in proportion to their total number in the population, over 7 percent of the patients in mental hospitals would be drawn from the teaching profession (9:287). Thus, teachers do not manifest psychoses out of proportion to their expected quota.

In numbers alone, personality disturbances among teachers is not a serious problem. The seriousness of this situation lies in the influence being exerted on millions of children who are forced to sit in the classrooms of these teachers. Therefore, it is vitally important for all educators to know how many teachers in the nation's schools are maladjusted and how many children are being exposed to them. Research studies of teacher maladjustment are woefully inadequate. In the following pages, 11 significant studies are summarized. These studies are not conclusive, nor are the techniques used entirely valid. They do, however provide us with an indication of the extent of this problem.

A study of the mental health of 600 teachers was made by Hicks (*12*) in 1933. He found that 17 percent of the total group were unusually nervous, and that 11 percent had had "nervous breakdowns."

Peck's survey (*33*) of the mental health of 110 women teachers using the Thurstone Personality Schedule found 21 percent to be emotionally maladjusted, and 12 percent in need of psychiatric advice. The symptoms of maladjustment discovered and the percentage of teachers evidencing these symptoms are shown below (*33:406*):

Symptom	*Percentage of Teachers*
Difficulty speaking in public	46
Discouraged easily	45
Feelings easily hurt	37
Moody	37
Nervous	33
Shy	33
Disturbed by criticism	31
Lack self-confidence	30
Confused easily	30
Dislikes responsibility	26
Frequent indigestion	26
Conflict between sex and morality	25
Often in state of excitement	25
Critical of other people	24
Frequently in low spirits	22
Desire to commit suicide	14

In 1942, a team of examiners under the direction of Dr. Emil Altman (3), Chief Medical Examiner of the New York City Schools, surveyed the adjustment of public school teachers in that city. They concluded that 33 percent of the teachers were maladjusted and 12 percent were in need of psychiatric service. Almost 4500 teachers in the city schools were diagnosed as in need of psychiatric treatment; 1500 were classified as mental cases. Yet all of these teachers were in the classroom at the time this study was made.

Boynton (5) through the use of an adjustment inventory found that in a group of 1500 teachers, maladjustment ranged from 33 percent for the teachers in the 46–50 year age group, to 49 percent for teachers in the 16–25 year age group. He found that elementary school teachers had more problems of adjustment than did high school teachers.

Broxson (6) used the Bell Adjustment Inventory with a group of 51 teachers and discovered that 35 percent of the group was emotionally maladjusted to a definite or serious degree.

Fenton's investigation (9) of 241 teachers in California schools uncovered 22.5 percent who were suffering from psychoneuroses or other personality problems which required mental hygiene assistance. His interpretation of these findings was: "Evidence of personality difficulties in over one-fifth of the teachers in good school systems is sufficiently serious to make the mental hygiene of teachers a major obligation of school administrators and one which can no longer be neglected" (9:290).

Blair (4) surveyed the mental health of 205 teachers using the Multiple-Choice Rorschach Test. On the basis of this technique he found that 9 percent of the teachers were seriously maladjusted.

Randall (35) used another approach to the evaluation of teacher maladjustment. She studied the lengthy absences of teachers during 1949–1950. It was found that of the 1036 absences in excess of 10 days, almost 10 percent were for "nervous conditions."

The National Education Association has made several important surveys of the adjustment of teachers. These studies are not highly valid from a scientific point of view, but they do have the virtue of including large numbers of teachers. The Department of Classroom Teachers made a questionnaire survey of 5150 teachers in 1938. On the basis of the responses received, it was concluded that 37.5 percent of the nation's teachers had worries intense enough to interfere with sleep, efficiency as a teacher, and physical health (26). Another study of 2200 elementary and secondary school teachers made by the Research Division of the

TABLE 8. Summary of Eleven Studies of Teacher Maladjustment

Study[a]	Number of Teachers Involved	Findings	
Hicks (12)	600	17	percent unusually nervous
		11	percent had nervous breakdowns
Peck (33)	110	21	percent emotionally maladjusted
		12	percent in need of psychiatric advice
Altman (3)	Approx. 35,000	33	percent maladjusted
		12	percent in need of psychiatric help
Boynton (5)	1,500	33–49	percent maladjusted
Broxson (6)	51	35	percent emotionally maladjusted to a definite or serious degree
Fenton (9)	241	22.5	percent with serious personality problems
Blair (4)	205	9	percent seriously maladjusted
Randall (35)	Approx. 10,000	10	percent of lengthy absences due to nervous conditions
Department of Classroom Teachers (26)	5,150	37.5	percent seriously worried and nervous
NEA Research Division (29)	2,200	43	percent working under considerable strain or tension
NEA Research Division (27)	4,167	20–30	percent unhappy and would not again go into teaching

[a] Italic numbers in parenthesis refer to references at the end of this chapter.

NEA found 43 percent of these teachers to be working under considerable strain and nervous tension (*29*).

In 1957, further evidence of unhappiness among teachers was secured through a nation-wide survey of 5602 teachers. It was found that 15 percent were so unhappy in their work that if given the opportunity to start over they would not choose teaching as a career, and another 11.7 percent were doubtful whether they would go into teaching again (*30*).

Implications of Teacher Maladjustment Studies

On the basis of the studies cited above and summarized in Table 8, we may draw the following conclusions regarding maladjustment among teachers:

1. From 27–43 percent are unhappy, nervous, dissatisfied, and working under considerable strain.
2. From 17–49 percent may be classified as maladjusted, although not seriously disordered.
3. From 9 to 35 percent are probably in need of psychiatric care.

Although these studies are sketchy and lack scientific exactness, we can get some idea of the significance of maladjustment among teachers by using the minimum percentages found in these investigations and applying them to the total teacher population. In 1957–58 there were 1,327,743 teachers employed in the public elementary and secondary day schools. The pupil-teacher ratio for that year was 25.2.[3] The *minimum* figures on teacher maladjustment derived from the 11 studies cited were: (1) Blair's data that 9 percent of the teachers are seriously maladjusted, (2) Hicks' finding that 17 percent are unusually nervous, and (3) the NEA reports that at least 25 percent of the teachers are so unhappy that they would not go into teaching again.

Applying these figures to the total teaching population in 1957 yields the following results:

Classification of Teacher Maladjustment	Percent of Teachers	Total Number of Teachers Affected, 1957	Total Number of Children Involved, 1957
Seriously maladjusted	9	119,497	3,011,324
Unusually nervous	17	225,716	5,688,043
Unhappy, worried, dissatisfied	25	331,936	8,364,787

[3] Research Division of The National Education Association, "Statistics for 1957–58," *NEA Research Bulletin* (February, 1958) 36:9–12.

There is probably much overlapping in these categories. The teachers classified as unhappy, worried, and dissatisfied may include those who were unusually nervous and those who were seriously maladjusted. Therefore, it is more accurate to consider only those children who were in classes with teachers described as seriously maladjusted. If Blair's data are accurate, and other studies show that his figures are low, then it is reasonable to conclude that *each day approximately 3 million youngsters are exposed to teachers who are so unbalanced that they should not be around children.*

The seriousness with which this situation is viewed by many educators in America is well expressed in this statement:

> . . . the emotionally unstable teacher exerts such a detrimental influence on children that she should not be allowed to remain in the classroom. The teacher with an uncontrollable temper, or one severely depressed, markedly prejudiced, flagrantly intolerant, bitingly sarcastic, or habitually scolding may endanger the emotional health of pupils as seriously as one with tuberculosis or some other communicable disease endangers their physical health. Such teachers need help, but while they are being helped they should be out of their classrooms so their pupils may be freed from the psychic injury and repression and fear which their presence creates. (25:138)

SUMMARY

The data on maladjustment in the schools indicate that educators have devoted too much of their attention to the development of intellect and not enough to the development of personality.

In schools, homes, and communities, youngsters are being subjected to experiences which may influence them to become the insane, the neurotics, the criminals, and the unhappy and ineffective citizens of tomorrow. Each year over a million youngsters come to the attention of the police; half a million appear before juvenile courts, and a large number are handled quietly by other social agencies—or never detected. Juvenile delinquency is today one of the major problems of society, and its incidence is increasing more rapidly than the rate of increase of juveniles in the population.

Any child who has emotional troubles is a potential delinquent, and research indicates that there are millions of such children in the public schools. Approximately one-fourth of our school-age children could be classified as maladjusted. In 1953, this amounted to almost 9½ million youngsters. Over 2 million children find so little satisfaction in school that they drop out between the first and the twelfth grades.

The problem of maladjustment among children is accentuated by the number of teachers who are ill-equipped to offer them any help because of their own personal difficulties. While no exact data on maladjustment among teachers are available, research indicates that in 1957 there were at least 120,000 seriously maladjusted teachers in the nation's classrooms. A group almost twice this size could be described as being unduly nervous. Almost one-fourth of the teachers now employed are so unhappy that they would not again become teachers if they had a chance to start over.

This is the problem which educators must face in the second half of the twentieth century. Mental illness and personality maladjustments are not things which happen outside the school door; they are in the school and in the classroom. If society is to be relieved of the financial burdens these ailments create, and if the human tragedies caused by these ailments are to be minimized, the schools of America must take upon themselves the responsibility for promoting mental health among children and among teachers.

PROBLEMS AND PROJECTS

1. Describe some children you have known whose behavior in school foreshadowed later delinquency.
2. Interview some school truants. Describe their feelings toward school.
3. Describe some maladjusted teachers you have encountered in your own school experience. What affect did they have on you?
4. What are some psychological reasons for finding a higher incidence of juvenile delinquency among lower socioeconomic groups?
5. Is it possible for a teacher to be maladjusted and still be successful in the classroom? Describe any such cases you may know of.
6. Interview some adults or youths who dropped out of school at an early age. Why did they leave school? Could the school have done anything to retain them?
7. Should secondary school boys and girls who want to leave school be forced to remain? If so, would the school program have to be altered in any way?
8. Select five teachers who are rated as poor or average. Determine if they would again go into teaching if they had the chance. What reasons are given for their decision?

9. Compare the desirable and undesirable aspects of tenure for teachers.
10. Does delinquency begin while children are of school age, or after they have left school?
11. What are the facts on juvenile delinquency in your state in terms of (a) numbers, (b) facilities for care, (c) cost, (d) age of offenders?
12. To what extent is delinquency connected with intellectual dullness? To psychoneurotic or psychopathic conditions?
13. What effects do movies, radio, television, newspapers, and magazines have on juvenile delinquency?
14. Ask several classroom teachers to rate their children as well adjusted, moderately maladjusted, and severely maladjusted. How do these ratings correspond with the data cited in this chapter?
15. Analyze some criticisms of the public schools. To what extent are schools being criticized for failing to promote the mental health of children? What are the implications of this situation?

SELECTED REFERENCES

1. Allen, Charles M., "What Have Our Drop-Outs Learned?" *Educational Leadership* (March, 1953), *10*:347–350.
2. Allen, E. B., "Psychiatric Disorders in Forty Male Teachers," *Journal of Nervous and Mental Disease* (October, 1942), *95*:204–206.
3. Altman, Emil, "Our Mentally Unbalanced Teachers," *The American Mercury* (April, 1941), *52*:39:401.
4. Blair, Glenn M., "Personality Adjustment of Teachers As Measured by the Multiple Choice Rorschach Test," *Journal of Educational Research* (May, 1946), *39*:652–657.
5. Boynton, P., "An Analysis of the Responses of Women Teachers on a Personality Inventory," *Peabody Journal of Education* (July, 1942), *20*:13–19.
6. Broxson, John A., "Problem Teachers," *Educational Administration and Supervision* (March, 1943), *29*:177–182.
7. *California Journal of Elementary Education,* vol. 22, November, 1953.
8. Federal Security Agency, Children's Bureau, *Juvenile Court Statistics 1946–1949,* Washington, D.C., Children's Bureau Statistical Series, No. 8, 1951.
9. Fenton, Norman, *Mental Hygiene in School Practice,* Stanford University Press, 1943.
10. Glueck, Sheldon, and Glueck, Eleanor, *Unraveling Juvenile Delinquency,* The Commonwealth Fund, 1950.
11. Hertzman, Jack, "High School Mental Hygiene Survey," *American Journal of Orthopsychiatry* (April, 1948), *18*:238–256.

12. Hicks, Francis P., *The Mental Health of Teachers,* Cullum and Ghertner Company, 1933.

13. Hoover, J. Edgar, "Crime Begins at Home," *Redbook Magazine,* October, 1946.

14. Hoover, J. Edgar, "Juvenile Delinquency," *Syracuse Law Review,* (Spring, 1953), 4:179–204.

15. Jaracz, William A., *Statistics of State School Systems 1950–51,* Federal Security Agency, Office of Education, Circular No. 367, March, 1953.

16. "Juvenile Delinquency," *Committee Print,* 81st Congress, 2nd Session, Printed for use of the Special Committee to Investigate Organized Crime in Interstate Commerce, 1950.

17. *Juvenile Delinquency,* Report of the Committee on the Judiciary, United States Senate, 85th Congress, 1st Session, Senate Report No. 130, March 4, 1957.

18. Kaplan, L., and Baron, D., *Mental Hygiene and Life,* Harper & Brothers, 1952.

19. Lowrey, Lawson, G., *Mental Hygiene Project at Kindergarten Level,* Mental Hygiene Committee, Vocational Adjustment Bureau for Girls, 1939.

20. Mangus, A. R., and Seeley, John R., *Mental Health Needs in a Rural and Semi-Rural Area of Ohio,* Ohio State Department of Public Welfare, Division of Mental Hygiene, February, 1950.

21. Mangus, A. R., and Woodward, R. H., *An Analysis of the Mental Health of Elementary School Children* (Hamilton, Ohio), Butler County Mental Hygiene Association, July 1949.

22. Mason, Frances V., "Study of 700 Maladjusted Teachers," *Mental Hygiene* (July, 1931), 15:576–599.

23. Murphy, Fred J., Shirley, Mary M., and Witmer, Helen W., "The Incidence of Hidden Delinquency," *American Journal of Orthopsychiatry* (October, 1946), 16:686–696.

24. Murphy, Melvin L., "The Mental Health Association Program: Its Place in Oregon," *Mental Health News,* Oregon Mental Health Association, 1950.

25. National Education Association, American Association of School Administrators, *Health in Schools,* 20th Yearbook, 1942.

26. National Education Association, Department of Classroom Teachers, *Fit to Teach,* 9th Yearbook, 1938.

27. National Education Association, Research Division, "A Teacher Looks at Personnel Administration," *Research Bulletin,* vol. XXIII, no. 4, December, 1945.

28. National Education Association, Research Division, "Schools Help Prevent Delinquency," *Research Bulletin,* vol. XXXI, no. 3, October, 1953.

29. National Education Association, Research Division, "Teaching Load in 1950," *Research Bulletin,* vol. XXIX, no. 1, February, 1951.
30. National Education Association, Research Division, "The Status of the American Public School Teacher," *Research Bulletin,* vol. XXXV, no. 1, February, 1957.
31. National Society for the Study of Education, 47th Yearbook, Part I, *Juvenile Delinquency and the Schools,* University of Chicago Press, 1948.
32. Palmer, H. D., "Common Emotional Problems Encountered in a College Mental Hygiene Service," *Mental Hygiene* (October, 1939), 23:544–557.
33. Peck, Leigh, "A Study of the Adjustment Difficulties of a Group of Women Teachers," *Journal of Educational Psychology* (September, 1936), 27:401–416.
34. Powers, Edwin, and Witmer, Helen L., *An Experiment in the Prevention of Delinquency: The Cambridge-Somerville Youth Study,* Columbia University Press, 1951.
35. Randall, Harriett B., "Health is for Teachers Too," *National Education Association Journal* (October, 1951), 40:467–468.
36. Rice, Sister M. Berenice, "A New Approach to the Diagnosis of the Mental Hygiene Problems of College Students," *Journal of the American Association of Collegiate Registrars* (October, 1938), 14:28–34.
37. Rogers, C. R., "A Study of the Mental Health Problems in Three Representative Elementary Schools," in *A Study of Health and Physical Education in Columbus Public Schools,* T. C. Holz, Director, Ohio State University Press, 1942.
38. Rogers, C. R., "Mental Health Findings in Three Elementary Schools," *Educational Research Bulletin* (March, 1942), 21:69–79.
39. Smith, Philip M., "The Schools and Juvenile Delinquency," *Sociology and Social Research* (November–December, 1952), 37:86–91.
40. Snyder, Louise M., "The Problem Child in the Jersey City Elementary Schools," *Journal of Educational Sociology* (February, 1934), 6:343–352.
41. Stone, Sybil A., Castendyck, Elsa, and Hanson, Harold B., *Children in the Community: The St. Paul Experiment in Child Welfare,* Federal Security Agency, Children's Bureau Publication No. 317, 1946.
42. Townsend, M. E., "Mental Hygiene and Teacher Recruiting," *Mental Hygiene* (October, 1933), 17:598–602.
43. Ullman, Charles A., *Identification of Maladjusted School Children,* Federal Security Agency, Public Health Service, Public Health Monograph No. 7, 1952.
44. U.S. Department of Health, Education and Welfare, Office of Education, *Biennial Survey of Education in the United States, 1952–54,* 1956, chapter 2.

45. U.S. Department of Health, Education and Welfare, Social Security Administration, Children's Bureau, *Some Facts About Juvenile Delinquency,* Children's Bureau Publication No. 340, 1953.

46. U.S. Department of Health, Education and Welfare, Social Security Administration, Children's Bureau, *Helping Delinquent Children,* Children's Bureau Publication No. 341, 1953.

47. U.S. Department of Health, Education and Welfare, Social Security Administration, Children's Bureau, *Juvenile Court Statistics 1955,* Children's Bureau Statistical Series No. 37, 1956.

48. U.S. Department of Health, Education and Welfare, Social Security Administration, Children's Bureau, *News Notes on Juvenile Delinquency,* October 13, 1953.

49. U.S. Department of Justice, Federal Bureau of Investigation, *The Crime Problem,* Mimeographed Bulletin, May, 1953.

50. U.S. Department of Justice, Federal Bureau of Investigation, *Uniform Crime Reports for the United States,* Annual Bulletin, 1956, vol. XXVII, no. 2, 1957.

51. U.S. Office of Education, Federal Security Agency, "Statistical Summary of Education 1949–50," *Biennial Survey of Education in the United States: 1948–50,* 1953.

52. U.S. Office of Education, Federal Security Agency, "Statistics of State School Systems, 1949–50," *Biennial Survey of Education in the United States, 1949–50,* 1952.

53. Wall, J. H., "Psychiatric Disorders in Fifty School Teachers," *American Journal of Psychiatry* (July, 1939), 96:137–145.

54. Witmer, Helen L., and Kotinsky, Ruth, *Personality in the Making,* The Fact-Finding Report of the Midcentury White House Conference on Children and Youth, Harper & Brothers, 1952.

55. Woodward, R. H., and Mangus, A. R., *Nervous Traits Among First Grade Children in Butler County Schools* (Hamilton, Ohio), Butler County Mental Hygiene Association, July, 1949.

56. Young, Pauline V., *Social Treatment in Probation and Delinquency,* McGraw-Hill Book Company, 1952, p. 422.

CHAPTER 4

Mental Health Programs in Schools and Communities

OUR discussion of mental hygiene has been confined thus far to the problem of mental illness and how it affects schools and society. In this chapter we shall view some of the promising mental hygiene programs which have been developed in recent years in an effort to prevent the spread of mental and emotional disorders.

These programs are much more extensive than generally realized. They range from the distribution of mental hygiene literature, to fully organized preventive health projects. For convenience of discussion, the mental hygiene programs described here are grouped under five headings: (1) programs of the federal government, (2) state programs, (3) community programs, (4) school district programs, and (5) school and classroom programs.

Since space will not permit a comprehensive discussion of the many mental hygiene activities now under way, the programs described are intended only to illustrate some of the efforts now being made to improve the quality of living in schools and communities.

PROGRAMS OF THE FEDERAL GOVERNMENT

The federal government has taken considerable interest in helping the states improve the conditions of living for their citizens. Agencies of the federal government are contributing both financial aid and professional services in an effort to stimulate human welfare projects in the states. These projects are so extensive that it is possible to mention here only two; the activities of the Children's Bureau, and of The National Institute of Mental Health.

The Children's Bureau

The United States Children's Bureau was organized over 40 years ago to promote the welfare of children. In 1921, Congress authorized this agency to give to the states $1,200,000 yearly for improvement of their health services for infants and for mothers during the childbearing period. Later, the Children's Bureau responsibilities were extended to include: (1) assembling facts needed to keep the country informed about matters adversely affecting the well-being of children, (2) determining what kinds of health and welfare measures and methods are most effective in aiding children and their parents, and (3) working with citizens and agencies in improving the conditions of childhood (3).

Financial aid to children has increased over the years. In 1954, federal funds available to the states for maternal and child health services, crippled children, and child-welfare services amounted to $31,367,-000 (1). Among the services which states are providing for children with the help of these funds are the following:

1. Increased services for mentally retarded children.
2. Improved services for children of migrant families.
3. Formation of small group-care units for orphans to replace large orphanages.
4. Increase in the number of full-time public child-welfare workers.
5. Improvement of services to children placed in foster homes.
6. Improved care of the physical health of children.

While not all of these services may be directly classified as mental hygiene projects, they illustrate some of the general efforts being made by the federal government to improve the welfare and happiness of children.

The National Mental Health Act

The federal government entered directly into mental health activities in 1929 when the Narcotics Division was established by the United States Public Health Service to conduct research on drug addiction, and to operate two institutions for drug addicts. In 1930, the Narcotics Division became the Mental Hygiene Division and was made responsible for investigating the causes, prevalence, and means for the prevention and treatment of mental and nervous disorders (*24*).

Toward the close of World War II, it became evident that the Division of Mental Hygiene could not adequately support the mental hygiene projects needed to combat mental illness, and that a larger effort was necessary. This need was met through the passage of the National Mental Health Act, which is probably the most significant piece of legislation ever enacted to protect the mental health of a nation.

The National Mental Health Act, passed by Congress in 1946, authorizes the federal government to participate in a comprehensive program for the prevention of mental illness and for the promotion of more positive mental health among the general population. In administering this Act, the federal government has been extremely careful to observe states' rights and provides its services to the states entirely on a volunteer basis.

The National Institute of Mental Health was established in 1949 to carry out the provisions of the Act. Through this agency the states are provided with certain financial grants and other services. The grants include

1. Grants-in-aid to states and territories for mental health programs conducted outside of mental hospitals. These grants are allocated on the basis of population, financial need, and extent of mental health problems. Each two federal dollars must be matched with one dollar of state or local funds. Annual grants issued by this formula may range from $20,000 to over $200,000 per State. (*27*)
2. Grants to universities, hospitals, laboratories and other non-Federal institutions, and to individuals for research projects. During the first three years that mental health research funds were available (1947–1950), support totalling $1,668,460 was given to research projects. These research grants have contributed to basic knowledge of schizophrenia, normal child development, micro-structure of the brain, psychosomatic aspects of arthritis, colitis and diabetes, causes and treatment of mental deficiency, evaluation of brain surgery techniques, diagnosis of mental disorders, and other problems in neurology, sociology, psychiatry and psychology. (*7*)
3. Grants to public and other nonprofit institutions for training and instruction, and for demonstrations in matters relating to psychiatric disorders. These grants are to promote the training of professional workers in order to make available more professional manpower to meet the needs of the population. (*27*)

The research and training programs of the National Institute of Mental Health are long-range programs intended to provide dividends in the future. For immediate aid to the states in developing mental hygiene services, the Institute has established a Community Services Branch. This Branch provides assistance in the forms of funds, clinical services, training programs, preventive and educational activities. States are not obligated to participate in these programs. However, in 1958 all states, Alaska, Hawaii, Puerto Rico, the Virgin Islands, and Guam were using federal grants-in-aid to establish programs of community mental health.

The National Mental Health Act involves an expenditure of over $10 million per year. During the years that this Act has been in effect, state mental hygiene programs have been expanded greatly. Before this Act was enacted, state-wide mental health programs were practically nonexistent. Now they are operating and expanding in every state and territory. Before the Act was passed, four states had no psychiatrist practicing outside the state mental hospital system. Today, every state has at least one psychiatrist. Before the Act, 15 states had no mental health clinics. Today, every state has at least one clinic, and through the aid of federal funds, clinic psychiatric services have increased approximately 50 percent (7).

STATE PROGRAMS

Each state has a Mental Health Authority which is responsible for the mental health activities conducted by the state government. In addition to this official agency, most states have volunteer mental health associations or societies supported largely by community contributions and memberships. Together, these agencies are exerting a great influence on the development of state mental health programs.

Mental Health Associations

The National Committee for Mental Hygiene, formally established in 1909, grew out of a need for some kind of organized effort on behalf of patients in mental institutions. At the time this Committee was created, state governments were being condemned for their inhuman treatment of patients in "asylums." Also, the preventive public health movement in America was gaining momentum, but few states showed any inclination of making preventive mental hygiene a part of their public health efforts.

The National Committee for Mental Hygiene stepped in to do what official state agencies were not doing in the way of improving the lot of patients in mental hospitals and organizing a preventive mental hygiene program. The Committee was instrumental in establishing volunteer mental health associations now active in most of the states. These associations are affiliated with the National Association for Mental Health which replaced the original Committee for Mental Hygiene.

At both state and national levels, these volunteer mental health associations carry on active campaigns to educate citizens in the facts of mental illness. They influence legislation, conduct reforms of mental hospitals, print and distribute literature, and in various other ways promote mental hygiene programs within the limits of their resources.

The scope of activities carried on by state mental health associations is illustrated by the program of the Mental Health Association of Oregon. This organization conducts or advocates the following projects:

1. Issuance of mental health leaflets for mothers of first babies.
2. Employment of a mental hygienist on the staff of well-baby clinics.
3. Utilization of a mental hygiene consultant as part of the preschool examinations of children.
4. Organization of classes in human relations in the public schools.
5. Promotion of institutes, study groups, and workshops for parents and teachers.
6. Offering psychiatric counseling for college students.
7. Orientation of teacher training toward the goals of mental hygiene.
8. Extension of school social-worker services.
9. Fostering interest among church and neighborhood groups.
10. Campaign for needed changes in legislation and in institutions.
11. Organization of county mental health units.
12. Expansion of state child-guidance clinics.
13. Development of adult mental hygiene clinics.
14. Establishment of private family-counseling centers. (12:46)

While programs in the various states will vary in terms of local needs, the Oregon projects will give some idea of the type of services these volunteer associations offer.

Official State Programs

In recent years there has been a tremendous growth in mental hygiene activities sponsored by state governments. Much of this growth is due to the federal support provided. However, many states have gone beyond the minimum programs made possible through federal funds and have developed noteworthy mental hygiene projects on their own.

The programs of each state vary greatly since they are geared to meet local conditions. Some states have organized extensive programs of mental hygiene education for public health officers, nurses, physicians, teachers, ministers, lawyers, and other special groups. The emphasis in these programs has been upon preparing public health personnel and community leaders to handle study and discussion groups and to give mental health information to the people whom they serve (14). Other states have based their mental hygiene activities upon expansion of clinical services, with less emphasis upon preventive education. The specific illustrations of state mental hygiene services which follow may help to outline further the scope of these programs.

PARENT-COUNSELING SERVICES. In many states the functions of the health department have been expanded to include mental hygiene instruction in their basic treatment programs for mothers and children. This has been done in New Jersey, Wisconsin, and elsewhere. The mental hygiene instruction conducted by various health department agencies seeks to prevent disordered parent-child relationships through influencing the parents' attitudes toward children before problems develop. The parents are prepared to expect certain types of normal child behavior so that they do not become disturbed when the behavior occurs. Seminars are conducted with small groups of parents under the leadership of a public health nurse who is trained in mental hygiene procedures. Well-baby clinics also are used as centers through which mental hygiene instruction is given to mothers.

This type of mental hygiene activity is of considerable significance as a relatively recent concept in state health programs. Instead of confining mental health education to the Department of Mental Hygiene, many states are beginning to include mental hygiene instruction in all of their health programs. Under this plan, nurses, doctors, social workers, and others who visit people in their homes provide instruction in mental hygiene in addition to ministering to the physical or social needs of their patients (13:39).

MENTAL HEALTH INSTITUTES. Another type of state mental hygiene program is represented by the College Symposium Project which was conducted in Ohio (5). To develop a program for a population of almost 8 million, the state was subdivided into several mental hygiene areas with the state college in each area serving as the nucleus of the program. A series of simultaneous statewide college symposia were held, organized around the mental health needs of each college district. The college programs were part of a whole series of institutes on mental health, the immediate aim of which was to arouse widespread interest in this subject and to focus attention upon the problem of mental health in the local college community.

COMMUNITY CLINICS. A number of states have organized traveling community clinics. These clinics commonly consist of one or more psychiatrists, assisted by psychiatric social workers, psychologists, and nurses. They provide services to areas unable to establish their own mental hygiene centers.

Since traveling clinics can spend only a short time in a community, often no more than a day or two, they are unable to provide patients with extensive therapy. Usually, these clinics deal with children and attempt to diagnose their cases and prescribe treatments which may be carried out by teachers, physicians, parents, or by community agencies. Although traveling clinics are not the most desirable type of therapeutic service, they do perform a valuable function in providing clinical services to areas where no other form of assistance is available.

TEACHER EDUCATION. A few states have experimented with teaching clinics organized at teachers colleges or schools of education. The purpose of these clinics is to promote the adjustment of teacher candidates and enrich their educational experiences.

One such project is the Mental Health Center established in Oregon through the combined efforts of one of the state teachers colleges, the County Health Department, and the State Division of Mental Hygiene. The college provided the center with a psychologist and a special education teacher. The County Health Department provided a physician, two public health nurses, and liaison with county welfare and attendance services. The State Division of Mental Hygiene furnished a psychiatrist who worked with the local staff one afternoon a week. The coöperative efforts of these specialists made possible two important mental hygiene services. First, clinical services were provided for children of the county. Secondly, teachers in training learned something about themselves as persons, extended their understanding of children, and developed greater insight into the use of mental hygiene techniques in teaching.

Student teachers were aided through experience gained in working up case histories for the children referred to the clinic and through participation in the case conferences. The clinical conferences proved to be an excellent technique for influencing the attitudes and understandings of teachers and student teachers. By dealing with actual cases, child psychology, mental hygiene, and classroom practices were integrated and made meaningful to the students. They were able to apply the principles derived from other college classes, and follow through the problems of a child under the guidance of a team of specialists. The case conference technique of instruction served as a focus around which both teachers and students developed significant mental hygiene attitudes toward children and toward teaching.

GUIDANCE CENTERS. Still another form of state mental hygiene service is illustrated by the Guidance Center organized in Miami County, Ohio (8). This center was established in a rural area which lacked previous experience with mental hygiene facilities and which had little social service of any type. The problem faced by the staff was how to meet the mental health needs of a county which had no private psychiatrists and no family service agencies.

To provide maximum service to the children and adults who were referred to the clinic, only about 10–15 percent of the cases were handled on a therapeutic basis. The remainder were handled on a consultative or diagnostic basis. The consultative services consisted of counseling with the people who handled problem cases, rather than dealing directly with these cases. Primarily, this involved showing teachers and mothers how they could improve their treatment of the children who were causing them concern. The diagnostic service consisted of examining individual patients and making recommendations to the referring agency for necessary action to be taken.

In addition to these services, the Guidance Center visited schools where they tested children, held discussion sessions with children and teachers, and organized weekly human relations classes for seventh and eighth graders. Lectures and programs for parent groups were also sponsored by center personnel. This project illustrates the efforts being made by some states to provide as much mental health service as possible with a minimum staff.

YOUTH COMMISSIONS. Some states have organized very extensive youth services administered through a central office. One of the most comprehensive of such programs is the New York State Youth Commission (16). This Commission was organized in 1945 to prevent delinquency and to promote the mental health of children and youth. It is composed of a chairman and the heads of seven state agencies: the Commissioners of the Departments of Correction, Education, Health, Labor, Mental Hygiene, and Social Welfare, and the Chairman of the Parole Board. Through financial assistance to cities, counties, towns, and incorporated villages, local governmental units are encouraged to expand existing public and private services for children and to create needed new services.

This Youth Commission has four major functions:

1. It provides state aid for certain types of youth services, youth bureaus, and recreation projects. Since its establishment, the Commission has provided more than $7 million to over 835 municipalities. It has blanketed the state with a variety of youth programs, psychiatric, guidance, and casework services.
2. It inquires into youth needs and problems. Teams of specialists have been organized to make a continuing study of what children need to facilitate their personality development.
3. It promotes understanding of youth needs and problems. Every medium of mass education is used to reach both youth and adult audiences. The Commission has used films, exhibits, publications, radio and television programs, and many other devices to bring to the attention of the people some basic understandings regarding the problems of youth.
4. It unifies efforts on behalf of youth. The Commission integrates plans, programs, and facilities of public and private agencies. It holds regular in-service training institutes which bring together probation and parole officers, psychiatrists, psychologists, educators, clergymen, and others who work with young people, so that they may work together on plans for dealing with their problems.

Many other state programs, which cannot be described here in detail, are now under way. The illustrations cited indicate that states are taking an increasing interest in the mental health of their people. It is hoped that as these programs are expanded and strengthened, there will eventually emerge a protection against mental illness which is comparable to the protection now provided against physical illness.

COMMUNITY PROGRAMS

Organized mental hygiene programs at the community level are most common in urban areas where personnel and facilities are available. Some of these programs have developed as a result of the leadership provided by school systems. Others were created independent of the schools to serve all social agencies in the community.

The programs described here will illustrate three types of community mental hygiene projects. First, regional programs which involve a number of school districts; second, coöperative school-community programs in which schools participate actively; and third, community programs which serve schools but operate independently of them.

Regional Programs

Some school districts have joined forces to make possible expanded mental hygiene services to the teachers and to the community. Two such programs which have received considerable attention are the Los Angeles County Human Relations Project and the Commission on Teacher Education Project.

THE LOS ANGELES COUNTY HUMAN RELATIONS PROJECT. In 1949, 21 school districts in Los Angeles County, California, organized an in-service education project on a coöperative basis. This project sought to: (1) Establish channels of communication whereby the good human relations practices under way in one area of the county could be shared with other school districts; (2) improve interpersonal and intergroup relations through the use of democratic techniques; (3) provide a new kind of in-service training for teachers, and explore and put into practice better ways of improving human relations in schools and communities; and, (4) make possible the immediate application of recent educational research in public school practice.

Funds were secured from the County Superintendent's Office, the city school districts, community organizations, and private foundations. By pooling these funds, it was possible to employ consultants whom individual school districts could not afford to employ on their own.

In 1950–1951, the project participants included 9500 teachers and other school personnel, 1000 parents and other citizens, 7 core staff, 49 visiting consultants, and 95 resource persons. The project began with the problems teachers faced in the classroom. The findings of scientific research were brought to bear on the solution of these problems. Under the direction of university people and nationally recognized consultants, workshops were held in sociometrics, role-playing techniques, intercultural education, and other areas. Classroom demonstrations were held by consultants using discussion techniques, reaction stories, and other devices. Numerous study groups were held in schools and communities. The subjects considered in workshops and study groups included curriculum revision, parent reporting, teacher personality adjustment, human development, group techniques, and other problems raised by teachers and parents.

This project was one of the largest coöperative ventures in human relations entered into by school districts. Informal evaluation of the benefits derived indicated that teachers succeeded in clarifying many of their problems. They learned new techniques for understanding children, and developed new classroom practices which enabled them to remove some of the blocks to learning which had troubled them (17).

THE COMMISSION ON TEACHER EDUCATION.   Another outstanding regional program was conducted by the Commission on Teacher Education of the American Council on Education (22). This project was started in 1938 with support from the Rockefeller Foundation and the General Education Board. Fourteen groups of school systems and 20 collegiate institutions coöperated in an experimental program which sought to devise means whereby the accumulated research on human behavior could be utilized by teachers.

The project consisted of sending a trained staff into a school system where teachers were enrolled in study groups on a voluntary basis. The study groups were limited in size to 14 people. Each person gathered data on a selected child and periodically presented this data to the group as a whole for manipulation in accordance with a graded series of processes designed to gradually build skill in understanding children. The study groups met several hours a week over a period of 3 years. Many of the teachers involved also attended workshops which helped them develop skills in studying children. Over a period of years, this project involved more than 20,000 teachers.

The Commission on Teacher Education believes that the teachers who participated in this project have been helped to understand and alleviate the misbehavior of children. About 80 percent of the teachers reported that they were much happier on their jobs. Principals and superintendents reported a decrease in the number of behavior problems—and a decrease in the number of parents complaining about teacher relationships with their children (5).

COÖPERATIVE SCHOOL-COMMUNITY PROGRAMS.   Schools and youth-serving agencies often tend to operate independently in a community, with the result that some mental hygiene programs suffer because of the lack of coördination. Many communities, however have succeeded in integrating the activities of social agencies and the public schools. A few examples of coöperative projects of this type are summarized below. They have been selected primarily because they represent several types of approaches now in operation (15).

In Canton, Ohio, the police department, recreation department, and the public schools work together to keep children busy after school hours. A unique feature of this organization is that the police department maintains a Child Welfare Bureau especially assigned to work with youth. This Bureau serves as a link between the public schools and the county guidance center.

Greensboro, North Carolina, Elizabeth, New Jersey, and Hartford, Connecticut, have developed coördinated community services in which the schools are represented directly. In Elizabeth, the Director of Guidance and Special Services for the public schools is one of the three referees of the juvenile court which hears cases of first offenders. In Greensboro, a Recreation Commission composed of representatives of the schools, the recreation department, the Parent-Teacher Committee, social service agencies, and other youth-serving groups coördinate all activities for youth in a year-around program. Hartford has a similar organization called the Recreation and Group Work Division of the Greater Hartford Community Council, which is concerned not only with recreation but all social problems affecting children.

In Passaic, New Jersey, a Children's Bureau is maintained to coördinate services for child study and treatment. The director of this Bureau is the Assistant Superintendent of Schools in Charge of Guidance and Special Services. Working with him are three policemen, a policewoman, a social worker, a psychologist, a reading specialist, and three attendance officers. This Bureau deals with school behavior problems, failure, truancy, atypical children, and delinquents. The police officers are housed in the Children's Bureau, rather than in the police department, and are assigned to the schools as investigators who emphasize child study and treatment rather than apprehension of wayward children.

An illustration of an extensive, city-wide organization for improvement of the welfare of children and youth is the New York City Youth Board (16). This Board includes the presiding justice of the Domestic Relations Court, the superintendent of schools, the chairman of the City Housing Authority, the Commissioners of Health, Parks, Police and Welfare, and private citizens. The Board employs a large staff of specialists in child welfare, recreation, group work, research, and community relations. This agency coördinates the activities of public, private, and religious youth-serving organizations in the city. It conducts systematic research into community and youth problems, provides financial assistance to public and private agencies, and disseminates information on the prevention, treatment, and cause of juvenile delinquency.

Among the youth-service projects which the Board conducts are programs of extended summer services to children, case work, psychiatric, psychological, guidance and employment services, group psychotherapy, and a program for antisocial gangs. Referral units are operated in 11 centers to locate and treat youngsters in the early stages of maladjustment. It also sponsers a camping program for youth with behavior difficulties, and has group work programs operating in settlement houses, Y's, housing projects, churches, and community centers.

These projects illustrate some of the organizational patterns which have been developed to integrate the activities of school and community agencies. They are significant because they represent a unified attack on mental health problems in communities. More adequate juvenile court facilities, juvenile police services, improved clinical, guidance, and recreational programs have resulted in many communities through the coöperation of social agencies, interested citizens, and the public schools.

Community Programs Serving Schools

A wide variety of organizations in many communities are supplementing the work of the schools through their own mental hygiene programs. Among such agencies are the courts, welfare bureaus, public health departments, medical and mental health clinics, guidance centers, YWCA, YMCA, service clubs, church groups, boys and girls aid societies, and the WCTU.

Community services provided by these agencies may include: (1) therapeutic work with individuals and their families, (2) advisory services to agencies and individuals regarding the mental health problems of clients or staff, (3) preventive services to groups who need assistance in developing a better understanding of themselves and the people with whom they work, and (4) community planning activities which attempt to coördinate and promote the activities of all agencies and institutions working for the betterment of mental health in the community (2).

In the large metropolitan centers may be found community agencies which perform all of these functions. Smaller municipalities must often limit their services because of restricted resources. In the following paragraphs are illustrated two types of extended community services and several less extensive forms of community mental health activities.

A METROPOLITAN GUIDANCE CENTER.   The Witchita Guidance Center is an example of a community agency which offers clinical, consultative, preventive, and promotional mental health services (2). Patients are referred to the Center by child-placing agencies, schools, juvenile courts, private physicians, the county welfare department, public health nurses, family case work agencies, the Red Cross, and others. Clinical treatment for these patients is supplemented by an instructional program for those who refer the patients to the clinic. The purpose of instruction is to help these workers learn how to handle emotional problems more constructively.

Consultation services are offered to help teachers, social workers, and others define the behavior problems they encounter and develop a plan of action within their ability to carry out. This is done through staff meetings based upon specific problems presented by the group, and in individual conferences with the workers.

The Guidance Center also carries on a program of preventive services. Study groups are conducted for parents to help them gain a better understanding of their children. In coöperation with the local health department, group discussions are held with teachers, school nurses, and mothers. Also, talks on mental health topics are given before community groups.

The Center is a part of the local Community Planning Council which develops plans for the total physical health, mental health, and social welfare needs of the community. It also conducts research relating to infant testing, parent discussion groups, orphans, and other problems relating to the mental health of the community.

The program described here illustrates a high degree of professional service to the community. Each member of the Guidance Center staff serves as a diagnostician, therapist, consultant, community educator, and scientist. Similar centers have been established in almost all of the large metropolitan communities.

Mental Health Associations

Community mental health organizations represent another type of mental health service commonly found in urban areas. The Southern California Society for Mental Hygiene is an illustration of such agencies.

This Society is a community chest agency which conducts a program of mental hygiene education and community service in and around Los Angeles. It is composed of citizens representing all segments of the community. The work of the Society is done by a small professional staff and numerous volunteer workers.

An information section, an education section, and a community service section are maintained by the Society. The information section advises citizens regarding psychiatric and psychological treatment services in the community. It distributes resource materials, such as a directory of psychiatric clinics in the area, operates a resource library of materials pertaining to mental hygiene, conducts a fact-finding service to evaluate the community mental health needs, and keeps the public informed of developments in the field of mental hygiene.

The educational section provides material for educational use by individuals and community groups. This includes distribution of mental hygiene pamphlets, a mental health film service, public exhibits of materials and literature, organization of public forums, and maintenance of a speaker's bureau which makes available professional speakers to community groups. It also has a program consultation service which aids groups to plan and organize long-range educational programs.

The community services section assumes responsibility for bringing together community groups for joint action in mental health activities. This service includes consultation with communities regarding the establishment of psychiatric clinics, organizing of local mental health chapters in smaller communities, legislative service for the education and information of legislative bodies regarding mental hygiene problems, and community liaison through members of the Society who serve on civic bodies and orient them toward mental hygiene activities (*21*).

Most urban centers have similar organizations which emphasize preventive mental hygiene rather than clinical or therapeutic services.

Other Community Programs

Operating on a smaller scale are other community agencies which do not attempt to cover the complete range of mental hygiene services. For instance, the Harlem Branch of the YWCA in New York City has held workshops in mental health for girls. Under the guidance of skilled discussion leaders, the girls were helped to clarify their problems and verbalize their attitudes and feelings. They discussed courtship, love, marriage, how to get along with others, and other problems which trouble teen-age girls. In this informal atmosphere, the youngsters were able to relieve many of their doubts and anxieties. Since this was a volunteer program with no authority figure present, such as a teacher, a great deal was accomplished in the way of influencing attitudes. Similar programs are conducted elsewhere at community centers, settlement houses, and other organizations where children gather voluntarily.

Another example of limited mental health service to a community is the work of the Portland (Maine) Mental Health Clinic. Here weekly discussion groups are held for mothers under the leadership of a staff psychiatrist. These discussions started with the immediate concerns of the mothers over problems of their children. As mothers learned to understand their children, they voluntarily yielded their places to new members. These discussion seminars were later broadened to include consideration of the mothers' personal problems (26).

In other communities, special homes or schools are maintained for children in trouble. These facilities are operated by nongovernmental agencies such as the Salvation Army, Volunteers of America, and Catholic Charities. They provide services for wayward girls, unmarried mothers, children of inadequate parents, young delinquents, and children whose problems cannot be handled entirely by official agencies or institutions.

Many communities have established boys' clubs and neighborhood recreation centers where gymnasiums, libraries, craft rooms, club rooms, and even camp facilities are available. Not only are individual children accepted into membership, but organized gangs are taken in and offered activities which supplant the delinquent activities such gangs might engage in outside the center.

From these few illustrations it may be seen that many communities are engaged in a variety of mental hygiene activities. The examples given here may be multiplied many times. Mental hygiene services are becoming increasingly available in communities, either through coöperative efforts of schools and community agencies, or through the efforts of local organizations and citizen groups.[1]

School District Programs

In the past 20 years, school districts have made great strides toward expanding their services to children and teachers. Described here are some representative mental hygiene programs conducted by school dis-

---

[1] For a detailed discussion of community programs, see R. Kotinsky and H. L. Witmer (eds.), *Community Programs For Mental Health,* Harvard University Press, 1955.

tricts, and a few interesting innovations which have been tried in recent years.

Services to Children

Special service personnel, many of whom were unheard of at the turn of this century, are now quite common among school systems. These include attendance supervisors, case workers, psychometrists, school social workers, visiting teachers, counselors, speech therapists, and school psychologists. In addition to these specialists, some large urban districts have fully equipped child-guidance clinics which are a part of the school system. These clinics not only treat children, but often do preventive mental health work with teachers and administrators.

Usually these special workers and clinical facilities are organized under a division or department variously referred to as the Division of Special Services, Department of Pupil Adjustment, Division of Child Welfare and Attendance, and so forth. Such organizations have as their primary function the detection and early treatment of maladjusted children.

THE PHILADELPHIA CASE WORK COMMITTEE. An unusual type of child-service organization is the Philadelphia Case Work Committee (23). This is a high-level committee composed of the Superintendent of Schools, the Directors of the Divisions of Pupil Personnel, Medical Services, and Special Education, and the District Superintendent. One morning each week the committee meets to consider problem cases submitted by school principals. Prior to the meeting, the Medical Service Division and the Pupil Personnel Division examine the child and prepare a history and analysis of the case. Since the committee members are all in strategic positions, they can cut red tape and swiftly mobilize the extensive resources at their command.

This committee has greatly encouraged teachers in their efforts to handle problem children. Teachers are assured of high-echelon backing. They know also that if the child's behavior cannot be improved in the school, he will be removed promptly. The Case Work Committee has authority to take legal action where parent coöperation cannot be secured, and it maintains influence over children after they leave school through liaison with the Crime Prevention Association and the Juvenile Aid Bureau of the police.

SPECIAL SCHOOLS AND CLASSES. Some schools handle the problem of child maladjustment through the organization of special classes or schools for disturbed children. The Detroit, Michigan, program is an illustration of this type of organization. Here a series of ungraded class-rooms are housed in the elementary schools to take care of younger children who have severe behavior disturbances. These children participate in many of the regular school activities, but are segregated most of the day for a modified program of instruction. For older children who cannot be handled in the regular school, special rehabilitation schools are conducted. These schools have the services of special teachers as well as psychologists, psychiatrists, and visiting teachers.

New York City has a similar organization, as does Newark, New Jersey, Philadelphia, Baltimore, and many other large school systems. Baltimore has an interesting modification of the usual rehabilitation program which involves operating a farm school for maladjusted boys. The program is centered around gardening and the care of farm animals, rather than the usual academic organization (10).

OTHER SPECIAL PROGRAMS.   Some school systems are utilizing camping experiences as an approach to the problems of maladjusted children. For instance, the Dearborn, Michigan, Public Schools conduct a camp for boys of age 15½ to 17½ who are potential school-leavers. The boys all have marked academic or personal problems. Through camp experiences much of their hostility is relieved; the boys become more friendly and coöperative, their attitude toward school undergoes change, and they develop better habits and improved personal and vocational skills. This program has proved so successful that drop-outs among the camp boys decreased to 7 percent, as compared to a total drop-out rate of 17 percent (10).

A variety of other services are provided for children in school systems across the nation. Cleveland employs two teachers who work with mothers of kindergarten children. They organize classes which run for six or seven weeks and in addition hold home conferences. Over 1000 mothers are reached each year with information regarding the behavior and personality problems of young children. In Portland, Oregon, Menlo Park, California, and elsewhere, special programs are conducted for gifted children. Other schools are examining their curriculums to bring them in line with pupil needs, reëvaluating their pupil administrative procedures, and otherwise attempting to make the school a place for wholesome living.

These are but a few highlights of activities in school districts where serious efforts are being made to meet the mental health needs of children.

Mental Hygiene Programs for Teachers

Many school districts are aware that no effective mental health program can be developed without an in-service education program for teachers. In the past decade, some very promising programs have been conducted in an effort to bring about constructive relations between teachers, children, parents, and school administrators. A few of the more notable activities in this field are summarized in succeeding pages.

THE DETROIT SCHOOL MENTAL HEALTH PROJECT. An extensive in-service training program was conducted in Detroit from 1947–1952 by Wayne University and the University of Michigan. Its purpose was to help the teachers and administrators of the Detroit Public Schools make living conditions in schools and classrooms more conducive to the development of mental health (20). Through financial support provided by private foundations, a new course in mental health was organized. Teachers attended classes on a voluntary basis one evening a week for 16 weeks. During the first half-hour of each class session, the entire group saw films and heard transcriptions dealing with various aspects of human relations and mental health. The next hour was used by a psychiatrist to discuss the essentials of child growth and the principles of mental health as related to work in the classroom. For the final hour, the class was divided into discussion groups of about 30 members. Under the leadership of a specialist in child growth and human relations, the teachers in these small groups discussed their classroom problems. About every third week, each discussion group had a psychiatrist available as a consultant.

Following this basic course, an advanced course was offered for teachers who wished further work in the field of mental hygiene. To reach those teachers who did not enroll in these courses, a special program was introduced in the various geographic areas of the city. This program included institutes and brief courses for small groups of teachers, a series of radio programs presented to coincide with regular teachers' meetings, consultation visits to schools by a traveling psychiatrist, and wide distribution of mental health pamphlets, books, magazines, plays, and other materials.

About 10,000 teachers and administrators were involved in this project over a 5-year period. Sponsors of the program observed that the teachers reached were living and teaching more than before in accordance with principles of mental health. They were more considerate and humane in their treatment of children and more conscious of the need for special service personnel.

THE RYE PROJECT. The public schools of Rye, New York, have initiated a mental health program to introduce from kindergarten through the twelfth grade a series of experiences designed to increase understanding of self and others (*9, 11*). This program involved (1) bimonthly seminars held with teachers and administrators of the high school and the two elementary schools, (2) weekly conferences with the guidance staff of the high school, (3) an experimental series of human relations classes in the schools, (4) a parent education program, and (5) a consultation service for parents and teachers who wished to discuss problems of individual children.

The bimonthly seminars were held after school on a voluntary basis. They consisted of lectures, films, and discussions related to child behavior problems. About 80 percent of the staff attended these seminars.

Consultations with the high school guidance staff sought to formulate school policies on important issues in terms of good mental hygiene practices. The human relations classes were conducted in the fifth, eighth, and twelfth grades. In the fifth and eighth grades, instruction consisted of reading and discussing stories indicating good human relations, dramatization and discussion of prevailing problems, and the use of films and filmstrips. In the twelfth grade, human relations lessons were integrated in the social science course where emphasis was placed on student discussion of mental hygiene problems.

Parent education was conducted by a consultant who ran weekly classes entitled "Psychology of Family Relations." These classes were limited in size to 10 or 15 parents and met once a month in the homes of members of the group. Consultation service was also made available to parents and teachers wherever the problems of children could be solved without use of psychotherapy. In the case of severe problems, children were referred to a child guidance clinic or to a private psychiatrist.

Directors of this project report some very encouraging results. The children in human relations classes responded with enthusiasm to the discussion of problems related to their own feelings and the feelings of others. Teachers and administrators believed that something significant was being done in an area of great concern to them. An improvement in teaching techniques and in personal relationships was noted throughout the schools.

THE FLINT, MICHIGAN, PROGRAM.   Another type of in-service project was carried out in the public schools of Flint, Michigan, by the University of Michigan and the Mott Foundation (5). Training for teachers was conducted by psychiatrists, psychologists, and psychiatric social workers to help teachers understand the effect of school experience on their pupils. In the introductory sessions of the program, teachers were given much material on individual differences in growth and development and were taught specific techniques in counseling, interviewing, and the gathering of pertinent data. Case conferences were held to help teachers develop skill in making recommendations for dealing with children, and to provide them with the experience of carrying out a plan of action. Teachers also made visits to the homes of their pupils and became steeped in the literature as well as the practice of mental hygiene as applied to the educational process. Teachers who completed one year of study in this program became resource persons in their respective schools and in this way spread the influence of their training.

CLINIC TEAMS.   Another approach to developing understanding of mental hygiene among teachers is the use of clinic teams which visit schools and consult with teachers. Two such programs are the Wellesley Project, and the Bronx Three Schools Project (22).

In Wellesley, Massachusetts, a clinic team from the Division of Mental Health of the Harvard School of Public Health conducted a regular program of weekly consultation visits to schools. A significant feature of these visits was the classroom visitations made by the clinic staff. This was done on the premise that the teachers' problems could not be understood without taking into consideration the dynamics of the classroom situation. Through classroom observation and in conferences with teachers, supervisors, and administrators, the clinic staff developed a realistic understanding of the problems presented to them. The clinic also organized human relations services as part of the preschool examination of children. Youngsters about to enter school were studied, and later, when they were in school, their behavior was observed and recorded. These data were used with teachers and parent groups to help them interpret the development and growth of the children.

The Bronx Three Schools Project was started in 1949 by the New York City Youth Board in an effort to combat the delinquency problem. A clinic team consisting of two part-time psychiatrists, three social workers, two psychologists, and two vocational guidance counselors were placed in an elementary, junior high school, and senior high school.

These teams did not attempt to tell the school what to do. They merely established offices in the schools and made it known that their services were available if needed. Over a period of time, school personnel gradually began to seek out the clinic staff for all types of services. At first the problems brought in related entirely to child behavior. Later, teachers and administrators consulted the clinic for help with all types of personal and administrative problems.

The informal atmosphere established by the clinic brought about a change in the attitude of school personnel toward clinic services. The teachers discovered that the clinic was there to help them become better teachers and not to correct their faults or criticize their handling of children. Over a period of years this approach was found to be a valuable technique for getting school personnel involved with the clinic and oriented toward a mental hygiene approach to school problems.

WORKSHOPS FOR ADMINISTRATORS. Workshop techniques have been used in several ways to secure administrative support for mental hygiene programs in the schools (5). In one instance, all of the principals of a school system, together with a number of their teachers, were invited to participate in a two-week workshop at a camp. The principals, by having the same experiences as the teachers, gained a real understanding of what was involved in classroom human relations. As a result, they were more receptive to suggestions for changes in the organization of the schools and in classroom procedures.

Another workshop project involved a group of superintendents from Texas who were brought to Chicago for a three-week session on child development. The superintendents gained considerable insight into what a mental hygiene program should accomplish and consequently were better able to understand the need for changes in the pattern of school organization, curriculum organization, and methods of dealing with children. This was something that could not have been accomplished except by getting them away from the pressures of their regular work so that they could relax and absorb new ideas.

The illustrations cited show how some school systems are incorporating mental health activities in their programs. In addition to projects such as those described, ideas relating to mental health are being included in study guides and in basic learning materials. Administrators as well as teachers are making progress toward understanding the mental health needs of the schools. There also seems to be more widespread concern about mental health throughout the communities where human relations projects are developed. These activities are having a beneficial effect on teaching techniques, morale, and general well-being of children and school personnel.

SCHOOL AND CLASSROOM PROJECTS

To round out our survey of mental hygiene practices, we shall examine a few programs conducted within individual schools or classrooms. Such programs appear most commonly in localities where mental hygiene projects are encouraged generally. However, some noteworthy mental hygiene activities are to be found in individual schools where teachers and administrators have been stimulated to deviate from conventional patterns of education and experiment with mental hygiene projects.

School Staff Programs

Some schools are conducting mental hygiene study programs within their own organization. The Des Moines, Iowa, and Battle Creek, Michigan, projects illustrate this type of activity.

Drake University in Des Moines has organized classes for teachers on a school-to-school basis. All of the teachers in one school building take these classes simultaneously. The children studied are those with whom the teachers are working every day and with whom most of the teachers are familiar. This system has the advantage of getting all the teachers in the building to work coöperatively on their problems. School principals are also included in these classes and benefit by relating their administrative problems to the teachers and children with whom they deal (5).

Battle Creek uses a camping technique to bring together teachers, children, and administrators in an informal setting. After working and playing together for two weeks or more in an atmosphere that makes them friends as well as colleagues, the staff develops a spirit of teamwork that carries over into the school (5).

Mental Hygiene Projects for Children

A number of attempts are being made to make mental hygiene instruction a part of the regular classroom activity. This is done in some schools by teaching mental hygiene incidentally as it arises in courses such as biology, social living, social problems, English, health, or contemporary affairs. Other schools have set up more fully organized programs in which mental hygiene is given a definite place in the curriculum. We shall describe in some detail four programs which fall in the latter category. These are the Forest Hills Village Project, the Bullis Project, the Ojemann Project, and the Force Project.

THE FOREST HILLS VILLAGE PROJECT.   This project was organized under the direction of the University of Toronto to bring mental hygiene directly into the classroom. The teachers of Forest Hills Village, a suburb of Toronto, were taught principles of mental hygiene by a team of clinicians. When the course was completed, the teachers conducted human relations classes with their children. These classes were held one hour per week in grades five through twelve. They consisted essentially in free discussions where children were allowed to talk about any problem which concerned them at the time. The teacher was completely permissive and made no attempt to direct the discussion (6).

These discussion sessions had all the aspects of a group therapy project. Children were permitted to relieve their anxieties regarding personal concerns, with no one sitting in judgment upon them or telling them what to talk about. It might be thought that under such circumstances the children would stray far from mental hygiene problems. In practice, however, it was found that no matter what the group started to talk about, before long they became involved with problems of living.

To supplement the classroom program, each school has organized "counseling teams," consisting of several teachers, the principal, a school guidance officer, and a special teacher who has had one year of training in mental hygiene principles and practices. This team works with children whose problems are not serious enough to warrant the intervention of psychiatric personnel, although clinic facilities are available and may be called upon when needed (22).

This project is a noteworthy experiment and has achieved some interesting results in its present setting. However, it has not been utilized very extensively in the United States or Canada, primarily because of the special training required and the clinical services which must be maintained to make the program effective.

THE BULLIS PROJECT.   In contrast to the Forest Hills Village Project in which human relations classes are nondirective, unstructured, and grouped determined, the Bullis Project has a definite organization and course of study.

This project originated in the schools of Delaware and New York, and has been used with over 200,000 children annually in about 21 states. The text for the course consists of three volumes entitled *Human Relations in the Classroom,* written by H. E. Bullis and E. E. O'Malley, and issued by the Delaware State Society for Mental Hygiene. These books provide the teacher with a discussion of basic mental hygiene principles, lesson outlines, and stimulus stories.

The procedure recommended to teachers is that the stimulus story be read to the children, to be followed by a class discussion, and a conclusion. The stimulus story features the emotional problem scheduled for a particular lesson. Its purpose is to stimulate children to discuss the problems presented in the story, and to relate their personal experiences which parallel this problem. Following this discussion the teacher summarizes the principles involved and children write down their conclusions in a diary or notebook.

The subject matter dealt with in this course relates to common emotional problems of preadolescent and early adolescent youngsters. Some of the specific topics are: "How Personality Traits Develop," "Our Inner Human Drives," "How Emotions Are Aroused," "Emotional Problems at Home," "Overcoming Personal Handicaps," and "Submitting to Authority" (3). Teachers require no special training to conduct human relations classes according to this plan. Consequently, the Bullis Project has gained widespread acceptance. However, some mental hygienists and educators criticize this approach as being too didactic and overly moralistic (6).

THE FORCE PROJECT.   This program came about as a result of complaints made by businessmen in Toms River, New Jersey, that graduates of the high school were totally unaware of the elementary rules of courtesy and were lacking in certain personality traits which would make them valuable as employees.

Mrs. Elizabeth S. Force, a teacher of English in the high school, set about to remedy this condition. She organized a course called "Social Techniques and Etiquette," which was offered on a voluntary basis to eleventh and twelfth grade students. In this course, rules of behavior at school, at home, and in the community were stressed. Students also learned good grooming, manners, and courtesy through a series of discussion and practice sessions. An indication of the practical nature of this course is the final examination, part of which consisted of taking the students to a large seashore hotel for a day where their conduct together and their behavior toward hotel employees were observed.

This course in social behavior was followed with another on family relations. Here students dealt with problems of love, courtship, marriage, and establishing a home. The students analyzed movies dealing with these subjects, evaluated radio programs, magazines, and advertising, studied children, and evaluated themselves as future husbands, wives, and parents. Through these activities, students became familiar with life problems and developed a realistic approach to some of the major concerns which lay ahead of them (6).

THE OJEMANN PROJECT.   At the University of Iowa an effort is being made to integrate human relations education into the regular public school curriculum (6, 18, 19). This is a long-range human relations project which involves revising basic text materials and adding special units to existing courses so that in grades one through twelve, children have before them recurring examples of typical behavior problems. Teachers are trained to encourage discussion of these problems whenever they arise in the normal course of class activity. Through this approach it is hoped that the basic principles of mental hygiene will become a part of the children's habitual way of thinking, feeling, and acting.

The technique used in the primary grades is for the teacher to read descriptive narratives, or work out with the children skits or plays dealing with human relations problems. In these narratives or skits, a situation involving some form of human interaction which the child can understand is developed. The children are led to investigate the causal factors involved in the problem presented. No attempt is made to relate this discussion to the children's own problems. The emphasis is upon learning that behavior has causes. When this basic understanding is achieved, children are ready to look into the causes of their own behavior.

In the intermediate and upper grades special units are developed to supplement the basic text material and adapt them to human relations instruction. At the seventh grade level, children have a series of units on "Guiding Our Own Development." In the community civics course there is a unit called "Where Do People Get Their Different Ways of Behaving." Other units are being developed to place a human relations emphasis on the various courses children take in junior and senior high school. In these units pupils are encouraged to examine their own behavior and their reactions to the various aspects of school and home life, and to seek possible causes for their behavior and reactions.

Much work remains to be done on this project since it entails rewriting much of the basic text material used in the schools. The investigators have found that most of the material written for children describes human relations in terms of surface behavior. If children are to understand the dynamics of behavior, this material must be revised to bring out the motivational forces involved: The end sought is not only descriptions of what people do, but why they do it.

To date, the studies made on the effectiveness of this program show that it has great promise. In the primary grades, children listen attentively and show much interest in discussions of human relations problems. In the intermediate grades, data show that children have improved their understanding of human relations and that definite changes have resulted in their attitudes toward themselves and others.

The projects mentioned illustrate some of the different approaches to mental health which are being tried in various schools and classrooms. There is a tremendous interest among teachers and administrators in such programs, and more and more schools are seeking to include human relations material in their curriculums.

SUMMARY

This chapter has described some of the mental hygiene programs which have been developed in recent years.

The federal government has provided great impetus to local programs through its child-welfare services, and particularly through passage of the National Mental Health Act. Grants-in-aid are made available to the states for developing mental hygiene programs, research is being supported, and the training of professional personnel is being underwritten by the federal government.

The states are taking an increasing interest in the mental health of their people. Most states have Mental Health Associations which are active in developing preventive health programs. Official state agencies have stepped up their clinical services and educational activities. Through the establishment of guidance centers, mental health institutes, traveling clinics, youth commissions, and other projects, the states are making a real effort to attack the problem of mental illness.

Many communities, school districts, and individual schools are making great strides toward organizing effective mental health programs for children and adults. Coöperative school-community projects have emerged to integrate the activities of youth-serving agencies. In-service mental hygiene programs for teachers are becoming more common.

Communities are placing increasing emphasis upon recreational programs, boy's clubs, community centers, and other services which keep children occupied after school and divert their energies into wholesome channels.

The public schools have added to their staffs specialized personnel whose primary function is the early detection and treatment of maladjusted children. Their work is being supplemented in the classroom through various types of mental hygiene education for children.

All of these activities hold great promise for the emergence of a mental hygiene movement in America which will do for mental illness what public health programs have done for physical illness. However, this movement is just beginning. As will be shown in succeeding chapters, much remains to be done before we can say that the problem of mental illness is being attacked effectively in schools and communities.

PROBLEMS AND PROJECTS

1. What is the name and address of the mental health authority in your state? What services does it perform? What use is being made of federal funds? How can schools utilize the services of this agency?
2. Does your state have a mental health association? If so, how is it supported? What are its activities?
3. Describe some community services available to schools in your locality.
4. Describe the mental hygiene activities being conducted in your school system.
5. Discuss your experiences with a teacher in-service program centered around mental hygiene or child study.
6. Talk with some teachers who have used the Bullis technique of teaching human relations. What results do they report? How do they evaluate this approach to mental health education?
7. Do high schools in your community have courses in family life? What is done in these courses?
8. How could you introduce human relations problems through regular high school courses such as biology, mathematics, or English?
9. Does the core curriculum in your schools have any units on human relations? If so, describe them.
10. If you were to organize a mental hygiene program for teachers in your school, what assistance could you secure from the National Association For Mental Health? From the Federal Government? From your local Mental Health Association?

SELECTED REFERENCES

1. "A Partnership Comes of Age," *The Child* (December, 1953), *18*:54–55.
2. Brewer, J. E., "A Community Program of Psychological Services," *Journal of Clinical Psychology* (October, 1951), 7:357–360.
3. Bullis, H. E., and O'Malley, E. E., *Human Relations in the Classroom,* Courses I, II and III, Delaware State Society for Mental Hygiene (Wilmington, Delaware), 1947, 1948, 1949.
4. *Children,* January–February, 1954.
5. Committee on Mental Health in Education, *Report of the Conference on Mental Health in Schools and Teacher Education Institutions,* Federal Security Agency, United States Office of Education and Public Health Service, 1949.
6. Committee on Preventive Psychiatry of the Group for the Advancement of Psychiatry, *Promotion of Mental Health in the Primary and Secondary Schools: An Evaluation of Four Projects* (Topeka, Kansas), Report No. 18, January, 1951.
7. Federal Security Agency, Public Health Service, National Institute of Mental Health, *The National Mental Health Program, Progress Report,* September, 1951.
8. Hackett, C. G., "How a Guidance Center Serves the Schools," *Studies in Higher Education,* Bulletin No. LXXIX, September, 1951.
9. Helfant, K., *The Rye Project For Education in Human Relations and Mental Health,* Rye Public Schools (New York), Mimeographed, 1953.
10. Hill, A. S., Miller, L. M., and Gabbard, H. H., "Schools Face the Delinquency Problem," *Bulletin of the National Association of Secondary School Principals* (December, 1953), 37:181–221.
11. Hoover, W. W., and Helfant, K., *The Rye Project the First Year, An Interim Report,* Rye Public Schools (New York), Mimeographed, 1953.
12. Kaplan, L., and Baron, D., *Mental Hygiene and Life,* Harper & Brothers, 1952.
13. Lemkau, P. V., *Mental Hygiene in Public Health,* McGraw-Hill Book Company, 1949, p. 39.
14. Maddux, J. F., "Psychiatric Consultation in a Rural Setting," *The American Journal of Orthopsychiatry* (October, 1953), *23*:775–784.
15. National Education Association, Research Division, "Schools Help Prevent Delinquency," *Research Bulletin,* vol. XXXI, no. 3, October, 1953.
16. New York State Youth Commission, *Blueprint For Delinquency Prevention* (Albany, New York), 1953.

17. Office of the Los Angeles County Superintendent of Schools, *Los Angeles County Cooperative Project in Human Relations: Annual Report,* Mimeographed, July, 1951.
18. Ojemann, R. H., "An Integrated Plan For Education in Human Relations and Mental Health," *Journal of the National Association of Deans of Women* (March, 1953), 16:101–108.
19. Ojemann, R. H., *Changes Needed in Subject Matter Content to Develop a Mental Hygiene Approach to Behavior,* Address presented at the 1953 meeting of the AERA (Atlantic City, New Jersey), Mimeographed.
20. Rankin, P. T., and Dorsey, J. M., "The Detroit School Mental Health Project," *Mental Hygiene* (April, 1953), 37:228–248.
21. Southern California Society for Mental Hygiene, *Annual Report, 1952* (Los Angeles, California), 1952.
22. State of New York, Department of Mental Hygiene, Mental Health Commission, *Third Annual Conference of Clinic Personnel on Clinic Relations With Other Community Agencies* (Albany, New York), 1953.
23. Taber, R. C., "Before It's Too Late," *National Education Association Journal* (December, 1953), 42:542–544.
24. "The Work of the United States Public Health Service," *Public Health Reprint 47, Number 6,* Reprints 1447, February, 1931, p. 30.
25. U.S. Department of Health, Education and Welfare, Public Health Service, National Institute of Mental Health, *The National Mental Health Program, Progress Report,* October–November, 1953.
26. U.S. Department of Health, Education and Welfare, Public Health Service, National Institute of Mental Health, *The National Mental Health Program, Progress Report,* February, 1954.
27. U.S. Public Health Service, *National Institute of Mental Health,* Public Health Publications, Series No. 20, Mental Health Series No. 4, rev., 1950.

PART II

ENVIRONMENTAL INFLUENCES ON PERSONALITY

A child's experiences begin in the home, move out into the neighborhood and community, and then into the school. At each step he takes with him the psychological and social learnings derived from the environmental forces he encounters. These environmental forces are an integral part of the child's life, and his behavior cannot be understood apart from them. As educators become aware of the total environmental milieu surrounding the child, they will be better able to guide his school experiences.

In the next four chapters we shall describe some of the forces in the home and community which influence personality development. Three chapters are concerned with the home, for it is here that personality and mental health originate. The fourth chapter discusses the culture surrounding the home, with emphasis upon how social class status influences behavior.

CHAPTER 5 ⎯⎯⎯⎯⎯⎯⎯⎯⎯⎯⎯

Psychological Forces in the Home

PSYCHIATRISTS have long maintained that our relationships with people are patterned by our early relationships in the home during the period of infancy and childhood. The home has been described as the psychological laboratory within which human nature is formed—the source of our most intimate and most lasting impressions. This power of the home cannot be disputed since the home has the child before any other social agency can get to him. Without question, the child's habits of thinking, feeling, and acting emerge out of the experiences he has in the family during the first five or six years of life. However, the growing child is constantly forming and reforming his personality as his horizons expand beyond the home into the school and community. School experiences, particularly, can have a significant impact upon his personality development. Therefore, educators need a clear understanding of what happens to a child at home so that they can guide his experiences in school more intelligently.

In this chapter, and the two which follow, we shall examine some of the more significant aspects of home life, especially those which are known to have an important influence upon the mental health of children. The discussion in this chapter is limited to (1) some characteristics of the modern home, (2) the significance of early life experiences, and (3) psychological effects of the child's position in the family. Subsequent chapters will treat the problems of parent-child interaction, and the emotional consequences of various forms of disciplinary control over children.

SOME CHARACTERISTICS OF THE MODERN HOME

Modern technological and social developments have introduced some major changes in the atmosphere of the home. These changes have not altered the importance of the family's influence on child growth, but they have definitely modified the kinds of influences which are brought to bear upon children in the home.

Influence of Technological Change

The industrialization of our society during the past half-century has broken down the wall which separated life outside the home from life within the family circle.

For one thing, the shift from rural to urban living has forced children out of the isolated protected environment of the home, into the stream of community life. About four-fifths of the nation's children live in urban areas (36). Here there is very little of the coöperative type of family enterprise commonly found on the farm. Children have little real responsible work to do in the modern mechanized household of the city. As a consequence, they tend to move outside the home for their recreation, work, and social activities. This movement out of the home not only removes children from the close observation of parents, but it also acquaints them with the ways of the world at a very tender age (10:6). The result is that children discover the cultural conflicts existing in society before they have the maturity to interpret them. They learn that the whole world is not centered in the home and that social practices often are in conflict with parental standards.

Moreover, mass media of communication, notably movies, radio, and television—have been instrumental in bringing the outside world directly into the home. The stories presented through these media sometimes complicate relationships in the home by challenging the child-rearing practices of parents. They even suggest to the child what standards of behavior to expect of parents, and they certainly have a powerful influence over what the parent buys for children to eat, wear, or play with.

These forces have taken from parents the almost complete control they once exercised over the personality development of their children. Today parents have of necessity surrendered some of this control to the cultural forces which cannot be walled out of the home. Modern family life no longer provides children with the secure, isolated, protected environment of pretechnological society. Therefore, parents can no longer be held completely responsible for what their children learn and do. They now share this responsibility with all the social forces and agencies which surround the home.

The Disruption of Family Units

The traditional prototype of an American family is a related unit of parents and their natural children living together. Modern events have altered this standard domestic organization for a great many people. Over 13 percent of the nation's children are living with either one parent, or have no parents at all (36). Divorce, desertion, separation, death, war, and the threat of war have disrupted many families, leaving millions of youngsters without the intimate family circle so important to their early security. The circumstances under which these children are living was described by the Midcentury White House Conference on Children and Youth in these words:

In 1948, about 2 million children under 18 were living with neither parent and nearly 4 million with one parent.

Among children living with only one parent, approximately 1,500,000 had a widowed parent, 900,000 had a divorced parent and 1,500,000 had a parent away from home. Absent parents include those in the Armed Forces, those employed away from home, those severely ill and cared for outside of the home, or those who had left the family by separation.

Among the 39 million children living with both parents, including step-parent and adopted parents as well as natural parents, nearly 6 million had at least one parent who was remarried. (36)

Evidence indicates that this problem was even more acute in 1953. In that year, about 7 million children were domiciled with only one or neither parent present (26).

While the break-up of the family unit does not inevitably result in emotional trauma for the child, it certainly introduces psychological factors which make growing up more difficult. In many cases family upheavals occur while children are still very young. For instance, two-thirds of the children affected by divorce are under 10 years of age (36). Also almost 2,700,000 children whose parents are now alive will lose their mother or father during the period of dependency (25). More often than not, as shown in Figure 4, the father is the first parent to die. This usually throws a heavy economic burden on the mother who must then earn a living as well as maintain a home.

Death and divorce are not, of course, modern phenomena. Such family disruptions have always occurred. Today, however, these events are more tragic than ever before because of the very narrow platform on which the modern home stands. When the American family consisted of many

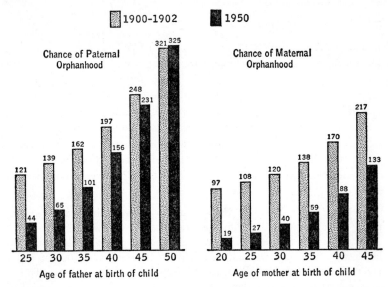

FIGURE 4. Chances in 1000 that a Newborn Child Will Be Orphaned Before Attaining Age 18, Mortality Experience of White Population, United States, 1900–1902 and 1950. (From Metropolitan Life Insurance Company, *Statistical Bulletin,* vol. 34, no. 10, October, 1953. See also, *Statistical Bulletin,* vol. 38, June, 1957.)

children together with their parents, grandparents, uncles, aunts, and other relatives, the loss of one member of the household did not imperil the entire family structure. Now about 70 percent of the families in the United States have only one or two children under 18 years. The typical urban family is the father-mother-children unit, largely cut off from other relatives. The child has few persons upon whom he can rely for emotional support. When one is taken from him, there is no one to fill the gap; the complete home life so vitally needed during the formative years is shattered. "This makes the parents relationship to the child far more intense than would be the case if there were additional intimate relationships available to diffuse the child's emotional attachment to any particular relative" (15:289).

The Working Mother

The most recent threat to the unity of family life is the working mother. When women left the home during World War II to work in defense industries, there was created a small army of "latchkey" children. These were the youngsters who returned from school, took the door key from around their necks, or from under the mat, and shifted for themselves until parents came home from work. Many children were cared for by relatives, friends, baby sitters, or no one at all during the years when they most needed parental guidance.

The emotional trauma which a young child may experience when he is left alone by his mother is vividly illustrated by the following case cited by Dr. Benjamin Spock:

Here is a typical story of a badly handled separation: A mother abruptly takes a job leaving her 22-month-old boy in the care of a woman with whom he is not familiar. The first day he is well behaved, but when his mother returns that evening he hangs on to her like a leech, refusing to let the other woman come anywhere near. The next morning there is a scene when his mother leaves and in the evening he not only refuses to let her out of his sight but also refuses to be put in bed. If she tears herself away he may cry anxiously for hours. Her slightest move toward the door brings him instantly to his feet crying.

I think that such anxieties can be largely avoided if the emotional dependence of young children is understood and respected. This brings up the whole subject of parental, foster parental, and group care. In the first place mothers should understand clearly that the young child, particularly up to the age of 3 derives his greatest security from a sense of belonging intimately and irrevocably to his parents. Generally speaking a mother should be discouraged from going to work during the child's early years unless it is really essential from the point of view of finances or of the mother's morale, and unless there is a relative, maid, friend, or foster mother to take her place who is familiar, loving, comfortable and can be counted on to last the job, or unless there is excellent nursery school care to which the child is mature enough to adjust. (38)

The mother's absence also may upset the emotional balance of older children. For instance, a study of 400 elementary school children referred to a guidance center revealed that the youngsters whose mothers were employed outside the home had a syndrome of behavior difficulties which distinguished them from a control group whose mothers were not employed. Children of working mothers were found to lack a feeling of independence; they had difficulty in establishing cordial relationships with people, and had symptoms of fantasy, withdrawing behavior and insecurity (35).

As adults look back upon their lives, the great majority say that their mothers were the greatest influence upon their personality development.[1] "She was always around" was a typical comment, "and we went to her with our troubles." By comparison, the emotional loneliness of a child whose mother was always away from home is revealed in the expression of a wartime adolescent: "They don't care what happens to me, why should I?"

The need of a young child for his mother cannot be exaggerated. In addition to the emotional comfort he derives from knowing that she is always present for emergencies, there is a need to tell somebody of his school experiences, his problems, and his plans. This cannot wait. The youngster who comes home from school and shouts, "Mom—I'm home," needs the comforting reassuring reply of a mother. So important is this factor that one psychiatrist has stated, "The distortion or maldevelopment of the child's character is usually in proportion to the sum total of physical and emotional absence on the part of the parents" (*31*).

Working away from home may also have an unwholesome influence on the mother herself. As Bossard has pointed out: "The combined strain of being wife, mother, and outside employee tends to make mothers unduly tired, with consequent feelings of impatience and irritability" (*1:284*). The mother's absence from the home affects her ability to render detailed services which children need, such as taking care of clothes, supervising their arguments, and just talking to them. As one adolescent complained, "My mother is so tired she won't even talk to me." Such behavior on the part of the mother, even when not intended, causes children to feel lonely and neglected. In some cases children seize upon the opportunity to run wild, inside the home and outside as well. This behavior commonly irritates tired, overworked parents until an emotional explosion results.

There is convincing evidence that a mother should weigh carefully the consequences of taking full-time employment outside the home when there is no familiar, loving, reliable person to take her place. Yet, it is becoming more and more common for women to work outside the home. During World War II the number of women employed in business and industry reached an all-time high. It was assumed that they would return to their homes when the emergency ended. But this did not happen. In fact after the war even more women left the home and entered the business world. In 1953, the United States Department of

[1] Gallup Poll, 1953.

Labor reported that almost 11 million married women were holding paying jobs—over three times the number who were working during the war period. Moreover, 5¼ million women workers were mothers of children under 18 years of age, and almost 2 million had children less than 6 years of age (28).

The Influence of Poverty

One of the inescapable realities of our culture is that people who can least afford children have large families, while people in the higher economic brackets have small families. In 1948, one-third of the families (accounting for one-half of the children) in large cities fell below the city workers' family budget standard of the Bureau of Labor Statistics. This standard is higher than the survival or relief budget, but far from a luxury budget. Yet, one out of every two children in large cities is found in families whose income is below this minimum level (36).

Thus, poverty must be considered as one of the major forces influencing home life. In many families just filling children's stomachs takes a great deal of the parents' energies and efforts. Parents who are uncertain about their own future, who subsist on marginal levels of poverty—with its usual attendants of disease and ignorance—can hardly be expected to develop in their children a feeling of security. If these children steal, skip school, or become like predatory little animals, it is often their living conditions which have made such behavior almost inevitable.

A case in point is the story of 10-year-old Jimmy who was referred to a child-guidance clinic because of truancy and stealing:

Jimmy was one of his widowed mother's six children. Asthmatic, and herself mentally ill, the mother tried to support her family of seven on a monthly welfare check of $105. Jimmy's medical history included repeated episodes of upper respiratory infections, earaches and scabies, the usual bedfellows of neglect and malnutrition. Often he did not go to school because he had no shoes to wear or food to eat for several days running. Asked what his most coveted wishes might be, Jimmy wished for money so there'd be enough to eat, clothes and books for school. When the children were placed for three months with their wise and devoted grandmother who supplemented the relief allotment with her meager life savings, Jimmy's "stealing"—it was for money for food —disappeared, and his school attendance became regular, though he remained a restless and deficient scholar. (7)

This case illustrates the direct link so often found between marginal living in the family and deviant behavior in children. There is little doubt that children living in slum areas or in homes deprived by low income are more likely than other children to have serious health and social problems. The Chicago study wherein a comparison was made of four slum areas with four good areas documents this conclusion. Here it was found that poor housing means poor chances for children. In the slum areas, juvenile delinquency was 20 times greater than in the good area, tuberculosis mortality 12 times greater, and truancy 3 times greater (*36*).

Despite such evidence it is encouraging to observe that not all children in the lower economic classes are destined to lives of social discord and unhappiness. One study of families on relief found that the psychological climate of the home rather than the level of subsistence of the family was the most important factor in determining the behavior of children (*11*). Anyone who has worked in slum areas knows that not all children turn out to be delinquents. Poverty may make it more difficult for children to achieve security, and for some it may be impossible, but where parents are kind and understanding children may have a wholesome home life despite economic hardships.

Mobile Families

The United States Department of Agriculture has estimated that from 500,000 to one million children in this nation are children of migrant families (*5*). These families include the hop-pickers, apple pickers, field hands, harvesters, and others who follow the sun for a living. Economically, they are among the most depressed workers in America. In 1949, the average migratory worker was employed 101 days and earned $514. About 92 percent of all migratory farm workers earned under $1000 a year (*5*).

This type of living has a marked effect on the children in migratory families. Many other children suffer from the conditions imposed by poverty and low income, but the child of migrants has the added disadvantage of belonging nowhere. He seldom gets a chance to establish firm relationships with children or adults, or to develop the kind of routines which children need to stabilize their worlds. Few children feel a greater insecurity in life, for each time they move, the routines of existence which they managed to establish are shattered. Their's is a life of poor housing, poor sanitation, inadequate home care, irregular schooling, no recreation, and little opportunity for normal friendships.

In general, the migrant child is a demoralized, displaced person. How alone and how completely worthless such a child can feel is described in the words of Mrs. Billie Davis, who as a little girl lived among the hobo families which John Steinbeck wrote about in his book, *The Grapes of Wrath.* These families did not even have the cabins or shacks which are provided for farm or ranch workers. They simply camped out wherever they happened to be. Here is how Mrs. Davis saw the world of her early childhood:

We squatted around the kettle every evening, put the beans in the kettle when the water boiled. Every morning my mother would put the kettle and water on the fire and cook mush. Each family had its big pan that was kept on the running board, we had no dishes except a pan and a spoon, and this big, black Dutch oven. Each of us took our pan. We recognized it by the way the enamel was chipped off on the bottom. We took this pan to the kettle, dipped out our portion of beans or mush, sat down under the tree, and ate with a spoon.

. . . . .

At night, the men would whittle little sticks, talk about "this dirty old world," how hateful, how the rich people crushed the poor, kicked them in the teeth, and all the society folks, rich folks did not like the hoboes, and never was there a chance in the world for dirty bums like us. We children got the idea that we were just the scum of the earth. I know when we talked together, my little sister and I, in our normal conversation, we talked about the "real people"—I never realized that until I looked back—the real people who lived in the houses. We felt we were sort of lower animals and often when I played with my little celluloid doll, with whom I had the most profound discussions, I would tell this little doll, pretending, of course, it was one of the real people who lived in one of the houses, I was its mother, and I would say to it, "Now listen, honey, don't go down to the river and play with any of those dirty campers because if you do, you might catch the lice." So I knew where I stood.

When children would laugh at me and call me a little gypsy, I was never bitter—I just simply agreed with them. I understood—I could see for myself the contrast, and I was not embarrassed to be among them because I went as a dog would go—I did not expect anything else, . . . (4)

Not only do migrant children develop such deep-seated feelings of worthlessness, they are exposed to many other emotional and physical dangers. In their unsanitary, overcrowded camps, children are often left alone all day to wander unsupervised around dangerous ditches, excavations, and other hazards. With little adult guidance to protect them, they become subject to all sorts of temptations and experiences. It is small wonder that studies of these families show that mobile children are more frequently delinquent and have more adjustment problems than children who live under more stable circumstances (*21, 3*). They are a problem to the community, to the school, and to themselves. How these children react to school, the difficulties they encounter, and what schools can do for them will be discussed in a later chapter.

Relatives in the Family

Another significant factor in the family environment is the presence of adult relatives. In some homes these relatives may make distinct contributions to the comfort and well-being of the children. In others, they become active competitors for the child's affections, or provide him with a refuge and comfort from the parents' demands, or even challenge the parents' authority and way of raising children. Often, too, these adults may become a special burden to the family. They may be uncles or aunts who were unsuccessful in finding a mate, or whose marriages have failed. They may be relatives who cannot support themselves, or who are too sick, feeble, or maladjusted to live alone. All of these conditions, quite apart from the direct influence of relatives on the children, may introduce unwholesome emotional overtones in the family.

Moreover, it is not at all uncommon to find considerable sniping among relatives living together under one roof. Sometimes this takes the form of sabotaging the relationships between parents and their children. Bossard cites the following case which illustrates this pattern of relationship:

The family consists of a father, mother and child. The home was comfortable with two servants in constant attendance. The mother's brother, a not too industrious person, made extensive visits during his lengthy periods of unemployment. Another brother, newly married, brought his wife for lengthy visits. Henry remembers distinctly the impression he received from these relatives. His father being away from home at work to maintain the establishment, was a recurring subject of conversation of these less occupied and economically strained relatives. Their attitude was that Henry's father was not friendly, that he was a hard and cruel man, that he was not cordial to a great many nice people, and that in all of these ways he somehow was doing a very mean thing to Henry's mother. Henry recalls how distinct this impression was, and how it bothered him, because to him his father was kind and generous. Henry reports that for several years he was greatly confused about his father. (*1* :62)

This type of conflict in the kinship group can undermine a child's security and leave him with feelings of guilt and doubt regarding his own parents.

Even when there is complete harmony among relatives, constant association with a large group of related persons may have adverse effects upon the child's personality development. This has been demonstrated in studies of primitive cultures. For instance, Margaret Mead (*23*) found that in the Samoan village of related families, 200 or more relatives may live together almost as a single unit. The Samoan child is brought up in a world of relatives who welcome him into their households as one of the family. As a result, the child's personal relationships are diffused among a large kinship group. He seldom develops any dependence upon his parents and establishes no binding ties with anyone. The Samoan child grows up lacking a sense of self-reliance. He shies away from responsibility and is passive or unassertive in his relationships with people.

A similar situation exists among the Arapesh Indians where the child learns to depend on a large group of relatives rather than upon his own parents. These relatives respond to his needs and hurts, cuddle and fondle him, and protect him from the frustrations commonly encountered by children in more individualistic cultures. The child grows up with a sense of emotional security in the care of others, and with a loving trust of all persons related to him. But this is a very insecure base for his character development. Never having found it necessary to learn how to manage his own environment, and having been protected from the painful lessons a child must learn as he develops his individuality, the Arapesh's loving trust of others can be shattered by a few disillusioning experiences (*24*).

Of course not all relatives have an undesirable influence on children. As pointed out earlier, relatives in the family may provide children with added security by broadening the family base. Yet it is also true that the presence of an outsider may upset the family atmosphere and introduce environmental influences which are detrimental to the mental health of children.

The Significance of Early Life Experiences

Personality development not only starts in the family—it starts in earliest infancy. Basic behavioral tendencies are laid down in the early months of life as a result of the infant's reactions to the kind of treatment it receives.

Some babies find the world a warm, comforting place where their cries are met with a ready response, where they are fed when hungry, cuddled and rocked, and treated with gentleness and love. They react to this treatment by becoming alert, pleasant, and responsive little persons. Other babies, treated more mechanically, develop quite a different set of reactions toward the world. Infants who are kept on a rigid feeding schedule, held as little as possible, and provided with plenty of opportunity to "cry it out" when they are not actually hungry or physically uncomfortable, may respond in several ways. Some learn that they can expect little satisfaction from their outer environment and turn to their own bodies for pleasure. This is one explanation for behavior such as thumbsucking, masturbation, rocking, head-banging, and various other stereotyped, repetitive movements.

Other infants learn that they have to yell to get any satisfaction out of the world. Later they may use temper tantrums and aggressive behavior as a means of controlling the persons around them. Still others find no way at all to gain control over their environment, so they withdraw from it. In infancy such children may lie passively in their beds, refusing to be stimulated, showing little animation, and even refusing to eat. They may become good babies, quiet babies—in some cases so quiet that they just shrivel up and waste away (*19*:208).

These responses are not intellectualized; they are preverbal behavior patterns which become deeply imbedded in the child's feelings. This makes it extremely difficult later to change these original reactions through an intellectual or reasoned approach.

Physical Reactions to Affectional Deprivation

In addition to affecting the infant's attitude toward the world, the absence of close, intimate affection may produce serious physical symptoms, intellectual deterioration, or mental abnormalities. For instance, inadequate fondling has been known to produce eczema in infants. Rosenthal (*33*) reports a study of 25 mothers of infants with eczema and 18 mothers of infants without skin disorders. He found that most of the infants with eczema had received inadequate soothing skin contact prior to the onset of the disorder.

At the University of Washington School of Medicine further information was gathered on the infant's physical reactions to parental attitudes (39). Investigators studied 18 infants from 13 families to determine how mothering affected the child's development. They found that as early as two weeks after birth there were distinct differences in the crying patterns of inadequately mothered babies. Eight babies in the group were observed to cry at least once a day for a period of not less than 90 minutes and could not be comforted.

At two months of age these inadequately mothered babies had an anxious, unsmiling facial expression. They had frequent respiratory infections, running noses, many skin rashes, numerous accidental falls, and excessive gas (colic) in the gastrointestinal tract. In studying the mothers of these babies it was found that there was much conflict over the acceptance of their roles as mothers. They did not know what to do for the babies. The feedings were erratic; sometimes the babies were fed when they were not hungry and sometimes they were not fed when they were hungry. The mothers held the babies excessively, or refused to hold them at all. When the baby was held, there was little close intimacy between mother and child, and much patting, jiggling, and excessive activity.

By contrast, the mothers of children who cried little were secure individuals who accepted their feminine roles and had close physical contact with their babies. The needs of their children were met adequately and at the right time, and the mothers felt sure of what to do for the children. These babies grew normally and functioned normally physiologically.

The investigators concluded that the infants who cried excessively were doing so in response to internal tensions resulting from the mother's behavior. These infants could not develop a feeling of security in interpersonal relations and were reacting in the only way they could, through crying and physiological upsets.

Research has found that the infant's physical reactions to inadequate mothering may become so intense that his life is impaired. This was disclosed in Escalona's study (8) of babies born to mothers confined to a reformatory for women. Ten cases of infants under four weeks old were observed to refuse either breast or bottle feeding from their highstrung excitable mothers. These mothers held the baby tightly, trembled, or babbled in a high-pitched, excited voice about their resentment over imprisonment generally and over the baby in particular. The babies responded by refusing to eat. In some instances there was vomiting, loss of weight, and other physical and emotional disturbances. In six cases the babies would accept formulas from other women prisoners, but would not eat when held by their mothers.

This study, and others such as those of Meyer (27) and Ribble (32), show how the improper handling of infants can damage the physical and emotional health of a child. These early experiences can influence deeply the physiological and psychological organization of an individual. If continued very long, they may result in irreversible changes which have a permanently damaging effect. Evidence on this point is discussed below.

Infantile Autism

Infants who have experienced continued affectional neglect sometimes develop a condition termed *infantile autism*. Children so affected behave much like idiots. They are characterized by extreme withdrawal and obsessive behavior. They do not talk, and rarely engage in any activity requiring intelligence, although their intellectual capacity may be normal (16). Because this clinical picture is found rather often among foundling-home children who receive little affection, it is sometimes referred to as "hospitalism."

A dramatic illustration of a developing case of infantile autism appeared in a newspaper story not long ago. At three months of age little Larry developed a torturous itching eczema. To keep him from scratching, his parents, who loved him, tied his arms so that he could not touch himself. They covered him with dressings and handled him as little as possible. He was merely fed and changed, never cuddled or held closely.

At first Larry fought against the dressings as any normal child would. Soon he became silent; his weight dropped from 21 pounds at 10 months to 14 pounds at 22 months. He did not coo or gurgle, and began to look like a half-dead, wizened old mummy. When seen by a doctor he had completely lost interest in life and was wasting away. The doctor's advice to the parents was to treat the child like a baby—to love and cuddle him, despite his skin ailment. The treatment worked. Larry increased in weight, and although his eczema did not disappear entirely, he was on his way back to becoming a normal healthy child (30).

Larry was fortunate in that his withdrawal from life had not proceeded so far that he could not be rescued. There are many other children who never recover from the effects of living in an emotional vacuum. The studies of Spitz (37), Roudinesco (34), and Goldfarb (13) are particularly revealing in this regard.

Dr. Spitz's first investigations involved 91 infants in two child-care institutions. One institution was a nursery in which infants were cared for by their own mothers. The other was a foundling home where there was one nurse for eight to twelve infants. Over a period of time it was noted that children in the nursery home developed normally. But in the foundling home where infants were picked up only occasionally by busy nurses, the children regressed in their behavior. They were unable to speak, walk, or feed themselves. Out of the original number studied, about 37 percent died, and the remainder behaved as hyperexcited or apathetic idiots. Spitz observed that deprivation of adult affection lasting more than three months, if it takes place during the first year of life, results in permanent damage that cannot be remedied by the mother's return.

Roudinesco summarized the studies of workers all over the world who were investigating the effects of separating very young children from their mothers. These studies included observations of children one to three years of age who had been separated from their mothers before the age of eight months and placed in institutions where no adequate substitute mothering was available. The responses of these children deteriorated progressively in the following manner:

First there was a stage of protest where the child cried loudly, shook the crib, threw himself about, looked eagerly toward sounds which might be the mother, and was demanding of adults—either clinging to them or fretting and crying when an adult approached. Following the stage of protest was a state of despair. The child's activity diminished, he cried intermittently, made no demands, and appeared to be in a state of mournful waiting. The final phase was one of denial. Adults having deserted him, the child became more and more self-centered and transferred his attention to material things like candy, toys, and food.

The most seriously neglected children presented the following clinical picture:

1. A lack of animation, movements slow and limited. Little or no use made of toys given to them. Some just sit and suck on a toy, or manipulate an object, or engage in other repetitive, stereotyped movements.

2. Each child isolates himself from others. If this isolation is disturbed by another child, there may be a sudden aggressive outburst.
3. Some children sit and rock themselves back and forth for hours. Others remain for many minutes in uncomfortable positions until they become distressed.
4. Little interest is shown in food. They eat passively when fed, but with no evident pleasure.
5. They have a sad, depressed attitude of mournful waiting. A child may watch the coming and going of adults in the room as if uncertain about what is going to happen. There is a lack of interest in people—no response when picked up or when put down. In some cases, children refuse to have any contact with adults. When picked up they shriek and fight as if terrified.
6. Many children refuse to walk. When held in a walking position a child may throw himself on the ground and remain there.

Psychiatrists are generally pessimistic about helping children who have suffered such severe damage through maternal deprivation. They feel that when a child is so affected in the first three years of life, his intelligence is impaired, distortion of personality occurs, and he becomes incapable of ever achieving harmonious human relations. When the child develops symptoms such as persistent rigidity, permanent rocking, abnormal movement of the hands, and absence of speech and facial expression, it is too late for mothering to do any good.

On the other hand, children who are separated from their mothers, but who receive good substitute mothering, do not experience any permanent damage. However, it is common to find among such children symptoms of insecurity, anxiety, and regression to more infantile types of behavior such as thumbsucking and overdependence on an adult.

Subsequent Effects of Emotional Deprivation

The Goldfarb study (13) throws some light on what to expect in later years from children who survive the effects of emotional impoverishment in infancy. This investigator followed two groups of children through their early school years and in some cases through adolescence. One group had been in an orphanage from the earliest months of life to about the age of three years, at which time they were transferred to foster homes. The other group, used as a control, consisted of children who had been brought up in foster homes from the beginning. The orphanage children had the best of physical care but no opportunity to relate themselves to anyone who would give them warm physical affection. They were cared for by a succession of nurses who had little time for emotional comforting.

The children in foster homes had adequate psychological satisfactions in a loving environment. They developed more or less normally. The orphanage children, however, showed distinct symptoms of personality difficulties, prominent among which were these:

1. They were unmanageable and unresponsive to normal motivation. They would wander off aimlessly from the school grounds and come home hours later than expected. This behavior persisted despite the warnings and punishments administered by the foster parents.
2. They had a history of extremely difficult behavior. In school they disregarded rules, accepted academic failure in a complacent manner, they were destructive, stubborn, given to severe temper outbursts, provoked fights frequently, and could not get along with other children.
3. Although these children had an insatiable appetite for love they did not know how to accept it. They were emotionally isolated and cold toward people, even those who tried to be affectionate toward them.

In general, Goldfarb concluded, these children even through adolescence showed characteristics similar in many respects to the personality structure found in children who had sustained severe head injuries early in life. They presented a picture of warped personalities who viewed the world as a cold hostile place, who could form no genuine attachments to people, and who displayed retaliatory, aggressive behavior.

Personality disturbances of this type are not limited to children raised in institutions. Wherever children are brought up in a frigid atmosphere, devoid of warm, human attention, the symptoms of personality disorganization may appear. To illustrate, Kanner (17) made an analysis of 50 children who had been treated in Baltimore clinics. He found among them many of the symptoms noted in institutionalized children. They were unresponsive to people, became absorbed in repetitive play, and were either mute or backward in language development. Those who did learn to speak made many irrelevant utterances with frequent pronoun reversals.

These children were not raised in institutions but came from homes of better-than-average socioeconomic standing. Their mothers, with few exceptions, were college graduates who before marriage had worked as nurses, physicians, librarians, and artists. The origin of their children's behavior lay in the fact that these parents were more interested in intellectual pursuits than in people. They were undemonstrative, cold, intelligent, perfectionistic individuals. Their children were raised as if each was a scientific experiment. In the home there was obsessive concern over routine and the performance of skills, accompanied by mechanical attention to the material needs of the children. They kept careful notes of their children's behavior and insisted upon obedience and rapid intellectual development. One parent had purchased an encyclopedia for his 2-year-old, another tried to teach his child to walk at three months.

Although these homes were not institutions, they were emotional refrigerators. The children in them had no fondling or cuddling as infants and never experienced the warmth of genuine parental affection. As a result they had little interest in human contact and their need for warm human relationships seemed to atrophy.

These studies underscore the significance of infancy and early childhood in personality formation. They lead inevitably to the conclusion that the early years without affection can leave an indelible impression on the child. Affection lost during this period of life can never be completely regained. If not delayed too long, children deprived of emotional warmth in their early years will respond, in some degree, to a warm-hearted, good-natured adult who will heap upon them the love they missed. But if they find no such adult during the first few years of life, not even psychotherapy can do much to help them achieve a normal state of adjustment.

PSYCHOLOGICAL EFFECTS OF THE CHILD'S POSITION IN THE FAMILY

A great deal of importance is attached to the ordinal position of children in the family. Whether a youngster is an only child, or the first, last, or middle child in a family, has considerable influence on his home environment and the way he reacts to it.

Despite the significance of a child's order of birth, it is difficult to ascribe a precise psychological role to children on the basis of this factor alone. So many other things play a part in shaping the home atmosphere that in any given instance they may overshadow the influence of the child's position in the family (40). The state of the family finances, the age of the parents, where the family lives, the age range between children, and the sex of children are but a few of the factors which may influence the psychological climate of the home. Any one of these can result in quite a different home environment for children, independent of their order of birth.

Nevertheless, enough clinical evidence has been accumulated to make some fairly accurate predictions about how children born at various times may be influenced by the environment they encounter in a normal family situation. It is helpful to keep these generalizations in mind as an aid to understanding children, even though the characteristics described are not invariably true and, in fact, may be only suggestive of the possibilities for which to look.

The Older Child

The first-born child enjoys certain relations with his parents which differ from those experienced by children who come along later. Usually, parents are excited and proud over their first offspring. He occupies the center of the stage, and although they may make mistakes by expecting too much of him in one way and too little in another, there is an exciting freshness about his accomplishments which is not quite duplicated with later born children.

Because the first child is older, bigger, and stronger, for a while at least, his life is one of firsts. He is first to cross the street alone, first to go to school, first to ride a bike, first to wear newly purchased clothes. He becomes the pioneer, the pathfinder, and the trail blazer in the family.

Accompanying his position of leadership in the family are certain responsibilities which he must assume. The older child is often expected to set an example for younger children, to take care of them, resist the temptations to which they succumb, and in general to demonstrate a level of maturity commensurate with his privileges.

However, certain unavoidable frustrations commonly enter the life of the older child and challenge his supremacy. By the time he becomes secure in his position as the center of attraction within the family, several things may happen to disrupt his security. For one thing, the passage of time usually brings a change in the parents' attitude toward children. The Fels Research Institute (20) noted that the child-centeredness of the home declines sharply from age two to five. Parents tend to be very solicitous toward the child for the first two years, then their attention declines to a moderate level, even before a second child arrives.

The arrival of a second child often introduces a real crisis in the life of the first-born. Dethronement by a new arrival causes the older child to react in several ways. If the first-born is still very young, he may show his disturbance through changes in his eating or toilet habits, by crying, or by temper tantrums. An interesting illustration of this situation occurred in a family where a new baby was born when the first child was just 18 months old. Nancy, the first-born, had been weaned of the bottle for several months. When her mother sat down to feed the baby his bottle, Nancy would try to climb on her mother's lap, making things difficult for everybody. When this tactic did not work, she would stand close to the mother and watch the feeding process with wide beseeching eyes. Then she would think of things she needed, or whine about something that had to be done for her immediately.

One day her mother jokingly offered Nancy the baby's bottle. Nancy took it, half in fun, but it turned out that this was just what she wanted. Thereafter, everytime the baby was fed, Nancy had to have a bottle too. With a bottle in her mouth she caused no trouble. But it was impossible to get the bottle away from her until the baby was weaned. Nancy was almost 2½ years old by that time and presented a rather incongruous picture with a bottle in her mouth, but she wouldn't give it up as long as the baby had it.

This treatment, while it cannot be recommended as a general practice, worked out very well. There was almost no friction between the children during the period they were nursing from the bottle. Today, they get along as well together as can be expected of normal siblings. There is relatively little rivalry for the parents' affections.

There appear to be some important implications in the reactions of a 2½-year-old to a new sibling. This is about the age when the first child has almost mastered the difficult tasks of keeping himself dry and feeding himself neatly. He becomes confused when he sees the new baby receiving his mother's love and approval despite the fact that it soils itself, messes with its food, and has none of the restraints which the older child had to learn. Margaret Mead (22:108) has suggested that this situation may be the seed "out of which grows the bitterness toward all those who 'have it soft,' or 'get away with it,' that is typical of the American personality."

If the first child is about school age when he is supplanted by a younger sibling, quite commonly he may express his resentment through various anxiety symptoms, including nightmares, nail biting, thumb-sucking, restless sleep, stammering, enuresis, excessive shyness, neurotic vomiting, negativism, or fantasies (1). These may persist as long as they are effective in attracting attention, or until other means are found to comfort the child.

With the passing of time, feelings of displacement and jealousy may be reflected in the child's social activities. He may have a chip on his shoulder, lack a sense of humor, and act more mature than is characteristic of his age. He may reflect a lack of security by seeking to be in a position of authority among his peers, and by failing to recognize the rights of others (40).

Feelings such as these may carry over into adult life. Even the choice of a marriage partner may be influenced by the unfulfilled strivings of the first-born child. It has been noted that the first-born son often tends to seek a wife who will make him feel important; someone whom he can take care of and dominate. This has been interpreted as a manifestation of the older child's unconscious desire to maintain his status of being first in the family (40).

In his choice of a vocation the first-born seems to gravitate toward positions of authority in which he will have responsibility for others. He is likely to seek executive positions or other authoritative pursuits such as police work, teaching, or nursing.

The resentment of the oldest child toward displacement and his hostility toward competitors may bring him into conflict with society. The studies of Harris (14), Rouman (35), and Brockway (2) disclosed that first-born children tend to have more adjustment problems and poorer relations with playmates than do other children in the family. They have more troubles associated with eating, elimination, and sleeping, and show more evidence of fear and tension. There is also some evidence that a relatively high proportion of first-born children have trouble with the law. Thieves are found more frequently among first-born children than among other siblings (29).

In summary, the first-born child has a tendency toward extremes. He may develop strong leadership qualities and become a dominating personality with a great capacity for handling responsibility. On the other hand, there is the chance that his struggles for supremacy in and out of the family may lead him into personal and social difficulties.

In-Between Children

Middle children are said to have the least enviable position in the family. They have neither the priority of the first-born nor the novelty of the last-born. As Faegre (9) has said, the second child ". . . often has hand-me-down clothes, a hand-me-down bike, and—just perhaps—a hand-me-down, somewhat matter of fact attitude from his parents when it comes to those thrilling things like a first formal, or the first loan of the family car to pick up a date."

Parents find it hard to recapture with the second child the excitement of their eldest's first events. They do not start off at as high a level of child-centeredness as prevailed with the first. But there is some consolation in the fact that their interest in the second child remains stable for a longer period (20). Yet, parents are likely to be less tolerant of the behavior of a middle child and tend to be more definite and prescriptive about the things he can or cannot do.

The in-between child must contend not only with the changed attitude of parents but, more significantly perhaps, with the personalities of older and younger children in the family. The middle child is wedged in among the other siblings. Always in front of him is the older child with whom he never catches up—the brother or sister who is bigger and stronger, with greater freedom of action and with constant priority on material things and experiences. Always behind him is the baby of the family whose claim for attention cannot be disputed and with whom he cannot compete.

This leaves the middle child with three possible choices of action, described by Bossard as follows:

> One is to drive himself forward, hard, relentlessly to catch up with or to overcome the oldest child. It is this which leads Adler to remark that the restless neurotics are to a preponderant degree, second-born children.
>
> A second possibility is to criticize and depreciate the older child and thus attempt to equalize the struggle. This leads to lasting animosities.
>
> The third possible course of behavior is for the in-between child to drop back and affiliate with the younger ones. This may result in an attitude of defeatism, a loss of initiative. Or there may be a sadistic turn with the in-between child becoming a tease and a bully taking out on the younger children the venom of his spite toward the oldest one. There may develop, however, an almost tender care for the younger children. (1:114)

Of course the path followed by the middle child will depend upon the characteristics of the other children. For instance, if the first child is particularly competent and successful, the second child may not have the courage to struggle against him. If the accomplishments of the first-born are not impressive, the second child may tend to be especially ambitious and develop a drive to overcome and surpass the first-born. In any event, the second-born child resents being bossed, he tends to be sensitive to criticism, and is somewhat of a revolutionary in that he would like to see the power in the family change hands, whether he takes any overt action to do so or not. Often he is an especially active youngster who speaks rapidly and is highly competitive (*40*).

Thus despite the fact that parents may say, "We love all our children alike and treat them equally," the in-between child lives in a rather sensitive environment and often needs special consideration.

The Youngest Child

The last-born child, because he is the baby and never really gives up this title, enjoys certain advantages. The parents, having now had considerable experience with children, are much more prepared for this child. They may be able to give him material things and cultural advantages which could not be provided for the older children. Other children in the family may also contribute to the welfare of the baby. They may fight his battles, intercede for him with the parents, make contacts for him outside the home, and steer him through his school and social experiences.

Life can become relatively easy for the baby of the family with all of these advantages to help him along. There are, however, some factors in the life of the last-born which may not have an entirely wholesome influence on his personality development. For one thing, parents may unconsciously be unwilling to let him grow up. They find it hard to end the good times they have had with him, or to give up the close physical contact he has permitted and which children tend to resist as they grow older.

Parents may have difficulty handling the youngster's insistence for independence. If they give in to him, the older children may resent his having the special privileges which they were denied. Also, the young one may develop some undesirable characteristics of domineering others and expecting to have his own way. If parents hold on to him too long, the young child may learn to accept the protection and domination of his family and make the most of it.

Where the baby of the family is coddled and given little opportunity to develop his own powers, he may become a pleasant, likeable, dependent person who goes through life leaning on others and feeling that things will work out well and someone will always help him. Or the child may learn to use other people. Discipline may break down with him because he uses his sweetness, affability, and ingratiating smile to control his parents. He may expect and demand much of others and never give much of himself in return. Or he may learn to enjoy being the center of attention and go to any lengths to remain so.

On the other hand, the fact that the younger child is always surrounded by larger and older individuals may result in a feeling of physical and mental inferiority. To overcome such feelings the child may become a rebel and try to compensate for his feelings of smallness by surpassing the others in some accomplishment, by choosing a vocation different from what is expected of him, or by emphasizing his distinctness from the rest of the family through asocial or nonconforming behavior.

Sometimes the youngest child develops considerable qualities of leadership and independence because of the necessity to resist the bossiness with which older children treat him. Commonly, this leadership takes the form of winning people over, rather than dominating or ordering them around.

In his choice of a vocation the youngest child may reflect his psychological experiences in the family. He may seek a vocation which will keep him in the limelight but impose little responsibility upon him. Stage careers are said to attract the last-born because here he can satisfy his need for being the center of attraction, with little responsibility to shoulder. Likewise in his choice of a marriage partner, the last-born child may reflect his tendency toward receiving rather than giving. He is likely to select a mate who is a strong parent figure, who will pamper and protect him, although on the surface it may appear that he is running the household (40).

Interaction of Siblings

When children live with other children of their own relative age and status, they create forces which cannot be duplicated outside the home. One such force is that of reality structuring. There is a natural tendency for children to create a world of make-believe—a tendency which movies and television have no doubt encouraged. The presence of other children in the family provides a safeguard against spending too much time in a private world of fantasy. The intrusion of a brother or sister quickly crowds out imaginary companions and forces the child to react in terms of reality rather than fantasy. Even when children engage in fantasy-play together, the presence and activity of several youngsters keep reality in its place and imagination separated from it. Although these children "shoot" each other and play dead, they know it is play and readily shift from imagination to reality as the occasion demands. The lonely, introvertive child, shut off from other children, may not make this distinction so easily. As in a dream, he may have difficulty with his fantasy world intruding in and overlapping the real world. With other children in the home this is much less likely to happen.

Living with other children also provides a relief from the unnatural environment created by adults. Children cannot compete with adults, nor match their accomplishments, nor join into their activities on a plane of equality. In their own little world, children understand each other, their interests and problems are common, they speak the same language and have the same kinds of experiences. The therapeutic benefits which children derive from each other is well expressed in the following statement:

> There is a sense of support, of consolation, of spiritual renewal that may come from a fellow sibling; opportunity to talk things over intimately, frankly, with one's own kind at odd moments, late at night, incidentally, while at play. There is a feeling of belonging, of not being isolated, of being fellow members of a group whose interests are irrevocably bound together. And it is this sense of security, this feeling of belonging, this conviction of the certainty of support which builds itself through succeeding days into the foundation of mental hygiene. (1:101)

Children have another way of healing each other's wounds. They provide each other with opportunities for catharsis and compensation. They pass along their humiliations and frustrations from the older to the younger. The older brother or sister takes out on his younger siblings the hurts, disappointments, and frustrations experienced at the hands of adults or older children. "What the nine-year-olds endure from the eleven-year-olds they tend to wreak on the seven-year-olds" (1:111). While this may be a difficult experience for the youngest in the group, it nevertheless appears to be a universal healing process among children.

Of course the benefits which children derive from each other are not without some disturbing aspects. Wherever there are children living together, there will be conflict. Parents usually are annoyed by the squabbles and noise of children in conflict, and sometimes someone gets hurt. Yet even conflict is an essential part of sibling relations. It is one of the ways in which children learn to take turns, to limit their impulses in the presence of others, and to appreciate the rights of others. In a large measure, these are lessons which children can learn only from other children—although this learning might at times appear to be distressingly painful.

The Only Child

The development of the only child in a family takes on particular significance in view of the lessons which children learn from growing up with brothers and sisters in the home. Since about 20 percent of all completed families have only one child (*1*:101), it is worth while to review the research and theory regarding the personality development of the child who grows up among adults.

Popular comments suggest that the only child is likely to be self-centered because of failure to learn give and take from siblings. He is also said to be more mature and serious-minded than the average child, and that too much adult attention makes him precocious, and therefore unpopular with children.

A review of scientific research both supports and contradicts these commonly held beliefs. This is not unexpected, since many factors influence the effects of being a sole son or daughter. For instance, a child may be an only child because his sibling died, or because his parents married late in life, or were divorced early, or for a large variety of reasons, each of which would influence the emotional atmosphere surrounding the child. Also, how the only child is treated in the family conditions his personality development. Some parents make a conscientious effort to find companions for their children—sending them to camp, nursery schools, and other places where they can be with youngsters their own age. Other parents baby their child, lavish him with gifts, protect him from social contacts, or force him to grow up too fast (*41*). This is why it is that a study of one group of only children may reveal these youngsters to be well adjusted personally and academically (*6*), while another study, using a different sample, finds only children to be more maladjusted than non-only children (*2*).

Scientific research has not come up with a consistent, reliable description of the personality characteristics of the only child. To learn that a child has no brothers or sisters may reveal nothing at all if we are seeking clear-cut, predictable characteristics. However, clinical studies of only children have uncovered some personality traits which occur with sufficient frequency to warrant attention. Although these characteristics cannot be used as blanket generalizations to be applied to all only children, they form a framework around which to interpret the behavior of such children.

Strauss' analysis (40) of numerous case studies of only children suggests that the only child has the same role as the first-born, except that he is never dethroned. This role may make it difficult for him to face competition when he enters school. Never having had to share, or fight for anything at home, he tries to recreate this situation in the classroom. As he encounters a strange new resistance from his peers, he may become aggressive and socially unacceptable, or he may adopt a passive acquiescent form of behavior.

The personal feelings of only children, Strauss found, often were associated with a sense of detachment, a feeling of being apart from things, of not belonging among children. The only child is not likely to be a joiner. When he does participate in group activity he may seek a small group where he can be a "big frog in a little pond." He is more at ease with adults than age-mates, and therefore may prefer to be left alone to work by himself rather than join in with other children. Carried over into adult life, the individualistic personal feelings of the only child may influence him to seek a vocation requiring a minimum of contact with other people. He may be intolerant of any opposition, noncoöperative, and impatient in his human relations at work and at home.

Not having learned the basic lessons of human relationships during early childhood, the only child may become the lonely child who does not know how to relate himself to his peers at any age. Both parents and teachers need to recognize this tendency and understand the vital importance of providing the only child with play companions at an early age. There is some evidence that one of the common childhood characteristics of schizophrenics is that they had few or no opportunities for contact with other children before the age of six, and had few or no friends at any time before their illness (12). This does not imply that among schizophrenics there are more only children than non-only children, but it does serve to emphasize again how important it is for children to grow up among other children.

SUMMARY

The home has been justly described as the nursery of civilization. Here the child encounters psychological and social forces which leave an indelible impression on his evolving personality. The human beings with whom he lives, the economic status of the family, the emotional climate of the home, and the experiences he has during infancy and childhood determine in a large measure his basic patterns of behavior.

Educators can influence the personality development of children only if they understand what has happened to them in their homes. This is particularly important for the millions of children who have been deprived of a wholesome home life by the death, divorce, desertion, or separation of parents, by economic necessity which takes the mother out of the home, by the disruptions caused by relatives in the home, or by the numerous other forces which undermine family cohesiveness.

As educators become aware of the significant influences affecting children in the home, they will be better able to meet the mental health needs of children in school. In subsequent chapters we shall discuss additional aspects of home life with which teachers and administrators must be familiar in order to achieve this end.

PROBLEMS AND PROJECTS

1. Describe some specific problems which television, movies, or radio have introduced in the home relationships of parents and children.
2. To what extent are the home conditions prevailing among migrant families duplicated in other mobile families, such as those where the father is in military service?
3. Discuss some wholesome influences you have observed resulting from relatives living in the home with the basic family unit.
4. How do the data on infantile autism apply to adopted children? What are the implications for parents who seek to adopt children?
5. Select some adolescents or preadolescents who have a history of difficult behavior. To what extent does their behavior seem to have been influenced by emotional deprivations in infancy?
6. Compare your own experiences as an only child, a youngest, a middle, or an oldest child, with the general patterns of behavior described in this chapter.
7. Examine the home and school behavior of children whose parents both work. Does the absence of parents seem to have any effect on these children?

8. Describe some situations where working mothers managed to maintain a wholesome home atmosphere for their children.
9. How can the subject of death be discussed with young children so as not to arouse feelings of dread, fear, or apprehension?
10. Do you know of any homes which are economically or sociologically below the average, but which rate high from the point of view of the mental health of children who live there? How do you account for this?

SELECTED REFERENCES

1. Bossard, J. H. S., *The Sociology of Child Development,* rev. ed., Harper & Brothers, 1954.
2. Brockway, I. V., "An Investigation of the Home Backgrounds of Some Problem Children," *Research Relating to Children,* Bulletin II, Supplement 1, U.S. Children's Bureau, 1954, p. 51.
3. Close, K., "Combining Forces for Migrant Children," *Children* (July–August, 1954), *1*:148–152.
4. Davis, B., "I Believe in Our Public Schools," *Addresses and Proceedings,* National Education Association, 92nd Annual Meeting, vol. 92, 1954, pp. 58–70.
5. Ducoff, L. J., *Migratory Farm Workers in 1949,* Bureau of Agricultural Economics, U.S. Department of Agriculture, Agriculture Information Bulletin No. 25, 1950.
6. Dyer, D. T., "Are Only Children Different?" *Journal of Educational Psychology* (May, 1945), *36*:297–302.
7. Eisenberg, L., "Treatment of the Emotionally Disturbed Pre-adolescent Child," *The Pre-adolescent Exceptional Child,* Proceedings of the 35th Conference of Child Research Clinic of the Woods Schools (Langhorne, Pennsylvania), May 23, 1953, pp. 30–41.
8. Escalona, S. K., "Feeding Disturbances in Very Young Children," *American Journal of Orthopsychiatry* (1945), *15*:76–80.
9. Faegre, M. L., *The Adolescent in Your Family,* U.S. Department of Health, Education and Welfare, Social Security Administration, Children's Bureau Publication No. 347, 1954.
10. Federal Security Agency, Social Security Administration, Children's Bureau, *Your Child from 6 to 12,* Children's Bureau Publication No. 324, 1949.
11. Francis, K. V., and Fillmore, E. A., *The Influence of Environment Upon the Personality of Children,* University of Iowa Studies in Child Welfare, vol. 9, no. 2, 1934.
12. Friedlander, D., "Personality Development of Children Who Later Became Psychotic," *Journal of Abnormal and Social Psychology* (July, 1945), *40*:330–335.

13. Goldfarb, W., "Psychological Privation in Infancy and Subsequent Adjustment," *American Journal of Orthopsychiatry* (April, 1945), *15:* 247–255.
14. Harris, D. B., "Parents and War-Born Children," *Children* (July–August, 1954), *1:*153–155.
15. Honigmann, J. J., *Culture and Personality,* Harper & Brothers, 1954.
16. Jervis, G. A., "Factors in Mental Retardation," *Children* (November–December, 1954), *1:*207–211.
17. Kanner, L., "Problems of Nosology and Psychodynamics of Early Infantile Autism," *American Journal of Orthopsychiatry* (July, 1949), *19:* 416–426.
18. Kanner, L., "Unwholesome Parental Attitudes and Children's Behavior," *Education* (January, 1949), 69:263–270.
19. Kaplan, L., and Baron, D., *Mental Hygiene and Life,* Harper & Brothers, 1952.
20. Lasko, J. K., "Parent-Child Relationships," *American Journal of Orthopsychiatry* (April, 1952), *22:*300–304.
21. Ludden, W., "Anticipating Cases of Juvenile Delinquency," *School and Society* (February, 1944), *59:*123–126.
22. Mead, M., *And Keep Your Powder Dry,* William Morrow and Co., 1942.
23. Mead, M., *Coming of Age in Samoa,* Mentor Books, 1950.
24. Mead, M., *Sex and Temperament,* Mentor Books, 1950.
25. Metropolitan Life Insurance Company, "The Chances of Orphanhood," *Statistical Bulletin,* vol. 34, no. 10, October, 1953.
26. Metropolitan Life Insurance Company, "Children in Broken Families," *Statistical Bulletin,* vol. 36, no. 2, February, 1955.
27. Meyer, G., *Studies of Children,* King's Crown Press, 1948.
28. "More Mothers Are Employed," *The Child* (December, 1953), *18:*51.
29. O'Kelly, Elizabeth, "Some Observations on Relationships Between Delinquent Girls and Their Parents, *British Journal of Medical Psychology* (1955), *28:*59–66.
30. *Oregonian,* November 11, 1951.
31. Reimer, M. D., "The Effect on Character Development of Prolonged or Frequent Absence of Parents," *Mental Hygiene* (April, 1949), 33:293–297.
32. Ribble, M. A., "Infantile Experiences in Relation to Personality Development," in J. McV. Hunt, *Personality and the Behavior Disorders,* vol. II, Ronald Press, 1944, pp. 621–651.
33. Rosenthal, M. J., "Psychosomatic Factors in Infantile Eczema," in *Research Relating to Children,* Bulletin II, U.S. Children's Bureau, 1953, p. 147.

34. Roudinesco, J., "Severe Maternal Deprivation and Personality Development in Childhood," *Understanding the Child* (October, 1952), *21*: 104–108.

35. Rouman, J., "Why They Misbehave," *California Parent-Teacher* (December, 1954), *31*:14–15.

36. Schwartz, E. E. (ed.), *Children and Youth at the Midcentury: A Chart Book,* Midcentury White House Conference on Children and Youth, The Working Committee on Statistics, National Publishing Co., 1950.

37. Spitz, R. A., "The Role of Ecological Factors in Emotional Development in Infancy," *Child Development* (September, 1949), *20*:145–155.

38. Spock, B., "Avoiding Behavior Problems," *Journal of Pediatrics* (October, 1945), *27*:363–382.

39. Stewart, A. H., Weiland, I. H., and others, "Excessive Infant Crying (Colic) in Relation to Parent Behavior," *American Journal of Psychiatry* (March, 1954), *110*:687–694.

40. Strauss, B. V., "The Dynamics of Ordinal Position Effects," *Quarterly Journal of Child Behavior* (1951), *3*:133–146.

41. Wattenberg, W. W., "Delinquency And Only Children: Study of a Category," *Journal of Abnormal and Social Psychology* (July, 1949), *44*:356–366.

CHAPTER 6

Patterns of Parent-Child Interaction

THE RELATIONSHIPS which parents establish with their children have a powerful influence upon the development of personality. Generally speaking, if parents are relaxed, affectionate, mature, and understanding, children will grow normally and become happy, socially useful adults. If parents fail to provide children with close, warm, emotional support, the possibility that their youngsters will become anxious, hostile, defensive, or confused persons is enhanced greatly.

The day-by-day relationships of parents and their children should be understood by those who deal with children outside the home. In this chapter we shall discuss three aspects of this relationship: (1) the effects of maladjustment in the family, (2) the types of emotional relationships existing among parents and children, and (3) the father's influence in the home. The following chapter will direct attention to the important problem of how various forms of control affect the behavior of children.

EFFECTS OF MALADJUSTMENT IN THE FAMILY

Personal relationships within a family are so close that when one person becomes emotionally disturbed the psychological equilibrium of the entire family may be upset (5). This is particularly true when a parent is so affected. The child who must live with a maladjusted parent is subjected to experiences so devastating in nature that his chances of becoming a normal, well-adjusted person are endangered.

Influence of Maladjusted Parents

Case studies of children seen at guidance clinics commonly reveal that the great majority of these youngsters come from homes where there is parental dissatisfaction, marital unrest, or emotional maladjustment (*10*). Speech defects among children have been associated with maladjusted parents (*48*); truancy, stealing, and sexual delinquencies have been linked with immature parental behavior (*21*); and the development of strong feelings of helplessness and worthlessness in children has been traced to disturbed family life (*47*).

When parents are emotionally disturbed, it can be expected that three-fourths of the children coming from these families will become involved in problem behavior in the same way and in the same area (*34*). Moreover, the twisted ideas and attitudes resulting from these unfortunate home experiences continue to affect the child long after the original conditions are corrected (*12*).

These studies, and many more, point to the conclusion that maladjusted or incompetent parents rear disturbed children. Although it is known that children are remarkably resilient and have the capacity to wall off or overcome many psychologically damaging experiences, few children raised in a disturbed home atmosphere can escape entirely the distorting effects of this experience.

Hereditary Factors in Maladjusted Families

The fact that emotional disorders and personality disturbances seem to run in families has been interpreted from the viewpoint that defective inheritance is involved. One of the major exponents of this view is Dr. Franz J. Kallman, head of the Medical Genetics Department of the New York State Psychiatric Institute. Kallman (*24*) has made painstaking studies of families in which severe mental illnesses existed. In one instance he collected data on familial patterns of schizophrenia. His studies disclosed that while the general expectancy of schizophrenia in normal populations varied from 0.7 to 0.9 percent, the comparative rate for relatives of schizophrenics increased directly with the closeness of their relationship. Children of schizophrenic parents have a 16.4 percent probability of developing this disorder; grandchildren of these parents, 4.3 percent; nieces and nephews, 3.9 percent; and brothers or sisters, 14 percent.

Studies of schizophrenia among siblings show even more clearly the effects of heredity in the family. If a child in the family has schizophrenia, a half-brother or sister has a 7 percent chance of developing this ailment, a fraternal twin a 14.5 percent chance, and in identical twins there is an 86.2 percent chance that if one twin is schizophrenic the other will be also (*25*).

Kallman also studied the hereditary transmission of the manic-depressive types of psychoses. The expectancy rate of this illness in the general population is somewhat less than one-half of 1 percent. But it appears in 26.3 percent of fraternal twins and in 95.7 percent of identical twins if one of the twins develops the ailment (23). Similar results were secured in studies of involutional psychoses. The expectancy rate was found to vary from 6.0 percent for brothers or sisters of an affected sibling, to 60.9 percent in the case of identical twins (25).

Further evidence on the relationship of heredity to abnormal behavior was derived by Kallman's study of homosexuality. He managed to locate 51 pairs of male fraternal twins and 44 pairs of identical twins in which homosexual behavior was identified. Only 11.5 percent of the twin brothers of homosexuals were also homosexual. But in the identical twin cases, every one of the twins was also homosexual and there was pronounced similarity in the role taken by twin partners in their individual sex activities (25).

On the basis of such studies, research workers in this field have concluded that severe mental illness is far more a hereditary matter than has previously been supposed. Environmental forces are not excluded as an influence in the development of psychoses, but, this view holds, the strength of the genes seems to outweigh even the most powerful environmental forces.

Environmental Influences in Maladjusted Families

Despite the evidence which Kallman and his associates have produced, it is not yet clearly established that genetic factors are prepotent in the transmission of mental disorders. Such studies as those of Rae, Burks, and Mittlemen (36) raise a doubt that heredity alone can account for the transmission of maladjustment from parents to children. These investigators examined children of alcoholic and psychotic parents 20 years after the children were removed from their original homes and placed in foster homes. They found that none of the children studied became alcoholic or psychotic. Although 30 percent of the children showed evidence of emotional disturbance, a significant finding was that the rate of maladjustment increased directly with the lack of love and increase of severity in the foster home. The implication that maladjusted family members, especially parents, provide a strong environmental influence on deviant behavior emerges from these investigations.

Other studies of how schizophrenic persons were treated as children lend additional strength to the environmental theory of maladjustment. For example, the studies of Kahn and Prestwood (22), and Mark (31) showed that children who later became schizophrenic were subjected to very restrictive parental controls. The mothers, particularly, had strong and rigid ideas about what is acceptable behavior in children. They allowed them no freedom of choice, dominated and overprotected them, drove them toward unrealistic goals, prescribed and channeled their behavior, and generally kept them bound tightly in a maternal vise. These children had no other recourse than to withdraw from so cruel and hostile a world.

Thus, what parents do to children must certainly be considered in interpreting the origins of personality disturbances. Often, too, children unconsciously pattern their behavior after the behavior of parents. If parents meet their problems in an immature or abnormal way, children learn to do the same, quite independent of any inherited tendencies. Or if parents cannot relate themselves to children, the consequences are often seen in the attempts of the child to solve his problems in unwholesome ways. This process is illustrated in the case of a 12-year-old girl who was well on the way toward becoming a hypochondriac when she was observed at a clinic:

Margaret was a good student who fitted nicely into her group at school. She was of normal intelligence, very conscientious about her school work, and good in creative art. Her trouble was marked anxiety over her health. Although she had never been seriously ill, she imagined herself sick with every disease she heard about. Usually her symptoms were in the form of internal pains and stomach flu. She wears glasses and is afraid that she is becoming blind, though she has no symptoms of eye strain.

Margaret lives in a neatly kept house with one brother and her parents. The family is not too well off financially, and often the child hears her parents discussing family finances, which worries her. Until Margaret was two and one-half, her mother was in a state of nervous anxiety and neglected the child. She was not answered or cared for when she cried. During this period she became very hostile to those about her, and slapped people who tried to be kind to her. She did not talk until the age of four. Now she gets very blue and sad over many things and is not able to talk things over with her mother.

The mother feels that nervousness is inherited in her family. She always has been afraid that her own emotional reactions would be picked up by the child, so she never became too intimate with her.

Margaret has no one at home who will accept her feelings and her hurt and give her opportunities to talk about them. She gets blue and sad over many things and seeks refuge in pseudo-illnesses.

Mental Illness as a Product of Heredity and Environment

A reasonable interpretation of the data on mental deviations can disregard neither heredity nor environment. Even the most ardent geneticist will agree that an aggravating environment may cause a genetically healthy person to break down. And the environmentalists cannot deny that some children succumb more easily than others to the influence of the presumably same environment, a fact which must to some degree be influenced by inherited tendencies toward emotional instability.

The interaction of environmental and hereditary factors is the explanation which best accounts for the familial occurrence of emotional problems. The operation of these factors is seen quite clearly in the following case:

> Clara and Doris were identical twin daughters of an illiterate Midwestern logger. He deserted his wife and the twins were given out for adoption when still infants. Clara grew up in a small town as the spoiled, loved, only child of an easy-going couple. Doris grew up in a large Eastern city as one of 4 children in a strife-torn religious family, where all pleasures were considered sinful. Despite these differences, both girls were dull pupils in school and suffered from the same physical ailments, including some that were clearly of a nervous origin.
>
> Clara married an older man who protected her and loved her. With him she led a comfortable, secure life. Nevertheless, she was always easily upset by trifles, unsure of herself and apt to have crying jags over the slightest problems. Doris married a neurotic war veteran who made her life a horror. By the age of 39, she had developed all the fantastic fears and the hallucinations of a full-blown mental illness and had to be committed to a mental hospital. (20)

In this case, heredity had given both girls a tendency toward emotional instability. Thanks to a warm, protected environment, Clara overcame this natural hazard and remained on the borderline of normality. Doris was not so fortunate and encountered a series of experiences which pushed her over into abnormality. On this basis it can be assumed that where the home and community establish a supporting environment for children, many youngsters who may have received a poor nervous endowment from their parents can be prevented from crossing beyond the borderline of normality. On the other hand, in an unusually restrictive environment even the best endowed child may be broken down by the pressures he encounters.

EMOTIONAL RELATIONSHIPS OF PARENTS AND CHILDREN

Parents differ widely in their motives for having children and in the emotional satisfactions derived from them. Children mean different things to different kinds of parents; therefore we might expect to find many different kinds of emotional relationships existing among families. Bossard and Boll (6:111–112) have identified and classified over 19 types of intra-family relationships, ranging from excessive affection to complete rejection. Since it is impractical to discuss all of these various forms of parent-child interaction, we have selected for emphasis four basic patterns which are encountered rather commonly. These are (1) the pattern of rejection, (2) the pattern of overprotection, (3) the pattern of domination or overcontrol, and (4) the pattern of submission or indulgence.[1]

As these relationships are discussed, keep in mind that there may be much overlapping in these patterns. In one home a child may be *rejected* and *indulged,* or *dominated* and *overprotected,* or *overprotected* and *rejected* at the same time. Also, there may be considerable fluctuation in the way parents act toward children at different times. For instance, it has been found that children at 9 years of age are treated differently from the way they were at 3 years of age. As children grow older parents tend to become less warm, less intellectually stimulating, less indulgent and more restrictive (4).

Because it is difficult to discuss the patterns of parent-child interaction while taking into account all of the possible variations and overlappings which may occur, we shall single out each form in order to emphasize the psychological factors involved, without attempting to qualify them any more than necessary.

The Pattern of Rejection

One of the ironies of life is that many people who want children cannot have them, while many others who have children reject them. No one knows exactly how many children fall into the latter category, al-

[1] For a more detailed discussion of parent-child relationships, see Symonds (45).

though some authorities believe that about one-fourth of all our homes contain children who are rejected (9:25).

HOW REJECTION IS EXPRESSED.   Parents may reject their children in many ways. Sometimes it is done openly and brutally, as in cases of infants who are abandoned in ash cans, or children who are beaten, chained to bedposts, starved, or surrendered to some institution.

More often, rejecting parents do not deliberately and consciously set out to make their children feel unwanted, but the end result is the same. We see this happening in families where children are sent out on a round of boarding schools, military schools, and summer camps, with only an occasional stay at home. Or when parents plan their vacations away from children, explaining, "It does us all good to get away from each other for a while." Or where the care and training of children is turned over to nurses, servants, or relatives who give the child everything except the love he craves.

Few children are deceived by the form which rejection takes or the explanations offered for it. They sense the emotional undertones, the lack of intimate response, the frustration of their desire to be loved, and in one way or another they must react to these feelings.

PASSIVE REACTION TO REJECTION.   Some children learn that it does no good to fight against feelings of being unwanted. They accept the situation passively and often with deep-seated feelings of worthlessness, defeat, and guilt, for they may blame themselves for the lack of parental approval. A typical case of passive reaction to rejection is the following, from the author's personal files:

Geraldine Bart, age 12, is a very quiet, shut-in child. She always looks sad and does not speak unless someone speaks to her first. In school she just sits in class and acts as if she doesn't want to be there. As might be expected, she is one of the most unpopular children in the room.

Geraldine doesn't do much at home either, other than wash dishes. The mother says she is lazy, although she has never taken the time to teach her how to do things at home.

In describing Geraldine's mother, the psychiatrist made this observation: "When I first saw her, the mother appeared to be quite vivacious, alert and pleasant. After talking with her for a while, she changed and became more reserved. One could see what Geraldine was up against. She really had two mothers. One she has a hard time getting to, and the other is a person she once knew who was quite comfortable to be around. This bothers the girl. The mother tells the girl she loves her, but her actions do not reflect her words. The girl doesn't know what to believe. She feels left out of her mother's heart, and has lost the emotional energy needed for normal aggressiveness."

Shy, withdrawn, rejected children like Geraldine sometimes may make feeble attempts to be noticed or approved by adults. They may even welcome punishment and abuse since it is better to be hurt than to be totally ignored. More often, however, these children continue to wall themselves off from people. Their lack of interest in life may give them the appearance of being stupid or feeble-minded. In extreme cases, an apathetic type of psychosis may be the end result.

There are many other paths these rejected children may take. Some of them seem to hold on to their feelings until they can be vented on children of their own, continuing the cycle of unhappiness. Some eventually are able to overcome their difficulties and grow up to be relatively well-balanced people.

THE AGGRESSIVE REJECTED CHILD.   Rejected children often build up much hate and hostility toward the world and seek to get even through retaliation against people and their property. They have been termed the "unsocialized aggressives" who seem to get great satisfaction from upsetting their teachers and parents. Symonds (45:45) describes them as attention-seeking, hostile, hyperactive, jealous, rebellious children who want group acceptance but whose behavior, paradoxically, only succeeds in making them outlaws to all except others of their own type.

The case of Lyle Dawson (age 11) is a rather typical picture of aggressive behavior in a rejected child. This case is also drawn from the author's files:

> Lyle is described by his teacher as being very cruel, disrespectful and high-tempered. He has a desire to crush things and often hurts children who get in his way. When he gets angry he is unable to control himself. He kicks the children viciously. After these outbursts he has no remorse; he only wishes he had kicked harder.
>
> Despite his behavior, Lyle really wants to play with other children, but they will have nothing to do with him. He has no friends and doesn't know how to make friends.
>
> The background of this boy's behavior was not difficult to discern. He lives with five sisters, a meek, insignificant father, and a hard, bitter mother. The mother is openly affectionate with the girls, but picks on the boy and gives him no affection. In fact all six females in the family are constantly riding Lyle for one reason or another.

This child's aggression is partly a request for love and attention, and partly an expression of the hostility he brings from home. Like most rejected children he has been hurt, and now he wants to hurt back. His behavior will have to be redirected since his kicking will only make things worse for him. What he needs is not more punishment, but more love and attention. This is very often the problem among aggressive rejected children. Those who are hardest to love usually are the ones who need it most. Their distrust of people, their hate, and hostility make it difficult to approach them. Therefore, they easily drift into gangs where the members find in each other and in their common struggle against society, more acceptance, security, and satisfaction than is offered anywhere else.

The aggression of rejected girls is less often of the attacking type found among boys. Girls have another way of securing affection and of hurting those who reject them. Sexual promiscuity often becomes their means for achieving these goals. A typical illustration of the etiology of this kind of behavior is shown in the following case:

> Jane was the only girl in a family of three boys. Her brothers received lavish attention from their parents. But Jane's mother, who was chronically unhappy over her lot as a woman, had no desire to bring another "woman" into the world.
>
> Jane seldom got any attention and when she did, it was usually criticism for something she had done. As long as she could remember Jane had tried to please her mother so that she, too, could have her love. But her efforts were in vain. Unable to get the attention she needed and wanted, Jane looked for it elsewhere. She wanted jewelry and perfume, so she would be noticed. And since she had no money to buy them, she stole them. She began to date older men, although she was only 15. In order to be sought after—and *wanted*—she became sexually promiscuous with all the men she dated. Eventually, her behavior led to court custody. (28)

In Jane we see a fairly clear-cut case of a rejected child seeking for the affection she did not get at home. Her case is repeated many times among young girls found in homes for delinquents and institutions for unwed mothers. For them sexual promiscuity is not only a way to secure affection, it is a means through which to express their hostility toward their homes, their parents, and all of society.

CHILDREN WHO REJECT.   Rejection works two ways. Not only do parents reject children, but the process often is reversed and children do the rejecting. Sometimes they rebel against the parents and all they stand for, as in the case of Jane. More often, this rejection is symbolic rather than physical or overt. For example, the child who wishes to move beyond the social status of his family may change his name, reject his religion, refuse to acknowledge his parents when he encounters them in a public place, or even secretly wish for their death. These feelings are revealed in the autobiography of a college student who wrote the following:

> I guess I became ashamed of my parents at about the time I left the neighborhood school and went across town to the large city high school. It wasn't that they didn't love me, or that they were not good to me, but I felt that I had grown beyond them and that they were now getting in my way. My parents were foreign-born; they spoke English with an accent and observed all the old-world Polish customs. My friends were from second- and third-generation American families. I couldn't bring them into my home. I couldn't bring my parents to school functions. I became sort of a social orphan.
>
> While I was in senior high school my parents died. First my father, then a few years later my mother. At the time I felt a deep sorrow. But this quickly vanished, and as I look back upon that period, I think that secretly I was relieved because fate had taken them from me. For the first time in my life I was free from the taint of foreign background. I could now be a real American. I made up stories about my parents having been born here, moved up state to a college, and cut myself off completely from the society into which I had been born. Fortunately my parents had legally changed the family name from Weszcynski to White, so this wasn't too difficult to do.

Many other children who are equally rebellious toward their parents and their old-world customs are unable to break away. They remain in the home where they chronically and stubbornly resist the control of their parents until this rebellion against authority becomes a habit response which is built into their personality.

The Pattern of Overprotection

Parents may seriously impair the growth of their children by over-protecting them. It appears that mothers are most often involved in such practices. Levy's studies (29) of maternal overprotection disclosed three common forms of overprotective mother-child relationships. These are:

1. Excessive physical contact of mother and child. This is manifested in excessive fondling, sleeping with the mother long past infancy, and careful protection of the child from any possible harm. The mother takes the

child to school, meets him after school, and never lets him out of her sight.

2. Infantilization—the prolonging of infancy by rendering services to the child far beyond what is customary for his age, as in the case of a 12-year-old whose mother still bathed him, shined his shoes, buttered his bread, and saw that he went to the bathroom.

3. The prevention of social maturity. The mother coaches the child, prepares his lessons, and fights his battles. She keeps him away from other children because of danger of infection, or because other children are too dirty, too rough, use bad language, etc. Their children are not permitted to go anywhere alone because they might get lost or kidnaped. Mother selects their clothes, chooses their friends, and even selects the courses they take in college.

EFFECTS OF OVERPROTECTION.   The child who has everything done for him may become a plastic personality with no will of his own. Usually he is an obedient, subservient, and docile child. Adults call him a "good" child because he is polite, neat, gentle, and respectful. Children usually call him a sissy or mama's boy. Usually these youngsters are timid and shy. If they play with children at all it is with younger children or girls. Some of them will not play with children unless their mothers are present. They seldom develop any interest in sports. They don't know how to make friends and as a result may grow up to be lonely, unhappy, isolated persons.

A typical picture of an overprotected child is the case of this little girl:

> Mona, though very bright, finds it an ordeal to speak in class. Hers is more than the natural shyness so common among children, and so endearing. She is so bashful that she has few friends. Other girls mistake her shyness for stand-offishness, and so don't go out of their way to be friendly. Her failure to enter into things is in all likelihood copied from her parents. They don't entertain much, rarely mix in crowds, and have strictly individual interests with which they are content. (15)

Here not only is the child overprotected and isolated from the world, the whole family has withdrawn to the extent that their children are unable to make good adjustments outside the home.

Overprotected children are likely to be the favorites of teachers because they present no discipline problems. Also, they are apt to be above average scholastically owing to their extensive contact with adults.

Many of these children continue their childhood interest in books and isolated activities, and follow an academic career in later life.

There are some more serious implications to the overprotection of children in terms of their later adjustment. As one psychiatrist put it (*42*), too much protection causes the infantile ego to be stifled, resulting, in extreme cases, in a parasitic type of psychotic or neurotic disorder. This view is supported by Strecker (*44*) who claims that a high percentage of neuropsychiatric casualties during World War II occurred among young men who had lived sheltered lives tied to their mother's apron strings. He terms their malady "Momism." These men were found to be immature and plagued by numerous physical symptoms such as headaches, tiredness, digestive disorders, and a chronic sense of not feeling right.

REVOLT AGAINST OVERPROTECTION. Most of the time overprotected children are satisfied to lead a docile existence, learning about life through books rather than living it. Occasionally there is an attempt at self-assertion, which may be coupled with an effort to injure those who deprived them of a normal life. Such was the case with quiet little Peter:

> Peter's mother gave him everything. Both his parents made every sacrifice to protect him from the problems of life. He was kept indoors at the slightest real or imaginary illness. If one teacher seemed "hard on him," his parents had him transferred to another. They not only protected him as any parent would, but they "overprotected" him by refusing to let him face the problems all children must face if they are to grow up.
>
> Peter was robbed of a sense of his own identity, of self-reliance and self-respect. His home environment was so suffocating that he actually became asthmatic.
>
> Peter somehow felt his inadequacy, his inability to face reality. He hated his mother for it. To hit back at her he stole a bicycle. He selected a form of self-assertion he knew would hurt his mother most. He was trying to prove to himself and others that he was a man. And because he chose a socially unacceptable way he became a delinquent. (*28*)

In other circumstances youngsters who revolt against a stifling home atmosphere may overthrow all restraint and go wild on their first occasion away from home. This is what happened to John who was never allowed to ride a scooter because he might hurt himself, who was taken to school by his mother every day until he reached the fourth grade and the children started to call him "sissy," and who never had a fist fight or went camping. John never learned how to act with other people. When he went to college and joined a fraternity, he went wild, began to drink, and finally was expelled.

WHY PARENTS OVERPROTECT CHILDREN. It is difficult to criticize parents who overprotect their children because usually they act either out of sincere motives or as a result of unrecognized psychological forces. Take Peter's mother, for instance. Obviously she loved her boy and was doing what she thought was best for him. But children can be loved too much for their own good. They can be overloved with an anxious, possessive sort of attachment of which the parent is not even aware.

This type of dependent attachment to children is not uncommon among older people who cherish their children because they can have no more; or among parents who have lost a child, or who have spent many years nursing a child through a physical disorder. These parents are as sincere about protecting their children as they are apprehensive over their welfare. Unfortunately, they cannot see that their children are becoming more yielding and submissive than is good for them.

In some families, overprotection of children is a form of control handed down through generations. Parents treat their children the same way that they were treated. To them it seems natural to think for their children and fight their battles. This is the way it was with them, and unconsciously they adopt toward their children the same type of control used by their own parents.

Other parents overlove their children, not for the child's sake, but in an attempt to satisfy their own basic craving for love. Their love for the child is a possessive love. They act as if the child is a reincarnation of themselves and they are going to give the child all the love, close physical contact, and security they never had. Because this love is selfish and stifling it has sometimes been called "smother-love," to distinguish it from real love, the kind that helps a child to mature and become a self-reliant, self-respecting member of society.

Sometimes the overprotection of children is an unconscious effort on the part of parents to disguise the basic rejection they feel for the child. By being solicitous of the child, babying him and protecting him, the parent avoids the necessity of facing the fact that he really doesn't want this child. His relationship with the youngster is a conveniently disguised strategy for obscuring a basic feeling of rejection. Some of the dynamics of this type of relationship is illustrated in the following instance:

Unlike most 12-year-olds, Doug Sterek doesn't like to engage in physical education. He does not seem to care for other children and during recreation periods he usually takes a ball and goes off to play by himself. After a few minutes of this he sits down complaining his side hurts.

In describing other aspects of his school behavior, Doug's teacher made this statement: "He acts like quite a little boy. He does a lot of whining. When we have committee work he goes off to work by himself. At noon instead of going out on the playground he stays in the room. When we chance to walk up the stairs together he takes my hand like a little boy might."

Doug's mother keeps sending notes to school asking the doctor to excuse the boy from P.E. The doctor has examined Doug and found nothing wrong with him which would justify such an excuse. But the boy's mother is not satisfied with this diagnosis. She said she had a difficult time raising him and does not want anything to happen. Everytime he is forced to attend P.E., she says, he comes home sick to to his stomach. She is sore at the school doctor and wants to take Doug to a specialist for a check up.

Analysis of the home environment found that the family consisted of Doug, an older brother, the father and mother. The older boy is a good athlete and very close to his father. Doug is close to his mother. As a child the mother had colitis for a number of years and is apprehensive over the possibility that Doug will get the same thing.

Psychiatric examination of the mother found that she had been disappointed when Doug was born. She had wanted a girl, but she has so completely disguised her feelings that she does not recognize the basic rejection she harbors for the boy. However, Doug senses this. He has unhappy, uncertain, depressed feelings his mother does not know about. He is not sure of his masculinity, and admits that he does not always like his father and mother.

This is an illustration of good people who are complicating their lives because of a mother's unrecognized emotional antagonism toward a child who should have been born a girl. Despite the basic hostility involved, she loves her boy. This love is complicated by a feeling of guilt. These emotions combine to make her an overprotecting, nervous, worrisome mother who is raising an immature boy.

This discussion of overprotecting parents must not be interpreted to mean that children do not need protection in the home. Children need the assurance that no matter what kind of trouble they get into, their parents will understand and help. They need to feel that while parents may at times disapprove of their behavior, they will not cut off their love because of it. This kind of protection is the basis of a happy home. Parents who love a child this way do not keep him from growing up by wrapping him in a protective blanket of oversolicitousness.

The Pattern of Domination

There are some parents who rule their children with an iron grip and drive them toward the achievement of goals which are often beyond their capacities. These parents usually act in the belief that for the child's own good he must have high standards set for him and be disciplined to work toward them.

Parental domination of this type is usually characterized by attitudes of perfectionism and overambition. The perfectionism is expressed through insistence upon perfect bowel habits at an early age, scrupulous cleanliness, absolute obedience, and other rigid rules of living. Overambition for the child may take the form of pressing children to read early, to bring home high grades from school, to play the piano or the violin, regardless of the child's talents, to take dancing lessons, or to do the many other things which ambitious parents think of that deprive a child of the normal enjoyments of childhood.

REACTION TO DOMINATION. Some children submit meekly to the demands of their parents and offer no overt opposition. If their capacities come anywhere near meeting the expectations of their parents, these children may internalize the drive and pressure of the parents and themselves become drivers. Quite often they achieve considerable academic success in school, and may become professionally successful in later life. They have more difficulty attaining happiness because they are tense, perfectionistic, worrisome people who seem unable to relax, and who must go on striving for one success after another.

People of this type have sometimes been classified as the "peptic ulcer" type—because they appear prone to this disorder. While this is not a perfectly scientific categorization of such individuals, it does appear true that their musculature seems to be in an almost constant state of tension, sometimes evidenced in the tightness of their jaw, or their constant drive to move around and be doing something.

Children of average or less than average capacities who are forced to strive for goals beyond their reach are caught between forces from which sooner or later they must seek some escape. The standards set for them are beyond their capacities; yet if they do not achieve them, they are denied parental approval. To escape from the frustrations of this situation, they may adopt tactics which will stall off unpleasant scenes at home by giving the impression that they are fulfilling the parents' expectations. These children may learn to cheat and lie in order to convince parents of their success.

Here is a rather common illustration of this type of behavior:

> Tom was an average boy but his mother got a thrill out of thinking him a budding genius. She made special efforts to get him advanced in school. Against the advice of his teacher he skipped his grade because his father had "pull." Tom could not carry the new work. In each class he arrived at the end of his rope in short time. He developed the habit of loafing and fooling away his time. It annoyed others in the class. He realized he was failing and tried to boost his standing by cheating. Why did Tom's mother want him to do the next grade? Why would she not recognize him as just an average boy? For the same reason that she had to "show him off" when company came. Was it for Tom or herself? Certainly not for Tom. (43)

As this case shows, well-meaning parents can make a child become deceitful and cause him to lose his ambition in an effort to escape the consequences of not satisfying the standards set for him. Children usually cannot keep up such pretenses indefinitely. The time may come when they become beaten and develop a feeling of hopelessness.

It has been noted that when a child's security depends upon placating a powerful parent, in later life he may tend to seek security in submission and passivity. If circumstances make it necessary to resist the demand of authority, this resistance may be accompanied by troublesome feelings of guilt (19:295). The child's reactions to domineering, overambitious parents may also result in stuttering (11), and in many other anxiety symptoms which often are accompanied by psychosomatic complaints (37:156). An interesting example of a problem of this type in the making is the story of Philip:

> Philip is 10½ and in the fourth grade. He is a pleasant, bright-looking boy, but he cannot read. During the reading period he becomes extremely nervous and stammers when called upon to answer a question. He seems to have some sort of block when under pressure. Things have to go just right with him or he gets panicky.

Philip's mother was formerly a teacher. She helps him read at home, turning the pages for him and scolding him when he makes a mistake. She thinks Philip's problem is the fault of the school. When she took him to the teacher to discuss his troubles, she hardly gave Philip a chance to talk. When the teacher asked the boy a question, the mother answered. When Philip did answer, he would look to his mother to see if he was right.

The mother is a big domineering woman with a lot of drive. She dominates her older boy and the two younger sisters. All four of them dominate Philip. They can't seem to leave him alone, and someone is always picking on him. Yet the mother thinks that she is being very gentle with Philip and careful not to hurt his feelings.

All of this pressure has made the boy feel that it is better not to try than to try and fail. He has many fears and hostile reactions toward the people who are pushing him around. As he said, "Sometimes I get mad and want to do the wrong things. Sometimes I feel like hitting my sisters. My mother bawls me out when I do something wrong. Then we get mad and don't talk to each other all day."

Here we have a capable child who could really go places if he could be relieved of his tensions, fear, and anxiety. He will probably learn to read someday, but may never realize his full capacities. Like other children subjected to the pressures faced in Philip's home, he can be expected to grow up a timid fearful person with many neurotic characteristics.

Some children do not knuckle down the way Philip did. They take so much pressure and then rebel. This revolt may come at any time, but often it is seen at the periods of preadolescence and adolescence when psychological forces normally reduce the influence of parents over children. For instance, Ted whose parents had no trouble with him at all, suddenly becomes unmanageable at the age of 12. He runs around with boys his parents disapprove of, doesn't turn up after school until long past his usual time, and refuses to explain where he has been. His sudden rebellion shows how a fire which has been smouldering a long time may break out as rebellion against parental domination (15).

Or take the case of 11-year-old Hilda, who tells her mother she is going to a girl friend's house to study, then surreptitiously meets Florence, an older girl, who knows how to "fool around" with boys—and the two go off to "get picked up." Hilda knows that there is no use talking to her mother about going out with boys, because her mother would be shocked at the mere idea of her being interested in boys.

These cases show how children who are brought up by dominating parents may never learn how to handle their own problems and make their own decisions. Often when the break comes and they leave home for the first time, they may place too much reliance on the judgment of their friends because they never learned to think for themselves.

There are many other variations of behavior seen among dominated children. Often there is intense conflict between the "conscience" built up under the strict control of parents, and the desire to be free of home influences. This conflict is a fertile soil for the growth of anxiety, doubt, and guilt. Sometimes children resolve this conflict by discarding entirely their home upbringing. Such behavior can be seen among youngsters who develop an aversion to religion because they had so large a dose of it at home that they can no longer tolerate the restriction and moral punishment inflicted by the parents' emphasis upon religious training.

Thus the child of domineering, overambitious parents may develop several patterns of behavior. He may turn out to be a driving energetic, perfectionistic sort of person who attains some economic success in life, but little inner peace. He may become a meek, timid, fearful person, a cheat, a neurotic, a rebel against all his parents stand for. Or he may turn out to be a relatively normal person if he survives the pressures of his parents while growing up. There are too many variables involved to predict exactly what will happen to a child whose parents have planned his life and try to fit him into it. However, in one way or another, the child will react to the upward drive of his parents, and the backlash of this reaction will be reflected in the school.

The Pattern of Overindulgence

The typical "spoiled child" is one who has been overindulged, or given too much of everything by the parents. This child usually has his own way at home. Parents are submissive to him and seem unable to assert their will against that of the child's. Indulgent parents are commonly heard to complain; "I have to read to her at every meal or else she won't eat." "I have to dress him every morning or he will be late for school." "I have to give him what he wants so he won't have a tantrum," and so on. These expressions reveal the typical feeling of helplessness found among parents of indulged children.

REACTIONS TO OVERINDULGENCE. Submissive parents who indulge their children produce youngsters who are egocentric, undisciplined, aggressive, negativistic, infantile, or worse. Let us look at Dotty Ward who is only 8 years old, but who already shows some of the behavior patterns commonly found in an overindulged child:

> Dotty is a very hostile, cruel little girl. In school she must be watched or she will squeeze the hamsters or do something equally sadistic. She can't get along with the other girls in the room because of her aggressiveness, so she plays with the boys when they let her. She demands much attention and physical contact from the teacher, and when she doesn't get it she will stir up a fuss in the room.

> Dotty's home was visited by a nurse who brought back this story: "The mother seems to have no control over the children. Dotty came in from skating and rolled into the front room on her skates. The mother told her to take them off. Dotty just sat down on the floor and wouldn't budge. She then started to talk baby talk. A younger child in the room was playing roughly with a dog. The mother told him to stop, but he paid no attention. She then took the dog out, but the child brought it right back in.

> Dotty's mother, Mrs. Ward, lives in a world of unreality. She has no contact with people outside the home, nor any understanding of her own feelings or those of others. As far as she is concerned life is one happy dream. Her parents live in the home, and although she thinks that they and Dotty's father tease the girl too much, she takes no responsibility in the matter. Her own mother recently was committed to a mental hospital. Mrs. Ward feels that if her brothers and sisters had been nicer to her mother, this wouldn't have happened.

There is no problem here of lack of affection. Dotty's mother certainly loves her, but she is so insecure herself and has had so much unhappiness in her own life that the only thing she knows to do for her child is to let her have her own way.

If such submission to children is carried on very long, the child is likely to become a demanding type of person who expects all kinds of special attention and services. Or he may develop into an aggressive, bullying, resentful sort of person who seeks to compel special considerations for himself. In long continued cases, these children may turn out to be egocentric tyrants who feel the world owes them all they can get.

Levy's studies (*29*) of mothers who made excessive concessions to their children showed a pattern of behavior which, fortunately, few parents condone. These children ate what they chose and when they chose. They left the table when they were ready, went to bed when they felt like it, threw their clothes around, told their mothers to go to hell, told them to shut up, struck their mothers, spat at them, and went into a rage whenever they were opposed in any way.

Four boys followed through to adulthood showed what can happen to such children. In school and at work they were unstable and did not profit from a succession of experiences which would have caused normal children to change their ways. They had ample maternal love, but little discipline, training, or socialization. Their impulses were never circumscribed, and they never learned to forego their own pleasures for the sake of others. They repaid kindness with increased demands. To their teachers and schoolmates they were bullies, showoffs, and nuisances. When seen in adult life, they were still making exaggerated demands on the world and interested only in satisfying their immediate desires.

However, not all of Levy's subjects became such psychopathic tyrants. Some of them encountered schoolmates and teachers who would not tolerate their demanding, egocentric behavior. Their tendency to show off was tempered to an innocuous clowning, their fighting and bullying were converted into an aggressive form of leadership, and their demanding ways developed into persuasive powers. Hence, the spoiled child need not become a lost child if he is treated with understanding and firmness, provided this treatment is started before habit patterns are fixed too firmly.

Many more types of undesirable parent-child relationships could be described. They all lead to the same conclusion, that is: Genuine parental love, untainted by overprotection, coercion, indulgence, or any other form of behavior that curbs a child's normal growth is the cornerstone of good family life. As a child grows up in a consistent atmosphere of acceptance and self-direction, he learns self-control, self-reliance, and self-regulation. He learns also to operate effectively within the framework of social limitations and becomes sensitive to the welfare of other people.

INFLUENCE OF THE FATHER IN THE HOME

Studies of the roles ascribed to parents by children show that the mother is selected as the one to take care of them and do the really important work of raising children. Fathers are reserved for such activities as play, reading, and providing fun (1).

Part of this attitude is probably due to the fact that in movies, radio, and television presentations, the American father is portrayed as a combination buffoon, banker, and lovable idiot to be outwitted whenever possible. Another important factor is that the father isn't around the home enough to provide the persistent and ever-present care expected of the mother.

This attitude is unfortunate since evidence suggests that the father has an important psychological role to play in the personality development of boys and girls. This role becomes increasingly important as children grow older, reaching its peak when they arrive at the stages of preadolescence and adolescence.

The Father's Role in the Family

There are two factors which affect the father's role in the family. These are (1) the time he can devote to the family, and (2) his own personality.

Probably if a father were with his children constantly and took care of them from earliest infancy, he would be looked upon as something more than a source of entertainment. This was observed to happen in a family where the father assumed responsibility for his first-born child, cared for his nightly feedings, ministered to him when he was sick, rocked him, burped him, and generally was always present to make the child comfortable. Later in life when this child was ill or hurt, no one but his father could comfort him. This case suggests that the father's role may be thrust upon him by economic necessities rather than by psychological forces.

The father's personality and attitude toward child-rearing also influence the role he plays in the family. If the father is a mild, unaggressive person who lets mother hold the reins, his masculine influence may have little effect on children. If the father goes to the other extreme and is a tyrant whose decisions have more weight than all others combined, he can hardly help having noticeable effects on his children. Given a relatively normal father who participates democratically in the affairs of the home and has a reasonable amount of time to spend with his family, there appears to be certain significant influences which he can exert on children (26).

First, he presents to children patterns of emotional response and social action associated with the aggressiveness, leadership, and objectivity which prevails in the world outside the home.

Secondly, he is of major importance in the sex-typing of boys. The personal contacts which the child makes with members of his immediate environment influence the patterning of his personality. Boys need male identification figures for the development of a masculine personality and an understanding of how men should behave. Through this process of identification the boy becomes masculine in his interests, habits, motives, and desires, and develops the characteristics which will enable him to assume the functions of a normal male adult.

Not only does the father set a pattern by which the boy may structure his own masculinity, but he also helps the child conform to the demands of reality, serves to broaden his interests, and stimulates the development of qualities of leadership, discipline, authority, and self-direction which are conducive to the normal emancipation of the boy from home.

Third, a father is important in the sex-typing of girls. The girl needs early contact with her father in order to gain an understanding of how men behave and how she should behave toward them. This helps to clarify her own femininity in relation to masculine modes of activity. Lacking the contact with desirable masculine patterns of conduct during childhood, girls may have difficulty in forming normal attachments with men in later life. The father provides the girl with the masculine protection and security usually associated with the male parent, and also acts as an agent through which the child makes a transition from the normal, homosexual stage of development to a secure and wholesome adjustment to the masculine sex (33).

Influence of the Father During Adolescence

A father means different things to children at different stages of development. The young child sees him as a big strong person who can do anything and who represents power, strength, and security. To the growing boy he becomes a model and an answerer of questions. When children reach adolescence, fathers have an even more important function to perform. Teen-age boys have a great need for some man to look up to. If the father is a person who can be admired and if he has a secure relationship with his son, the boy is better prepared to accept the responsibilities of manhood. The maleness of his father's interests helps the boy to build interests that will make him acceptable to his peers, and frees him from the constant association with women which is the lot of the great majority of American boys.

Lucky is the boy whose father has been able to live his parental role in the full sense, who is close enough to his son so that they have interests in common and can share their lives and experiences. Boys welcome being taken into their dad's confidence, whether it is political views they discuss, a father's boyhood work experience, or the problems a man comes up against day by day (*14*).

It has been noted that where a father is missing at this stage of life, boys attach themselves to other male figures in their environment to satisfy their desire to be influenced by a person corresponding to the father. In this manner, teachers, scout leaders, recreation directors, and even imaginary and fictional males may become more important in the child's life than the real father if he is seldom seen (*17*).

The adolescent girl likewise needs a close relationship with her father. Girls in their teens are building an image of the man they would like to marry. They need to measure the boys they meet against an ideal marriage partner and depend greatly on the father, or some father figure to provide a standard. The girl whose father is absent from the home builds dreams around him and produces an idealized standard of a husband which is sometimes difficult to fulfill (*14*).

Undesirable Father-Child Relationships

Where father-child relationships are unpleasant or unsatisfactory, the effects on children become evident early in life. Studies of nursery school children show that youngsters in such homes are lacking in rivalry toward other children, have passive, colorless personalities, are often isolates, and exert little influence over other children (*35*).

Unsatisfactory father-child relationships have been found to be significantly associated with sex delinquency in girls. One study of 29 unwed mothers found highly disturbed relationships among fathers and their daughters. The girls had little concept of the roles of a father, husband, or man in the domestic or social world. These feelings were coupled with the lack of a close emotional bond with either parent. This led to compensating activity in an effort to find love—usually from a man (*8*).

The effects of poor father relationships among adolescent boys was impressively described in Kimball's study (*27*) of educational failure among adolescent boys of superior intelligence. These boys had IQ's ranging from 125–139, but their scholastic achievement was very low. Their underlying difficulties were found to be poor father-son relationships, and identification with the mother.

In almost every case the father expected too much of his son, set high goals for him, and was a strong disciplinarian. There were no warm interpersonal feelings between the boys and their fathers. The boys were forced to inhibit the direct expression of hostility felt toward the father, and instead expressed their feelings through indifference toward school achievement, sulking, and passive rebellion. They turned to their mothers for emotional support. This identification with the mother made it difficult for them to form friendly associations with a masculine figure. Particular difficulty was experienced in getting along with masculine authority figures.

These observations have been confirmed in other studies (7). When a boy is rejected by his father, he may have trouble adjusting to be a man, or he may develop feminine mannerisms as a reaction against his father's influence (30). Such boys also may be slow in learning masculine roles and may lack interest in sports and other motor activities (32:398).

Effects of the Father's Absence

Children who are without fathers, or whose fathers are away most of the time, appear frequently among those referred to guidance clinics for academic failure. Rouman's study (39) of such children found that they lacked motivation and had an inadequate sense of personal worth. Also, these children emancipated themselves from the home earlier in life than did other children.

It appears that preschool children suffer less than older children from the father's absence. Beginning among school-age youngsters and increasing in importance as children reach the 9- to 12-year-old stage, boys especially need their fathers to help them develop masculine forms of behavior. It has been noted that boys who are constantly in contact with their mothers may develop effeminate characteristics and interests which become a source of great disturbance during the teen-age period. Sometimes these boys retain effeminate voices long after their vocal chords are capable of forming the deeper male sounds.

For these reasons, the mother who is left alone to raise her children must make efforts to see that they have opportunities for close association with an adult who can serve as a father figure. The family friend or relative who can offer intimate companionship to a fatherless child performs a great service. Many youth agencies have assumed this responsibility and secure the help of fathers who devote their time to scout and club activities (46).

Return of an Absent Father

The attitude of children toward an absent father has been studied through projective techniques such as doll-play and picture stories. As might be expected, a child's attitude toward his absent father is influenced to a great extent by his mother's attitude. If she is antagonistic or contemptuous toward her husband, the children show a great deal of aggression toward their father. If the mother is affectionate toward the absent father, children picture him as an ideal person who is kind to everyone (3).

Sear's study (41) of preschool children found an interesting relationship between aggression in boys and girls and the presence or absence of the father. The aggressive behavior of boys diminished when the father was away from home, while the aggression of girls remained about the same. This is explained on the basis that the father is an important influence in the sex-typing of boys and provides greater frustration and more rigid controls than he does with girls. Thus, when the father is away, pressure on the boy is relieved; he has fewer frustrations and less need to be aggressive. This might be the reason why some children are more difficult to control when their fathers are at home than when they are away.

Another explanation for this phenomenon is that when fathers return to their families after a separation they tend to be critical of the behavior of their children and of the wife's child-rearing methods. They become more severe and restrictive in controlling the children in an effort to correct the damage they think has been done. After a while, readjustment takes place in the family relationships and peace is reëstablished.

It thus appears that in some cases at least the father's return to the family may cause more emotional disturbance than his absence (18). Fathers should be aware of this and not attempt to correct the behavior of children immediately after return from an absence.

The Authoritarian Father

In some homes the father's personality dominates the household. He is the undisputed source of authority, the court of final appeal, the administrator of punishment, and bestower of rewards. This role is exemplified by Erikson's description (13:490) of the typical father in a middle-class German home. When the father comes home from work the whole atmosphere is electrified. The mother hurries to satisfy the father's whims and does everything possible to avoid angering him. The children hardly make a sound for the father does not approve of nonsense. There is little open affection between husband and wife. The father disapproves of intimacy and affection, so the mother also inhibits any demonstration of warmth toward the children once they are past infancy. Her personality is submerged into that of the father, and she identifies with him as closely as possible (*40*:15–40).

The dictatorial German father does not hesitate to punish his children for fear that he might lose their love. He expects not love from his children but respect. His role is that of the omniscient, undemonstrative, irreproachable authority whose word is law. Although the German father loves his children, worries about them, plans their future, makes toys for them, and gives them presents, he can never unbend lest he reveal his own limitations and impair his reputation as a wise, powerful, infallible father.

Anthropologists believe that this type of family life breeds people who have strong dependency upon authority—stoic people who cannot unbend, display sentiment, or admit their limitations. Girls grow up to feel the same respect for, and compliance to, men that they saw displayed by their mothers. In the case of German women, it is said that even their sexual behavior is probably motivated more by passive compliance to the wishes of men than any desire for affection (*19*:297).

The consequence of such family patterns is a mass respect for authority. Rodnick's interviews (*38*:57) with children in the American Zone of postwar Germany supports this point. He discovered an almost universal identification between the father authority-figure and the National Fuehrer. ". . . just as father takes care of the needs of his children," he was told, "so there must be a Fuehrer to take care of the unfortunates who exist in German society."

This discussion is not intended to stereotype the German father as a dictatorial, authoritarian figure. There is, of course, as much variation in family patterns among Germans as there is among the families of any other nation. The illustrations used merely exemplify the possible consequences to a family and to a culture where the father is cast in an autocratic role.

Although many Americans feel that the father should exercise more authority in the family, we are, perhaps, fortunate that the typical American father is not treated with greater respect or awe. The democratic participation of the father in the family facilitates identification between the father and his children, and tempers the American's attitude toward people in authority (19:299).

SUMMARY

By and large, most American families provide their children with the warm supporting human relationships which build mental health. Yet, we cannot overlook the many children who are growing up in homes where such an atmosphere does not exist.

In some cases, parents are themselves so maladjusted that children have little opportunity to develop adequate patterns of behavior. Their emotional lives are in such turmoil that help must be provided by agencies outside the home if children are to be given a reasonable chance to grow up normally.

In other families, parents may reject their children, or children their parents; they may overprotect the youngsters to a point where character formation is impeded; they may push children beyond their capacities, or overindulge them to a point where they become egocentric, undisciplined outlaws.

The emotional interaction of parents and their children may take many other forms which are detrimental to personality development. Parents may be inconsistent in their attitudes and behavior toward children, causing them to become confused and insecure. The father, either because of his absence, his own personality inadequacies, or his dictatorial attitudes may inject discordant factors into the home atmosphere.

Children who come to school from such home backgrounds need understanding and help. They carry a heavy load of emotional problems not of their own making. Somehow the school must find ways to create an atmosphere in which they can work out some of their emotional difficulties and learn how to relate themselves to people.

PROBLEMS AND PROJECTS

1. Select some children who stutter or have other functional speech defects. Search for factors in their relationship with parents which might help to account for these difficulties.
2. Review Strecker's *Their Mothers' Sons.* Do you feel that the author is too critical of mothers? Do fathers have any responsibility for the problems he describes?

3. Discuss: Under what circumstances is it common for normal parents to reject their children? What are the long-range effects of such behavior?

4. Is it a good technique for a teacher to inform a parent that he is rejecting his child? How can parents be helped to understand the effects of their relationships with children?

5. What are the implications of the father's influence on children for having more men teachers in our schools?

6. Describe the home atmosphere of some families in which the father is away on business trips for extended periods.

7. Children who come from homes where the father is very strict are said to be well behaved. Discuss this in terms of your observations.

8. Discuss the claim that overprotected children are likely to be favored by their teachers.

9. How might the discussion of patterns of emotional relationships among parents and children provide an explanation of why so many parents are critical of the school's methods of teaching reading?

10. Is there any evidence that American children are exposed to too much feminine influence?

SELECTED REFERENCES

1. Ammons, R. B., and Ammons, H., "Parent Preferences in Young Children's Doll Play Interviews," *Journal of Abnormal and Social Psychology* (October, 1949), 44:490–505.

2. Anderson, J. E., *The Psychology of Development and Personal Adjustment,* Henry Holt and Company, 1949.

3. Bach, G. R., "Father-Fantasies and Father-Typing in Father-Separated Children," *Child Development* (1946), 17:63–80.

4. Baldwin, A. L., "Differences in Parent Behavior Toward 3- and 9-Year-Old Children," *Journal of Personality* (December, 1946), 15:143–164.

5. Berman, S., "Adjustment of Parents to Children in the Home," *Journal of Pediatrics* (1948), 32:66–77.

6. Bossard, J. H. S., and Boll, E. S., *Family Situations,* University of Pennsylvania Press, 1943.

7. Browning, C. J., *Differential Social Relationships and Personality Factors of Parents and Boys in Two Delinquent Groups and One Nondelinquent Group,* Unpublished Doctoral Dissertation, University of Southern California (Los Angeles), 1954.

8. Cattell, J. B., "Psychodynamic and Clinical Observations in a Group of Unmarried Mothers," *American Journal of Psychiatry* (November, 1954), 111:337–342.

9. Cole, L. E., and Bruce, W. F., *Educational Psychology,* World Book Company, 1950.

10. Dawson, W. M., "An Investigation of Social Factors in Maladjustment," *Occupational Psychology* (January, 1944), *18*:41–51.

11. Despert, J. L., "Psychosomatic Study of Fifty Stuttering Children," *American Journal of Orthopsychiatry* (January, 1946), *16*:100–113.

12. Eisenberg, L., "Treatment of the Emotionally Disturbed Pre-adolescent Child," *The Pre-adolescent Exceptional Child,* Proceedings of the 35th Conference of Child Research Clinic of the Woods Schools (Langhorne, Pennsylvania), May 23, 1953, pp. 30–41.

13. Erikson, E. H., "Hitler's Imagery and German Youth," in C. Kluckhohn, and H. A. Murray (eds.), *Personality in Nature, Society and Culture,* Alfred A. Knopf, 1948.

14. Faegre, M. L., *The Adolescent in Your Family,* U.S. Department of Health, Education and Welfare, Social Security Administration, Children's Bureau Publication No. 347, 1954.

15. Federal Security Agency, Social Security Administration, Children's Bureau, *Your Child From 6 to 12,* Children's Bureau Publication No. 324, 1949.

16. Field, M., "Maternal Attitudes Found in Twenty-Five Cases of Children With Behavior Primary Disorders," *American Journal of Orthopsychiatry* (1940), *10*:293–311.

17. Harms, E., "A Fundamental Concept for Analytical Psychology of Childhood: Paternis and Materna," *The Nervous Child* (April, 1946), *5*:146–164.

18. Harris, D. B., "Parents and War-Born Children," *Children* (July–August, 1954), *1*:153–155.

19. Honigmann, J. J., *Culture and Personality,* Harper & Brothers, 1954.

20. Hunt, M. M., "Doctor Kallmann's 7000 Twins," *Saturday Evening Post,* (November 6, 1954), *227*:20–21.

21. Johnson, A. M., "Etiology of Antisocial Behavior in Delinquents and Psychopaths," *Journal of the American Medical Association* (March, 1954), *154*:814–817.

22. Kahn, S. W., and Prestwood, A. R., "Group Therapy of Parents as an Adjunct to the Treatment of Schizophrenic Patients," *Psychiatry* (May, 1954), *17*:177–185.

23. Kallmann, F. J., *Heredity in Health and Mental Disorder,* W. W. Norton and Co., 1953.

24. Kallmann, F. J., "Modern Concepts of Genetics in Relation to Mental Health and Abnormal Personality Development," *Psychiatric Quarterly* (1947), *21*:535–553.

25. Kallmann, F. J., and Baroff, G. S., "Abnormalities of Behavior (In The

Light of Psychogenetic Studies)," *Annual Review of Psychology* (1955), 6:297–326.

26. Kaplan, L., *The Status and Function of Men Teachers in Urban Elementary Schools,* Unpublished Doctoral Dissertation, University of Southern California (Los Angeles), 1947.

27. Kimball, B., "Case Studies in Educational Failure During Adolescence," *American Journal of Orthopsychiatry* (April, 1953), 23:406–412.

28. Leonard, C. W., "The Corrective Institution and Crime Prevention," *Crime Prevention,* Report of the Second Annual Conference, Chicago Crime Prevention Bureau, October 20, 1953.

29. Levy, D. M., *Maternal Overprotection,* Columbia University Press, 1943.

30. Lidz, T., *et al.,* "The Role of the Father in the Environment of the Schizophrenic Patient," *American Journal of Psychiatry* (August, 1956), 113:126–132.

31. Mark, J. C., "The Attitude of Mothers of Male Schizophrenics Toward Child Behavior," *Journal of Abnormal and Social Psychology* (April, 1953), 48:185–189.

32. Martin, W. E., and Stendler, C. B., *Child Development,* Harcourt, Brace and Co., 1953.

33. Merloo, J. A. M., "The Father Cuts the Cord," *American Journal of Psychotherapy* (July, 1956), 10:471–480.

34. Phillips, E. L., "Parent-Child Similarities in Personality Disturbances," *Journal of Clinical Psychology* (April, 1951), 7:188–190.

35. Radke, M. J., "The Relation of Parental Authority to Children's Behavior and Attitudes," *Monographs,* no. 22, University of Minnesota, Institute of Child Welfare, 1946.

36. Rae, A., Burks, B., and Mittleman, B., "Adult Adjustment of Foster Children of Alcoholic and Psychotic Parentage and the Influence of the Foster Home," *Quarterly Journal of Studies on Alcohol,* no. 3, Yale University Press, 1945.

37. Redl, F., and Wattenberg, W. W., *Mental Hygiene in Teaching,* Harcourt, Brace and Co., 1951.

38. Rodnick, D., *Postwar Germans: An Anthropologist's Account,* Yale University Press, 1948.

39. Rouman, J., "Why They Misbehave," *California Parent-Teacher* (December, 1954), 31:14–15.

40. Schaffner, B., *Fatherland,* Columbia University Press, 1948.

41. Sears, R. R., Pintler, M. H., and Sears, P. S., "Effects of Father Separation on Preschool Children's Doll Play Aggression," *Child Development* (1946), 17:219–43.

42. Starr, P. H., "Psychoses in Children: Their Character and Structure," *Psychoanalytic Quarterly* (October, 1954), 23:544–565.
43. Stevenson, G. S., "Are We Helping Our Children or Hindering Them?" *Mental Hygiene Bulletin,* The National Committee for Mental Hygiene, Inc. (May, 1927), 5:1–5.
44. Strecker, E. A., *Their Mothers' Sons,* J. B. Lippincott Co., 1946.
45. Symonds, P. M., *The Psychology of Parent-Child Relationships,* Appleton-Century-Crofts, 1939.
46. Tasch, R. J., "The Role of the Father in the Family," *Journal of Experimental Education* (1952), 20:319–361.
47. Wahl, C. W., "Some Antecedent Factors in the Family Histories of 392 Schizophrenics," *American Journal of Psychiatry* (March, 1954), 110:668–676.
48. Wood, K. S., "Parental Maladjustment and Functional Articulatory Defects in Children," *Journal of Speech and Hearing Disorders* (December, 1946), 11:255–75.

CHAPTER 7 ─────────────────────────

Disciplinary Practices in the Family

WITH the increase of juvenile delinquency has come a mounting pressure for a return to the discipline of the woodshed. A typical expression of this point of view is the following opinion voiced by a parent as a solution to the delinquency problems of today:

> Our present upsurge of delinquency is simply a result of the silly sentimentality of parents who refuse to do their duty to rear good citizens.
>
> If these adolescents had been inculcated with proper standards of behavior by force of a small switch at the age of 3 or 4 when the experience is nearly painless and correction easy, they wouldn't have become the violent rebels they are today.
>
> This writer has the good fortune to have been raised by a wise mother who never spared her strength in due correction of an unruly son by agency of a leather strap. It was painful, but necessary, and we continued that course in rearing the following generation of boys who developed a sound moral tone and respect for authority.

This attitude is quite prevalent among parents, despite the fact that the severe disciplining of children is known to produce fear and hostility as well as respect for authority. But many parents, having been disillusioned by "permissive" principles of child care, tend to disdain all modern practices and adopt the old-fashioned techniques of their own parents (*11*). These problems of home discipline are of direct concern to educators because they are reflected in the school behavior of children. In this chapter we shall examine some of the basic ideas and practices related to home discipline and point out how these factors influence the mental health of children.

PERMISSIVENESS IN THE CONTROL OF CHILDREN

Some years ago the term "permissiveness," was applied to the concept that growth proceeds along natural, developmental lines and that the function of adults is to so order the child's environment so as not to impede or distort the natural unfolding of his capabilities.

Somehow this idea has been distorted to mean that children must have complete freedom to do exactly as they please. Many parents have become afraid of curbing their child's desires because they fear that in doing so they may lose his love.

Effects of Too Much Freedom

Actually, children do not want complete freedom to do as they wish, regardless of how much they clamor for it. Too much freedom is bewildering and leads to dread and anxiety beyond the capacity of the child to handle. Children who have things their own way may even feel that their parents do not love them since they seem not to care what they do. Parents do no kindness to children when they permit them to become a law unto themselves, lacking in self-control and unable to meet the ordinary social requirements of our culture.

This point is illustrated in the case of a 4-year-old boy whose father was a physician and whose mother was a clinical psychologist (10). These parents believed that inhibiting a child would build frustrations that lead to the development of a neurotic personality. Consequently, there was a complete lack of parental control in the home. But instead of growing up to be an uninhibited, unfrustrated child, this boy showed alarming symptoms of aggressive behavior and extensive hallucinations. The parents passed this off as a temporary state which would disappear with maturity. That this is not always the case is shown by Mosse (24) who describes a 22-year-old girl with a history of sexual relations, restlessness, and suicidal ideas. One of the principal reasons for this girl's behavior is found in her statement:

> My parents always let me do what I wanted but I've decided not to go back to them anymore. Yes, I got all the clothes I wanted. I have everything I wanted. They never forbade me anything, but they never gave me any direction. They were not religious. I am not either. That's

O.K., so far. But you must have something to believe in—to fight for, and they didn't give me anything to fill the gaps . . .

One night I came home very late. The next morning mother began to reproach me but dad interrupted her and said, "If the child wants to stay out 'til 3 it's her business," and that was all. Of course I felt neglected. It doesn't strengthen you. It only makes you weak . . .

Thus parents who do not set limits to their children's behavior may do as much damage as parents who are overly stringent in their control.

The Need for Limits

Because children are immature in judgment and lacking in self-control they need to express their aggressive tendencies to find out how far they can go in asserting themselves. If no limits are set to their behavior, these aggressive tendencies may carry them too far and lead to feelings of intense guilt and confusion. Parents must act as a brake on children by keeping their behavior in bounds. This means that a "space of free movement" must be established for a child so that he learns he may go so far and no farther and becomes capable of distinguishing acceptable from unacceptable behavior.

Of course children will argue and storm over such restrictions. This is a normal reaction to restraint and should be handled as such without fear of future effects. Usually there are none. The child accepts his limitations in a matter of fact way just as long as they are set with judgment and understanding and enforced with love and fairness. From this ordered, structured environment he draws security and comfort because there are controls to protect him from anxiety. He feels secure in knowing that there are certain places where he can play, and others where he cannot; places where he may cut and color, and others where he may only read; places where he may be as noisy as he likes, and places where he must be quiet. Knowing these things stabilizes his environment and enables him to play in comfort and security without the fear that he might be doing the wrong thing (*11*).

The need for limits in a child's life is shown in the case of this youngster:

Bobby is a 9-year-old whose family say they have not been able to control him since babyhood. He was always determined to get his own way and the parents soon gave up the struggle. When he was about

4 or 5, he began wandering from home, going farther and farther each day. The mother often could not find him for hours at a time, but he always came back, so she resigned herself to doing nothing about it. She scolded, and nagged but this did not change the pattern of behavior.

Now at 9 Bob rarely reports home from morning until late at night. Often he does not appear for meals but begs or buys them from neighbors. Recently his adventures have led him afield in other ways; he was apprehended in a neighborhood drug store for taking things. He has constantly been in trouble in school for fighting and disturbing others; he knows no rules but his own desires, and cannot conform to group regulations even though he desires to.

The family feels lost in trying to establish any limits for Bobby at this point, even of knowing where he is and what he is doing. He is exhibiting many symptoms of insecurity such as stuttering, biting his nails, bedwetting, and inability to concentrate. In talking with the psychologist he verbalized bitterly that nobody liked him. When asked why he thought so, he said, "Because they don't care what I do." (16)

Bobby's difficulties are summarized in the expression, "Because they don't care what I do." He resented having to take complete responsibility for his conduct at an age when other parents were still exerting some control over their children. He wanted parents whose love meant protection from himself, who would let him be a little boy, approved and taken care of. Doing wrong things left him guilty and anxious; yet he felt compelled to do them.

With the help of social agencies, Bobby's parents set definite limits for him. He had to report home promptly after school and not leave without permission. In many other ways they made him realize they did care enough for him to be interested in what he does. After a while, Bobby became a happier and more secure child. But his willful behavior was strongly ingrained and for a long time he will need continued attention and reassurance if he is to develop habits of doing the right things.

This case emphasizes the child's needs for boundaries. Parents must establish limitations for him and stand ready to enforce the established prohibitions. As the child continues to live in a way acceptable to his parents and consistent with his own developmental needs, he will internalize the controls of the home. His parents' code of behavior will become his own code of behavior and he will learn to regulate his interaction with other people in terms of these internalized controls.

Firmness with kindness helps the child build his threshold of frustration tolerance so that he learns to be strong in the face of trials.

EFFECTS OF SEVERE DISCIPLINE

Parents who undertake to make their children good by beating goodness into them usually are disappointed with the results. The case histories of juvenile delinquents and mature criminals are filled with instances of overly strict, cruel and punishing parents. But such strict control did not prevent the delinquent or criminal behavior. For instance, Hartogs' study (15) of male sex offenders found that 92 percent of these men had been frequently and severely beaten during childhood. In some cases these beatings were started as early as 2 years of age and continued as late as 17 years of age. The parents did not merely spank their children; they beat them with leather belts, razor strops, broomsticks, or electric cords. Yet this severe punishment did not deter these boys from forms of behavior which they knew their parents would condemn, and which would invoke more punishment.

Children's Reactions to Severe Discipline

Such studies indicate that the woodshed has been overrated as a corrector of child behavior. Even though the child may show surface compliance to the will of his parents, there is likely to be an undercurrent of resentment, rebellion, and hostility toward them and toward the authority they represent (20).

HOSTILITY. The child who is physically mistreated is likely to feel rejected and may develop a feeling of distrust toward all adults. If his aggression has not been beaten out of him he may harbor feelings that somehow, someday he is going to get even. This may not necessarily lead to delinquent behavior, but usually it leads to trouble with human relationships.

An illustration of how a young child may develop intense hostility in an atmosphere of rigid discipline is shown in this instance:

Barry is only 6 years old but he is already a behavior problem in school. He has terrible temper outbursts and gets terrifically resentful over minor things. One day in the lunchroom the teacher asked him to pick up some crumbs he left. Barry nearly exploded: "I don't want to," he said, "I wasn't sent to school to clean up after hogs." He has had other troubles too, such as refusing to pay for his lunches at school, and taking other children's money.

Barry has intensely hostile feelings toward adults. His responses on picture tests showed adults being punished quite severely. Many were eaten by animals or taken to jail. Women in particular were cruel. As Barry said, "They eat people."

Barry's parents keep a strict control over him. There is considerable religion in the home, including nightly Bible meetings. Barry must attend these meetings. When he is naughty one of his punishments is to memorize sections of the Bible. Because of this harsh environment, the boy has learned to keep his feelings to himself while at home. But his father is a strict disciplinarian and beats Barry when he won't talk.

Barry doesn't like his parents. He said his father was the meanest man in the world. These feelings generate guilt which forces Barry into aggressive behavior that usually gets him into trouble.

Unlike Barry, there are some children who cannot express their hostility through overt aggressiveness. They find other forms of expression, or, failing this, their hostility is turned inward and becomes a gnawing nucleus of anxiety and disturbance.

PREJUDICE.   Prejudice seems to be a fairly common mode of expression for severely disciplined children. Youngsters from authoritarian homes have been observed to be much more prejudiced than children raised in democratic or permissive homes. Often the home of the prejudiced child contains a mother who believes that obedience is the most important thing a child can learn. And she often uses a heavy hand to teach that it is wicked for a child to disobey his parents (14). These children seem to displace their hostility toward the parent onto others who are unable to defend themselves, or who represent a minority group. In this way they rid themselves of the hostility engendered in the home.

It would seem, however, that this mechanism of behavior does not solve the problems of these children. Intolerant children have been found to be more constricted, cynical, fearful, less confident and secure, and more suspicious than children of greater tolerance (13). Their arrogance toward others who are weaker or more vulnerable than they may well be a reflection of this inner turmoil, rather than an expression of superiority as is commonly thought.

EMOTIONAL DISTURBANCES.   Other children react to authoritarian parents by developing social maladjustments, inability to get along with other people, and infantile dependency patterns. They act as if they are trying to resist growing up, perhaps because they secretly wish for a return to infancy when the parents loved them and treated them with kindness.

Sometimes we see a form of persistent negativism or stubbornness among children who have been disciplined too severely. This pattern of behavior is evident in the following case:

> Betty ran into trouble the first week she was in kindergarten. She was a shy, unhappy child, afraid to mix with the other children.
>
> Betty's difficulty was not hard to understand. The mother, intent on having her child do everything right, was always correcting and instructing her, and the child had never been left alone long enough to learn. She was afraid to do anything on her own initiative and sure that anything she did would be done wrong. The only possible course for her in any situation was to do nothing at all.
>
> Scolding having failed to make Betty the child she thought she ought to be, the mother had resorted to severe punishment. She talked chiefly of Betty's stubbornness and the different punishments she had used to make her mind, all without effect.
>
> The mother was gradually brought to see that the child's stubbornness was in reality fear and bewilderment, which no punishment could cure. She began to use more patience in handling her. This combined with the work of an understanding kindergarten teacher eventually had results. At the end of the year, Betty was giving no more trouble. (8)

Not all parents can alter their attitude toward children as readily as did Betty's mother. In many children the fear and bewilderment which Betty exhibited grows into something worse as parents continue to punish and restrict them in an effort to change their behavior. A child's stubbornness and resentment may change to a withdrawal from the unpleasantness of life. He may reach the point where he refuses to do anything for fear it will be wrong or will result in pain or abuse. If his home environment is particularly repressive, this type of child may be forced into a psychotic maladjustment.

WITHDRAWAL. A sensitive child who is overcontrolled, repressed, punished, and prohibited from satisfying his natural drives may withdraw from this painful environment and create his own world of unreality where things are more pleasant. This is what Mark (22) found in his studies of schizophrenics. He examined 100 mothers of schizophrenics in a veteran's hospital and compared their child-rearing practices with an equal number of mothers of nonschizophrenic patients and found that the mothers of boys who later broke down had maintained a very autocratic form of control. They believed a child should be allowed no freedom or choice of activity. It was the mother's duty, they said, to know everything the child was thinking, to select his friends, and to protect him from sexual information. They did not believe in playing with a child because it would spoil him. Their concept of a good child was one who was nice and quiet and did not annoy parents with unimportant problems. This form of control over children was continued well beyond childhood, and in some cases into adulthood. These were the children who later became patients in the psychiatric wards of a veteran's hospital.

It cannot be concluded that an authoritarian home environment will inevitably produce children with schizoid tendencies. Nevertheless, such an atmosphere can provide great impetus toward the development of personal and social maladjustment in children. Those children who escape being driven into severe maladjustment tend to be unhappy isolates who are ineffective socially and lacking in personal warmth (25).

Fear as a Technique of Control

Basically, all types of severe discipline are based upon fear. The purpose of punishment, essentially, is to make the child afraid to do the wrong things so that approved behavior remains as his only course of action. However, punishment is not the only way in which fear is utilized as a control technique. Other devices can be more effective determents to behavior, and psychologically more traumatic than a beating.

Primitive cultures regularly make the inculcation of fear in children a part of their rituals. Among the Hopi Indians, for instance, the "Soyoko" descends upon the village once a year, or oftener if children misbehave, leaving sleepless children in her wake. Between the ages of 7 and 10, Hopi children undergo a severe initiation at the hands of their spirits as an additional reminder of what might happen to them if they stray from the paths laid out by their kinsmen (6:288).
Here is how one Hopi Indian recalls his childhood training:

> . . . we children were never denied food, locked in a dark room, slapped on our faces, or stood in a corner—those are not Hopi ways. . . . Our relatives warned us that the Katchinas would bring no gifts to naughty boys and that giants would get us and eat us, or the Spider Woman would catch us in her web. My parents often threatened to put me outside in the dark where a coyote or an evil spirit could

get me, a Navaho could carry me off, or the whites could take me away to their schools. Occasionally, they threatened to throw me into the fire or warned me that Massaúu the Fire god would appear in the night and cause my death. (27:70)

There is no doubt that these techniques are effective and that they minimize the conflicts between parents and children. Parents rarely have to discipline a Hopi child. But the price of such built-in controls is a lifetime of nightmares. In our society, devils, witches, and spirits are not called upon to instill fear in children. But we have equally devastating techniques—the use of sarcastic, derogatory, and critical remarks or commands, or the constant threat of withdrawing the parents' love.

As Katz (18) has shown, many parents subject their children to a constant barrage of critical, faultfinding, and disparaging remarks. In his study of 1000 parents of preschool children, he found that by their own admission, 75 percent made uncomplimentary or disapproving remarks to their children at least five times a day, while 65 percent stated that they complimented or approved their children only once every other day. In other words, this average group of parents criticized their children ten times more often than they approved or encouraged them.

Does it harm children to be told over and over, "You are a bad boy," "You will be the death of me yet," "I wish you were never born"— or other things which are calculated to instill fear in him? Often it does. While it is true that some children develop a protective mechanism which insulates them from the psychological effects of negative treatment, many others, particularly young or sensitive children, tend to believe the things they hear about themselves. The constant negative comments of their parents threatens the security of such children and makes them feel something is wrong with them. Children of emotionally cold parents are prone to suffer most severely when exposed to criticism, nagging, or threats because they have no cushion of parental love to comfort them.

EFFECTS OF INCONSISTENCY AND DISCORD

There are many homes in which parents disagree over policies of child discipline, or are guided by no policies at all. Their discipline is casual and opportunistic, and children's problems are handled according to the impulses of the moment. This erratic, inconsistent behavior plays havoc with the morale of a child. The parent who overlooks recurring offenses, only to explode at the next time the offense is committed leaves the child with no stability (*23*). The youngster cannot learn how to act because he cannot predict how his parents will react to his behavior. This situation has been described by Stevenson (*28*) in the following anecdote:

> Dick's mother ruled that he must not get up from the table during a meal unless necessary, in which case he must ask her. But five times out of six, when he disregarded the rule, she said nothing about it, making a great uproar the sixth time only because he broke a dish or spilled the beans. Dick never knew where he stood. To Dick the kitchen stove was more sensible; since the first warning of its burning flame that fixture had had a perfect understanding with the boy, and he respected it. When he wanted to do something which involved the danger of burns from the stove, he did not hesitate, or question the stove, or wonder what mood it was in, or stop to see if the stove were looking, nor did he become emotionally upset or sullen. He proceeded cautiously to gain his end without disrespect for the qualities of the stove.

This reference to Dick's sensible relationship with the stove emphasizes the fact that children whose parents agree upon methods of control, and who are consistent in their use, have fewer problems than children whose parents disagree on methods of discipline (*19*). In homes where there is discord, such as many restrictions on behavior or violent reactions toward the child alternating with periods of almost complete neglect, the child may be completely uprooted from his moorings. This was the pattern of home relationships which Hartogs (*15*) found among the sex criminals and delinquents he studied. Not only were they beaten severely, but there was marked inconsistency in the parents' disciplinary behavior. The punishment administered was determined not by the child's behavior but by the parents' mood. Sometimes an act was completely ignored by the parents; the next time this same act brought on a severe beating. Many times these children were punished without even understanding what they had done to merit the punishment.

Parents must have a basic agreement on how children are to be controlled—and they should stick to it until it proves itself inadequate. When changes of policy are made, the child must be helped to understand what the changes are and the reasons for them. In the absence of such clearly defined policy, the child's behavior becomes subject to the moods of his parents. This leaves him with no standards for evaluating the adequacy of his behavior, or for formulating a pattern of action which will be acceptable to the parents.

MENTAL HYGIENE IN CHILD DISCIPLINE

We have seen how the mental health of children may be influenced by parents who use undesirable disciplinary practices. Does this mean that parents must never punish a child, or scold him, or let him take the bit in his teeth and run? Not at all. It is entirely possible to correct undesirable behavior, and control children in such a way that they become self-disciplined, mentally healthy people. In the discussion which follows we shall describe some of the control techniques and, more important, discuss the general atmosphere in which these techniques should be applied.

CREATING AN ATMOSPHERE FOR WHOLESOME DISCIPLINE

It is not easy to isolate specific control devices and say to parents, "Here is a formula for raising your children in a positive way." Individuals differ so much that no one formula can be prescribed to fit all families. There are some parents who can spank their children with excellent results for both parents and child. Other parents create an emotional crisis whenever they punish their children. It is not so much a matter of *what* is done to control a child, but *how* it is done, and the general emotional atmosphere is which these controls are applied.

Research has disclosed that a democratic home provides the kind of atmosphere in which children can best learn acceptable modes of conduct. In such a home human beings, with all their weaknesses, live together naturally on an experimental, coöperative basis. Because people, young and old, are not perfect, we expect some disharmony in the home. Sometimes parents will lose their patience and do unwise things. They may spank or scold their children, use them as a target for the release of personal frustrations, or do many other things which in another type of emotional climate would have serious consequences for the children.

The stabilizing element of a democratic home is that underlying the surface interplay of the family members are certain basic attitudes and principles which bind them together into a harmonious group. Prominent among these are the following:

A warm parent-child relationship. There is an abundance of warm, physical affection in the family. The parents are themselves reasonably well-adjusted persons who have the capacity to love and receive love. There is relatively little discord among parents and a relatively consistent attitude toward children.

A willingness and patience to help children learn. Parents understand the necessity for helping children learn the skills that will ready them to take part in social life outside the home. The underlying capacities of a child are given a chance to develop, without sacrificing too much the comfort of adults.

An appreciation of the nature of childhood. The child's need for happiness, security, and activity are recognized. The home should be a place where children behave as children, under the insightful guidance of parents—a place where happy children are more important than unscratched furniture. Parents understand and tolerate the normal activity of healthy growing children and do not demand more of them than they are able to deliver at a particular age. In other words, children are not hurried into growing up in order to simplify life for parents.

Firmness with affection. Parents know how to keep their reactions to themselves when necessary and can apologize when they make mistakes. They are just, fair, and loving toward their children. However, there is adequate control and guidance in the home. Since children at all ages want to know what they can or cannot do, they need rules to go by. A certain amount of grumbling and resistance is expected of children, but no issue is made of this since often it is the infant side of a child seeking an outlet in unreasonable demands and behavior. Over a period of time children normally learn to accept these rules. They want to be become good because they need the approval of parents to make them happy. There is a balance of control and permissiveness which keeps the child on the right track with a minimum of adult interference.

Children have a voice in their affairs. While a child is very young parents need to exert a maximum of control and can give him little freedom of choice. As the child becomes more capable of regulating his own behavior, he should be consulted more often, be given opportunity to exercise more freedom within the limits of his capabilities, and experience a relaxation of parental controls accordingly.

In summary, the democratic home is one in which there is an appropriate balance of permissiveness and control, resting on a foundation of love and mutual trust. Given these conditions, almost any system of handling children can be expected to produce persons who are kind, tolerant, just, understanding, and constructive.

The Use of Coercion

In even the most ideal home atmosphere, few parents can escape the necessity for using coercion to control their children. Although it is often possible to anticipate the reactions of children, and so prevent crises from arising, such planning will minimize the need for using coercion techniques, but will not eliminate it. It is the very nature of childhood to run afoul of adult standards of conduct, to challenge authority, and sometimes to be just plain naughty or obstreperous. Parents should anticipate such behavior and not become greatly concerned over it.

When disciplinary problems do arise, the child should have a chance to make choices and discuss remedial action. This develops self-reliance and gives him relief from constant direction by adults. Children need as much latitude as they can handle for solving their own problems. The wise parent will overlook many quarrels and minor infractions of rules, and exercise his authority only when serious matters are at stake. If coercion must be used, it should not develop into a battle of wills. Parents are bigger and more powerful than children and usually can impress their will upon them. But this type of coercion does not develop the inner controls which will continue to function when parents are not around. The more a child's behavior is controlled from without, the less opportunity he has to develop internal controls.

Nevertheless, there are times when parents must use their power to curb or redirect the behavior of children. When this necessity arises, parents should not be afraid to act. Children will take a lot of abuse from a mother or father who really loves them. In fact, they would prefer to be scolded or punished by a warm-hearted parent to whom they have a close emotional attachment, than be treated well by a parent who is inwardly cold, selfish, resentful, or constantly afraid of doing the wrong thing (9).

In succeeding paragraphs we shall discuss the mental hygiene implications of some control techniques commonly used by parents.

PHYSICAL PUNISHMENT. It is not uncommon to find considerable confusion among parents concerning the use of physical force on children. This is not suprising since even psychiatrists are not agreed on this question. For example, English (7) has said: "A little spanking in early childhood, when it is relatively harmless, may be preferable to waiting for the world to mete out more severe punishment for offenses later. Certainly it is preferable to having a youngster grow up indifferent to the rights and wishes of others, bent on pushing people around."

The contrary view is represented by Selling's statement (26) that: "Great harm can result from physical force. Children can learn to dread their parents and have great feelings of apprehension."

Confusion arises not only from such diametrically opposed points of view, but also from the fact that there is a great deal of truth in each. Take the problem of spanking, for instance. Few parents can live with growing youngsters without resorting to a spanking once in a while. According to some clinical evidence, children actually may have a need for punishment. A child may be so filled with guilt over hostile feelings or wishes which he harbors toward his parents that he unconsciously goads them into punishing him so that he can pay for these guilt feelings and get rid of them (5).

Another illustration of a child's need for punishment is rather familiar to parents of young children. When a 3- or 4-year-old becomes overtired or overstimulated, he usually becomes hyperactive and hard to quiet. At bedtime he cannot sleep. Parents may read to him, tell him stories, do everything they can think of to get him relaxed—but nothing works. When all else fails, a spanking is sometimes the only thing that will get such a child unwound so that he can relax. The crying and emotional explosion accompanying the spanking may be a form of catharsis which releases accumulated energy. Often after such an episode the tired child will quietly go to sleep and in the morning all will be forgotten.

This does not mean that physical coercion is to be recommended as a technique for rearing children. It simply implies that punishment may have a place in the disciplining of children. However, parents must understand that physical coercion can build up considerable humiliation and resentment if it is used consistently as a form of control. Because the child is dependent upon the parents' approval for his happiness, punishment at the hand of a loved parent may produce feelings of hate or anger which he does not dare express. Sometimes these feelings are not even acknowledged because so much guilt is associated with them. But pent-up feelings are hard to keep in, and soon they lead the youngster to misbehave again, resulting in another spanking and more hostility.

Some children grow up within this circle of misbehavior, punishment, hostility, and more misbehavior. Others get rid of their hostile feelings by striking out at children younger and smaller than they are. Or they may learn techniques of evasion and become sly, tricky persons adept at managing their behavior so that they don't get caught. Punishment also may make children timid and spineless, as was described in our discussion of the overdominated child.

These undesirable consequences of physical punishment need not occur if parents use this form of coercion wisely. There are a few simple precautions which will help make punishment an effective tool for controlling the average child. First, the discomfort of punishment should be associated with the act which is to be eliminated. Secondly, something must be done about the child's emotional reactions to his punishment. Third, punishment should be gradually replaced by more positive forms of control.

ASSOCIATION OF PUNISHMENT AND ACT.   Parents have sometimes been advised never to spank a child in anger, but to wait until both parents and child have cooled off. For instance, at a meeting of parents, this procedure was suggested: "Punishment given in anger is quickly recognized by the child who rightly assumes, 'Mom licks me because she is mad, not because I got it coming.' Resentment is inevitable and correction is nil. But by postponing action and delivering the punishment later in coolness and explaining the reason for that postponement, the child grasps the point that he has nobody to blame but himself for invoking justice."

Although there may be times when this advice should be followed, in general, it violates a fundamental principle of psychological conditioning. Experiments with laboratory animals have shown that the stimulus administered must be closely associated in time with the response desired, or the animal will react not to the original stimulus but to some substitute stimulus, such as the experimenter himself. The following experience with a pet dog will illustrate how this can happen:

Mac was a sheep dog acquired as a puppy by my family when we were living in the country. When he was about a year old we moved to the city. Here he developed a penchant for chasing cars, barking at them furiously and arousing the whole neighborhood.

I undertook to cure him of this disturbing behavior by spanking him gently with a stick every time he returned from one of these escapades. After a few spankings, Mac learned his lesson; but it was not the lesson I had tried to teach. He continued to bark at cars; the change which had occurred in his behavior was that after chasing a car, he would slink back to the house, cower in the grass and wait to be spanked. After he was spanked, he would bound away and repeat his activities.

What happened to Mac happens to many children when they are told, "You'll get spanked when Daddy comes home," or "I'll get to you later." Instead of associating the punishment with his act, the child associates the pain inflicted with the person inflicting it. His earlier behavior is not a part of this experience. If his behavior is changed, it is changed because of fear for the punishing parent rather than a negative conditioning toward the original act.

Punishment, if it is to be effective in curbing behavior without instilling great hostility toward the parent should be immediate, consistent, and tempered to the occasion. If a child is forbidden to strike his brother, then every time the act occurs, punishment should be swift and inevitable. In this way the child may learn to refrain from the forbidden behavior. If punishment is deferred, he may learn that its all right to hit your brother, but you must not get caught. Or if he is punished long after the act is forgotten, he may only learn to hate his parents.

Of course, it is not always possible to punish a child at the psychologically opportune time because parents are not always able to catch him in the act. But the less time that elapses between the act and the punishment, the better it will be in terms of the child's psychological reactions.

HANDLING THE CHILD'S FEELINGS.　The psychological pain of a spanking is usually more acute than the physical pain. If parents understood this and consoled their children after one of these unpleasant incidents, the psychological wounds would heal as quickly as the physical ones.

Every parent who has had to spank a preschool child knows that after the spanking if he takes the child in his arms, reassures him of his love, and explains why he had to punish him, in a few minutes the youngsters will be off running around as happy as ever. Young children hold few grudges; they recover rapidly and before long the whole incident is forgotten. The older child becomes more sensitive, however, and his emotions are not so easily calmed. But he too needs the same kind of reassurance that the parent is not unhappy with him, but only with what he did. He wants to let bygones be bygones, and it is hard for him to do this if parents continue to be upset and disapproving of him after the punishment is over.

If parents would dissipate their own emotions as readily as the child dissipates his, they would be more reasonable in their treatment of children. The purpose of punishment is to condition a child against a forbidden act. Once it has been inflicted, the lesson is learned—if it is to be learned at all. There is no point in continuing to be upset long after the child has forgotten the whole thing (3).

REPLACING PHYSICAL PUNISHMENT. When the child is able to reason, when he can understand the meaning of his acts and the reason for his punishment, physical control should gradually give way to other forms of discipline.

At approximately the age of 2½ years, it is said that the child reaches the height of spanking (12). After that point he gradually learns how to inhibit his impulsive behavior, and psychological forms of control begin to function more effectively. In a normal home, spanking will be a relatively rare occurrence after the age of 5 years, and will be used only for extreme situations. Isolation, the withdrawal of privileges, talking things out, redefining the rules, and similar practices should become more effective means of controlling child behavior.

Physical coercion, then, does have a place in the upbringing of a child. Some children need an occasional spanking to reorganize their emotional balance. Parents need have no fear that children will grow up hating them if the punishment used is associated with the child's act, if care is taken to handle the child's feelings after he is punished, and if physical punishment is replaced with other forms of control just as soon as the child is psychologically able to respond to them.

CONTROL THROUGH REWARD. It is unwise, usually, to pay or reward children for doing what is asked of them. Rewards may weaken the parent's authority by teaching children to bargain for good behavior. This can turn into a form of juvenile blackmail where the child increases his demands, using the threat of misbehavior as a weapon. There are times, however, when rewards serve a useful purpose. Sometimes parents need to buy a little peace of mind and are willing to pay almost anything for it. Rewards of this type will do no great harm, provided they are used only in emergencies.

The use of long-term rewards may have a beneficial affect on children. For instance, a child who is promised a bike for Christmas if he keeps his room neat is being rewarded, but he is earning his reward. In the process of reaching his goal, he learns certain standards of conduct and develops habits which may carry on. This technique may be used with older children quite effectively because they have the ability to restrain their impulses in order to achieve later rewards which are of greater value. With young children delayed rewards may not work too well because the young child has difficulty in controlling his daily behavior in terms of distant goals. He is opportunistic and usually will expect immediate rewards and the future reward as well.

CONTROL THROUGH THREATS. When mothers of nursery school children get together to compare notes on control techniques, one of their favorite topics of conversation is how to control youngsters without having to yell at them or threaten them so much. It is hardly possible to live with lively young children without using such verbal control techniques.

How children react to verbal harrassment depends upon their emotional stability. The sensitive, insecure child may be hurt by a few harsh words, while the secure, fearless child often tosses them off like a boxer parries a blow. Normally, children learn to gauge rather accurately from the tone of the parent's voice how seriously to take his threats. Of course, they sometimes misjudge and pay the penalty. But often this is a game which they learn to play with skill, particularly if there is a warm relationship between parent and children, and if threats do not carry with them the implication of rejection. Children even learn to threaten back. For example, when 3-year-old Janet was told, "You can't go to the party until you brush your teeth," she replied, "If you don't let me go to the party I'll never brush my teeth."

This type of interplay usually places a greater strain on the parent than on the child. Therefore it is wise to keep threats to a minimum and to use suggestion whenever possible. By suggesting to a child that he do certain things and pointing out the possible consequences of the action he chooses to take, parents often can secure the results they wish without a struggle. Suppose a parent wanted a 7-year-old to pick up his toys. He might say, "I would like you to see a special program on television, but I can't because your toys are scattered all over the house." There is a threat implied here, and a bribe as well, but it is a positive approach because the child has a choice in the matter.

These suggestive techniques will work well with children who love their parents, and with parents who follow through on their agreements. However, as Selling (26) points out, suggestion usually will not work when children are very negativistic, or when immediate results are desired with children whose conduct is habitually unacceptable. It works better with older children, particularly with those who are amenable to verbal controls.

THE USE OF SOCIAL PRESSURES. The wise use of social coercion can be a powerful form of control over children. It is known that when a child is in a group his behavior often changes radically. He will eat things which he wouldn't touch when he is alone, and he will maintain a different standard of cleanliness and dress. Many parents are surprised to see how differently their children act at school than they do at home. Here is a rather typical example of how social pressure can affect a child's behavior:

> Five-year-old Dicky was once hit by a car and spent a year in the hospital during which time he was thoroughly conditioned to fear the man in the white jacket. Almost a year after his release from the hospital his mother took him to the dentist. One look at the dentist's white jacket sent Dicky into such a frenzy of crying that they couldn't even get him to sit in the chair. However, when the dentist came to school a few months later, the boy had his teeth examined without a whimper.

What happened here is rather obvious. Dicky couldn't let the other children see him cry. So he controlled his intense fear of white jackets and submitted to the examination. Similar behavior is seen among school children who stand in line for their injections and vaccinations, bravely assuring each other that it does not hurt. Individually, in the doctor's office, these same children may act as if an injection were the most distressing thing in life. Social pressure exerts a powerful force on children and parents will be alert to circumstances under which it may be used in a positive way.

LATER EFFECTS OF COERCION. The coercion techniques described here do not exhaust the list of devices which parents may use to control children in ways which safeguard their mental health. It is quite impossible to prescribe disciplinary techniques suitable for all children because youngsters may be handled in a variety of ways and still turn out to be normal, well-adjusted persons. Such factors as the child's inherited constitution, the personality and experiences of parents, and the atmosphere of the home will influence the kind of controls which should be used. So long as the methods of control adopted are accompanied by warm, physical affection and sincere concern for the welfare of children, they will leave few emotional scars.

However, parents must anticipate that certain unpleasant emotions will be experienced by a child in reaction to the coercion imposed upon him. Here is a typical illustration of how children may react to coercion, and what often happens to their feelings in later life. The person who describes her feelings is now a mature, well-adjusted mother:

> Because I was the first child in the family and my parents, un-schooled in modern child adjustment methods, wanted me to turn out right, I was spanked often and for everything. Several years later when my brother came along, father and mother decided that perhaps the spanking had done me little good, so brother was almost never spanked. Now we are both grown and seem to be fairly well-adjusted, happy people and apparently good citizens.
>
> But I do remember a time of hating my father. However, mother had spanked me as often as father had, so perhaps physical pain was not the only reason for the hate. In the years after I became 16, a deep love and respect replaced the hate feelings harbored toward my father.

As seen here, children commonly have ambivalent feelings toward parents who punish them—hating and loving them alternately. But time is a great healer of the emotional wounds of childhood. If parents really love their children and know how to express their affection, the child's feelings of hate will be overcome by his feelings of love and he will sustain little damage from his experiences with coercion in the home. What emotional distress he does sustain will be far less severe than what might happen to him if parents do not channel his behavior.

OUTCOMES OF DEMOCRATIC CHILD-REARING PRACTICES

Studies of the personality adjustment of boys and girls in relation to their home environments show that parents often predetermine the personality of their children through their choice of disciplinary techniques.

As was shown earlier, authoritarian homes tend to produce children who are either quiet, well behaved, and restricted in curiosity, originality, and forcefulness, or children who are prejudiced, hostile, and aggressive (1). When parents go to the other extreme and allow children too much freedom, the outcome may be youngsters who are self-indulgent, anxious, insecure; who lack skill in muscular coördination and are apprehensive of physical activity.

What about children who receive neither too little nor too much control, who are encouraged to develop self-direction under consistent and loving parental guidance? From the point of view of many adults, the behavior of such youngsters is far from ideal. In fact, they may be hard to live with because they tend to be active children who make much noise, damage furniture, give their parents little privacy, and are difficult to control (4). However, from the mental health viewpoint, this type of child-rearing can be expected to pay great dividends in terms of future happiness and accomplishments. Studies of nursery school children conducted at the Fels Research Institute (21) show that children raised in democratic homes are active, outgoing, aggressive, bossy, and competitive youngsters—but they are also intellectually alert and show a high incidence of originality and creativeness.

Similar studies of adolescents (29) have found these youngsters to be realistic in their thinking, mature in their judgment on ethical questions, and more at peace with themselves and with the world than children raised in nondemocratic homes. Adolescents from democratic homes also are significantly more self-reliant, more sensitive to the feelings and wishes of others, have better emotional control and a greater sense of responsibility.

From such data it may be concluded that if parents desire children who are well adjusted, intellectually alert, and outgoing in their relationships with others, they may have to put up with some personal inconvenience during the growing-up period. These children really live in their homes; they refuse to be manipulated like puppets and they insist upon being a part of the family. They ask questions, want to know reasons for things, express their emotions, and in many other ways demonstrate that life is something to be understood through experimentation rather than through dictation from adults. In this way they learn to assume responsibility for their own conduct and develop the ability to handle life situations and work in harmony with their environment.

SUMMARY

The type of disciplinary procedures used in the home is reflected directly in the school behavior, mental health, and general personality development of children.

Parents cannot escape the responsibility for exercising control over their children. This is not only a social obligation but a psychological requirement of children as well. Boys and girls need to be assured that their parents love them enough to be concerned over what they do.

They want to be protected from the bewilderment and anxiety which results when their behavior is not limited.

However, the control of children can be carried too far. Parents who use severe disciplinary techniques may generate in children feelings of hostility, prejudice, aggression, emotional disturbances, infantile dependency, fear, and negativism. Social maladjustment and withdrawal or isolation from people and from reality may also result from the imposition of too rigid controls.

Such severe discipline is not limited to physical punishment but involves other fear-producing forms of coercion such as criticism, nagging, and threats. Even more damaging to a child's emotional balance than either discipline which is too lax or too severe is the inconsistent treatment of children. Erratic behavior on the part of parents plays havoc with a child because he cannot predict how his parents will act and therefore is unable to stabilize his own behavior.

Parents can control their children without undermining their mental health. If coercion techniques are used in an atmosphere which is characterized by mutual regard, love, patience, and an appreciation of the nature of childhood, children will respond by becoming well-adjusted, self-reliant persons. Although children may temporarily harbor antagonistic feelings toward their parents, eventually these feelings will be replaced by positive emotions. The end product of such treatment is children who are active and aggressive, but they will also be intellectually alert, self-reliant, responsible, and mentally healthy.

PROBLEMS AND PROJECTS

1. What are the major areas of conflict between parents and their adolescent sons and daughters in the modern home? How can these conflicts be reconciled in accordance with mental hygiene principles?
2. Should children be payed to do chores around the home? What disciplinary problems may arise out of this situation?
3. How can you account for the fact that many children who experience strict discipline at home grow up to be well-adjusted persons?
4. Describe a permissive home environment with which you are acquainted. How are freedom and control balanced in the handling of children?
5. What are some ways in which parents can handle the emotional reactions of young children who have been punished? How should adolescents be treated under similar circumstances?
6. Describe a situation in which a child had a psychological need for punishment which was expressed through provoking behavior.

7. Study the home background of adolescents whom you know to harbor prejudices against minority groups. To what extent are their attitudes related to the disciplinary procedures used in the home?
8. What are some devices used by parents to instill fear in children in order to control their behavior? What is the effect on children?
9. What can parents do about children who sulk or isolate themselves after they have been disciplined?
10. Discuss: Should children be permitted to express their hostility toward parents by saying such things as "I hate you"?
11. Evaluate the psychological effects of withholding a child's allowance as a disciplinary technique.
12. What are some ways in which a parent can use social pressure to control a child in the home?

SELECTED REFERENCES

1. Baldwin, A. L., "Socialization of the Parent-Child Relationship," *Child Development* (September, 1948), 19:127–136.
2. Baldwin, A. L., Kalhorn, J., and Breese, F. H., "The Appraisal of Parent Behavior," *Psychological Monographs* (1949), vol. 63, no. 4.
3. Baruch, D. W., *New Ways in Discipline,* McGraw-Hill Book Company, 1949.
4. Blood, R. O., Jr., "Some Differential Child-Rearing Philosophies, Practices, and Their Consequences: A Study of the Attitudes and Experiences of "Traditional" and "Developmental" Middle-Class Parents," *Research Relating to Children,* Supplement No. 4, U.S. Children's Bureau, April, 1951, p. 102.
5. Bower, E. M., "The Need for Punishment," *California Journal of Elementary Education* (February, 1953), 21:41–48.
6. Eggan, D., "The General Problem of Hopi Adjustment," in C. Kluckhohn and H. A. Murray (eds.), *Personality in Nature, Society and Culture,* Alfred A. Knopf, 1953.
7. English, O. S., and Foster, C. J., "How Bad Is it to Spank Your Kids?" *Better Homes and Gardens* (June, 1950), 28:197, 253, 255.
8. Federal Security Agency, Social Security Administration, *Helping Children in Trouble,* Children's Bureau Publication 320, 1947.
9. Federal Security Agency, Social Security Administration, *Your Child From 6 to 12,* Children's Bureau Publication No. 324, 1949.
10. Forrer, G. R., "Parlor Psychiatry," *Psychiatric Quarterly* (January, 1954), 28:126–133.
11. Geisel, J. B., "Discipline Viewed as a Developmental Need of the Child," *The Nervous Child* (March, 1951), 9:115–121.
12. Gesell, A., and Ilg, F. L., *Child Development,* Harper & Brothers, 1950.
13. Gough, H. G., Harris, D. B., Martin, W. E., and Edwards, M., "Chil-

dren's Ethnic Attitudes: I. Relationship to Certain Personality Factors," *Child Development* (1950), 21:83–91.

14. Harris, D. B., Gough, H. G., and Martin, W. E., "Children's Ethnic Attitudes: II. Relationship to Parental Beliefs Concerning Child Training," *Child Development* (1950), 21:169–181.

15. Hartogs, R., "Discipline in the Early Life of the Sex Delinquent and Sex Criminal," *The Nervous Child* (March, 1951), 9:167–173.

16. Huston, H. F., "Isn't It The Limit?" *California Parent-Teacher* (November, 1954), 32:16–17.

17. Hymes, J. L., Jr., *Behavior and Misbehavior,* Prentice-Hall, Inc., 1955.

18. Katz, B., "The Inferiority Complex: Some Essential Causes," *Education* (January, 1949), 69:293–295.

19. Koshuk, R. P., "Development Records of 500 Nursery School Children," *Journal of Experimental Education* (December, 1947), 16:134–148.

20. Lafore, G. G., "Practices of Parents in Dealing With Preschool Children," *Child Development Monograph,* No. 31, National Research Council, Society for Research in Child Development, 1945.

21. Lasko, J. K., "Parent-Child Relationships," *American Journal of Orthopsychiatry* (April, 1952), 22:300–304.

22. Mark, J. C., "The Attitudes of the Mothers of Male Schizophrenics Toward Child Behavior," *Journal of Abnormal and Social Psychology* (April, 1953), 48:185–189.

23. Meyer, C. T., "The Assertive Behavior of Children as Related to Parent Behavior," *Journal of Home Economics* (February, 1947), 39:77–80.

24. Mosse, E. P., "Social Psychiatry as an Aid to Child Analysis," *The Nervous Child* (April, 1946), 5:199–203.

25. Radke, M. J., "The Relation of Parental Authority to Children's Behavior And Attitudes," *Monographs,* Series No. 22, University of Minnesota, Institute of Child Welfare, 1946.

26. Selling, L. S., "Coercion: Pathogene or Therapy," *The Nervous Child* (July, 1946), 5:226–234.

27. Simmons, L. (ed.), *The Sun Chief, the Autobiography of a Hopi Indian,* Yale University Press, 1942.

28. Stevenson, G. S., "Are We Helping Our Children or Hindering Them?" *Mental Hygiene Bulletin,* The National Committee for Mental Hygiene, Inc. (May, 1927), 5:1–5.

29. Stott, L. H., "Mental Health and Developmental Hygiene," *Education* (January, 1949), 69:271–274.

30. Wolf, A. W., *The Parent's Manual,* Simon and Schuster, 1941.

CHAPTER 8

Social-Class Influences on Mental Health

EVERY major area of family life is directly or indirectly affected by the social and cultural forces acting upon it. Habits of speech and thought, modes of handling children, forms of worship, systems of values—all of the basic human characteristics developed in the family are molded by the culture. All of us are culture-bound, and, in a sense, personality and mental health are expressions of cultural influences.

Interpreting the highly diverse social matrix which constitutes our American culture is no simple task, since we do not have a single culture but a complex of loosely organized subcultures about which it is difficult to generalize. Factors such as rural or urban conditions, religion, race, occupation, education, or ethnic origins may produce subcultures which vary greatly in their methods of child-rearing, the values they hold, and their modes of living.

In this chapter a composite cultural characteristic termed *social class* has been selected for emphasis. For the past three decades, psychiatrists, sociologists, and anthropologists have been studying the social and cultural factors which contribute to the social-class structure of our society. Their studies indicate that social class has a pervasive influence on the mental health of children and that educators need to know what it is, how it works, and what it does. Particularly significant for educators are the data pointing to the strains imposed upon children when schools challenge the cultural values and customs of a social class.

191

SOCIAL-CLASS STRATIFICATION IN AMERICA

Most laymen are aware that social stratification exists in our society. This is evidenced by references to people who "live on the wrong side of the tracks," the "slum dwellers," the "common man," the "Four Hundred," or the people who belong to country clubs as distinct from those who are in labor unions. These are terms commonly used to divide people into various socioeconomic groups. They are rough, rule-of-thumb criteria by which we judge each other's station in life.

The Measurement of Social Class

Social anthropologists have refined these rough criteria and developed measures which make it possible to classify people with greater accuracy. To the sociologist, a social class consists of a group of people whose members have common ideas, feelings, attitudes, values, and forms of behavior (17:59). A person is a member of that social class with which most of his interests are identified, and whose members have similar patterns of living (62).

Extensive research has been conducted in an effort to discover how persons derive their social-class status. Warner and his associates have been among the most active workers in this field. Through community studies in New England, the Midwest, and the South, they arrived at a unit of measurement called an "Index of Status Characteristics." This index is composed of four major items; occupation, source of income, house type, and dwelling area (67). While some sociologists have criticized this classification as an oversimplification which omits many pertinent factors (47, 51), it still appears to be a useful approach to the interpretation of social stratification in America.

Distribution of Social Classes

While it is generally known that social classes exist in our society, the average person has only a vague notion of how he fits into this class structure. This was illustrated in a national poll conducted by the Institute of Public Opinion. When people were asked, "To what social class in this country do you think you belong, the middle class, the upper class, or the lower class?" 88 percent answered "middle class," and the remaining 12 percent divided themselves equally between upper and lower classes (26:169).

However, Warner and his associates found quite a different social stratification in their investigations. Instead of a bulging middle class overshadowing very small upper and lower classes, they found the population to be made up of a six-step pyramid, as follows (65):

Upper-upper class	1.44 percent of the population
Lower-upper class	1.56 percent of the population
Upper-middle class	10.22 percent of the population
Lower-middle class	28.12 percent of the population
Upper-lower class	32.60 percent of the population
Lower-lower class	25.22 percent of the population

Even if these six classes are combined into three, the pyramidal structure of society remains unchanged. The base of the pyramid is the lower class with 57.82 percent of the population, followed by a middle class of 38.34 percent and an upper class comprising only 3 percent of the population.

This picture of social classes in America has been contested because the New England community investigated had a large proportion of foreign-born inhabitants. However, similar studies in Midwest and Southern communities reveal relatively the same pattern of stratification (see Davis, *12, 13, 14, 17,* and Hollingshead, *35*). This fact is of particular significance to educators because it means that over 70 percent of our elementary school children come from the lower socioeconomic groups, while more than 95 percent of the teachers come from the middle socioeconomic groups (*13*). The implications of this situation will become evident as we discuss the differences which characterize these social groups.

Characteristics of Social Classes

Each social class has characteristics which are sufficiently distinctive and powerful to impress on its members different values, forms of behavior, habits, customs, and attitudes. For convenience, we shall summarize these differences in terms of three broad groups: the upper, the middle, and the lower social classes.

THE UPPER CLASSES. The New England studies revealed that one must literally be born into an upper class to be accepted as a member of that group. The upper-class group is made up of native-born whites with long residence in the community and long family histories of upper-class aristocracy. People in this group own spacious homes located in the most desirable areas of the city. Over 83 percent are in the professional and higher managerial occupations. Almost all are college educated. They belong to social clubs and charitable organizations, but not to lodges or secret societies. Their children go to special preparatory schools rather than to the public high schools. In their homes are found magazines such as the *National Georgraphic, The Saturday Evening Post, Time, Atlantic Monthly, Fortune, Sports Afield, Harpers, The New Yorker, Current History,* and *Field and Stream* (65).

Women play a dominant role in the upper classes, due partly to the abdication by men of social leadership, and partly to the fact that women live longer than men and inherit their wealth. Women dominate social organizations, clubs, and other groups which operate upper-class social activities (43:194).

The general impression left by studies of upper-class society is that members of this group are unconcerned with ordinary economic cares, and unaffected by the pressures for improvement of status commonly found among the lower classes. Theirs is a secure position at the top of the social ladder, a position automatically protected by tradition and inherited wealth. Upper-class members are concerned about prestige, social graces, tradition, the family, and diplomacy (43:194).

THE MIDDLE CLASSES. As one goes down the status scale, income is derived more from personal effort than from inheritance. In the middle classes are found persons who receive their income from fees, salaries, and profits of their business or investments. Here we find white-collar workers, foremen and highly skilled craftsmen, small businessmen, and the like (65).

Members of the middle class are not born to security and tend to be fearful about loss of steady income. They set a high valuation on owning property and other concrete symbols of achievement. They learn to build their security by resisting immediate pleasures and investing in future status. From their anxiety over security comes a drive toward self-improvement which makes them willing to endure sacrifices in order to insure socioeconomic status (30:195). In the middle classes, women are accorded a position more nearly approaching equality with men than is true in the upper or lower classes. Here marriage is more of a partnership; men are expected to participate in housework and child care, while women often contribute to the family income.

The emotional life of middle-class persons follows a pattern of control and reserve. They are striving, competitive persons who value progress and who conform rigidly to group standards. They conduct their lives in accordance with generally accepted patterns, attending church, PTA functions, discussion groups, book clubs and other organized forms of recreation (*35*). They emphasize cleanliness, tidiness, restraint, and sublimation of aggressive tendencies. Education is valued highly. Moral conformity is stressed, and strong pressures are exerted against stealing, property destruction, sexual immorality, bad manners, and carelessness in dress and speech (*37*:319).

The middle class, while it is not numerically the largest class, is said to be the official culture of this country. It is the culture which is taught in the schools, and practiced by recreational agencies, social agencies, and churches. The middle class is the "public" toward which advertising, sales campaigns, movies, magazines, and other media of mass communication are directed (*60*).

THE LOWER CLASSES. Life in the lower classes is so different from that of the upper and middle classes that it must be examined in some detail. Actually, we need to speak of two lower classes; the upper-lower, which is the class of the "common man," includes skilled and semiskilled workers and laborers with steady jobs; the lower-lower class is composed of unskilled laborers, the foreign-born, tenant farmers, migrant workers, and persons with little education (*65*). It is from these two classes that most of our school children come.

The upper-lower class is more like the middle class in its aspirations, anxiety over insecurity, and some of its customs and values. It resembles the lower-lower class in its struggle for economic existence. However, lower-class people are sufficiently similar in their basic living patterns to be differentiated from the lower-middle-class group (*16*:264).

Lower-class people are conscious of their group identity to the extent of differentiating between those in the group and those outside of it. They feel little responsibility toward people outside the circle of the family, neighborhood, or friends. Within this sphere it is important to be honest and loyal. Outside of it, disloyalty and deception are more likely to be overlooked or condoned (*37*:319).

The lower classes do not emphasize cleanliness and tidiness to the extent that the middle class does, nor do they place so high a value on accomplishment. Their aggressive impulses are less restrained or sublimated, and sexual restrictions are much more loose in this group. The incidence of premarital sexual intercourse in the lower classes is said to be seven times higher than among the upper or middle classes. From one-fourth to one-third of all lower-class births are illegitimate births (*16*:264). Relations between husband and wife are also different in lower-class families. Wife beating is almost entirely a lower-lower class characteristic. Women work harder in these families. Lower-class men enjoy more leisure than do their wives, and their leisure activities usually are shared with male companions (*43*:194).

Members of the lower-lower class marry early and enter the semi-skilled and unskilled occupations at an early age. They experience the greatest distress in times of unemployment and usually comprise the bulk of relief cases. Very few lower lowers own their own homes. The houses in which they live are of little economic value, being small, run down, and located in the least desirable sections of town. These people almost never join a charitable, social, or economic organization other than labor unions, and only occasionally are they found among the members of fraternal organizations. They make little use of the public library, subscribe to few magazines, and usually read a tabloid or "yellow journal" type of newspaper. The lower-lower class furnishes more than its share of criminals and delinquents. In Yankee City (*65*) 65 percent of all those arrested came from this class, although they comprised just 25 percent of the population.

Where middle-class people have anxieties about social and economic security, the lower lowers are more concerned with the basic essentials of life. They alternate between periods of depression when they have nothing or almost nothing to periods when they have all they desire. Unlike middle-class people, they do not learn to be moderate in their habits so that life is not so much an all-or-nothing matter (*13*).

Understanding this background of lower-class anxieties over the fulfilling of basic organic needs, we can better interpret the behavior of these people when they get a relatively large increase in income. In a Northern industrial city, it is common to find large, new, shiny cars standing in front of run-down, unpainted wooden shacks. Here lower-class workers from other parts of the country are able to secure temporary but well-paid factory jobs. Just as soon as they accumulate a little money, they purchase large new cars which they seldom retain very long because they are unable to meet the payments. Similarly, slum dwellers who come into money have been observed buying fur coats, expensive clothes, new furniture, and, for a short time, enjoying a high standard of living.

In the judgment of middle-class citizens, such behavior is improvident and extravagant. But to the lower-lower class person this extravagant spending is a defense against anxiety. Even if he can buy these things only once or twice in his life, they help to increase his self-esteem by providing him with some of the prestige symbols of the higher classes (37:322).

Race and Social Status

Research discloses that the class order of society is not the result of color or race groupings. It is commonly assumed that the lower classes are made up predominantly of Negroes, Mexicans, and other racial minorities. While it is true that large numbers of such people are in the lower classes, they are there not because of race or color, but because these conditions of living have been imposed upon them. When circumstances channel these minority groups into inferior types of employment, deny them equal access to housing, education facilities, and cultural opportunities, they are forced to live according to lower-class patterns. Comparisons which have been made between middle- and lower-class whites and Negroes show that their similarities and differences follow social class rather than color lines. That is, there is more similarity among middle-class whites and middle-class Negroes than there is among middle-class and lower-class Negroes, or middle-class and lower-class whites (16, 18, 19).

Psychoses and Social Status

Certain mental disorders appear to be significantly related to social-class membership (24). Schizophrenia, for example, occurs more frequently among the lower classes. One study of all schizophrenics under treatment in a large community noted that the incidence of this ailment in the lowest social class was ten times greater than in the highest social class, and about six times greater than the middle class (36). This circumstance was explained partly on the basis that upper-class people seek treatment earlier than do lower-class people. However, the poorly integrated family life existing among the lower classes is known also to be a critical factor in their emotional adjustment.

The upper classes appear to be more susceptible to manic-depressive psychoses, while the middle class suffers most from psychosomatic disturbances, said to be related to their tendency toward conformance and their repressed aggression (41:201).

Social-Class Mobility

While there is no question that social classes have pervasive influences over their members, it is wise to interject a note of caution against interpreting too literally the limitations imposed upon an individual by his social-class status. Social classes are not rigid divisions in our society. There are no official criteria of class position, nor are there legal demarcations or restrictions. Theoretically, individuals may move from one class to another unhampered by official barriers (47).

Ours is an open class system which allows for vertical movement, and, compared with other countries, there is much mobility in American society. Through the acquisition of money or education, and through talent, skill, or marriage, a person can move up from the social level into which he was born (68). Yet, as we shall point out later, there are certain forces in our society which deny to the lower classes the opportunity to rise above the conditions of life which their class status imposes upon them (55).

SOCIAL-CLASS DIFFERENCES IN CHILD-REARING

Nowhere do social-class differences express themselves more definitely than in the patterns of family living. Social classes live in different worlds, psychologically as well as economically. Their families reflect the world of their class and mold oncoming generations in the class likeness (5:323). This section is devoted to a discussion of the important aspects of child-rearing in terms of class differentials.

Child-Rearing in the Upper Classes

The upper-class child is likely to live in a large house where he has his own room. He will have space to be by himself and a place to bring his friends without disturbing adults or having adults intrude upon them. Here will be found ample closet space, drawers, play space, a great variety of play equipment, toys, books, and educational materials. These physical advantages give the upper-class child a chance to develop a feeling of property ownership and enable him to grow up in a quiet, rich environment (5:327).

Commonly, there are servants in the home to relieve parents of household chores and provide time for leisurely family life and relaxed parent-child relations. Parents are well educated and are likely to be familiar with modern views on child training. Their children have all the recommended vaccinations and receive regular medical examinations (2:327). Upper-class parents are not overly anxious about masturbation or sex play. Children are allowed considerable freedom to show aggression toward their parents. Discipline takes the form of reasoning, rewards, praise, and deprivation of privileges, rather than spanking or scolding (57).

Despite the apparently relaxed relationships between upper-class parents and their children, these youngsters are under considerable pressure to uphold the family name, tradition, heritage, and status. It is assumed that they will attend college and learn the social graces required of their class, that they will marry "right," and that they will maintain or develop the family fortune. This pressure comes not only from the immediate family, but from all relatives who bear the family name, including those who are dead (5:330).

Child-Rearing in the Middle Classes

Middle-class homes are smaller and more crowded than those of the upper class. However, parents recognize the child's need for some privacy and do what they can to provide it. The middle-class family is concerned with appearances—with what people will say or how things will look (5:333). Children are trained early and vigorously to develop habits of cleanliness, respect for property, control of aggression, and sexual inhibitions. The middle-class child is taught to assume responsibility in the home early. Girls are expected to help with the cooking and sewing and to assume the care of younger children. Boys help with the chores around the house and often are payed an allowance for such services. Both boys and girls are required to be in the house earlier at night and to work harder on school lessons than are lower-class children (13).

Middle-class fathers are anxious that their sons develop qualities of aggressiveness, competitiveness, and initiative, and they stress athletics in an effort to promote these qualities. At the same time they insist upon obedience and emotional restraint, and teach their children not to fight or inflict physical pain upon others (1).

In general, middle-class children are sheltered, intimidated, and highly supervised. The middle-class family tends to be less permissive than upper- or lower-class families and more inclined to stress responsibility, self-control, and individual achievement. It is possible that the anxiety reactions noted among middle-class children result from this form of child-rearing. Observers have found masturbation to be two or three times more common among middle-class children than among lower-class children, and thumbsucking is found three times more common among the middle-class youngsters (12, 22).

Despite these pressures, parents and children in middle-class homes enjoy close emotional ties. Children are said to have considerable psychological freedom, even though their physical freedom is curtailed. This is one explanation offered for the low incidence of submissiveness, bullying, and hierarchical behavior observed in middle-class play groups (45).

Child-Rearing in the Lower Classes

Lower-class families live close together in small, thin-walled crowded houses, flats, or apartments. Their families are large, and low income often necessitates the inclusion of relatives or boarders in the household. These factors make it almost impossible to find privacy in the home. Children get in each other's way and must share life more intimately with their siblings than is true in other classes (5:325). Crowded conditions of living influence the attitudes of lower-class parents toward their children. In lower-class homes, children are taught not to be a nuisance, not to disturb adults, to cause no trouble, and to stay out of the way. Physical punishment is used liberally to induce obedience and prompt response to commands (70).

Lower-class parents appear to be very permissive in their relationship with young children. They probably nurse their children longer than middle-class mothers do, and they are not quite so anxious over such matters as toilet training, weaning, or masturbation (22, 40, 46). Children are even less sheltered and protected as they grow older. Lower-class children are permitted to go to movies alone at an early age and may stay out later in the evening than their middle-class peers. There is less family pride and less concern for appearances or for upholding family status. As a result, children are free to roam the streets with relatively little parental supervision. They form their own associations and are often forced to accept adult responsibilities at an early age.

The apparent permissiveness of the lower-class home appears to be more a matter of not wanting children around to interfere with parental activities than any concern for developing the child's capacities. Consequently, the physical freedom of lower-class children does not result in psychological freedom. These children tend to fear their parents and to feel rejected and unworthy because of the lack of close parental ties (45, 46).

Parent-child relationships are influenced also by the rate of family disorganization in lower-class homes. There are frequent changes of residence among these people, and a high rate of divorce, desertion, and transitory illegal unions. In these exchanges of sex mates, children usually accompany their mother, and it is not unusual to find among lower-class children many youngsters who do not know their own fathers (5:331). In this setting of freedom, lack of privacy, and sexual promiscuity, lower-class children begin their sexual experimentations very early. Parents, by their own example, tend to make sexual relations among children a natural outcome of the home environment.

Living in crowded, disorganized homes tends to stimulate the development of aggression among lower-class people. In the slum family, parents may fight and beat each other, and children enter into these conflicts as soon as they are able. Moreover, children are taught to defend themselves and to strike first whenever possible. They learn to fight children of either sex and to attack adults as well, using clubs, rocks, or knives if their fists are not adequate. Both mother and father may join these fights if the occasion warrants. Fighting is so integral a part of lower-class life that unless the child becomes a ready and proficient fighter he loses prestige among his peers and in his family as well (13, 16).

SOCIAL-CLASS INFLUENCES ON CHILD BEHAVIOR

As the child grows up in his social-class environment he takes on the values, ideas, beliefs, and customs of his class. He is conditioned to behave as the culture would have him behave, becoming so firmly imbedded in his culture that only a long-term process of reconditioning will enable him to live comfortably in another culture (3:108). In this section we shall illustrate the ways in which social-class membership affects children in terms of their family attitudes, play interests, and attitudes toward discipline. This discussion is supplemented in the following section with an analysis of how this behavior is reflected in the school.

Attitudes Toward the Family

It has been noted that the interpersonal distance between parents and children becomes greater as social status decreases. In Smitter's study (57) of the relationships between parents and their adolescent children, definite class differences were observed. When these youngsters were asked to name the person to whom they turn for advice on personal problems or worries, their choices were as follows:[1]

[1] Adapted from Smitter (57), Table 34, p. 37.

Person Chosen	Percent of Children Making Choice			
	Class I (Lowest)	Class II	Class III	Class IV (Highest)
Father	37	43	45	55
Mother	54	70	77	83
Sister	25	19	14	12
Brother	11	7	9	12
Friend	19	25	21	25
Teacher	8	11	11	26

The relationships between parents and their children in the lowest class is reflected by the fact that only 37 percent sought the advice of their fathers, and 54 percent looked to their mothers for help. As social status increases, children are more inclined to approach their parents for assistance with personal problems.

These interpersonal relations may be explained in part by the attitudes of children toward their parents' occupations. Children have definite feelings about the respectability of the work their parents do. The traditional professions, high-level executive positions, ownership of creative businesses, and the semiprofessional and socially useful positions, such as social welfare workers, commonly are esteemed. Proprietors of small businesses with little or no prestige, or salesmen working on a commission are accepted but not particularly respected. Occupations from which parents return home with dirty clothes or bodies, or where the product handled is not a nice one, are held in low regard (25).

In higher-status families there is much identification among children and their parents. Boys are proud of their father's work and tend to follow similar occupations. As social status decreases and the respectability of the father's occupation is lowered, there is less admiration for the father and less tendency for a boy to identify with him (25).

This factor, together with others mentioned earlier, brings frustrations and disappointments into the home experience of lower-class children. They may learn to have little confidence in people and to assume that the world is a hostile place (39:308). Such attitudes carry over into adult behavior and impose serious barriers to the development of mental health among lower-class people.

Play Interests

Children's play interests vary with social-class status. A study of the out-of-school play activities of 11-year-olds in a Midwestern community

(*61*) found the upper-lower-class child to be more active and adventurous than children from any other class. Some 45 percent of the children in this group expressed a liking for rough play, whereas 33 percent of the middle-class youngsters and just 10 percent of the lower-lower-class children participate in such play. Middle-class children are more inclined toward team play and sports, since fighting and rough behavior are not approved by their families.

The lower-lower-class children have fewer play interests and are the least active of all children (*57, 61*). These are timid youngsters who stay at home or near home, even when their parents are away. They do not like to fight, and will endure much heckling and punishment before being goaded into retaliating. It has been suggested that poverty and lack of social status in the community have made lower-lower-class children so inhibited, fearful, and insecure that they seldom become aggressive. This appears to be more true of children of migrant families and tenant farmers than of urban slum children. However, lower-lower-class children in general tend to have few friends and lack confidence in social relationships. They are the children who have the most need for nursery schools, club experiences, summer camps, and other socializing activities.

Attitudes Toward Discipline

Another way in which children reflect their socioeconomic backgrounds is in their feelings about how misdeeds should be handled. In a study made in New York City (*20*), lower-class fifth grade children in a public school and middle- and upper-class children in a private school were given this problem:

> Tommy, age 10, and Jimmy, age 6, were brothers. Jimmy constantly interfered with Tommy. Whenever Tommy entertained his friends, Jimmy intruded. Jimmy always broke up Tommy's games, took his toys, and in general was considered a poor sport.

The children were asked to write out the way they would handle this problem. Later they were interviewed individually and asked a series of questions related to discipline and behavior. From this study it was learned that lower-class children tended to hold the individual responsible for infractions of the rules. They would punish him and avenge his misdeeds, using truant officers, reform schools, and other law enforcement agencies if necessary. Private school students took a more generous view toward misbehavior. They suggested situational and environmental changes to correct misconduct and had a much more tolerant attitude toward children who misbehave.

A possible interpretation of these findings is that upper- and middle-class children, because of their greater economic and emotional security, have the capacity to be understanding and lenient toward misbehavior. Also, they have themselves experienced kindness and consideration and know the meaning of these forms of treatment.

On the other hand, lower-class children are so accustomed to being whipped and punished that they accept it as a matter of course and do not feel this is too severe a form of treatment for children who have done wrong (*42*). In their emphasis on retaliation, rather than forgiveness, they merely reflect the upbringing of their social class.

SOCIAL INFLUENCES IN THE SCHOOL

In many ways, children of lower-status families live in a different world than that of upper-status children. Although they may sit side by side in school and rub shoulders on the playground, they are products of different cultures and have had different experiences, ideas, attitudes, and values impressed upon them.

Theoretically, our public schools should reduce these differences by providing all children with a common education so that they may have equal opportunities in life. However, the school is essentially a middle-class institution employing middle-class teachers and administrators and teaching a middle-class way of life. As a result, lower-class children find themselves in an unreal environment which often contradicts the teachings and practices of their homes and neighborhoods. These children profit less from the academic program, enjoy fewer social privileges, share less in the school recreation program, and have more scholastic, emotional, and social problems than upper-status children.

Class Status and Academic Achievement

The effects of socioeconomic status are reflected in the school achievement of lower-class children. By the time these youngsters reach the eighth grade they are, on the average, two years retarded in achievement. Vocabulary items, reading, and arithmetic present the greatest difficulties to these children, and these difficulties increase with the passage of time (*13, 21, 57*). So common is this occurrence that it is said socioeconomic status is a better predictor of academic expectation than is intelligence (*34*).

Teachers are aware of the learning difficulties of lower-status children and expect less of them. The teaching process in lower-class groups often becomes a struggle to get across a few basic skills. A principal in a slum area school describes the problem this way:

The children come into our upper grades with very poor reading ability. That means that all the way through our school everybody is concentrating on reading. It's not like at a school like S_____ (middle group) where they have science and history and so on. At a school like that they figure that from first to fourth you learn to read and from fifth to eighth you read to learn. You use your reading to learn other material. Well, these children don't reach the second stage while they're with us. We have to plug along getting them to learn to read. Our teachers are pretty well satisfied if the children can read and do simple number work when they leave here. You'll find that they don't think very much of subjects like science, and so on. They haven't got any time for that. They're just trying to get these basic things over . . . (4)

This restricted kind of education aggravates the problem of educating lower-class children. In each grade, the gap between what the children should know, as judged by grade norms, and what they actually do know becomes wider and wider. Many of these youngsters start dropping out of school before they finish the eighth grade, and they continue to do so in increasing numbers in high school. Only about 5 percent of the lower-class children go on to college, while 80 percent of their upper- and upper-middle-class schoolmates and 20 percent of the lower-middle-class children get there (31).

Intelligence and Social Status

Inferior intelligence has been the most frequent explanation offered for social-class differences in academic accomplishment. There is no doubt that IQ's derived from the ordinary intelligence tests show typical social-class variations. For instance, a study of eighth graders in California found the average IQ in the lowest class to be 87.8, the next higher social group had an average IQ of 99, the next group 105.8, and the highest social group 108.6 (57). These findings are consistent with other studies which reveal that at age 14 the average IQ of the lowest socioeconomic group is 20 to 23 points below that of the higher-status groups (12).

However, there is quite a large body of evidence which indicates that these differences in intelligence test scores are not differences of capacity but of culturally derived information. When the cultural biases of the common intelligence tests are removed, and only such words, grammatical constructions and situations as are about equally common in the environment of all socioeconomic groups are used, the resultant test gives a different picture of the distribution of intelligence among socioeconomic groups.

Using such "culture fair" tests, Davis, Eells, and others have shown that the average real intellectual ability is in general at the same level for all social groups. On such tests there is no difference in the percentages of the upper and lower social class groups who answered the problems correctly. In other words, the usual intelligence tests measure the cultural and economic opportunities which the child has—not his real intelligence (*11, 13*). On the basis of such evidence, Warner, Meeker, and Eells (*68*) have concluded that the school failure of lower-class children cannot be blamed on their lower intelligence. Many slum children who do poorly in school, as measured by present tests, have higher natural ability than upper-class children who do well in school.

Loeb (*44*) suggests another possible explanation of the inferior test performance of lower-class children. In judging test scores it is assumed that the child taking the test is motivated to do his best. When we note that most achievement tests concern behavior which is not meaningful to the lower-class child, it raises a serious question about how well motivated he is. For the lower-class child much school learning is concerned with meaningless content and incomprehensible goals. Therefore, his test results may be a reflection of his conflicting motivation and his rejection of what the school is trying to teach.

Social-Class Emphasis in the School Curriculum

There is good reason to believe that a major cause for the academic difficulties of lower-class children is a curriculum which does not meet their needs. The usual school curriculum places a high premium on language, draws its illustrations and problems from middle-class culture, and regards as extracurricular or nonacademic those skills which lower-class children tend to develop. Because of these factors, lower-class children often look upon education as impractical and unrelated to their own goals or problems. The school curriculum becomes to them an artificial creation which demands skills they do not possess and teaches things which have no utility in their lives.

EMPHASIS ON LANGUAGE.   Child-rearing practices in upper- and middle-class homes usually produce children who have a high verbal facility. In the upper-class home, children become acquainted with good grammatical usage, they learn the subtleties and shades of meaning in our speech, acquire an extensive vocabulary, and know how to use it. Middle-class children likewise are taught a language and form of word usage which is directly transferable to the school situation. Lower-class children, however, enter school with a severe language handicap. They have a meager vocabulary and are accustomed to poor grammar, profanity, and improper word usage. Therefore when they come to school they must relearn the language before they can fit into the school program (5:339). By the time they have accomplished this, they have become retarded learners.

Moreover, the initial verbal handicap of lower-class children is accentuated by intelligence and achievement tests which have high verbal components. On the basis of these tests, children are stigmatized as "slow learners" and are commonly separated into groups which receive narrow, attenuated programs of instruction and which have last call upon the school's facilities and equipment. Such grouping tends to strengthen the socioeconomic discrimination within the school by narrowing the scope of education for lower-class children (11, 13).

TEXTBOOK BIAS. From the time the lower-class child is first handed a book, the pattern of life presented to him in the classroom is the typical middle-class culture. In his primer he will read about the Joneses who have two children, a boy and a girl. They live in a pleasant little suburban house in a well-cared-for neighborhood. Each child has a private room with closets, dressers, and play space. The bathroom is clean and sparkling with separate towel racks for each individual and a place for each person to keep his toothbrush. Father is pictured as coming home from work nattily dressed and carrying a brief case. Everyone is clean, happy, emotionally secure, and well adjusted.

All of this is the prototype of the middle-class, white, liberal Protestant, Anglo-Saxon, politically and religiously apathetic, middle-of-the-road pattern of life (23). At least one-fourth of the children who read about this "typical" American family will find no resemblance to their own home life in the congested slum areas of the city or the shanty dwellings on farms and in rural areas. They are familiar with crowded quarters where they sleep two and three in a bed, share a bathroom with other families, if they have a bathroom, hang their clothes on nails or hooks fastened to the wall, and do most of their washing in the kitchen. Their father comes home dirty and tired. Family life is congested, noisy, and not at all like the idyllic storybook conception of what home life ought to be. Lower-class children are often hurt by this contrast and confused by the unreal picture it presents (3:120).

CONCERN FOR LOWER-CLASS NEEDS. This unrealistic pattern of education continues throughout the school life of the lower-class child. Seldom does he learn anything that will help him with his own problems of living or prepare him for the realities of his own world. It is always the middle-class values, customs, behavior, and problems which fill his classroom hours.

The interests and aptitudes of lower-class children are neglected in the usual school program, both in designing the curriculum and in evaluating the achievement of children. These youngsters have been found to have considerable interest and aptitude in the areas of athletics, music, and art, due perhaps to their need for achieving individual status and for escaping from the drab routine of their existence (57, 5:342). But few schools build on these interests, tending more often to emphasize the verbal and academic aspects of the school program which is best suited to middle-class needs, while nonverbal abilities and interests are given secondary consideration.

The emphasis on reading and the disregard for the realities of life confronting the lower-class child creates an artificial environment for these children. As Davis has said, the lower-class child

. . . is in school primarily to learn how to think, to develop his reason, his insight, his invention, his imagination. The materials now used in reading are felt by the pupils and particularly the lower socioeconomic group, to have little importance in his life outside of school. . . . Learning the skill of decoding written communication is important, but not so important for the development of mental ability as the pupil's analysis of his own experience, and his drawing of correct inferences from this analysis. (11)

These conditions have created in the schools an educationally neglected group of children. At the beginning high school level, this group may be distinguished by the following characteristics:

1. They come from families the members of which are engaged in unskilled and semiskilled occupations.
2. Their families are in the low-income and low-cultural environment group.
3. They begin school later than other children and are retarded in their progress.

4. They make considerably lower achievement test scores for their age and for their grade.
5. Their intelligence test scores are below average.
6. They make lower grades than other students.
7. They are less emotionally mature, tending to be nervous and insecure.
8. They lack interest in school work. (56)

Within this educationally neglected group are children with a great untapped potential of intellectual ability. As Anderson (2) points out, while highly gifted children occur seven times more frequently in professional homes than in lower-class homes, it is in the unskilled labor homes of America that the reservoir of gifted children exists, for there are ten times more such homes than professional homes. If our society is to make use of the brains and talents of this group of young people, schools must learn how to educate them. For schools to do this, the children must be kept in school long enough to learn the skills they need to function adequately in our economic and social world (68). At the present time these youngsters become disillusioned with school at an early age, and leave just as soon as they can.

Cultural Opposition of Home and School

In addition to the unrealistic curriculum presented to lower-class children, cultural conflicts between the home and the school often place children under stress. Certain kinds of behavior which are considered quite normal and natural by persons in the lower classes are strongly disapproved in school. Conversely, much of what is taught and recommended by the school contradicts the values and customs of the lower-class home.

SCHOOL CONFLICTS. In lower-class families, physical aggression is a normal, socially approved and socially inculcated type of behavior. Lower-class children are therefore more inclined to settle playground disagreements by violent means than are middle-class children (12, 13). Also, they are more likely to use profane and obscene language and to refer to physical organs and physiological process by names which they learn at home and in the streets. Such behavior and speech is offensive at school and meets with punishment and criticism. Children are thus disapproved for behaving in a way they have been taught to behave by their culture.

Another source of conflict between home and school is seen in the dietary habits of children from lower-class homes. In one instance, two little Spanish-American children refused to eat their lunch where they might be seen by the teacher or other pupils. It was learned later that their daily diet of tortillas had been ridiculed by the other children, causing the youngsters much embarrassment (69:323). Similar incidents have been noted among children who bring their lunch wrapped in newspapers and eat with their heads concealed by the newspaper.

Even the patterns of discipline used in the home and in the school may create sources of conflict. The home dominated by an autocratic parent cannot tolerate the freedom allowed children in school. This is illustrated in studies of German-American families in New York City, where it was found that mothers and grandmothers of nursery school children often were troubled by the general laxness of discipline in the school and the encouragement of spontaneity. They tried to balance this by increasing rigidity at home, although the behavior of the children did not provoke such treatment. With several children the schism between home and school led to behavior problems in school because at home they were not permitted to act out their feelings (50).

Teachers have been criticized by parents for many other practices which conflict with home standards. They have been rebuked for referring to the theory of evolution during a study of dinosaurs, for permitting children to recite from the Bible, and even for teaching Christmas carols during the holiday season (69:324). These are more than just misunderstandings between the home and the school; they represent areas of cultural conflict.

HOME CONFLICTS.   In many cases, schools attempt to teach children to live in a world entirely foreign to them and to their parents. The lower-class child who is taught the virtues of thrift, nonaggression, and respect for authority, who is urged to be a model of good deportment and to better himself through education is often being asked to adopt customs and values which differ in many important respects from his way of life. If children attempt to bring these teachings into their homes, they encounter violent antagonism from their families. In one instance, a boy from a lower-class home used the word "preference" at home. His father swore at him, shouting, "Preference, preference, I'll preference you. You with fancy words. You can't high hat me as long as I pay the bills" (5:184).

In another lower-class family, Mary was praised by her teacher for being quiet and anxious to please. But at home this behavior caused her mother and sisters to condemn her for being a schemer and an apple polisher. Her sister Paulette was a problem at school because of her profanity, fighting, and disrespect for authority. But at home she was accepted as a good child, popular, and highly admired (*18*:14, *54*). Consciously or unconsciously, both children made a choice in adjusting to the conflicting pulls of home and school. Mary will probably get along well at school, but will have problems to face at home. Paulette will have difficulties at school and will continue to be influenced mainly by the home.

Children are torn between home and school, not only in terms of the overt behavior demanded of them but in terms of their values and ideals as well. When they learn from books, teachers, and classmates that the customs and values established in their homes are inferior or improper, their security is threatened. By rejecting the behavior and values of their parents, the school rejects their parents also. Since lower-class children often lack security in their home relationships, they usually are reluctant to jeopardize what security they have by adopting the values of the school. To do so would drive a psychological wedge between them and their already tenuous attachment to the family. Consequently, children tend to adhere to their culture and resist the teachings of the school and the culture it represents.

Social-Class Attitudes Toward the School

There is a reciprocal relationship between the extent to which schools contribute to family goals, and how children and their families feel toward the school. These feelings are both an expression of social stratification and an evaluation of the school as a social institution.

In the upper classes the importance of education is taken for granted. Here education is not so much a matter of preparing for a vocation as it is a means through which one equips himself with the competencies and standards of his class. Upper-class children often look with disfavor upon the public schools, particularly the public high schools which some consider to be factories bogged down with great numbers of students who are not going to college, and whose values, ambitions, and codes of behavior are so inferior to their own that it does not pay to mingle with them (*10*, *52*). For these reasons, many upper-class students attend college preparatory schools, finishing schools, and the well-established private colleges.

To middle-class parents the school represents an agency through which their children may rise in the world. Almost all middle-class boys and girls go through high school. Large numbers go to state universities and colleges where scholarships, stipends, or work opportunities are available. Throughout their school careers they are admonished to: "Behave yourself, do well in your studies, be a go-getter, search out all the facilitating aids that society offers for higher training, and you will get along in the world, i.e., raise your status" (5:339).

Middle-class students have conscientious work habits; they believe that rules must be obeyed, and that to be a good citizen one must do boring jobs if the school wants them done (*31*). They are likely to endorse the ideas that children who do not work hard in school won't amount to much when they grow up; that children who do not act as others do are not popular in school; that good citizens should support community projects and public activities, and that if you have ambition you can succeed (*52*).

Lower-class attitudes toward school and education are very different from the other classes. This is true particularly of slum dwellers, tenant farmers, and migrant workers who frequently view the schools as a device to deprive the family of the income that might be received from a working child (*12*:23). These parents have little contact with the schools—and then only when their children are in trouble. One study (*57*) found that 78 percent of the lower-class parents never attend a parents' meeting, and 81 percent never visit their child's classroom. The comparable figures for upper-class parents were 42 percent and 48 percent. Lower-class parents seldom seek help from a teacher and are more likely to go to a minister or priest for help with school problems. They tend to feel that neither the school nor the community are of particular value to them in rearing their children. As social status increases, parents are more likely to value the contributions made by school and community to the development of their youngsters (*57*).

Coupled with these attitudes are other factors which affect the school relationships of lower-class people. Frequently children must work before and after school; there is a high incidence of disturbance in the family, changes of school are frequent, and children are not encouraged to do well in school. These factors provide a mileu which furnishes few incentives to the child for learning (5:339).

Because they feel out of place in the middle-class school, lower-class children attend only as long as the law forces them to, and where attendance laws are loosely enforced, they do not attend at all (*35*). They are likely to feel that boys and girls who stay in school after the legal attendance age are trying to avoid going to work (*52*).

In a study of school attendance among lower-class high school students in New Haven, Connecticut, Davie (*10*) found that most of the lower-lower-class youngsters who were in school at all tended to be in trade schools where they could learn something practical that would help them get a job. In their homes where both parents worked to earn enough for the basic essentials of life, sickness and industrial accidents often forced children to leave school in order to help out. Even when children were not needed at home, they left school anyhow to earn money for the things parents could not provide. The one thing which kept many of them in school was the knowledge that employers were requiring high school diplomas. However, the attraction of earning money was too great for most of them. They left school just as soon as they reached the legal age limit, only to find that the jobs available to them were the low-paying ones as laborers, bus boys, or waitresses.

Class Status and Adjustment

The school world of the child may be pleasant, rewarding, and enhancing to his self-esteem if he can adjust to the values and standards of a middle-class institution. Middle-class children can do this, and they are generally content with the school's rules, procedures, teachers, and social life. The lower-class youngster tends to make a poor adjustment to the school and experiences many frustrations before he finally leaves it.

TEACHER RELATIONSHIPS. Lower-lower-class children often feel that teachers overemphasize good order and conduct, are overly strict, and do not praise them when they do good work. They see upper-status children receiving awards and praise while little recognition is accorded them (*35*:180–198).

Moreover, the barrier between teachers and lower-class children is raised higher when the teachers' demands and standards contradict the child's out-of-school experiences. These children come to feel that education and learning are unfriendly things; they resent the authority of the teacher and seek ways to circumvent his supervision, ways which usually lead to trouble (*3*:124). Their inability or unwillingness to learn and their insubordination or misbehavior have been interpreted as the natural consequences of the discouragement and rejection felt by lower-class children (*12*). These youngsters have no great respect for academic accomplishment. They do not boast about good school marks and may, in fact, conceal high grades if they receive them. Both family and friends teach the lower-class child to guard against being taken in by the teacher, or of being a softie to her. He is in disgrace if he pursues homework too seriously (37:323). His reputation is likely to be based upon how well he can fool the teacher, how many aggressive acts he can commit without being caught, or how much punishment he can absorb at the hands of school authorities.

Such behavior is the result of general class feelings toward the school, together with the personal feeling that the teacher is hostile or that the whole school is against the lower class. These attitudes generate feelings of inadequacy, insecurity, and discouragement. The lower-class child would like to escape from such unpleasantness, but finds himself a captive. Therefore he may adjust by becoming a withdrawn, dependent youngster who leans heavily on the teacher, or by developing defense mechanisms which make him a behavior problem and increase the tensions in his personal relationships (33).

PEER ACCEPTANCE.   One of the most powerful of the social-class influences operating in the school is the acceptance and rejection which occurs among children. It is in this sphere that the lower-class child feels most isolated.

In Neugarten's study (49) of elementary school children in a Midwestern community where the population was about 90 percent native-born whites, social acceptance was distinctly linked with class status. Upper-class children were described by their classmates as being fair, well mannered, and the ones most desired as friends. Lower-class children were mentioned often as persons not liked and not desired as friends. They had the reputation of being poorly dressed, not good-looking, unpopular, aggressive, dirty, and bad mannered. These youngsters experienced social isolation as early as the fifth grade.

Cook's study (9) of the friendship preferences of high school students revealed an even more pronounced awareness of social-class symbols. Upper-status children were credited with positive personality traits such as; "best dressed," "best liked," "most fun," or "real leader." Lower-class children were seldom mentioned as possessing these traits, except by other lower-class children. Both upper- and middle-class students referred to the lower group as "drips" and "jerks" and described them as dirty, smelly, aggressive, and dumb.

Other studies (29, 32, 35, 59) support the conclusion that lower-class boys and girls are rejected by their upper-status peers. They are not welcome in school clubs and are unwanted in the classroom or on the playground. Only when they excel in athletics and can make an important contribution to the school team do they receive recognition from their classmates. Most lower-class children never attain this status and experience only futility and bitterness in their social contacts.

These conditions force lower-class children into association with their class equals. They seek to achieve a feeling of belonging by developing a group spirit among themselves—sometimes expressing this spirit through aggression toward those groups who rejected them. Lower-class children's groups set their own standards of behavior, and their members are likely to earn status through street fighting, cursing, and early sexual relations. They may disdain the overtures of institutions, clubs, and agencies established to provide recreational opportunities and guidance for them, preferring their own unsupervised freedom. Such attitudes frequently carry over into the school, since children do not completely cast off these patterns of conduct when they leave the street.

Despite the efforts of lower-class children to find acceptance among their own kind as a compensation for their rejection by other social groups, these youngsters show more problem tendencies and greater evidences of emotional instability than do children of higher status (58). This is significant in light of the fact that among preschool children it is the middle-class that shows more symptoms of tension as evidenced by thumbsucking and masturbation. Evidently, failure of the home and school to meet the emotional needs of lower-class children becomes more critical as the child grows older.

This conclusion is further supported by data on admission to psychiatric clinics. For example, in California, 3680 persons were admitted to outpatient psychiatric clinics in 1951. Of these, 3172 were classified as economically dependent or marginal (6:76). It is possible, of course, that persons of higher socioeconomic status do not go to state mental hospitals for treatment, but to private psychiatrists. However, other studies support the interpretation that low social status, and its attendant economic insecurity, has an adverse effect on personality from the earliest years (68).

Social-Class Influences on Teacher-Pupil Relationships

Teachers bring their own social-class backgrounds into the cultural conflicts which exist in the school. Davis (13) claims that 95 percent of our teachers are from the middle socioeconomic groups. They come predominantly from hard-working families engaged in the skilled and clerical occupations and from the farms of the nation. Only a few come from homes of professional people, and these tend to teach either in private secondary schools or colleges (8).

Teachers try to be democratic and fair in their relationships with children, but they cannot escape their middle-class indoctrination. They have difficulty understanding and relating themselves to children from the lower classes and reflect this in their attitudes toward these children, their disciplinary approaches, and their teaching techniques.

ATTITUDES TOWARD CHILDREN. Teachers have been found to display a bias in favor of upper-status children. According to the study made by Heintz (33), teachers like children who are clean, neat, orderly, quiet, courteous, discreet, and respectful of authority. They appreciate children who are interested in books, who work hard on assignments, are adept in the use of words, and attentive and interested in what the teacher says. These characteristics obviously are those of middle-class children. Rated low are children who lack interest in school, fail to respect adults, use profanity, have uncombed hair, unwashed or unpressed clothes, and whose parents do not attend the PTA.

These attitudes lead to different ways of treating children. Upper-class children are expected to provide leadership in the school and are handled considerately and with concern for their educational welfare. Lower-class children are handled with more directness and with less regard for their feelings or their educational welfare (4).

The teacher's preference for upper-status children has a direct influence on academic achievement. Heintz (33) and Hollingshead (35) have noted that lower-status children must do better work than their higher-status classmates to obtain similar grades. The higher a child's position in the prestige structure, the better are his chances to receive high grades.

Few teachers are able to project themselves into the lives of lower-class children and understand their strivings for acceptance and recognition. The social distance between teacher and pupils is too great to encourage such identification. For this reason, teachers find it difficult to communicate with members of lower social groups. Communication depends upon insight into the patterns of living, the ideas and attitudes, feelings, values, and prejudices of people. Lacking these insights, the middle-class teacher is not equipped to handle the many problems encountered in the classroom.

The social distance between status groups is not a problem confined to education. Even psychiatrists have been frustrated by their inability to communicate with lower-class patients. A recent study (53) of 17 therapists working with lower-class people showed that these therapists frequently disliked their patients because they couldn't understand their values and disapproved of their lack of responsibility and discipline, their dependency, and their incapacity for facing and correcting emotional problems. The recommendation of this study was that if therapists are to help lower-class patients, they must first overcome their own social prejudices and learn more about the values and modes of living of these people. This appears to be precisely the task which confronts our teachers. This problem is more pressing because the teacher must go the entire way and can expect little coöperation from lower-class pupils and their families.

DISCIPLINE. Teachers and school authorities tend to administer discipline harshly and somewhat unfairly in dealing with lower-class children, and to be more lenient with children in the upper-status groups (35:331). This appears to be an outcome of basic class antagonisms. When a child from a culture which encourages aggression and rejects the middle-class values of the school faces a teacher who considers aggression a misdemeanor and lack of learning a vice, then one of two things must happen: Either the teacher must adjust his values and meet the children on their own level, or he must attempt to change the value standards of the children. Most teachers have taken the latter course. Out of a sense of responsibility to society and to their profession, they conscientiously attempt to raise the cultural level of the students. To do this, they increase the pressure to make the children conform to existing curriculums and to the pattern of behavior prescribed by the schools. This reinforces and intensifies the already existing hostility of lower-class children. Often the result is a persistent atmosphere of tension. This makes it necessary for teachers to devote a major part of their time to discipline, while teaching becomes a secondary activity.

Sometimes this conflict assumes rather serious proportions. In Becker's Chicago study (4), instances were found where first graders carried razor blades and jagged pieces of glass to school. Teachers reported being tripped and pushed on the stairs and having their cars damaged by pupils who wanted to get even for what was done to them in the classroom.

To counteract such behavior, teachers developed various methods of dealing with these children. They established their authority by assuming a "tough" attitude at the first meeting of the class and then easing off as conditions permitted. Physical force was commonly employed to control children. Where such methods of control were prohibited, means were found to circumvent this restriction. One teacher, describing a disciplinary device in use, explained how a child was stood up against a wall and chucked under the chin so that his head was knocked back against the wall. "It doesn't leave a mark on him," she explained, "but when he comes back in that room he can hardly see straight, he's so knocked out. It's really rough. There's a lot of little tricks like that you learn about" (4).

Upper-class children who are overindulged at home may also create disciplinary problems for the teacher. If they do not take orders at home, they are inclined to be independent at school. Accustomed to having maids and servants do things for them, they may be uncoöperative toward the teacher, who is often placed in the same category as a maid. Many teachers do not like to work in such schools, preferring the more submissive middle-class children with whom they have more in common (4).

ACADEMIC PROBLEMS.   Teachers normally derive a great deal of personal satisfaction from seeing their efforts reflected in the form of pupil achievement. They find their work rewarding when children are interested in school, work hard, and are trained at home to be coöperative and respectful.

The attitudes of lower-class children toward learning and their seeming lack of ability are disturbing and incomprehensible to teachers. Confronted with children who do not appreciate the value of education, who have no desire to improve themselves, and who are indifferent to school work, they feel frustrated and bewildered. They have difficulty motivating these children because prestige and social acceptance in their own slum groups are earned without much education (15:99). Teachers cannot feel successful with children who are unresponsive, and they often resort to dramatics in order to interest them. An illustration of this situation is the case of a high school science teacher who describes the techniques he must use in a lower-class school:

. . . if you had demonstrations in chemistry they had to be pretty flashy, lots of noise and smoke, before they'd get interested in it. . . . If you were having electricity or something like that you had to get the static electricity machine out and have them all stand around and hold hands so that they'd all get a little jolt. (4)

Not only is this situation discouraging to teachers, but the inferior education which lower-class children receive tends to perpetuate the inequalities existing among social classes (4). The atmosphere in lower-class schools may take the form of an academic "cold war," where teachers try to keep the students entertained until they reach the legal age for leaving school.

How Schools Affect the Class Structure

Education and economic position have become intimately linked in modern life. Very few men now start at the bottom of the ladder and move into top places in business and industry. There is a trend for the sons of executives to replace their fathers, and for top jobs to be filled by men educated at technical colleges and universities (68). The route up the economic and social ladder is from grade school to high school to college, rather than from janitor to supervisor to manager. Today the individual must prepare himself by education if he wishes to fill an important position.

Since the school conveyer belt drops lower-class children early on the educational route, their opportunities for social mobility are curtailed. It is only the unusually bright or exceptionally ambitious lower-class child who will go the whole route and rise above his class. Most lower-class youngsters are defeated before they start out in life. The jobs they can look forward to are those commonly filled by members of their class, the ones requiring little education and having low social status.

Thus, while the ideal of equal opportunity for all is a primary goal of American schools, what actually happens is that schools perpetuate the class system by feeding children into occupational pursuits characteristic of the social-class level from which they come (10). As things stand now, being born into a family of a particular social class will predetermine a child's academic success and the limits of his social mobility. Even among children of equal intellect and ability, it can be predicted that a large percentage of those from the lower classes will drop out before their sophomore year in high school, while almost all of the upper-class children will continue on through (68). This is one of the most serious challenges faced by our society, for inequality in educational opportunity means inequality in social and economic opportunity. These inequalities result in frustration, thwarted ambition, and the loss of much human potential.

SUMMARY

Social classes in American society consist of informal but distinct groups having different standards, values, and patterns of behavior.

We can expect members of the upper classes to be concerned about prestige, social graces, tradition, and the family. They have a secure position at the top of the social hierarchy, a position which is protected by tradition and wealth.

Middle-class persons have considerable anxiety over economic security and social status. They are striving, competitive persons who value progress, are concerned over appearances, and are willing to forego immediate pleasures in order to insure future rewards.

Lower-class persons are said to be aggressive, less concerned about moral and ethical behavior, improvident, and more anxious about satisfying their immediate organic needs than building toward future security than are members of the middle class.

Membership in a given social class often defines the social and economic opportunities of an individual. Lower-class status is synonomous with economic and social disadvantage, while privileges accrue to the upper social groups.

Education commonly is considered the leavening agent which equalizes the disparities existing in society so that all children have the same opportunity to enjoy the advantages of the American way of life. However, the schools are middle-class institutions designed to meet the needs of the "average" American, which turns out to mean the average middle-class American. As a consequence, public education does not alleviate the differences which exist in the opportunities for children. Children of the lower classes with fewer home advantages receive fewer services at school and profit less from education, while both school and community make a significant contribution to the lives of upper-status children.

If educators are to help lower-class people, they must first overcome their own social prejudices and learn more about the values and modes of living of these people, so that school life may be made a positive force for their betterment.

PROBLEMS AND PROJECTS

1. What social-class consciousness have you observed among kindergarten children? Third graders? Junior high school students?

2. What success do community youth organizations such as Boy Scouts or Girl Scouts have in slum areas?
3. Describe the characteristics and behavior of children who come from families of migrant workers.
4. Recall the development of your own awareness of social-class distinctions. When did they begin? What actual human contacts influenced your attitudes?
5. How might a lower-class social origin handicap or help a teacher?
6. Appraise the socioeconomic status of the children you teach, using the father's occupation as an index (see Remmers and Gage, p. 435). Combine these evaluations in class. To what degree do the composite results coincide with Davis' statement that 70 percent of all children in the elementary school are from the lower classes?
7. Examine textbooks at various educational levels. Do you agree that they emphasize middle-class life and give little consideration to life in the lower classes?
8. Cite some cases of lower-lower-class children who rose above their class position. What factors account for this? What problems do these children face?
9. Study some lower-class youngsters who are seniors in high school. What factors keep them in school?
10. Examine the conduct and values of middle-class white children and middle-class children of a racial minority group. What similarities and differences do you note? How does the behavior of these children compare with their lower-class counterparts?

SELECTED REFERENCES

1. Aberle, D. F., and Naegele, K. D., "Middle-Class Fathers' Occupational Role and Attitudes Toward Children," *American Journal of Orthopsychiatry* (April, 1952), 22:366–378.
2. Anderson, J. E., *The Psychology of Development and Personal Adjustment,* Henry Holt and Company, 1949.
3. Beck, R. H., Cook, W. W., and Kearney, N. C., *Curriculum in the Modern Elementary School,* Prentice-Hall, Inc., 1953.
4. Becker, H. S., "Social Class Variations in the Teacher-Pupil Relationship," *Journal of Educational Sociology* (April, 1952), 25:451–465.
5. Bossard, J. H. S., *The Sociology of Child Development,* rev. ed., Harper & Brothers, 1954.
6. California Department of Mental Hygiene, *Biennial Report for 1950–1952* (Sacramento), 1953.
7. Centers, R., "Social Class Identifications of American Youth," *Journal of Personality* (1950), 18:290–302.

8. Commission on Teacher Education, *Teachers for Our Times: A Statement of Purposes,* American Council on Education, 1944.

9. Cook, L. A., "An Experimental Sociographic Study of a Stratified Tenth Grade Class," *American Sociological Review* (1945), *10*:250–261.

10. Davie, J. S., "Social Class Factors and School Attendance," *The Harvard Educational Review* (Summer, 1953), *23*:175–185.

11. Davis, A., "Poor People Have Brains, Too," *The Phi Delta Kappan* (April, 1949), *30*:294–295.

12. Davis, A., *Social Class Influences on Learning,* Harvard University Press, 1949.

13. Davis, A., "Socio-Economic Influences on Learning," *The Phi Delta Kappan* (January, 1951), *32*:253–256.

14. Davis, A., "Socio-Economic Influences Upon Children's Learning," *Understanding the Child* (January, 1951), *20*:10–16.

15. Davis, A., "The Motivation of the Underprivileged Worker," in Whyte, W. F. (ed.), *Industry and Society,* McGraw-Hill Book Company, 1947.

16. Davis, A., and Dollard, J., *Children of Bondage,* American Council on Education, 1940.

17. Davis, A., Gardner, B. B., and Gardner, M., *Deep South,* University of Chicago Press, 1941.

18. Davis, A., and Havighurst, R. J., *Father of the Man,* Houghton Mifflin and Co., 1947.

19. Davis, A., and Havighurst, R. J., "Social Class and Color Differences in Child-Rearing," *American Sociological Review* (1946), *11*:698–710.

20. Dolger, L., and Ginandes, J., "Children's Attitudes Toward Discipline as Related to Socio-Economic Status," *Journal of Experimental Education* (1946), *15*:161–165.

21. Driggs, D. F., "Relationship Between Intelligence Test Items and Occupation of Parents of School Children," in *Research Relating To Children,* Bulletin II, Supplement 2, U.S. Children's Bureau, 1954, p. 23.

22. Ericson, M. C., "Child-Rearing and Social Status," *American Journal of Sociology* (November, 1946), *52*:190–192.

23. Fingarette, H., "Backgrounds of American Values," *California Journal of Elementary Education* (February, 1955), *23*:155–172.

24. Freedman, L. Z., and Hollingshead, A. B., "Neurosis and Social Class," *American Journal of Psychiatry* (March, 1957), *113*:769–775.

25. Galler, E. H., "Influence of Social Class on Children's Choices of Occupations," *The Elementary School Journal* (April, 1951), *51*:439–445.

26. Gallup, G. H., and Rae, S. F., *The Pulse of Democracy: The Public Opinion Poll and How it Works,* Simon and Schuster, 1940.

27. Ginzberg, E., "Sex and Class Behavior," in D. P. Geddes, and E. Curie (eds.), *About the Kinsey Report,* New American Library of World Literature, 1948, pp. 131–145.
28. Green, A. W., "The Middle Class Male Child and Neurosis," *American Sociological Review* (February, 1946), *11*:31–41.
29. Hand, H. C., *Principal Findings of the 1947–48 Basic Studies of the Illinois Secondary School Curriculum Program,* Superintendent of Instruction (Springfield), 1949.
30. Harsh, C. M., and Schrickel, H. G., *Personality: Development and Assessment,* Ronald Press, 1950.
31. Havighurst, R. J., and Taba, H., *Adolescent Character and Personality,* John Wiley and Sons, 1949.
32. Heintz, E., "Adjustment Problems of Class Status," *The Phi Delta Kappan* (April, 1949), *30*:290–293.
33. Heintz, E., "His Father is Only the Janitor," *The Phi Delta Kappan* (April, 1954), *35*:265–270.
34. Hieronymus, A. N., "A Study of Social Class Motivation: Relationships Between Anxiety for Education and Certain Socio-Economic and Intellectual Variables," *The Journal of Educational Psychology* (April, 1951), *42*:193–206.
35. Hollingshead, A. B., *Elmtown's Youth,* John Wiley and Sons, 1949.
36. Hollingshead, A. B., and Redlich, F. C., "Schizophrenia and Social Structure," *American Journal of Psychiatry* (March, 1954), *110*: 695–701.
37. Honigmann, J. J., *Culture and Personality,* Harper & Brothers, 1954.
38. Janke, L. L., and Havighurst, R. J., "Relations Between Ability and Social Status in a Midwestern Community," *Journal of Educational Psychology* (1945), *36*:499–509.
39. Kardiner, A., and Ovesey, L., *The Mark of Oppression,* W. W. Norton and Co., 1951.
40. Klatskin, E. H., "Shifts in Child Care Practices in Three Social Classes Under an Infant Care Program of Flexible Methodology," *American Journal of Orthopsychiatry* (April, 1952), *22*:52–61.
41. Kluckhohn, C., *Mirror for Man,* Whittlesey House, 1949.
42. Krugman, M., "The Psychocultural Approach in the Three Schools Project, Bronx," *American Journal of Orthopsychiatry* (April, 1953), *23*:369–390.
43. Lindgren, H. C., *The Psychology of Personal and Social Adjustment,* American Book Company, 1953.
44. Loeb, M. B., "Implications of Status Differentiation For Personal and Social Development," *The Harvard Educational Review* (Summer, 1953), *23*:168–174.

45. Maas, H. S., "Some Social Class Differences in the Family System and Group Relations of Pre- and Early Adolescents," *Child Development* (1951), 22:145–152.

46. Maccoby, E. E., Gibbs, P. K., and others, "Methods of Child-Rearing in Two Social Classes," in W. E. Martin, and C. B. Stendler, (eds.), *Readings in Child Development,* Harcourt, Brace and Co., 1954.

47. Mayer, K., "The Theory of Social Classes," *The Harvard Educational Review* (Summer, 1953), 23:149–167.

48. Murray, W. I., "The Concept of Social Class and Its Implications For Teachers," *The Journal of Negro Education* (1951), 20:16–21.

49. Neugarten, B. L., "Social Class Friendship Among School Children," *American Journal of Sociology* (1946), 51:305–313.

50. Opler, M. K., "Cultural Values and Attitudes on Child Care," *Children* (March–April, 1955), 2:45–50.

51. Pfautz, H. W., and Duncan, O. D., "A Critical Evaluation of Warner's Work in Community Stratification," *American Sociological Review* (1950), 15:205–215.

52. Phillips, E. L., "Intellectual and Personality Factors Associated With Social Class Attitudes Among Junior High School Children," *Journal of Genetic Psychology* (1950), 77:61–72.

53. Redlich, F. C., Hollingshead, A. B., and Bellis, E., "Social Class Differences in Attitudes Toward Psychiatry," *Psychosomatic Medicine* (January–February, 1955), 17:60–70.

54. Remmers, H. H., and Gage, N. L., *Educational Measurement and Evaluation,* rev. ed., Harper & Brothers, 1955.

55. Rennie, T. A. C., *et al.,* "Urban Life and Mental Health," *American Journal of Psychiatry* (March, 1957), 113:831–837.

56. Segel, D., "Intellectual Abilities in the Adolescent Period," United States Office of Education, *Bulletin 1948,* no. 2, part 2, 1948.

57. Smitter, F., *Experiences, Interests and Needs of Eighth-Grade Farm Children in California,* Bulletin of the California State Department of Education (Sacramento), vol. XX, no. 5, July, 1951.

58. Springer, N. N., "Influence of General Social Status on Emotional Stability of Children," *Journal of Genetic Psychology* (December, 1938), 53:321–328.

59. Stendler, C. B., *Children of Brasstown,* University of Illinois Bulletin No. 59, April, 1949.

60. The Committee on the Family of the Group for the Advancement of Psychiatry, *Integration and Conflict in Family Behavior,* Report No. 27 (Topeka, Kansas), August, 1954.

61. Volberding, E., "Out-of-School Living of Eleven-Year-Old Boys and

Girls from Differing Socioeconomic Groups," *The Elementary School Journal* (February, 1949), 49:348–353.

62. Warner, W. L., "A Methodological Note," in St. C. Drake, and H. R. Cayton, *Black Metropolis,* Harcourt, Brace and Co., 1945, pp. 772–773.

63. Warner, W. L., *et al., Democracy in Jonesville,* Harper & Brothers, 1949.

64. Warner, W. L., Havighurst, R. J., and Loeb, M. B., *Who Shall Be Educated?* Harper & Brothers, 1944.

65. Warner, W. L., and Lunt, P. S., *The Social Life of a Modern Community,* vol. I. "Yankee City Series," Yale University Press, 1941.

66. Warner, W. L., and Lunt, P. S., *The Status System of a Modern Community,* vol. II, "Yankee City Series," Yale University Press, 1942.

67. Warner, W. L., Meeker, M., and Eells, K. E., *Social Class in America,* Science Research Associates, 1949.

68. Warner, W. L., Meeker, M., and Eells, K. E., "Social Status in Education," *The Phi Delta Kappan* (December, 1948), 30:113–119.

69. Willey, R. D., *Guidance in Elementary Education,* Harper & Brothers, 1952.

70. Woolworth, W. G., "A Basis for Character Education—A Study of the Problem by Teachers and Parents in a School District," *California Journal of Elementary Education* (February, 1954), 22:148–164.

PART III

TOWARD A BETTER UNDERSTANDING OF
CHILD BEHAVIOR

Each child fashions his own private world as he grows out of the family into the broad social environment. His external appearance and overt behavior may reflect this inner world, or disguise it. The extent to which schools may influence the growth of children depends, in a large measure, upon the ability of teachers to interpret the meanings of behavior and to understand the underlying forces which motivate it.

The three chapters which follow are designed to enhance the teacher's insight into the dynamics of growth. Here we discuss the needs of children, the pattern of growth, and some of the behavior deviations and adjustment problems which may be encountered in the classroom. As educators become aware of the factors which shape the personalities of children they will comprehend more clearly what might be done to help them reach a satisfactory state of maturity.

CHAPTER 9

Dynamic Forces in Human Behavior

PRECEDING chapters have emphasized some of the major environmental forces which may influence the personality development of children. To understand more fully the nature of human behavior, we must look beyond overt action into the inner life of the child where the mainsprings of behavior lie. Here, below the level of awareness, many psychological forces motivate behavior quite independent of the individual's conscious desires.

In this chapter we shall examine some of the basic psychological processes at work within the individual. An understanding of these processes will make it possible to interpret child behavior in terms of fundamental forces rather than superficial or symptomatic reactions.

THE BASIC HUMAN NEEDS

Behavior may be viewed as arising from certain urges, desires, wishes, or drives which are collectively called needs. These needs create a tension or disequilibrium within the individual, and to relieve this tension he strives for certain goals or satisfactions. When these ends are attained, the stress is removed and the individual is in harmony with himself and his environment (6).

Psychologists have identified two groups of needs which together provide the major motivating forces for human behavior. They have been called (1) the biological needs, which every individual must satisfy to preserve his organic integrity; and (2) the psychosocial needs, which are vital to the person's psychological and social well-being. These needs are present in everyone and generally are regarded as the primary internal determinants of adjustment and mental health (*31*:186).

The Biological Needs

Because we are living organisms, there are certain basic needs which all people must satisfy. These are primarily physiological in nature, inherited as part of our organic structure, and vital to the maintenance of life and physical well-being.

When normal organic functions are impeded, distressing tensions arise which motivate the individual toward relieving these tensions. The action undertaken to restore physiological equilibrium has been termed *homeostasis*. It is an imperative, and often an automatic process, set in motion whenever organic equilibrium is disturbed (*23*).

The operation of homeostasis is familiar to all who have experienced deprivation of essential organic elements such as food, air, or water. Less familiar, but equally important, is the expression of disturbed organic functioning through psychological rather than physical symptoms. For instance, Eisenberg (*8*) describes the case of a 5-year-old girl who was referred to a guidance clinic for treatment of temper tantrums and general irritability. Laboratory studies revealed the girl to have a hemoglobin concentration 30 percent below normal. This child needed a blood transfusion rather than treatment for her behavior problems.

Similar misinterpretations of behavior symptoms may occur when parents or teachers are not aware of the physical processes going on within a child, and the necessity for satisfying his organic needs.

The Psychosocial Needs

Because we live among people, there are certain social and psychological experiences which we must have in order to attain emotional security. These experiences are learned during the process of growing up in a social environment. They begin in infancy with the pleasurable feelings derived from being cared for by other people. The child seeks to have these feelings repeated until the need for them becomes incorporated into his personality structure (*10, 19*).

Psychologists are not agreed on how many psychosocial needs a child acquires as he grows, or which are vital to his emotional well-being. It is generally thought that there are three groups of psychosocial needs: (1) the need for interpersonal satisfactions, (2) the need for group status, and (3) the need for self-development (*19*).

THE NEED FOR INTERPERSONAL SATISFACTIONS. All children seek love and affection from those who are important to them. To be loved and to have willing recipients for his love makes a child feel warm and wanted. It gives him an inner strength and a feeling of being important. These are the feelings which make a youngster secure and enable him to face life's problems and hardships.

A child's affectional needs are at first all one-sided. He receives, but has nothing to give. As he grows older, a child must have someone who will accept his love. Through giving his love to someone who wants it, he enhances his security and develops an outgoing attitude which will help him build wholesome relationships with other people. Thorpe (39:339) has referred to this as the "mutuality need"—the need to give as well as to receive. It has been noted that children who have no one to receive their love may lavish affection upon a bird, an animal, or a fantasy figure, so strong is this need to share one's emotions with others (31:187).

THE NEED FOR GROUP STATUS. Growing out of the need for love and affection is the need to belong to somebody. At first it is a need to belong to one's parents, then the family, then a gang, team, school, or larger social group. Eventually this search for belongingness leads the individual back to the family as a parent.

Status in a group gives a child assurance that he is an acceptable being. He gains personal strength from being wanted by others, from identifying with others, and from being a part of something larger than himself. Without the companionship of other people he becomes lonely, loses self-confidence, and begins to question his own adequacy.

Even the normal functioning of the human brain is affected by social interaction. Experiments with male college students who were isolated in a cubicle and cut off from social and perceptual stimulation revealed that when kept alone long enough, and when levels of physical and human stimulation are low enough, normal individuals will experience intellectual deterioration, hallucinations, and impairment of problem-solving abilities and the power of concentration (4).

THE NEED FOR SELF-DEVELOPMENT. At each stage of life, as the growing organism gains awareness of his potentialities and capacities, there arises a compelling urge to test and use these powers. A child pursues self-initiated and self-directed activities because to do things for himself gives him a sense of personal worth. Yet, with all his insistence on self-directed activity, he wants others to note what he is accomplishing. He needs to be independent and self-sufficient, but he also needs the approval of other people if he is to achieve success in the struggle to establish his own adequacy.

Human Needs and Mental Health

Although we have separated the biological from the psychosocial needs for the sake of discussion, the child, himself, cannot be so fragmentized. Mind, body, and emotions are inextricably related. The satisfaction of biological needs produces a healthy organism which is physically capable of adjusting to the environment, while satisfaction of psychosocial needs yields the emotional security so essential to a child's well-being. Both physical health and emotional security are manifested in the child's behavior, appearance, and the energy with which he meets the demands of life. This behavior is integrated into his personality and is reflected in mental health, as shown diagramatically in Figure 5.

Not all of a child's needs can be fully satisfied at a given time. But if most of his requirements are met at home and at school, particularly at the time when certain needs become most pressing, he has a good chance of achieving mental health and becoming a stable, well-adjusted person.

PSYCHODYNAMIC INTERPRETATIONS OF BEHAVIOR

Many psychiatrists and psychoanalysts consider the *needs concept* too superficial an explanation of why people act as they do. As a result of clinical experiences they have postulated a psychodynamic interpretation of behavior based upon the operation of an *inner self,* of which the mind is the major aspect (*11,* 13, 12, 7). The word *mind* is not synonomous with brain, but represents the mental processes, including thinking, reasoning, memory, volition, and other mental activities. These mental processes occur on three levels of awareness: the conscious, the subconscious, and the unconscious.

Levels of Mental Activity

The mind has been described as an iceberg. About seven-eighths of its content is submerged below the surface of awareness, while only a minor portion of mental activity is ours to command.

THE CONSCIOUS MIND.   The conscious mind is the seat of our aware-ness. It is here that we do our thinking, remember past events, and plan future activities. The individual normally controls what goes on in his

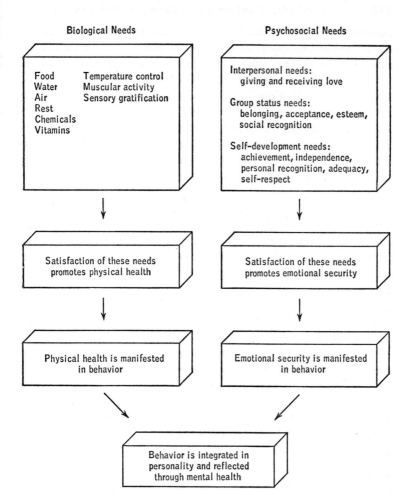

FIGURE 5. The Integration of Biological and Psychosocial Needs. (Adapted from L. Kaplan and D. Baron, *Mental Hygiene and Life,* Harper & Brothers, 1952, p. 37.)

conscious mind, but in certain illnesses and during sleep these controls are relaxed and he experiences dreams, hallucinations, and various sensations or perceptions which seemingly come and go as they wish.

THE UNCONSCIOUS MIND. In the great unconscious mind lies a mass of thoughts, feelings, memories, desires, and experiences which we have either forgotten or never knew. The unconscious serves as a reservoir for inherited forces and instincts, as well as for past experiences. Nothing which is once experienced is ever lost. The past is stored in the unconscious, and there it remains throughout life. Each experience, together with the emotions which it originally engendered, is tucked away in the unconscious where it may influence us to say things we do not mean to say, do things which we later regret, or feel things which shame us.

Most of the time the content of our unconscious mind is unknown to us. On occasion, while under the influence of hypnotism, alcohol, or drugs, a person will reveal facts which were not known to him in his normal state. But even under these extreme conditions only an infinitesimal part of the unconscious mental content can be revealed.

THE SUBCONSCIOUS MIND. Somewhere between the indefinite end zone of the conscious mind and the darkness of the unconscious is a twilight area called the subconscious or preconscious mind. In it are stored forgotten facts and experiences which under proper conditions may be returned to awareness. At one end, the subconscious merges into the unconscious, causing things we should remember to become irretrievably lost. At the other end, the subconscious is linked with the conscious mind, and by association or concentration we can bring back experiences and use them.

Psychic Forces in Mental Life

Within the three levels of the mind exist psychic forces or energies called the id, the ego, and the superego. The id energies are limited entirely to the region of the unconscious. The ego functions primarily on a conscious level, although part of it extends down into the subconscious and the unconscious. The superego is distributed over all three levels of the mind but performs most of its functions on the conscious and subconscious levels. These spatial relationships are illustrated in Figure 6.

THE ID. Created with the unconscious mind, and permanently located there, is a seething mass of energy called the id. What little is known of this aspect of personality has been learned through dream analysis, or through interpretations of mental activity made when a person is under the influence of drugs which relax the centers of conscious control.

The id is thought to be the repository of our sex drives, mastery drives, pleasure drives, aggressive drives, and other instinctual drives which strive for expression. These are the base, primitive, uncivilized, and uninhibited aspects of man. In every way possible these drives seek gratification in accordance with what has been called the *pleasure principle*. This principle relates to behavior which provides for the pleasurable satisfaction of id drives, with little concern for the consequences.

The id does not change as we grow older, although its influence is not so evident in the adult as it is in the infant or young child. The hates, passions, destructiveness, and cruelties of adults bear testimony that the id continues to operate throughout life. Not being in contact with reality, the id knows of no good or evil, no morality or self-control. It speaks no words but works entirely through feelings. Therefore, as long as there is life the id will influence feelings and behavior.

THE EGO. One can well imagine the type of world this would be if the id maintained complete control over our behavior. Fortunately, the id energies are gradually brought under control through the process of socialization. The infant is at first permitted free id expression because of his physical helplessness. Gradually he learns that there are things he may do and things he must not do. These restrictions force the child to modify his instinctual, pleasure-seeking activities because he is dependent upon the love and protection of the people who impose them.

As the child grows he consciously begins to take over some of these controls. Out of repeated experience a part of the id is built up as a psychological wall between the demands of reality and the internal primitive energies. This psychological wall is the self or the ego. When the ego emerges, the child becomes aware of himself as a separate entity. He distinguishes between his internal demands and the outside world through which these demands may be satisfied.

This differentiation between self and non-self begins during the preverbal stages of infancy. With the development of language, ego formation takes a tremendous spurt and by 2½ years its development has reached the point of self-assertion, commonly reflected by a stage of negativism (*1, 33*).

Once it has been created, the ego undertakes the function of interpreting reality to the id so that the latter in its blind struggle for expression will not lead the individual into pain or destruction. In the young child the ego is small and can exercise only a very weak control over the id. As the child grows, the ego develops and becomes capable of sensing external situations and of using thought and reason to create conditions whereby the id may express itself safely. In this way the ego

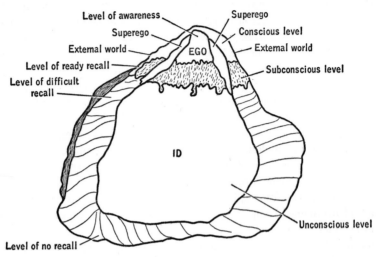

FIGURE 6. Schematic Representation of Psychic Forces in the Levels of the Mind. (Adapted from L. Kaplan and D. Baron, *Mental Hygiene and Life,* Harper & Brothers, 1952, p. 123.)

serves his well-being by protecting him from the destruction which might be caused by the undisciplined id.

Because the ego is in contact with reality and makes the id abide by the demands of society, it is said to function in accordance with the *reality principle.* The reality principle recognizes the necessity for adapting to environmental forces, and while it may deny us immediate satisfaction, in the long run it promises greater success and security. The work of the ego is to substitute the reality principle for the pleasure principle as a guide to behavior, so that life does not become a series of painful frustrations and rebuffs.

As this process goes on, the ego becomes that aspect of mental functioning which organizes and controls perceptions, protects us against unreasonable pleasure-seeking tendencies, and tests reality. Its development is influenced by environmental forces and the strength of id drives.

The ego will be strong if its genetic equipment is good, if environmental forces aid in its development, and if id drives are not overpowering (2).

THE SUPEREGO. The constant making of decisions and the struggle of putting the id energies to use place a great strain on the ego. To aid in the control of id energies, a third psychic force appears on the mental scene just when the ego is finding its duties most burdensome. This is the superego which takes over the function of discriminating between right and wrong behavior and provides the ego with an interpretation of reality. The ego and superego working together release the id energies in small doses, thus pacifying the id while at the same time abiding by the social and moral laws which govern social behavior.

There are two aspects to the superego: the conscience and the ego-ideal. The conscience is the prohibitive and punitive aspects of mental life which distinguish right from wrong behavior. The ego-ideal establishes goals or standards toward which the ego is compelled to strive.

Formation of conscience. First in genetic emergence is that part of the superego which consists of internalized symbols of parental authority. In the beginning there are no moral overtones to these symbols, for young children conform to the rules of their parents because they have to, not because they feel any moral compulsion to be good, generous, or honest. After many months of coercion and persuasion, of receiving rewards for good behavior and punishment for bad behavior, the child begins to develop habits of acting in the way adults want him to. By the time he reaches the third or fourth year of life, he has absorbed so many parental prohibitions and moral concepts that part of the ego becomes differentiated as the conscience. Two or three years later this conscience is fully formed and firmly established. Although later contact with teachers, ministers, other adults, children, and ideas may alter the conscience somewhat, its nucleus is defined in the preschool period (26).

The ego-ideal. In addition to its punitive functions, the superego is responsible for establishing goals or standards by which the ego measures itself and toward which it seeks to grow. This goal-oriented aspect of the superego is the ego-ideal which controls the ego, not by fear of consequences as does the conscience but by setting up a self-image which the ego strives to attain.

The ego-ideal emerges gradually out of a series of identifications. Parents are usually the first ideal incorporated into the superego. Later this image is influenced by other persons, and by ideals derived from movies, comics, radio, television, books, and stories. These images become merged into the ego-ideal, and children consciously or unconsciously seek to mold their lives in accordance with its pattern.

INFLUENCE OF PSYCHODYNAMIC FORCES ON PERSONALITY FORMATION

The genetic development of the ego is an extremely important process in personality formation. If the ego is sufficiently dominant, it will be able to perform its three primary functions of regulating the release of id energies, making suitable compromises with the superego, and recognizing the demands of the external world. When the ego is inadequately developed, it may succumb to the influence of the id or superego, causing personality changes which sometimes proceed to the point where the individual feels depersonalized, or lacking a self.

Factors Affecting Ego Development

A home atmosphere where security, affection, and approval are wisely tempered with respect, control, and encouragement is the matrix out of which strong egos emerge. The growing child must be assured of parental love, but to develop an adequate *self* concept he must also be permitted to think for himself and allowed to grow up slowly without undue pressure (*14*).

When the child enters school he has an immature self concept which reflects the quality of his early home experiences. In school this self concept may be expanded, changed, or undermined, depending upon the success and acceptance he encounters in his academic and social relationships (*21*). All children strive to enhance their egos; they seek feelings of personal worth and want to be appreciated and made to feel important. If they are provided with opportunities for experiencing such feelings in school, ego development will proceed in wholesome, constructive ways. If they are denied these opportunities, subjected to too much failure, isolated by other children, or rejected by the teacher, they may seek to counteract the resulting feelings of inadequacy through a-social forms of ego-enhancing behavior. These circumstances are often found to underlie the misconduct problems commonly encountered among school children.

Reformation of the Ego in Adolescence

During the prepuberty years the child manages to establish a rather stable self concept based on childhood values and relationships. With the onset of puberty these values and relationships change. The youngster's body undergoes a major transformation, leaving him with new sensitivities toward his physical appearance and physiological functions. These bodily changes, together with the altered social relationships brought on by adolescence, cast the ego loose from its childhood moorings. The self concept must be reëstablished in terms of the child's new body image and the changes which occur in his economic role, social status, and personal relationships. For many months, and sometimes years, his ego will be unstable and insecure as he searches for new attachments, new competencies, and new channels through which his sense of adequacy can be restored. Gradually, as the adolescent reëstablishes himself in terms of these new perceptions and relationships, the ego emerges in its mature form (*21, 33*).

Thus the process of ego formation is never quite finished. At all stages of life the individual seeks experiences which provide support for his ego and make him feel adequate and approved. Parents and teachers must recognize this tendency among children and guide their ego-building experiences while guarding against making the child overly self-centered or egocentric.

The Superego in Personality Formation

Psychiatrists generally agree that the superego is fully formed by about the fifth year of life. Therefore the family plays an extremely important role in the formation of the superego. As was mentioned previously, the superego is compounded out of pressures exerted on the child to act in a desired manner. These pressures are soon forgotten, but the habit patterns, feelings, and attitudes they engendered remain with the person throughout life.

The type of superego a child will develop depends upon how much pressure is imposed upon him. If the controls are imposed too rapidly, or if they are too severe, the superego may become so strong that it dominates mental life. When this occurs in early childhood, an infantile neurosis may result from the ego's inability to cope with stringent moral pressures (*29*). Sometimes this neurosis takes the form of specific phobias or obsessions associated with the lessons which parents overemphasized. This was observed to happen in a family where Mary, an only child, was carefully supervised by her highly moralistic, conscientious parents. From early childhood great emphasis was placed on keeping clean. Now she is 15 years old; Mary never goes to picnics or eats out because of insects. She washes her hands so frequently that she uses two cakes of soap each day. She carries tissues in her pockets which she uses to open doors and turn on lights. Cleanliness has become such a ritual with her that she is ridiculed by other children.

Children with such rigid superegos tend to become perfectionists, or hard-working, severely conscientious individuals who must have everything just so. They have little fun in life and cannot tolerate others whose standards of conduct are less severe.

Parents can help a child develop a normal, wholesome superego by regulating the demands they make upon him, and by accompanying these demands with ample love and affection. The child who does what his parents want him to do because he loves them and wants to please them develops a more effective superego than the child who is coerced by threats and punishment. Wanting to do the right thing is the essence of superego formation. When love is lacking in the parent-child relationship, a youngster may learn to control his behavior because of fear of punishment, but never develops internal controls which will function when such threats are absent. These circumstances result in an undeveloped superego such as is found among delinquents and psychopaths.

The school as well as the home plays an important part in superego development. Although the superego is said to be fully formed during the preschool years, the child's morals and values can be changed by experiences with age-mates and teachers. The values of the group, and the standards established by teachers affect a child's psychological functioning in significant ways. While these conditions cannot build a superego in cases where parents have not done their work effectively, they can reinforce a child's inner controls, or help modify the behavior of youngsters who are overly inhibited.

Personality and the Id

Although the id itself is unconscious and unalterable, much can be done to help the child control its expression. The young child with his growing ego and immature superego cannot suppress his id energies. If he is forced to do so, they may accumulate until they explode into destructive behavior. Every parent is familiar with the "growing days" so common in childhood. These are the days when the child's inner controls seem not to function and he becomes particularly aggressive, irritable, difficult to handle, and impossible to please. This behavior may be the result of accumulated id energies which should have been released regularly in small doses, but which have piled up and assumed temporary control over the individual. It implies that children need ample opportunity to satisfy their pleasure drives and release energy through active play.

If the child is not constantly restrained, if his innocent pleasures are not condemned as sinful, and if he is given an opportunity to indulge his desires and release his aggressive energies, the id will follow a normal pattern of domestication. Sexual drives will mature into love, sadism may become a desire to build and construct rather than destroy, aggression is converted into wholesome competition, and the child will grow up with properly balanced internal controls.

Psychodynamics and Growth

No matter how well parents and teachers do their jobs, each individual carries into adulthood some vestiges of his childhood struggles between gaining satisfaction and conforming to social pressures. Each person has his own peculiar pattern of childhood anxieties left over from his earlier psychological struggles; sensitivities which he has not been able to outgrow and which flare up from time to time.

Growth is a continuous process of struggling with internal psychic forces and trying to bring them into harmony with social demands. In the course of these struggles the ego finds certain forms of reaction more effective than others in reducing the pressures brought to bear upon it. Each individual develops his own behavior patterns in terms of what makes him feel more comfortable. He uses these repeatedly until they become automatic habit systems.

Many people develop habits of resolving their anxieties by enhancing their egos. They seek situations and companions which bolster their self-esteem, and avoid situations which make them feel insignificant or unimportant. Other people attempt to modify their superegos through various psychological mechanisms which take the sting out of the conscience so that life is more bearable. Still others get so accustomed to indulging the id that they find it impossible to exercise much self-control and are unable to conform to social requirements.

Each of us is a different person because of his psychic energies and the manner in which he reacts to them. What the individual does and what he will become depends not entirely on his own will and desires but upon the resultant of all internal and external forces which act upon him. How individuals will behave and the personality patterns they develop are dependent upon the relative influence of these internal and external forces.

FRUSTRATION AND EMOTION IN HUMAN BEHAVIOR

Whether we interpret behavior from the viewpoint of needs and their satisfaction, or in terms of psychodynamic theories, it is evident that many of the child's reactions are motivated by inner forces of which he is unaware. In reacting to these inner forces and attempting to reconcile them with environmental conditions, he inevitably encounters obstacles both within himself and in the social world. These obstacles are the frustrations of life which no child can avoid, and to which each must adapt in some way for they threaten his ego integrity and intensify his emotional reactions.

Emotional Correlates of Frustration

When an individual driven by compelling inner forces encounters frustration or failure, he is likely to experience emotional reactions. These may be of the intense, expressive variety, known as hyperemotional states, which prepare the individual for fight or flight, or they may be repressed, restricted reactions, termed hypoemotional states, through which an individual withdraws from frustration (30, 42).

HYPEREMOTIONAL STATES.   Externally, hyperemotionalism is evidenced by physical tension, changes in facial expression and bodily posture, heightened color, and other symptoms which indicate that extensive changes are going on within the individual. Internally, the adrenal glands pour increased secretions into the blood stream causing the heart to beat more rapidly, the liver releases more sugar, metabolism is increased, and great quantities of energy are made available for muscular activity. Also, there is an increased supply of blood to the musculature and brain, blood pressure increases, more air is admitted to the lungs, and the kidneys store up water and minerals.

The function of this internal upheaval is to prepare the body for emergency physical activity. There is nothing the individual can do about these internal changes because they are under the control of the parasympathetic division of the autonomic nervous system which is beyond voluntary regulation. Once the physiological processes accompanying hyperemotionality are started, they must run their course and some way must be found to release the excess energy produced. If expression of this emotional energy is prohibited, the internal reactions which result may have more serious consequences than the overt behavior. Constipation, ulcers, hypertension, and numerous other psychosomatic disorders, as well as general anxiety, are said to result from this internalization of emotional energy (15).

HYPOEMOTIONAL STATES. In hypoemotional states such as grief, depression, gloom, sorrow, or sadness, the person, in effect, withdraws from life. His physiological processes slow down, there is a decrease of metabolism, and the individual feels apathetic and lethargic both physically and mentally. Externally, this condition may be reflected in a withdrawn, vacant, slack look; there may be a lack of timbre and inflection in the voice, and often facial pallor and a general feeling of malaise.

Hypoemotional or depressive states are among the least desirable of the emotions from a mental health viewpoint because they consume a great deal of the individual's emotional energies and leave him with little energy to direct toward solving his problems. If this becomes a chronic condition, the person may develop an overly inhibited, restricted personality, which borders closely on the abnormal (41).

THE LIBIDO. The psychoanalytic concept of libido is useful in explaining the dynamics of this type of emotional restriction. The libido is the supply of psychic energy which each person has at his disposal. The source of this energy is the id. Each of us has just so much libido to power our life activities. If an extra amount of energy is called upon to support some particular aspect of our behavior, there is correspondingly less for other activities.

This process may be likened to that of an electrical circuit represented in Figure 7. The electric motor represents the id or source of energy supply which produces a current (libido) to operate the various appliances attached to the circuit. If an inordinate amount of power is drawn off by any one appliance, the functioning of the others will be impaired. In like fashion, when excessive energy must be diverted from the human energy system, the supply available for other purposes is decreased.

The ego has first call upon our human energies. This is represented in Figure 7 by the electric iron which may be adjusted to use varying amounts of power. When full power is required to operate the iron, little is left for the light, radio, or other appliances. Such is the case when the ego is threatened, when frustration is intense or protracted, or whenever the person is made to feel inferior or inadequate. In such events, great stores of libidinal energy are employed to bolster the ego. Energy which would ordinarily be directed outward in the activities of living are turned back upon the self or directed toward those activities which minister most to ego needs.

Hence, any child or adult who encounters more frustration than he can tolerate may devote his energies to enhancing his ego through fanciful successes, or expend most of his energies in achieving success in a limited area while his basic problems remain unsolved. These internally directed energies leave the person with relatively little force to direct toward socially useful, productive, happy living.

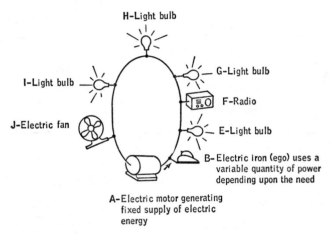

FIGURE 7.   A Schematic Likeness of the Human Energy System. An electric motor (A) generates power which operates a variety of appliances attached to the circuit. The iron (B) uses a varied quantity of power depending upon the need. When the power used to operate the iron is increased, the supply of power available to operate the other appliances is limited. When this happens the lights are dimmed, the radio volume is reduced, and the power supply for the fan is reduced. The motor is analogous to the Id, the energy supply to Libido and the appliances to the thwarting incurred in the process of living. (Adapted from L. Kaplan and D. Baron, *Mental Hygiene and Life,* Harper & Brothers, 1952, p. 231.)

ROLE OF FRUSTRATION IN ADJUSTMENT.   This discussion of the emotional concomitants of frustration does not imply that all frustration should be avoided, or that frustration has no useful function in human living. It is true that frustration interferes with the normal flow of emotional energy and places the individual under stress. But sometimes this stress may stimulate personality development and encourage the individual to put forth his best efforts. We see this taking place when individuals match their strength, wits, or skill with others in competitive activities. Many persons seek out stress situations because they wish to test themselves and because their self-sufficiency and self-confidence are increased when they master difficult situations.

It is also necessary to encounter frustrations to learn how to handle failure and disappointment. No one can realize all his desires or satisfy all his needs. We must all develop a degree of frustration tolerance which will enable us to encounter frustrating experiences without becoming demoralized. These experiences may, in fact, have considerable value if they teach an individual to accept his own limitations and to establish realistic goals for himself. Frustrating experiences may also increase an individual's personal effectiveness by encouraging him to develop initiative and resourcefulness in attacking his problems.

Because we all encounter many obstacles in life, some people feel that children should be provided with frustrating experiences early and consistently so that they may develop frustration tolerance. This attitude is based on the premise that a few small hurts in childhood will teach the individual to tolerate greater hurts later in life. However, this viewpoint receives little support from scientific evidence. Experimental studies have shown that the majority of children respond aggressively and destructively when faced with consistent frustration (*34*). Frustration, as we have shown, is linked with the emotions, and if children are introduced to stress before they have the capacity to handle their emotions, the resulting behavior may be disruptive rather than adaptive. Children can learn frustration tolerance only when they have developed sufficient emotional security, self-confidence, and emotional control. If they are exposed to too much stress before reaching this stage of development, they may never learn to face or respond adequately to frustration (*27*).

Experience with stress may be a positive force in developing mental health if the individual is sufficiently secure and if his ego is strong enough to accept frustration as a challenge. The person who is exposed to stress situations which threaten his security usually responds by adopting ego-protective devices to preserve his sense of self-integrity. These devices may facilitate his adjustment, or they may lead to serious personality problems, depending upon the circumstances under which they are used.

Techniques of Ego Defense

No one learns to accept completely and gracefully all the frustrations and inconveniences imposed by society. No matter how adequate a person may be, his ego can be threatened by stresses or upheavals emanating from the external environment or from his own psychological functioning (*33*). When this occurs, the individual resorts to protective devices which will relieve him of the sense of threat and provide means through which he may maintain his self-esteem (*35*).

These ego-protective devices, commonly called adjustment mechanisms, are involuntary, tension-reducing techniques which provide convenient ways for a person to extricate himself from tensional situations. They may or may not enable the individual to cope with his problems or conflicts. Their primary purpose is to relieve anxiety and defend the ego from threat (*19, 38*). Ego-protective devices may be classified in terms of how they serve the individual's quest for security. For discussion purposes we shall group them as (1) mechanisms of deception, (2) mechanisms of substitution, and (3) mechanisms of avoidance.

MECHANISMS OF DECEPTION. A person may protect his ego by excluding tension-producing stimuli from his center of awareness, or by reconstructing his attitudes and feelings so that he senses no threat to himself. This may be accomplished through the following devices:

Rationalization: Providing plausible reasons for behavior when the actual reasons are too painful to acknowledge.

Projection: Transferring the responsibility for an act or thought from oneself to an outside agency or to other persons.

Displacement: A special form of projection where a response or reaction is shifted from its original object to another which is less dangerous.

Repression: An unconscious process wherein shameful thoughts, guilt-laden memories, or distasteful tasks are removed from awareness or forced below the level of consciousness.

Suppression: The deliberate, conscious control of one's hazardous and undesirable thoughts or impulses so that they are removed from awareness.

ADJUSTIVE VALUE OF MECHANISMS OF DECEPTION. Mechanisms of deception protect the ego by removing the feeling of threat. They do not remove the threat itself but enable a person to dodge the reality of a menacing situation. Such self-deception may have some adjustive value, since the passage of time often results in a reorientation in the attitudes and feelings of an individual or the alteration of circumstances so that what was a crisis earlier becomes less threatening at a later date. This phenomenon occurs quite commonly among children. At a given stage of life, disappointments and frustrations may be acutely painful and threatening. However, when people reach maturity, they look back upon many of these feelings as inconsequential growing pains. Mechanisms of deception may earn for the individual a little time relatively free from harassment so that changes may occur in the conditions which threaten his ego.

MECHANISMS OF SUBSTITUTION. When a person feels thwarted or is made uneasy by a tensional situation, the most wholesome thing he could do would be to make an active attack upon the obstacles which interfere with the attainment of his goals. But many obstacles, threats, and tensional situations are of such a nature that no amount of added effort will enable him to overcome them. Under these circumstances, he may use mechanisms of substitution to relieve his anxieties and extricate himself from a disagreeable situation. Mechanisms of substitution enable a person to find release from tension by altering his goals. They involve the following devices:

Compensation: A mechanism which enhances self-esteem by overcoming a failure or deficiency in one area through achieving recognition in another area. This mechanism is usually used to cover up a weakness, counterbalance a failure, or achieve prestige.

Substitution: A device which makes it possible to discharge tensions by diverting one's energies from a desired goal to a substitute goal. It differs from compensation since there is a change of goal as well as of activity.

Reaction formation: The substitute activity adopted to relieve guilt feelings is a complete reversal of the original behavior, as, for example, the alcoholic who becomes a rigorous crusader against drinking.

Sublimation: The redirection of emotional tension or primitive energies into socially acceptable modes of behavior.

ADJUSTIVE VALUE OF MECHANISMS OF SUBSTITUTION. The mechanisms of substitution are potentially more adjustive than those mechanisms which distort the perceptions of threat. The person who uses mechanisms of substitution is making an active attack on his problems, rather than merely disguising them. He senses the threatening situation and tries to do something about it by changing his goals or activities so that he does not remain trapped by an emotional block. Compensation and sublimation are probably the most effective of the adjustive mechanisms in that they may lead to real emotional satisfaction and stable adjustment.

However, these mechanisms are only potentially adjustive. If they are misused or overused, then the person will overcome one conflict, only to create another. Like all adjustive mechanisms, substitution devices serve primarily to make a person feel more secure and comfortable. They do not alter the factors which create insecurity or discomfort. The person remains sensitive to the original threatening circumstances even when he finds other channels of satisfaction.

MECHANISMS OF AVOIDANCE.   Avoidance mechanisms enable a person to remove himself from the scene of conflict. He does not solve his troubles, but creates for himself a life where there are no troubles, where his wishes are fulfilled, and where he is no longer threatened. These devices enable the individual to protect his ego by substituting psychological satisfactions for the actual satisfactions denied to him in real life.

Fantasy: A device which enables a person to escape into a self-created, fanciful world. Includes daydreaming, sleep, reading, music, drama, and commercial forms of fantasy.

Regression: A process of relieving anxiety or threat by falling back upon the thoughts, feelings, or behavior which worked successfully during an earlier period in life.

Negativism: The refusal to participate in a tensional situation. The individual protects his ego by resisting attempts to involve it in distasteful activities.

Motor hysteria: The development of physical symptoms which enable a person to withdraw gracefully from a difficult situation.

Identification: A process of attaining satisfactions through the accomplishment or status symbols of another person, group, or object.

ADJUSTIVE VALUE OF AVOIDANCE MECHANISMS.   The tendency to take flight from a distressing or dangerous situation is a normal characteristic of living things. The snail escapes danger by withdrawing into its shell, the sow bug rolls itself up into a hard little ball, the clam snaps itself shut. When it is no longer threatened, each organism resumes its normal mode of living.

Man may use this same technique to insulate himself from disruptive reactions and protect his nervous system from unbearable irritations. Such behavior has a self-protective value as long as the person can control his insulation from life and return to his problems. If he can keep his escape mechanisms under control and does not develop anxiety over using avoidance devices, he may make a fairly good adjustment to the frustrations of life. However, withdrawal may generate feelings of guilt, shame, and hurt pride. The feeling of being a quitter or a helpless puppet who cannot direct his own destiny may increase the individual's anxiety.

The Utility of Ego Defenses

While we have categorized and classified the mechanisms of adjustment, it should be emphasized that actual behavior cannot be simplified in this manner. The borderline between mechanisms is indistinct and rarely can a single mechanism be used to explain such a complex phenomenon as adjustive behavior. In reacting to tensional situations, the individual commonly employs several mechanisms simultaneously. This selection is not made deliberately but is an automatic process based upon feelings rather than reason. Frequently the individual may know what he is doing, but does not know why he must do a particular thing, or why it makes him feel better. Children, for instance, do not consciously desire to be negativistic or to develop sick feelings when faced with threatening situations. Reactions of this sort are outward signs of stress-relieving habits which have become an integral part of personality. The individual clings tenaciously to these habits because they protect his ego and to part with them would precipitate him into the anxiety from which these devices protect him (20).

EGO DEFENSES AND MENTAL HEALTH. Everyone uses ego-defense techniques at one time or another to protect himself from the minor irritations of everyday life and to conserve his energies so that major problems can be met more effectively. One's mental health is influenced not so much by the defense mechanisms used as by the use to which they are put. The maladjusted individual uses defense mechanisms to protect himself from the major problems of life as well as from minor irritations. So much of his libidinal energy is consumed in dodging the forces which menace him, or in artificially expanding his own ego concept, that he has little energy left to direct toward constructive adjustment.

The merits of adjustment mechanisms may be judged by the extent to which fundamental problems are affected. In evaluating defense techniques, the following criteria may be applied:

1. Does the technique used reduce the felt tensions of the individual and minimize his anxieties?
2. Is the device socially approved?
3. Does it facilitate further adjustment?

If the defense mechanism does not relieve tension, it is obviously nonadjustive. However, internal tensions must not be relieved at the expense of incurring the disfavor of society, for this would create new tensions as rapidly as the old ones are relieved. Finally, unless the adjustment technique enhances the individual's ability to analyze his problems and attack the fundamental origins of his anxieties, then he is making no progress toward an adequate adjustment to life.

SUMMARY

This chapter has focused attention on the inner dynamics of human behavior. The primary forces which motivate behavior may be viewed as originating from certain basic needs that create tensions within an individual and cause him to seek satisfactions which will relieve these tensions.

The basic needs are the biological needs which must be satisfied in order to preserve organic integrity and insure physical comfort, and the psychosocial needs derived from the culture. How a person behaves is dependent upon the particular constellation of needs to which he must react at a given time, the situational factors that determine the satisfactions he may achieve, and the habit patterns he has established for attaining need satisfactions.

Another way of interpreting the origins of behavior is in terms of psychodynamic forces acting within the individual. Operating on various levels of consciousness are certain psychic forces called the id, the ego, and the superego. What a person makes of himself is largely dependent upon his ability to keep these psychic forces in proper balance with each other and with relation to environmental requirements.

While these viewpoints differ in their theoretical structure, they have a common application to behavior. A person's actions are motivated to a significant degree by inner forces, many of which operate below the level of awareness. In reacting to these forces and attempting to reconcile them with the demands of society, the individual encounters frustrations within himself as well as in the social world. These frustrations may stimulate personality development, or they may give rise to emotional reactions and conditions which threaten the ego or *self* concept. When faced with such threats the individual may resort to various ego-defense mechanisms which protect the ego from threat and diminish the feeling of anxiety.

Human behavior is the result of a complex network of internal psychological forces, together with responses to environmental conditions. As teachers and parents appreciate this fact, they will look beyond the symptomatic aspects of a child's behavior and be sensitive to the deeper motivating forces which underlie his actions.

PROBLEMS AND PROJECTS

1. What is meant by emotional security? Is this a motivating force or an end product?
2. In what ways might the superego be affected by school experiences?
3. Interpret from a psychodynamic viewpoint why it is so difficult to teach a young child to share.
4. Why are children unwilling to part with their possessions even after they have outgrown them? What are the implications for child care?
5. What evidence can you cite for or against the possibility of altering one's personality after the age of 15?
6. Describe some techniques which may be used with (a) preschool children, (b) elementary school children, and (c) high school children to provide acceptable forms of id expression.
7. What are some ways in which the school can contribute to the formation of the ego-ideal in children?
8. Should competitive, emotion-arousing contests of a nonathletic nature be encouraged among school children?
9. What are some common school experiences which contribute to the frustration of children? How do these affect ego development?
10. Describe some instances where a child's use of projection or displacement resulted in misinterpretations of what was going on in the home or at school.

SELECTED REFERENCES

1. Ausubel, D. P., "Negativism as a Phase of Ego Development," *American Journal of Orthopsychiatry* (1950), *20*:796–805.
2. Bellak, L., "Toward a Unified Concept of Schizophrenia," *Journal of Nervous and Mental Disease* (January, 1955), *121*:60–66.
3. Benedek, T., *Insight and Personality Adjustment,* Ronald Press, 1948.
4. Brosin, H. W., "The Primary Processes and Psychoses," *Behavioral Science* (January, 1957), *2*:62–67.

5. Cameron, N. A., *The Psychology of Behavior Disorders,* Houghton Mifflin Co., 1947.

6. Carmichael, L., "The Experimental Embryology of Mind," *Psychological Bulletin* (January, 1944), 38:1–28.

7. Cole, L. E., *Human Behavior,* World Book Company, 1953.

8. Eisenberg, L., "Treatment of the Emotionally Disturbed Pre-Adolescent Child," in *The Pre-Adolescent Exceptional Child,* Proceedings of the 35th Conference of the Child Research Clinic of the Woods Schools, (Langhorne, Pennsylvania), May 23, 1953, pp. 30–41.

9. English, O. S., and Pearson, G. H. J., *Emotional Problems of Living,* W. W. Norton and Co., 1955.

10. Fisher, V. E., *Auto-Correctivism: The Psychology of Nervousness,* The Caxton Printers, 1937.

11. Freud, S., *A General Introduction to Psychoanalysis,* Garden City Publishing Co., 1938.

12. Freud, S., *An Outline of Psychoanalysis,* W. W. Norton and Co., 1949.

13. Freud, S., *New Introductory Lectures on Psychoanalysis,* Carlton House, 1933.

14. Fries, M. E., "The Child's Ego Development and the Training of Adults in his Development," *Psychoanalytic Study of the Child* (1946), 2:85–112.

15. Funkenstein, D. H., "Nor-Epinephrine Like and Epinephrine Like Substances in Relation to Human Behavior," *Journal of Nervous and Mental Disease* (July, 1956), 124:58–68.

16. Guetzkow, H. S., and Bowman, P. H., *Men and Hunger,* Brethren Publishing Co., 1946.

17. Hebb, D. O., "The Mammal and His Environment," *American Journal of Psychiatry* (May, 1955), 3:826–831.

18. Hendrick, I., "Instincts and the Ego during Infancy," *Psychoanalytic Quarterly* (1942), 11:33–58.

19. Kaplan, L., and Baron, D., *Mental Hygiene and Life,* Harper & Brothers, 1952.

20. Katz, B., "Children in Distress," *Education* (May, 1946), 66:573–577.

21. Klein, D. B., "Self-Respect and Self-Esteem as Educational Goals," *Education* (May, 1946), 66:562–568.

22. Kraines, S. H., and Thetford, E. S., *Managing Your Mind,* The Macmillan Company, 1947.

23. Kubie, L. S., "Instincts and Homeostasis," *Psychosomatic Medicine* (January, 1948), 10:15–30.

24. Maslow, A. H., "Conflict, Frustration and the Theory of Threat," *Journal of Abnormal and Social Psychology* (1943), 38:81–86.

25. Masserman, J. H., *Behavior and Neurosis,* University of Chicago Press, 1943.

26. Menninger, W. C. and Leaf, M., *You and Psychiatry,* Charles Scribner's and Sons, 1948.

27. Milner, M., "The Toleration of Conflict," *Occupational Psychology* (1943), *17*:17–24.

28. Morgan, C. T., *Physiological Psychology,* McGraw-Hill Book Company, 1943.

29. Peto, A., "The Interrelations of Delinquency and Neurosis: The Analysis of Two Cases," *British Journal of Medical Psychology* (1954), *27*:1–14.

30. Saul, L. J., *Emotional Maturity,* J. B. Lippincott Co., 1947.

31. Schneiders, A. A., *Personal Adjustment and Mental Health,* Rinehart and Co., 1955.

32. School Health Bureau, Health and Welfare Division, Metropolitan Life Insurance Co., *Children's Behavior Problems,* December, 1948.

33. Sherif, M. and Cantril, H., *The Psychology of Ego-Involvement,* John Wiley and Sons, 1947.

34. Sherman, M., "The Education of Personality," *Education* (May, 1946), 66:556–561.

35. Snygg, D., and Combs, A. W., *Individual Behavior,* Harper & Brothers, 1949.

36. Stott, L. H., "Mental Health and Developmental Hygiene," *Education* (January, 1949), 69:271–274.

37. Strecker, E. A. and Appel, K. E., *Discovering Ourselves,* The Macmillan Company, 1943.

38. Symonds, P. M., *The Dynamics of Human Adjustment,* Appleton-Century-Crofts, Inc., 1946.

39. Thorpe, L. P., *Child Psychology and Development,* Ronald Press, 1955.

40. Thorpe, L. P., *The Psychology of Mental Health,* Ronald Press, 1950.

41. Wilson, D. C., "Dynamics and Psychotherapy of Depression," *Journal of the American Medical Association* (May, 1955), *158*:151–153.

42. Young, P. T., *Emotion in Man and Animal,* John Wiley and Sons, 1943.

43. Zander, A. F., "A Study of Experimental Frustration, *Psychological Monographs* (1944), vol. 56, no. 3.

CHAPTER 10

Developmental Characteristics of Normal Children

AS NORMAL children pass through various stages of growth, their behavior undergoes many changes. In some periods of development children are coöperative, predictable, and nice to have around; in others they become exasperating, irrational, and difficult to understand.

Although such inconsistent behavior may be disturbing to adults, it is nonetheless a normal part of growing up. Therefore, adults who work or live with children must learn what to expect of them during various stages of development. This understanding will prevent a great deal of the strife and anxiety which results when adults, mistaking normal behavior for maladjustment, try to force youngsters into patterns of living which are incompatible with their growth tendencies.

To provide a perspective which will help teachers and parents interpret the strivings of normal children as they pass through the developmental sequence from infancy to maturity, this chapter presents, in broad overview, four stages of growth: the preschool period, early and middle childhood, the puberty years, and the adolescent period. There are no sharp divisions between these stages, for growth is so continuous that one stage merges into another like colors in the spectrum. Moreover, there will be many individual deviations from the behavior descriptions provided since the factor of individuality is so strong that no two children are exactly alike at a given age. Yet, individual variations occur around a central trend, and for any selected age it is possible to sketch a portrait which roughly delineates the behavior characteristics typical of the age (19:60). The descriptions of behavior which follow are thumbnail sketches of the common characteristics and behavior which may be expected of normal, middle-class children in the American culture.

THE PRESCHOOL CHILD

From birth to 5 years of age, growth is so rapid that a month in the life of a preschooler is like many months in the life of an adult. Physically, socially, and psychologically, the first 5 years are years of transformation. Some authorities say this is the most vital single period in a child's life—a period during which he learns more new things than he will learn during the rest of his years (*2, 12*).

Physical Development

Physically, the child's growth is as rapid from birth to 5 years of age as it is from 5 to 15 years (*23*). He starts out at an average birth weight of 7½ pounds, and a length of 22 inches, then proceeds to grow about an inch per month during the first year. After the first 18 months, he gains 2 to 3 inches and 3 to 6 pounds a year, until at the age of 5 the average boy is 37 to 45 inches high and weighs 33 to 45 pounds, and the average girl is 36 to 44 inches in height and weighs 31 to 42 pounds (*24:89*).

The child's body does not mature evenly. At about 6 years, the circumference of his head is 90 percent of its adult size. He is far-sighted and his eyes tire if he spends much time looking closely at small things. His muscles contain relatively more water and less solids and proteins than they will at maturity. Also, they are more delicate, less firmly attached, and not completely under voluntary control. As a result, the child can use his large muscles quite skillfully, can run, skip, dance, climb, and jump, but he is still rather awkward and inefficient in his movements and often spills things or knocks them over when he reaches beyond arm's length (*24:89*).

At 5 the heart and lungs are small, while veins and arteries are large. These factors cause the 5-year-old to tire easily. He is an active, noisy, vigorous child, in short bursts, but becomes cross and irritable if he is not made to rest or play quietly at intervals. Often he will voluntarily retire from active play until physiological balance is restored and his energy renewed.

Social and Psychological Development

When the child reaches 5 years of age he is a well-domesticated home-body, strongly attached to his mother and father. He is feeling the pull of the outside world, the attraction of other children, and his own developing individuality, but still seeks refuge and comfort in his parents. He is eager to do things which lie within his own capacity, tries to build his own ego and self-integrity, and likes to feel the satisfaction of achievement and social acceptance.

In his play with children, the 5-year-old has come far from the nursery school stage where quarrels occur about every 5 minutes (*23*: 304). He gets along peacefully with playmates in small-group play, if it is closely supervised, but does better with one or two children than with larger groups. He can take turns, respect other people's property, ask for things instead of snatching them, and knows how to use bribery and barter to get what he wants (*19, 20*). He can settle his disagreements by compromises such as name calling or appeal to adults, rather than physical retaliation (*1, 37*).

The 5-year-old's play is spontaneous and unorganized, with rapidly changing roles and much motor activity. Yet, his activity has direction and purpose and is accompanied by much creativity and imagination, as well as reflections of his home life and experiences with television and movies. Boys and girls play together when their interests are similar. Frequently they form attachments to each other and decide whom they will marry when they grow up.

Accomplishments of the Preschool Years

Although encompassing just a few calendar years, the progression from bassinet, to crib, to high chair, to play pen, to backyard, sidewalk, nursery, and schoolroom is a long and swift journey. Gesell summarizes the sweep of these growing years as follows:

In the first quarter of the first year, the infant, having weathered the hazards of the neonatal period, gains control of his twelve oculomotor muscles.

In the second quarter (16–28 weeks) he gains command of the muscles which support his head and move his arms. He reaches out for things.

In the third quarter (28–40 weeks) he gains command of his trunk and hands. He sits. He grasps, transfers and manipulates objects.

In the fourth quarter (40–52 weeks) he extends command to his legs and feet; to his forefingers and thumbs. He pokes and plucks.

By the end of the second year he walks and runs; articulates words and phrases; acquires bowel and bladder control; attains a rudimentary sense of personal identity and of personal possession.

At three years he speaks in sentences, using words as tools of thought; he shows a positive propensity to understand his environment and to comply with cultural demands. He is no longer a mere infant.

At four years he asks innumerable questions, perceives analogies, displays an active tendency to conceptualize and generalize. He is nearly self-dependent in routines of home life.

At five he is well matured in motor control. He hops and skips. He talks without infantile articulation. He can narrate a long tale. He prefers associative play. He feels socialized pride in clothes and accomplishments. He is a self-assured, conforming citizen in his small world. (19:62)

All things considered, the normal 5-year-old is a delightful, super-infant. He is in excellent equilibrium with the cultural world and ripe for enlarged community experience. He is comfortable in his home and child groups, displays a pleasing seriousness of purpose and interest in the world, is beginning to distinguish between truth and falsehood, is self-sufficient, friendly, and ready for the years of growth which lie ahead (19:247).

To be sure, perfection is not to be looked for or expected among preschool children. It is inevitable that their precipitous, pell-mell growth from helpless infancy to the chattering, roaming, adventurous, curious zestfulness of the young child will be accompanied by occasional thwarting and emotional outbursts. But on the whole, teachers may expect the school beginner to have established his basic attitudes toward himself and other people, to have developed reasonable control over his own reactions, and to be prepared to loosen his hold on the home and start the journey toward becoming a part of the wider social world.

EARLY AND MIDDLE CHILDHOOD

Development moves along at a fairly even pace between the age of 6 and the onset of puberty. Some writers have called these years a latency period in which children and parents gain a breathing spell before embarking on the stormy seas of puberty and adolescence. Actually, there is no cessation of growth during these years; the developmental changes which occur are merely not so striking as those of the first 5 years.

Aspects of Physical Growth

The growth of bones, muscles, and nervous tissue is the most dramatic physical change occurring in this period. Soon after he enters school, the child goes through a stage where the long bones of arms and legs grow rapidly, giving him a tall, thin appearance as contrasted with his stocky, rounded figure of earlier years. Skeletal growth is followed by muscular development which increases the child's weight about 5 pounds per year (*13*).

As the large muscles of the legs, back, arms, shoulders, and wrist develop, children have an organic need for strenuous physical activity which exercises these muscles. They learn skills easily and practice them enthusiastically, dashing breathlessly from place to place, climbing, swinging, and chasing. Their increased strength and resistance to fatigue makes it possible for them to carry on such activities over a long period of time. This inexhaustable energy, usually accompanied by much shouting and loud talking, often brings them into conflicts with adults.

Girls are less prone than boys to encounter difficulties over noisy, boisterous activity. The reason for this is cultural, rather than physiological, since girls mature more rapidly than boys. At the age of 11, girls are approximately a full year ahead of boys in physiological development, and can match or excell them in tests of skill and endurance (*4*:138).

The nervous system reaches its maximum rate of development at age 10, and at 12, the brain attains mature size (*23*:150). These neurological changes lead to the development of imagination, creativity, and interests which are at a higher level of maturation than the muscular dexterity available to carry out the projects conceived. As a result, the child often gets into trouble by starting things which he is not physically able to complete.

At around the age of 8, fusion of the eyes for depth perception usually is complete. The eyes reach adult size and function at 10 years of age, making it possible for the child to spend more time with books.

While many other physical changes occur among 6- to 12-year-olds, their skeletal, muscular, and neurological development is particularly significant. Maturation of these structures provide the child with capacities for dealing with life outside the home. As may be expected, these new capacities lead them into new problems and produce behavior characteristics which distinguish this period of life.

Social Behavior

Interpersonal relations among primary grade children are on a very casual basis. They can have fun with a group of their age-mates, but often are just as well satisfied to play by themselves or with another child.

Their play is loosely organized, and there is constant maneuvering to be first or to win. A checker game among these youngsters may start out peacefully enough but often ends with tears, quarrels, or an appeal to adults for arbitration.

Although primary school children show less overt hostility toward each other than do nursery school youngsters, the quarrels which do occur are more intense. Fighting may reach a peak between ages 7 and 8, a time when the timidity common to younger children reaches a low point. At this age, suggestibility is high, and misdemeanors among boys may be quite common. These are not misdemeanors in the legal sense, but the kind of behavior that results from taking "dares" or urging each other into some kind of mischief (23:312).

After the eighth year, group life among children takes on a new meaning and significance. Having passed through the stage of individualism, which usually extends from kindergarten through the second or third grade, they begin to crave the companionship and approval of other children. At about 9 years of age, the drive toward emancipation from the family begins, and youngsters enter the gang stage. They develop an engrossing interest in, and conformity to, the activities and standards of their age-mates (42). Tremendous comfort and encouragement are derived from membership in groups. Elaborate rituals, secret signs, passwords, and even a code language may be established in order to retain the intimate character of these group associations (48).

However, youngsters in this age range are still on an immature level in terms of their ability to engage in coöperative group activities. Team games are not too successful below the age of 10 because groups do not remain homogeneous for any length of time. When adults attempt to supervise them, the groups disintegrate. Team spirit means very little, and the children prefer individual competition or competition in pairs or double pairs rather than in larger, more formally organized team play (4:46).

Adjustment to Authority

Adults loom large in the life of the primary school child. He has a strong admiration for his parents and is still possessive of them, even to the point of resenting their attentions to other children. He strives to please his teachers, and, in general, knows what adults expect of him and is anxious to fulfill these expectations.

Gradually, this beautiful state of compliance and conformity vanishes.

As the child arrives at an age when the approval of his friends becomes a significant force in his life, adults, and the authority they represent, become less important to him. This stage may be ushered in by rude, blustery behavior, sassiness, arguing, or defiance. At the age of 9, boys and girls may show a disregard for adult standards, fight against previously accepted routines like brushing teeth or going to bed, question the decision of their parents, and compare their rules and regulations with those which prevail in other homes (*4, 30*).

At about 10 or 11, the child seems to prefer almost any home to his own, and is very critical of his parents and alert to ways in which he can prove them wrong, unfair, or discriminatory. He learns a whole new set of techniques for controlling his parents and becomes quite skillful in knowing when to deceive, when to ignore, flatter, wheedle, cry, throw a tantrum, or act like a little angel (*37:81*).

This mixture of good and bad behavior often is quite discouraging to parents and teachers. Wilson's survey (*48*) of parent attitudes toward intermediate grade children found many parents criticizing their youngsters for talking back, talking too much, being sloppy, slow, lazy, deceitful, or unruly. Teachers say they have more problems with children in this age group than with any others in the elementary schools (*4*).

These negative reactions to the behavior of middle and upper elementary school children are not without cause. In a large part, the American culture permits the development of such behavior. Parents must expect children in this age group to go through certain troublesome phases of behavior which in less permissive societies are uncommon or nonexistent. Studies have shown that in this country aggressive behavior, unruliness, running with the gang, disobedience, stubborness, and rudeness all reach a peak between the ages of 9 and 12 (*4*). Parents find it difficult to exhibit warmth and affection toward children of this age, and previous rejections and emotional conflicts which had been smoothed over, often arise again and create crises in parent-child relationships.

These struggles have an effect on the child's emotional life. Rebelling against people for whom he has a deep emotional attachment produces strains which may be expressed through the formation of benign obsessional symptoms (*42*), through physical symptoms such as restlessness, facial tics, nail biting, skin chewing, and scratching, or through the return of outgrown speech disorders (*36*). But despite the problems of this period, parents and teachers find many satisfactions in children of elementary school age. Their bustling activity, enthusiasm, spirit of helpfulness, eagerness to learn, inquisitiveness, and underlying need for adult protection and reassurance are wholesome qualities which outweigh the negative aspects of their behavior (48).

Sexual Interests

The period of middle childhood is one in which sex feelings or drives are relatively quiescent. By the time children enter school the question of anatomical differences between the sexes has been pretty well settled. There may still be some experimentation to satisfy curiosity, but this occurs more rarely than in the preschool years.

From the ages of 5 to 7, children are not greatly concerned about sex in their selection of play companions. Boys show no special courtesy to girls and accept them for what they can do. Infantile "love affairs" are common, generally taking the form of definite, although temporary, attachments to a girl friend or boy friend. This picture begins to change at around 8 years of age. Boys and girls accept each other less openly at this time, and by the time they are 9 years of age they are definitely segregated. At first this segregation appears as aloofness, then it becomes apparent contempt, then active hostility, and finally shy withdrawal (6, 13). At about 10 years of age, definite sex antagonisms are expressed. Boys are more aggressive about this, expressing their disdain for girls frequently and loudly. Girls are indifferent toward boys, rather than antagonistic. They think boys are silly, dirty, and noisy, but are less openly hostile toward boys than are boys toward girls (4). Despite their disdain for each other, boys and girls are quite conscious of the opposite sex and usually express this consciousness through playful hair-pulling, teasing, or pushing.

The apparent lack of sexual interest in the elementary school child does not imply that he has no interest in sex information. By the time a child is 10 years old, he has stored up considerable knowledge about the "facts of life," gleaned usually from reading, or from conversations with adults and age-mates. Studies of the sex knowledge of boys indicate that at age 10, 70 percent knew that babies come from the mother, 57.5 percent knew about intercourse, 43.2 percent had learned about masturbation, 23 percent knew about prostitution, 10 percent knew about contraceptives, and 3 percent had heard of venereal diseases (35). It must be conceded that the sex information of children is rather well advanced by the time they leave the elementay school. This appears to be true regardless of whether the school or parents take an active hand in imparting this information (*10, 34*).

Ethical and Moral Development

There is a growing concern during these years over the rightness and wrongness of behavior. At 7 and 8 this concern may be expressed through tattling to parents or teachers. The 7-year-old's ethics are still on a practical, personal, and largely verbal basis. He doesn't like to be in the wrong and tends to alibi and blame others to avoid disapproval. Eight-year-olds become more truthful and more capable of accepting responsibility for their behavior.

The idea of fairness develops progressively from 8 to 12, and by the end of this period practically all children believe in justice and fair play. Although they do not grasp the full implications of the personal sacrifices required to achieve real justice, they can make excellent progress toward developing a sense of morality (*4*).

However, ethical behavior and morality are not matured during this period, and elementary school youngsters are quite capable of getting temporary satisfaction out of acts of mischief (*37*). Self-centered, unsocialized behavior is common, particularly among boys—so much so that one psychiatrist expressed concern over finding a boy of this age who is honest, obedient, truthful, and considerate of others. These are considered to be abnormal, or at least unusual, qualities for boys around 9 years old (*3:38*).

Intellectual Development

The elementary school years is a time for the eager absorption of ideas and information. Children take a great deal of pride in what they know, and have an insatiable appetite for learning and for using what they learn. They develop an interest in reality, in natural and technological phenomena, and are no longer satisfied with pretending and imagining. They want to try things for themselves, to explore and experiment. Sometimes this craving for direct experience leads them into trouble. This is the age when children stick their fingers into electric sockets to feel the electricity, dig up flowers to see what makes them grow, and experiment with cigarette lighters and matches.

It is an age for collecting and hoarding all kinds of treasures, for learning to play cards, checkers, dominoes, or monopoly, for guessing games, riddles, and jokes. They plunge into all kinds of projects hastily and enthusiastically, and drop them just as fast. At around the age of 9, reading becomes an increasingly interesting occupation, reaching a peak at 12 or 13, and dropping off steadily thereafter (4:163). Perhaps the commonest of all free-time activities of 9-, 10-, and 11-year-olds is reading the comics in either newspapers or books. Comics are as much a part of their daily life as eating.

From grades two to six, children become less interested in animals and personal activities, and more concerned with current happenings in the world. Concepts of natural causes and physical relationships become remarkably clear and accurate by age 12. Interest in the expressive arts diminishes, except for those youngsters whose special talents are encouraged.

From ages 10 to 12, children can memorize meaningless material as well as adults (1). It is possible that much of their learning is on this memorized, verbalized basis, since concepts of time in terms of the historical past are very hazy until at least 11 years of age. Thus, the teaching of history through units on ancient Egypt, early American Indians, or primitive man is largely wasted as far as time concepts are concerned (4, 23).

An Overview of Middle Childhood[1]

In general, elementary school youngsters are lively, eager, light-hearted creatures, tremendously interested in the things and life around them, and experiencing them with all their senses. Many of them cease to be responsible, compliant children and become talkative, noisy, daring youngsters who flaunt their courage and bravado and are willing to try anything once. Boys are likely to be careless in their appearance, language, or work. Both boys and girls are amazingly self-dependent and often openly hostile to the adults they love best. They are absorbed in their juvenile world, and while they still appreciate adult attention, they are striking out for themselves, making friends, showing individual tastes, and exploring many fields (5, 20, 31).

THE PUBERTY YEARS

Between late childhood and early adolescence there is a period in which growth changes are rapid and dramatic. These are the years of

[1] See H. H. Remmers and R. H. Bauernfeind, *Examiner Manual for the SRA Junior Inventory*, September, 1951, for further data on the personal problems, interests, and attitudes of children in grades four through eight.

puberty or preadolescence—a time when old personality patterns are loosened up in order to make room for what the child must become (36).

Physical Growth

The puberty period is ushered in by a growth spurt which occurs between the ages of 10 and 14 for girls, and between 12 and 16 for boys. Girls gain in height most rapidly from 9 to 12 years, and undergo weight increases from 10 to 12. In these years, there is an average annual weight gain of 14 pounds. At the time of maximum weight increase, menstruation usually begins (36:20).

Boys gain in height most rapidly from 11 to 14 years, and add about 15 pounds in weight each year between the ages of 12 and 14 (23:141). Because of these differential growth rates, girls are larger than boys between the eleventh and thirteenth years (43).

In addition to these dramatic increases in height and weight, other significant physiological changes are taking place. The cartilage framework of the nose develops, causing the nose to become larger and to assume a definite shape. By the age of 13 or 14, the nose has attained mature size and may be disproportionately larger than other features. At about this same time the hands and feet reach maximum size. These temporary anatomical exaggerations of nose, hands, and feet cause the youngster much concern and embarrassment.

Changes in the visceral organs influence the child's physiological capacities. The heart increases in size just before and during puberty; arteries, however, grow less rapidly. As a consequence, the ratio between the opening of the heart and the width of the arteries is five to one. The heart pumps blood into an opening only one-fifth as wide as itself; therefore strenuous exercise may cause faintness, dizziness, heart strain, or enlargement of the heart (23:151).

The digestive tract becomes mature at puberty, resulting in an enormous, but often uncertain, appetite. Also, the gonads in boys and girls increase in weight about four times as fast as the body as a whole, resulting in accelerated hormonal activity (30: 214).

Skin eruptions are quite common during the puberty years because the small ducts through which oil is carried to the skin do not grow fast enough to take care of the increased activity of the glands supplying this secretion. Consequently, the ducts become plugged and a comedo, or blackhead, forms at the opening. The glands continue to function even though drainage is blocked, until the ducts become overfilled and raised places, or pimples, appear on the surface of the skin (*29, 44*).

Typical Reactions to Physical Changes

The physical changes of puberty introduce a number of disturbing influences in children's lives. Youngsters who have been playing together for years suddenly begin to notice differences in each other. The girl who enters puberty early loses her childhood interests, begins to dress more maturely, uses makeup, and becomes interested in boys. This creates a gap between her and her friends who are still in the late childhood stage of growth.

The boy who matures early may gain considerable status in his group because his size, strength, and competency in group games are important determiners of prestige. Also, his aggressiveness, daring, and willingness to experiment with prohibited actions, such as smoking, make him something of a hero in the eyes of his slower growing peers. Late-maturing boys, on the other hand, may develop anxiety over their size and physical abilities. They may be left out of games and sports because at this age a premium is placed on skill, and those who cannot compete effectively are forced into spectator roles. Slow-growing boys also are likely to experience much bullying and pushing around from their larger contemporaries.

Another area of disturbance in preadolescence involves adjusting to new physical proportions. These youngsters find it hard to realize how radically their bodies are changing. They may knock things over and appear clumsy or awkward because the 24-inch arm they are accustomed to has suddenly grown to 25 inches. They may not know what to do with their hands, and often suffer much embarrassment over a new pair of shoes, which inevitably looks so much larger than their old ones. Also, there is considerable sensitivity over skin blemishes, developing breasts, increased weight, and other external manifestations of growth. Parents and teachers must refrain from making personal remarks about the child's size or physical features because there is already much distress over these characteristics. Children need to be reassured that their bodies will grow up to their feet and hands, and that in a few years the disparities in size among themselves and age-mates will be leveled out.

The child's energy output is another source of concern to him and his parents. Growth is taking place so rapidly that the preadolescent may seem lazy. Often this is due to physical fatigue; so much energy is required for growth that the youngster is too tired to exert himself. Because his actions contrast so sharply with his alert, energetic behavior of preceding years, the lassitude of preadolescence may cause considerable anxiety in the family (24:185).

School work may be noticeably affected during the puberty years. Cornell and Armstrong (9), studying the Harvard Growth Data, found evidence of a definite break in the mental-age growth curve among children going through puberty changes. Very little advance in mental age was noted during this period. Other investigators have found that children often become school problems during periods of rapid growth. Their restlessness, lack of initiative, and behavioral difficulties may be related to disturbed physiological functioning (4:141).

Socio-Sexual Adjustment

The socio-sexual problems of earlier years are intensified during preadolescence. Girls develop earlier than boys and become interested in heterosexual relationships while boys are still interested in baseball. To complicate matters, girls are taller and heavier than boys during these years and feel conspicuous among them. Their overtures toward boys in their own class often are met with a complete lack of response, making the girl feel even more self-conscious and socially frustrated (45).

The criteria for acceptance among boys' groups differ from those prevailing in groups of girls. At the age of 12, the socially successful boy is aggressive, boisterous, unkempt, fearless, and skilled in games and sports. Girls at this same age derive prestige from being neat, attractive, friendly, demure, docile, good-humored, and acceptant of adult standards. At 15, social requirements for acceptance among boys have changed to a point where boisterousness and hyperactivity are regarded as childish. Higher value is placed on personableness, social ease, and poise in heterosexual situations, but athletic ability and aggressive leadership qualities are still important prestige factors. Girls at the age of 15 achieve acceptance and popularity through being attractive to boys and through buoyant good-fellowship in mixed groups (16, 46).

These divergent values are effective in keeping apart girls and boys of the same age. They will mix together at school activities, but tend to gather in groups of their own sex when left on their own. The behavior that can be expected at a preadolescent social gathering is described by Lane and Beauchamp in this little anecdote:

> The mother of a thirteen year old girl spent many evenings with her daughter planning and re-planning a Hallowe'en party that the girl was giving for her friends. Hours were spent discussing the party. Games were planned and food was decided upon. Most of this planning was initiated by the teen-ager. How surprised the mother was when she discovered that none of the plans (except the consumption of the food) was carried out. The kids arrived from an hour to two hours later than they were invited. When they got together, they just sat around and listened to the record player and giggled and visited a bit. One or two of the couples danced. They descended upon the kitchen like locusts, ate all the food, and abruptly departed. (28:290)

Emotional Characteristics

Emotional disequilibrium commonly accompanies the physical and physiological changes of puberty. Preadolescent youngsters are restless, they giggle and whisper incessantly, and often are moody, brash, or irritable. Their moods change quickly and often. They may be cheerful and exuberant in the morning, and blue or rebellious in the afternoon, capable and responsible one day, and dependent or childish the next. As one author has said of their behavior, "If you don't like it, wait a minute" (28:291).

Depressed and negativistic states seem to be sufficiently common among preadolescents to constitute a typical characteristic. Girls enter this phase some time between the ages of 11 and 13. It lasts for two to six months and generally ends with the onset of menstruation. Boys go through this stage for a slightly longer period somewhere between the ages of 13 and 15, ending when the secondary sex characteristics appear. Hurlock describes their behavior in this manner:

> Typically, the boy or girl at this age carries a chip on his shoulder. He is apt to misinterpret what others say or do and to feel that those who were formerly his friends are now his enemies. Both at home and in school, the spirit of antagonism is displayed in a critical attitude toward home, parents, and society in general. The preadolescent seems to resent the happy, carefree spirit of others, just as he resents it if he is urged to take part in the activities of his schoolmates. No matter what is done for him, it is not right, and his attitude toward all with whom he comes in contact is apt to be suspicious, unfriendly and critical.

The desire to withdraw from his former friends and playmates is a natural accompaniment of the socially antagonistic attitude. The preadolescent wants to escape from those who he feels are responsible for making him unhappy. It is not at all an uncommon thing for boys and girls at this age to break away from their former play companions and to spend their leisure time alone. Many childhood friendships of long standing are broken at this age because of the misunderstandings and hurt feelings which result from the preadolescent's withdrawal from his old play groups or from criticism of his former friends for being rowdy, childish or silly. (23:315–316).

Preadolescents spend a great deal of time reading, daydreaming, or just moping. At the ages of 12 and 13, reading may become a craze. Boys devour books of legendary or historical heroes, and biographies of great men as they feed their hero-worship hunger. Books about invention, athletics, and adventure also are popular. Girls show a preference for books relating to home, boarding school, college life, adventure, nature, and Bible stories (23:367). Such stories not only provide children with identification figures, but also offer a channel through which to drain off hostility toward adults which tends to rise in the puberty years.

Daydreams and fantasies provide the preadolescent with another way to retreat from unpleasant reality. Typically, their daydreams are of the cartoon adventure type in which the self-image is a martyr who is treated badly by parents, teachers, or friends, until the end when he emerges as a much maligned hero. Often their fantasies seem to have no content at all; youngsters simply stare into space with nothing on their conscious minds, or their minds may be filled with quickly changing flights of ideas which have no pattern or theme (23, 36).

The Preadolescent in School

Relatively few intellectuals are found among preadolescent youngsters. Generally, children of this age find sustained concentration difficult. They tend to avoid responsibility, are easily discouraged, and are quite satisfied to turn out products below their level of ability. However, preadolescents are capable of conscientious and enthusiastic work if the school program is centered around their interests. They are eager for information about growth and vitally concerned with problems of modern living and what makes people act as they do. They like an informal school setting which deals with life problems, and they need teachers to whom they can talk and who let them express their thoughts and feelings. This type of academic atmosphere, rather than a formal classroom environment, will help youngsters pass through the difficult puberty years with the least amount of strain or anxiety (*23, 24, 28*).

THE ADOLESCENT PERIOD

Adolescence usually is considered as the period extending from puberty to the late teens or early twenties. We have described the puberty years as a separate phase of growth in order to emphasize the critical changes which occur during this period. Therefore, our discussion of adolescence will be confined to the post-puberty years when the child's growth is decelerating and most of his major physical development has been completed.

In this post-puberty period, the adolescent's life is dominated by three major concerns; his emotional reactions, reëstablishing a sense of selfhood, and stabilizing his social roles. Many other growth problems confront the teen-age youngster, but these three stand out as major concerns.

Emotional Reactions

Many unsolved problems are carried over from the puberty years and continue to produce emotional distress in adolescence. Included here are frequent changes of mood, sensitivity over physical appearance, and many old fears which crop up and press more vividly than ever before.

Normal adolescents worry constantly about these old problems and many new ones. School achievement looms as one of their chief worries. Although intellectual abilities are on the rise during this period, large numbers of high school youngsters say they cannot concentrate on their studies (*11, 39*). Confusion about religion, feelings of inadequacy, anxiety over social status, and problems of vocation, sex, and marriage are also common concerns of the typical adolescent.

These problems contribute to the unintegrated, diffusely anxious personality patterns found so often among adolescents. The emotions of adolescents are of such depth and intensity that they must not be treated lightly by adults. Frequently, a series of neurotic symptoms arise, beginning, usually, with difficulties involving concentration, sleep and appetite, and progressing to minor depressive swings, strong tendencies toward introversion and fantasy, and sometimes hypochondria (*33*). According to the studies of Fleege (*14*) and Knoebler (*27*), these reactions occur so commonly that they may be regarded as a normal adolescent syndrome.

The Search for Selfhood

Closely associated with these emotional reactions, and contributing directly to them, are the adolescent's need to reform his ego and re-establish his sense of selfhood. Out of the disorganization of the puberty years he must reweave the pattern of his life into an adult image. This does not come about rapidly or easily, for the adolescent has many major conflicts to reconcile. Prominent among these is the conflict between himself and his family. Before he can become an individual in his own right he must alter his position in the family from that of a child to that of an equal with adults and a superior to younger brothers and sisters. Adolescents undertake this quest for independence with varying degrees of intensity. Some teen-agers overreact to adult authority and reject their family and the ethical, moral, or religious concepts which were taught them. Sometimes they even defy the dictates of their own conscience since it, too, was shaped by adults.

More often the teen-ager's rebellion is less intense, particularly where parents understand his need for freedom and give him some leeway. Various surveys have found that from 10 to 50 percent of high school students have serious conflicts with their parents. Usually these conflicts center around matters such as going out at night, using the family car, sharing work in the home, allowances, and understanding each other's personal problems (*11, 41*).

Most teen-agers go through a period of disillusionment when they begin to see their parents as sadly human and fallible. Their identifications may be transferred to youth workers, teachers, counselors, older youths, or religious leaders. Almost anyone but a parent is selected as a confidant with whom to discuss personal problems and concerns over ethical, moral, and philosophical issues. Quite often teachers and counselors become exceedingly important adult figures to the adolescent because they do not demand dependency of him but encourage his development as an individual.

Actually, most adolescents do not want to cast off their parents. Despite their protestations, many adolescents are not prepared to relinquish their dependency. Complete independence frightens them, intensifies their existing feelings of inadequacy, and makes them feel rejected. Many of the teen-ager's outbursts are not so much against parents as they are a cover-up against these feelings of doubt and inadequacy. What they are seeking is not absolute freedom but a relationship which permits them to love and receive love from their parents without clinging to them as children. Once they attain recognition as equals, they are prepared to accept parental guidance and attention, if it is offered with consideration and respect.

It is no easy matter for parents to walk this narrow line between too much and too little concern over the adolescent. Parents, too, are confused by the teen-ager's contradictory behavior and sometimes do not have the foresight and patience needed to help him work out his problems (*24, 29*).

Social Behavior

As in earlier years, status in social groups is of paramount importance to adolescents. Through sharing the mistakes, successes, and problems of their peers, and functioning as an equal among equals, adolescents bolster their self-confidence and ease their anxiety.

Conformity to group standards still has a strong hold over teen-agers. Sometimes boys and girls even disguise their talents or decrease their effort toward academic accomplishments to avoid being different from others in their group. Later on, when they are more sure of themselves, they can risk being different by pursuing individual talents and interests. But in the early teens, security and social acceptance comes from being exactly like others.

Teen-agers further protect their social security by barring some of their peers from membership in the group. There is much snobbishness and discrimination in adolescent society, and considerable emphasis on social and economic position. This has been described as a defensive reaction, through which adolescents build a protective wall around their social units and thus enhance their egos by making it a mark of accomplishment to be accepted in these groups (*15, 47*).

The friendship patterns of boys and girls take on a more personal meaning in adolescence. Children begin to look for different things in their friends, whereas in earlier years they were happy with the companionship of anyone who had similar interests. Boys tend to have a larger number of friends than girls, and their friendships are less intimate. The group loyalties of boys are still quite strong, while girls are less likely to participate in large group efforts and more inclined to break up into small cliques or sets composed of six to twelve favored individuals (*30, 47*).

Heterosexual relations assume a new significance in the middle teens, particularly for boys. This is a romantic period, with a succession of crushes, hero-worship, and falling in and out of love. Relationships between the sexes do not run smoothly because of oversensitivity, self-consciousness, and fear of being rejected or rebuffed (*32*). The most prominent boy-girl problems, according to the studies of Remmers and Shimberg (*41*) are, in order of frequency:

For Boys	*For Girls*
Seldom have dates.	Seldom have dates.
Don't have a girl friend.	Don't have a boy friend.
Bashful about asking girls for dates.	Don't know how to keep boys interested.
Don't know how to keep girls interested.	Don't know how to refuse a date or break up an affair without causing hard feelings.

Among their other serious concerns were problems such as how far to go in love relations, petting and necking, selecting a mate, and preparing for marriage and family life. As adolescents grow older these problems diminish in intensity. But for 25 to 50 percent of teen-agers, these are serious concerns for several years.

An Overview of Adolescence[2]

If the adolescent is moody, confused, or oversensitive, he may have good cause. He is faced with the tremendous task of reconstructing his childhood self-image into an adult pattern. This entails clarifying his masculine or feminine role, coming to terms with social requirements, and revising his many childhood beliefs and fantasies in accordance with his real potentialities and limitations.

The adolescent is experiencing a period of insecurity, accentuated by drives and desires which he feels intensely but does not completely understand. He wants to be accepted and loved, but is afraid of showing this desire or demonstrating affection for others. He needs adult guidance, but rebels against it and demands freedom and independence which he cannot assume. He has high ideals, a strong sense of morality, and great confidence in himself and the opportunities which lie before him. Yet, he is anxious over his own abilities and unsure of his values and goals.

[2] See H. H. Remmers and D. H. Radler, *The American Teen-Ager*, Bobbs-Merrill Company, 1957, for a summary of the problems, interests, and attitudes of adolescents derived from 15 years of polling by the Purdue Opinion Panel.

It is clear that these are difficult problems for a youngster to handle. It takes time to put the scattered pieces of a previously integrated personality into place on a new level of maturity. However, with understanding, wise guidance, and adequate support, most normal adolescents, by the time they are in their late teens, reconcile their various problems and arrive at a reasonable state of maturity and integration (*17, 18*).

SOME BASIC PRINCIPLES OF GROWTH

Now that we have viewed the broad panorama of growth, certain basic principles of development should be emphasized to facilitate interpretation of child behavior.

It is obvious that growth is not a continuously pleasant upward jaunt through which children progress joyfully and carefree. We have discarded the idea that normal children are free of problems. The nature of psychobiological development is such that few children mature without encountering some physical, mental, or emotional distress. As Jersild has said:

> Every hurdle in development involves a hazard, and every gain is made at a price. When a child is able to walk, he is able to walk not only into new interests but also into new troubles. In social development, as he becomes capable of tasting the experience of being an accepted member of a team, he also faces the possibility of being rejected by his fellows. When, in his mental development, he becomes able, through his imagination, to anticipate a future pleasure, he also becomes able to worry about what the future will bring. A gain in power does not mean a gain in composure. In addition, the more a child can do for himself, the more there is for him to do. Gain in ability usually brings increases in responsibility. (*25:25*)

Youngsters who are permitted to function fully and freely at each stage of development suffer less than those who have frustrations, deprivations, and coercions imposed upon them. This is why adults need to understand some of the basic principles underlying the growth process, as well as the typical behavior to be expected of children at various ages.

Individual Variations in Growth

All normal children follow an essentially similar sequence of growth, but we can only generalize about an individual's course of development since each child follows a different calendar and a different clock as he goes through the growth sequence. There is no universal, detailed timetable for human growth. A child must meet the demands of development, maturation, and socialization at his own rate of progress. In doing so he attains the size, shape, functional capacities, and personality which are uniquely his own (7).

Because of this individual variation, the number of years a child has lived provides only a rough indication of his level of development. In every age group there will be some children ahead of their peers in terms of physical, mental, social, or emotional development, and there will be others who lag behind. For example, an extensive study of first grade classrooms found that the range of mental ages among these youngsters was from 4 years 7 months, to 9 years 3 months (32:216). As children grow older, differences in the various aspects of their development are accentuated.

Spurts and Plateaus in Growth

Growth is continuous but does not proceed in a straight upward and onward direction. At times a child's development goes on at a rapid rate; at other times his growth seems to be at a standstill, and sometimes he may even appear to slip backward in his rate of maturing (24). The path of development consists of steep places where growth is difficult, interspersed with plateaus where the child moves along smoothly. Gesell describes growth as a spiral wherein the child makes progress upward in a particular line of development, only to revert downward to an earlier stage before going upward again to a new and higher level. The downward gradient is nature's way of giving the child a chance to consolidate forces. It is an important and necessary part of the growth spiral because by repeating behavior characteristic of a previous stage in development the child builds up enough strength to forge upward to higher levels of achievement.

This irregularity of growth has its emotional concomitants. When growth is most rapid, or when it slows down noticeably, emotional problems are accentuated. At these times children may be irritable, or show frequent up and down swings in mood (31). Spurts in growth often are accompanied by a tendency to go all-out in the use of a new skill or capacity. Children become intensely absorbed in a new mode of behavior or phase of development. As time passes, this fascination for the new power loses its novelty and the new behavior becomes a part of the broad pattern of development (25:42).

Growth and Behavior

Growth is not necessarily accompanied by an improvement of behavior. Often as a child matures, changes occur which create new problems, or accentuate older ones (37). Also, a child never completely leaves one phase of growth when he enters another. He retains older ways of behaving even though they may be obscured by new mannerisms and affectations. Much of the child is contained in the adolescent, and much of the infant in the child.

While children tend to cling to old patterns of behavior as they grow, it is true also that they undergo a developmental revision of habits. At every stage of growth children will show forms of behavior which they will change or abandon in their own time. It is difficult to predict which characteristics will remain with children as they mature, and which will be revised or discarded. Because a certain form of behavior is strongly entrenched at one stage of growth it does not mean that it will carry over to a later stage. Yet, there is always a possibility of this because what we see in a child at a particular time is often a precursor of things to come (25:44).

Developmental Tasks

Part of growing up consists of developing the skills, understandings, feelings, attitudes, and modes of behavior appropriate to each new stage of development. As a child's physical and psychological capacities mature, he is confronted with new expectations and new demands. These are crucial life problems, termed "developmental tasks," arising partly from the pressure of cultural processes and partly from the individual's own desires, aspirations, motives, and values (8).

Many of the common developmental tasks of childhood have been described in preceding pages. They range from learning sex differences and sexual modesty in early childhood, to achieving socially responsible behavior in adolescence. Havighurst (21, 22) has suggested a series of life tasks which confront children at various stages of growth. The ease and speed with which these tasks are accomplished vary as individuals vary. However, society does not countenance too much deviation from the time period within which the various developmental lessons must be learned. Moreover, failure to learn the lessons of one period may jeopardize the mental health of children by making it difficult, or even impossible, to learn these tasks at a later period. For instance, the child who does not learn to distinguish right from wrong during the period when his superego is being formed, and when he is not required to pay fully for his errors, may have great difficulty later in acquiring such learning. In the case of psychopaths, this task may never be accomplished.

Facilitating the Growth of Children

The guidance of a child's growth requires much skill, knowledge, and discretion. At any stage of development parents or teachers can make demands which intensify the problems of growing up, or they can ease the course of development by supporting the child's natural growth patterns (26). Adults must acquire a sense of timing; they must learn to detect the emergence and recession of a stage of development and know when to step in with aid or encouragement, and when to leave the child to his own learning. Each child has his own rate of growth and cannot be pressured into growing up any faster than his pattern will permit. If he is not pushed too hard, but accepted for what he is at each stage of growth, his development can be expected to proceed normally and naturally (19, 25).

SUMMARY

This brief overview of the behavior of normal children should help parents and teachers understand what might legitimately be expected of children at various stages of growth. From the preschool years through adolescence, the way a child acts is dependent upon the experiences he has had at an earlier stage of life, together with the life tasks which currently confront him.

Given an average inheritance and home environment, normal, middle-class children can be expected to go through a rapid growth period during their preschool years, followed by a "latency period" in middle childhood, a growth spurt in puberty, and a period of reorganization in adolescence.

The preschool child develops the physical and psychological competencies required for adapting to social life outside the home. In his elementary school years, the youngster becomes a bigger and better child, learning to get along with other children, exercising his growing muscles, and developing his self-reliance.

In the puberty years, the child goes through a metamorphosis, emerging from this period with a changed body and a fluid personality which is no longer cemented by childhood bonds. Adolescence is the period of reforming personality in a new matrix. The early teens are disturbing years for the youngster as he tries on new faces and experiments with new feelings and roles in order to find the ones which fit him best. If given enough leeway, understanding, and wise guidance, the adolescent will reconcile his conflicts and arrive at a reasonable state of integration in his late teens.

This, in broad perspective, is the course of growth for normal children. By understanding their developmental tasks and the behavior commonly displayed as children seek to solve their life problems, adults will be less disturbed by the sometimes distressing actions of children. With wise guidance and discreet support, most children will negotiate successfully their temporary periods of maladjustment and emerge from the growth process as normal, mentally healthy individuals.

PROBLEMS AND PROJECTS

1. Examine the following studies:
   (a) Wilson, F. M., "Mental Health Practices in the Intermediate Grades," in *Mental Health in Modern Education,* University of Chicago Press, 1955, pp. 195–215.
   (b) Kaplan, Louis, "Annoyances of Elementary School Teachers," *Journal of Educational Research* (May, 1952), 45:649–665.
   What do these studies reveal about how well teachers understand the behavior of normal children?
2. Discuss the question of "Life Adjustment Education vs. Classical or Traditional Education," in terms of the growth characteristics of junior and senior high school students.
3. The "teachable moment" has been defined as that point at which a child is ready to learn something and society requires it. Describe some teachable moments you have experienced, utilized, or missed.
4. Discuss some cases of the "developmental revision of habits" which you either experienced or observed.
5. Discuss the problem of competitive athletics in terms of the physical and psychological development of children.
6. From the viewpoint of the adolescent's social and emotional development, should high school fraternities and sororities be discouraged or encouraged? Cite some illustrations of the effects of fraternities and sororities in high schools.
7. Why is the emphasis in this chapter placed on middle-class children?

What differences in growth patterns might be expected of lower-class youngsters?

8. To what extent should parents or teachers interfere with a child's selection of friends? Illustrate your reply through experiences or observations.

9. How should a parent or teacher handle fighting among boys? Should fighting be accepted as a normal means of expressing hostile feelings?

10. Review for the class the "developmental tasks" set forth by Havighurst. Select an age group with which you are acquainted and discuss some of the problems commonly encountered by children as they seek to master these developmental tasks.

SELECTED REFERENCES

1. Baldwin, A. L., *Behavior and Development in Childhood,* Dryden Press, 1955.

2. Benton, P. C., "The Pre-School Years," in Oklahoma State Department of Health, *The Teacher and the Road to Mental Health,* Mimeographed Report of the Mental Health Workshop for Teachers (Norman, Oklahoma), 1953, pp. 14–19.

3. Beverly, B. I., *In Defense of Children,* John Day Company, 1941.

4. Blair, A. W., and Burton, W. H., *Growth and Development of the Pre-adolescent,* Appleton-Century-Crofts, Inc., 1951.

5. Blos, P., *The Adolescent Personality,* Appleton-Century-Crofts, Inc., 1941.

6. Campbell, E. H., "The Social Sex Development of Children," *Genetic Psychology Monographs* (1939), no. 21, pp. 461–552.

7. Children's Bureau, United States Department of Labor, *Mental Hygiene for Children and Youth,* Mimeographed, February, 1945.

8. Corey, S. M., and Herrick, V. E., "The Development Tasks of Children and Young People," in F. Henne, A. Brooks, and R. Ersted (eds.), *Youth, Communication and Libraries,* American Library Association, 1949, pp. 3–13.

9. Cornell, E. L., and Armstrong, C. M., "Patterns of Mental Growth and Factors Related to Their Classification," in *Research Relating to Children,* Bulletin II, Supplement 2, 1954, U.S. Department of Health, Education and Welfare, Social Security Administration, Children's Bureau, pp. 22–23.

10. "Do You Favor Sex Education in Our Schools?" *McCall's Magazine,* January, 1952, pp. 28, 29, 90, 91.

11. Elias, L. J., *High School Youth Look at Their Problems,* The State College of Washington (Pullman), 1949.

12. Federal Security Agency, Social Security Administration, Children's Bu-

reau, *Your Child from 1 to 6,* rev. ed., Children's Bureau Publication No. 30, 1945.

13. Federal Security Agency, Social Security Administration, Children's Bureau, *Your Child from 6 to 12,* Children's Bureau Publication No. 324, 1949.
14. Fleege, U. H., *Self-Revelation of the Adolescent Boy,* Bruce Publishing Company, 1945.
15. Frank, L. K., "This is the Adolescent," *Understanding the Child* (June, 1949), *18:*65–69.
16. Furfey, P. H., "Case Studies in Developmental Age," *American Journal of Orthopsychiatry* (April, 1931), *1:*292–297.
17. Gallagher, J. R., "A Clinic for Adolescents," *Children* (September–October, 1954), *1:*165–170.
18. Gardner, G. E., "The Mental Health of Normal Adolescents," *Mental Hygiene* (October, 1947), *31:*529–540.
19. Gesell, A., and Ilg, F. L., *Infant and Child in the Culture of Today,* Harper & Brothers, 1943.
20. Gesell, A., and Ilg, F. L., *The Child From Five to Ten,* Harper & Brothers, 1946.
21. Havighurst, R. J., *Developmental Tasks and Education,* Longmans, Green and Company, 1951.
22. Havighurst, R. J., *Developmental Tasks and Education,* Longmans, Green and Company, 1952.
23. Hurlock, E. B., *Child Development,* McGraw-Hill Book Company, 1950.
24. Jenkins, C. G., Schacter, H., and Bauer, W. W., *These Are Your Children,* Scott, Foresman and Co., 1953.
25. Jersild, A. T., *Child Psychology,* Prentice-Hall, Inc., 1954.
26. Joseph, H., Thieman, A., and Hamilton, E., "Preventive Psychiatry at the Henry Street Settlement: A Five Year Experimental Project," in State of New York, Department of Mental Hygiene, Mental Health Commission, *Third Annual Conference of Clinic Personnel on Clinic Relations with Other Community Agencies* (Albany), 1953, pp. 115–127.
27. Knoebler, M., *Self-Revelation of the Adolescent Girl,* Bruce Publishing Company, 1936.
28. Lane, H., and Beauchamp, M., *Human Relations in Teaching,* Prentice-Hall, Inc., 1955.
29. Lawrence, H., "The Importance of Emotional Problems in the Acne Patient," *The Merck Report* (July, 1955), *64:*7–10.
30. Lemkau, P. V., *Mental Hygiene in Public Health,* McGraw-Hill Book Company, 1949.
31. McDaniel, I. C., "Growing Pains Need Attention," *California Journal of Elementary Education* (November, 1954), *23:*109–120.

32. Morse, W. C., and Wingo, G. M., *Psychology and Teaching,* Scott, Foresman and Co., 1955.

33. Murray, J. M., *Normal Personality Development,* National Committee for Mental Hygiene, 1949.

34. Olson, W. C., *Child Development,* D. C. Heath and Co., 1949.

35. Ramsey, G. V., "Sex Information of Younger Boys," *American Journal of Orthopsychiatry* (April, 1943), *13*:347–352.

36. Redl, F., *Preadolescents, What Makes Them Tick?* The Association for Family Living (Chicago), 1944.

37. Redl, F., and Wattenberg, W. W., *Mental Hygiene in Teaching,* Harcourt, Brace and Co., 1951.

38. Remmers, H. H., and Bauernfeind, R. H., *Examiner Manual for the SRA Junior Inventory,* Science Research Associates, September, 1951.

39. Remmers, H. H., and Hackett, C. G., *What Are Your Problems?* Science Research Associates, 1951.

40. Remmers, H. H., and Radler, D. H., *The American Teenager,* Bobbs-Merrill Company, 1957.

41. Remmers, H. H., and Shimberg, B., *Examiner Manual for the SRA Youth Inventory,* Science Research Associates, 1949.

42. Spock, B. M., "The School-Age Child. Some Behavioral, Anthropological and Physical Implications of the Latency Period," in F. J. Braceland (ed.), *Abstracts and Reviews of Selected Literature in Psychiatry, Neurology and Their Allied Fields,* The Institute of Living, Series XXIII February, 1955, p. 51.

43. Stuart, H. C., "Normal Growth and Development During Adolescence," in J. M. Seidman (ed.), *Readings in Educational Psychology,* Houghton Mifflin Company, 1955, pp. 11–15.

44. Thom, D. A., *Guiding the Adolescent,* U.S. Department of Labor, Children's Bureau Publication No. 225, 1933.

45. Tryon, C. M., "The Adolescent Peer Culture," in *Adolescence,* Forty-Third Yearbook of the National Society for the Study of Education, University of Chicago, 1944, pp. 217–239.

46. Tryon, C. M., "Valuation of Adolescent Personality by Adolescents," in R. G. Barker, J. S. Kounin, and H. F. Wright (eds.), *Child Behavior and Development,* McGraw-Hill Book Company, 1933, pp. 545–566.

47. U.S. Department of Health, Education and Welfare, Social Security Administration, Children's Bureau, *The Adolescent in Your Family,* Children's Bureau Publication No. 347, 1954.

48. Wilson, F. M., "Mental Health Practices in the Intermediate Grades," in *Mental Health in Modern Education,* the 54th Yearbook of the National Society For the Study of Education, Part II, University of Chicago Press, 1955, pp. 195–215.

CHAPTER 11

Behavior Deviations in Children

ABOUT one-fourth of the children and youth in American schools have adjustment problems which are more persistent and more serious than those described in the preceding chapter. The early detection and insightful guidance of these troubled youngsters is a responsibility of the school, since the law requires children to attend school during the years when their problems are taking form. Teachers, in particular, should learn to recognize the early symptoms of maladjustment so that help may be brought to these children while it is still effective and before too much damage has been done.

This chapter will indicate the types of disturbed behavior which may be encountered in the school. Particular emphasis is directed toward symptoms of chronic maladjustment, the behavior of children who later become psychotic, sex differences in adjustment, and the problems of atypical children.

IDENTIFYING DEVIATE BEHAVIOR

In most cases of behavior deviation the child gives ample warning that trouble is brewing. Bolton (4) observed that 74 percent of the children referred to a clinic for treatment of emotional disturbances had shown evidence of their difficulty in the first 5 years of life. Unfortunately, many educators do not recognize these early symptoms of disturbance, or interpret them incorrectly. As a result, disturbed youngsters often receive no assistance until their problems become so acute that they attract the attention of clinical or law enforcement agencies.

Teachers' Perceptions of Maladjustment

Studies of teachers' attitudes toward child behavior indicate that teachers may unwittingly contribute to the maladjustment of children by being concerned more with aggressive youngsters than with those who are withdrawn or submissive. An early study by Wickman (79) demonstrated that teachers are more disturbed by children whose behavior disrupts the smooth operation of the classroom than they are by quiet, complacent, withdrawn youngsters who cause no trouble. These reactions are significant when it is learned that clinicians consider the behavior of the good, obedient, withdrawn child more prognostic of serious maladjustment than that of the troublesome child.

Later studies by Thompson (71), Hayes (32), and Mitchell (49) found teachers becoming more aware of the fact that the amount of trouble a child caused in school was not an adequate measure of his mental health. However, recent investigations (39, 59, 63, 65) show that teachers still consider aggressive, troublesome behavior to be more significant than the withdrawing types. The findings of Pilzer (54) and Harris (30) suggest that this misplaced emphasis often results in providing therapeutic services to the wrong children. They believe that over one-third of the youngsters whom teachers select as being well adjusted in school would be diagnosed as rather seriously disturbed when judged by clinical workers.

These findings emphasize the need for acquainting teachers with the symptoms and implications of various types of deviate behavior. One cannot blame a teacher for being upset by aggressive, asocial, destructive, or dishonest children. Yet, from the viewpoint of future adjustment, these youngsters are taking an active approach to their problems and will either attract assistance or work out their own solutions. The shy, withdrawn, submissive, agreeable child may be even more disturbed than the aggressive youngster and may harbor feelings more detrimental to himself and to others, but he is more likely to escape detection; therefore, his problem goes unnoticed until it reaches an acute stage.

This does not mean that the teacher should ignore aggressive or antisocial behavior. Indeed, behavior of this type may lead to delinquency and quite serious forms of maladjustment. It implies that equal attention must be given to youngsters who do not impress their problems upon adults in a dramatic way, but who, nevertheless, suffer quite intensely.

Recognizing Symptoms of Chronic Maladjustment

The variety of behavior problems which teachers encounter in school requires them to make some discriminating judgments and interpretations. It is quite important that teachers be able to distinguish forms of behavior which are harmful to the individual from those which are temporary consequences of environmental upsets, by-products of normal growth, or expressions of emotional release. Also, they must be able to predict which characteristics may be outgrown, and which can be expected to become progressively worse and lead to serious behavior problems.

These judgments are not always easy to make. However, various research studies and clinical reports reveal certain clusters of symptoms which are considered indicative of chronic maladjustment. The following list, adapted from a compilation made by the Minneapolis Public Schools, indicates some of the behavior characteristics commonly associated with serious adjustment problems:

1. *Nervous behavior.* Habitual twitching of muscles, scowling, grimacing, twisting the hair, continuous blinking, biting or wetting the lips, nail biting, stammering, blushing or turning pale, constant restlessness, frequent complaints of minor illnesses, head banging, nervous finger movements, frequent crying, body rocking, frequent urination.
2. *Emotional overreactions and deviations.* Undue anxiety over mistakes, marked distress over failures, absent-mindedness, daydreaming, meticulous interest in detail, refusal to take part in games, refusal to accept any recognition or reward, evasion of responsibility, withdrawal from anything that looks new or difficult, chronic attitude of apprehension, lack of concentration, unusual sensitivity to all annoyances (especially noises), inability to work if distracted, lack of objective interests, frequent affectations and posturing, inappropriate laughing, uncontrolled laughing or giggling, explosive and emotional tone in argument, tendency to feel hurt when others disagree, unwillingness to give in, shrieking when excited, frequent efforts to gain attention, sudden intensive attachments to people (often older), extravagant expressions of any emotion.
3. *Emotional immaturity.* Inability to work alone, tendency to cling to a single intimate friend, inability to rely on own judgment, unreasonable degree of worry over grades, persistent inferiority feelings, unusual self-

consciousness, inability to relax and forget self, excessive suspiciousness, overcritical of others, too docile and suggestible, persistent fears, indecision, compulsive behavior, hyperactivity.

4. *Exhibitionistic behavior.* Teasing, pushing or shoving other pupils, trying to act tough, trying to be funny, wanting to be overconspicuous, exaggerated courtesy, marked agreement with everything the teacher says, constant bragging, frequent attempts to dominate younger or smaller children, inability to accept criticism, constant efforts to justify self, frequent blaming of failures on accidents or on other individuals, refusal to admit any personal lack of knowledge or inability, frequent bluffing, attempting either far too little or far too much work.

5. *Antisocial behavior.* Cruelty to others, bullying, abusive or obscene language, undue interest in sex (especially efforts to establish bodily contact), telling offensive stories or showing obscene pictures, profound dislike of all school work, fierce resentment of authority, bad reaction to discipline, general destructiveness, irresponsibility, sudden and complete lack of interest in school, truancy.

6. *Psychosomatic disturbances.* Reversals or complications in toilet habits, enuresis, constipation, diarrhea, excessive urination, feeding disturbances, overeating, nausea or vomiting when emotionally distressed, various aches and pains. (*48*)

It will be recognized that many of these characteristics appear in the behavior of normal children. However, as a general rule, whenever a combination of these symptoms appear frequently and consistently, and do not yield to usual controls, it should lead the teacher to suspect a serious problem. We may generalize even further and say that regardless of the symptom, whenever a child's behavior is exaggerated beyond what is customary for youngsters of his age, an adjustment problem is indicated (*21, 64*).

Interpreting Symptoms of Maladjustment

Behavior symptoms are meaningful only when they lead to an interpretation of the factors which create them. Here the teacher must proceed with caution, for the symptoms of children often are deceiving. Aggression, for instance, may stem from hostility, fear, inferiority, or sheer exuberance. The overt behavior resulting from these causes may appear the same, but have vastly different psychological roots. Likewise, the fat, passive, submissive child may present a deceiving appearance of good-natured joviality. Beneath this mask often lies a basic hostility which has been repressed and is kept under control through overeating.

Even dull children have been noted to appear so bright and interested in their work that their intellectual inferiority is obscured. These false signs can easily lead astray an inexperienced observer.

Another complicating factor in the interpretation of behavior symptoms is that a given set of symptoms may stem from a variety of causes; or a single basic cause may yield several seemingly unrelated symptoms. For example, nail biting is a common tension-relieving device used by normal children, particularly at the ages of 12, 13, and 14. However, fatigue, vitamin deficiency, self-punishment, guilt feelings, or neurotic anxiety are conditions which also give rise to this symptom (*14*). Thus, the significance of nail biting may be exaggerated in some cases, whereas in others it is not given sufficient consideration.

Similarly, the child who shows considerable variability of disposition, quarrelsomeness, hypermotility, and fluctuations in ability to concentrate may be undergoing the typical ups and downs of preadolescence—or he may be reacting to something far more serious. These symptoms are known to result from certain physical ailments, such as convulsive disorders, epidemic encephalitis, or asphyxiating illnesses in infancy, and are associated also with the behavior of children who later become psychotic (*58, 60*).

A third factor which makes difficult the interpretation of symptomatic behavior relates to predictions of future adjustment based upon earlier behavior characteristics. The evidence on this point is quite conflicting. Kanner's extensive studies (*37*) showed that there is no way of telling for certain whether behavior problems will carry over into later years. On the other hand, Despert's work (*19*) with stutterers revealed a definite relationship between early manifestations of poor adjustment and the later development of speech disorders. Similar relationships were found by Barber (*1*), Marcus (*47*), and others, who studied retarded readers. They found that children who show educational disabilities almost invariably have a history of immature interpersonal relationships and a lag in psychological maturity.

These difficulties are mentioned primarily to emphasize the danger of reaching hasty conclusions regarding the problems of children. By becoming keen observers of gross deviations from normal behavior, teachers can learn to distinguish forms of adjustment which have clinical significance. This does not require teachers to become diagnosticians, but stresses the need to look beyond superficial symptoms of behavior to discover the causes underlying them. Diagnostic thinking of this type can be done even by teachers who have a minimum of training in child study.

Handling Maladjustment in the Classroom

Ideally, the teacher's responsibility for maladjusted children should be to identify these youngsters early and refer them to qualified therapists for treatment. The lack of clinical facilities and trained clinical workers makes this procedure impractical in many schools and forces the teacher into the role of a therapist.

There are some definite limitations to what teachers can or should do for disturbed youngsters, and these limitations must be clearly understood by parents, teachers, and administrators. In general, it is the teacher's function to provide a climate favorable to the development of mental health. If a teacher goes beyond this and attempts to correct deep-seated behavior problems without having the necessary training in therapy, he may intensify a child's problems. There are several reasons why teachers who are not specifically trained in therapeutic procedures should not attempt to probe too deeply into a child's psychological problems.

First, a disturbed child will develop a series of protective devices to allay his anxiety. These protective devices may not be conducive to mental health, but they make him feel more comfortable and are the best techniques at his command. The adult who seeks to set matters right by causing the child to cease using these devices, and is unable to provide him with other sources of comfort, releases the child's anxiety and leaves him unprotected. This is why clinicians advise parents and teachers to avoid meddling with a child's anxiety-relieving behavior. If the protective devices a child develops are not too harmful to himself or to others, they must be accepted until they can be replaced with more positive modes of adjustment. Usually, if the modification of environmental factors do not relieve a child's anxiety or change his anxiety-reducing practices, he needs the help of a skilled therapist.

Secondly, many behavior deviations may run a normal course determined by the sequence of growth and need not reach permanent or pathological dimensions (27:295). The inexperienced person may unwittingly interfere with this course of development by trying to correct behavior that later may correct itself. For instance, studies of shy, withdrawn children show that the matter of "bringing out" the shy child may have been overemphasized. A report on the adjustment of 54 adults who as children had been shy, withdrawn, anxious, and fearful, showed that two-thirds of the group achieved satisfactory adjustment without any particular therapeutic help. They had been allowed to develop in their own way and at their own pace, and they succeeded in becoming self-supporting stable persons, although they continued to be quiet and retiring (50). This suggests that not every lonely child is unhappy. Some children prefer their own company to that of others, and if they are not made to feel guilty about this, or taught it is abnormal, they can be well-adjusted, happy persons.

Third, a person who is not trained to use many kinds of therapeutic procedures commonly resorts to symptomatic treatment. Usually, they succeed only in eliminating one set of symptoms which is soon replaced by another set, while the basic causes of maladjustment go unattended. This may be harmful to the child in that it delays bringing to him the therapeutic help which may prevent the further development of his difficulties. For example, it has been found that Amphetamine can be used to control enuresis, stimulate the quiet, withdrawn child, or calm down the child who is hyperactive, aggressively noisy and antisocial (7, 9). If these conditions are treated superficially by a person who is not authorized to use medical therapy, a child's difficulties may be intensified and his recovery impeded.

These precautions are offered not to discourage teachers from efforts which may help alleviate children's problems, but to emphasize that they should not attempt more than they are qualified to do by their training and experience. The skilled and understanding teacher can offer children great stimulus and support in the classroom. Chronic maladjustment often can be averted by controlling the pressures upon children, and by adapting the school program to their needs. So long as the teacher's efforts are confined to modifying the physical, social, and emotional environment of the classroom to fit children's needs, to helping children express and clarify their troubles, to helping them work out their own adjustment problems, and to providing emotional support, he need have no fear about aggravating the problems of disturbed children.

Moreover, teachers should not become discouraged if they cannot salvage all the maladjusted children who pass through their classrooms. Many of these youngsters require the best efforts of medical or clinical workers. If professional treatment is not available, the teacher must do what can be done through the rather simple therapeutic procedures at his disposal without becoming frustrated over his inability to do more.

PREPSYCHOTIC AND PSYCHOTIC BEHAVIOR IN CHILDREN

As a rule, teachers encounter very few cases of active child psychosis. However, most of the children who will later develop serious mental disorders are in our schools, and if the teacher can help identify these youngsters and refer them to specialists before they reach the most serious stages of their disturbance, some important preventive work can be accomplished.

There is no sure way of detecting the prepsychotic child unless his symptoms are pronounced. Very often the child who later becomes psychotic appears on the whole not very much different from the average run of boys and girls. Even skilled examiners have not succeeded in predicting which of the children they examine at a guidance clinic will later become psychotic (3). Some worth-while investigations have been made of the early behavior of children who later became psychotic, and the findings will interest those teachers who encounter cases of this type. These studies deal mainly with youngsters who developed schizophrenia, manic-depressive psychosis, or psychopathic personality.

The Preschizophrenic Child

There is perhaps more evidence on the behavior of preschizophrenic children than on the early stages of other forms of psychoses. Bradley's extensive studies (8, 10) of boys and girls under 13 years of age who were residents in a children's mental hospital found that the most striking characteristics of the preschizophrenic child, in rank order of significance, were as follows:

1. *Seclusiveness.* A strong tendency to remain aloof from other children for no apparent reason.
2. *Irritability.* A reaction of anger when the seclusive activities are interrupted.
3. *Daydreaming.* Beyond that usually noted in children of normal development.
4. *Bizarre behavior.* Posturizing, repetitive, purposeless motions, unintelligible language, and irrelevant expression of emotion.
5. *Diminution of interests.* Attracted to fewer objects and activities than normal children.
6. *Regressive personal interests.* Selection of amusements and occupations common for younger children.
7. *Sensitivity to comment and criticism.* Excessive emotional response to praise and blame.

8. *Physical inactivity*. Less motor activity than children of similar age and development.

The findings of Friedlander (*26*) and Demerath (*17*) essentially confirm Bradley's findings. In addition to the characteristics described above, these investigators found that the preschizophrenic child is likely to be apprehensive, tense, easily upset, and overdependent on parents; he has few or no friends, lacks self-confidence, is often depressed or low in spirits, and is sometimes aggressive.

Other studies (*55*) have found the preschizophrenic child to be a sweet, gentle child who is easy to get along with, passive, and dependent. His school work may be average or better than average, and his general appearance that of a shy, seemingly well-behaved youngster who is preoccupied with his own problems. If observed over a long period of time, the future schizophrenic becomes increasingly self-involved, sensitive, and serious. Often it is after puberty, when he has to face problems of sex, social relationship, and relinquishing of dependence, that he becomes acutely upset and develops psychotic symptoms. At this time, like a dam giving out, everything bursts at once.

The Schizophrenic Child

Few children develop schizophrenia before puberty. Those who do have definite symptoms which set them apart from other children. Prominent among these are the following:

1. Hormonal imbalance, resulting in premature or delayed onset of puberty.
2. Gastrointestinal symptoms, including colic and difficulty with eating and elimination.
3. Disturbed homeostasis, as evidenced by vasomotor instability, such as cold extremities and even cyanotic nail beds; abnormal adrenal response to stress situations, and sleep rhythm irregularity, with either too much or too little sleep. At times they are torporous during the day and wide awake at night.
4. Lack of muscle tonus; the muscles are soft, yielding to the touch without firmness, cheeks are full and there is a pouting expression to the lips.
5. Outstanding language disturbance, ranging from complete mutism to highly elaborate language and symbol formation. (*51, 60*)

The young schizophrenic child, age 6 to 8, is usually a pretty child with puffy cheeks, pouting expression, and a delicate complexion. He is alternately withdrawn and alert. He may suddenly shriek and hold his hands over his ears, or he may become aggressive and destructive. He repeats sudden questions over and over again. Despite such reactions, many of these children learn to read and write by the age of 7 or 8, and cover endless pages with their lettering. They may have a large vocabulary and are able to memorize songs and poetry, but cannot use language effectively for expression and communication.

The child schizophrenic apparently is confused over his body image. He often treats parts of his body as if they were foreign objects. He is abnormally preoccupied with space relations and has a great interest in circling and spinning. He outlines objects with his fingers, or traces around them, seemingly concerned more with geometric design than with the object itself. Touch is used conspicuously in dealing with objects; he even smells and tastes them. In all these activities, the child seems to behave as if each toy or object is a series of details, while the function of the object is not perceived (51).

Schizophrenia at the age of 10 or 11 may be ushered in with sadistic or impulsive behavior, a sudden increase in anxiety, withdrawal, phobias and obsessive-compulsive defenses. Bizarre somatic complaints are frequent, such as fear that one extremity is growing longer than the other, or that a rod is running down his back and if it comes out, he will no longer be able to stand.

Phobias often are associated with body image problems. They may be concerned with ghosts, skeletons, the feeling that a man will steal into the window and kill him, the illusion that a little man, an Indian, the devil, or a little voice that tells them what to do is in the head, heart, or stomach (60).

Manic-Depressive and Psychopathic Manifestations

These disorders have not been studied as extensively as schizophrenia, but enough is known to describe some of the typical symptoms seen in children.

The young manic-depressive usually is friendly and outgoing in his interests and strives for group approval. He may manifest a high degree of insecurity that is reflected in a drive for accomplishment and anxiety to succeed. He has a serious, anxious, and worrying attitude toward life, shows no negativism or rebellion, and often is so warm and altruistic toward teachers and friends that he is well liked.

These children manifest many autonomic disturbances, such as gastric distress, nausea, vomiting, headaches, anorexia, loss of weight, delay in menstruation, and insomnia. Also, they experience hypomanic and depressive moods, fear reactions, psychomotor retardation, phobias, insecurity, and crying spells (13).

The child psychopath seldom fails to attract attention. He seems unable to exercise control over antisocial impulses. He is particularly envious and competitive and readily resorts to cheating and foul play if these methods will insure success. He apparently does not learn from experiences with authoritative discipline and attempts to avoid punishment by acting remorseful when apprehended. He tries to manipulate people through extortion or ingratiation and seeks to satisfy his desires without giving anything in exchange (47).

Friedlander's study (26) found almost all psychopathic children exhibit tenseness and an easily upset emotional balance. About half daydreamed frequently and showed symptoms of general apprehension. Rejection or ambivalent feelings toward parents were evidenced by 78 percent. Poor school work was part of the picture in 87 percent of the psychopaths. These children were more aggressive than normal children of their age, were excitable, and usually were leaders among their age-mates.

These are some of the behavior characteristics to which teachers should be particularly alert. A seriously disturbed child does not belong in an ordinary classroom. He constitutes so serious a problem that no teacher should have to deal with such a youngster, other than to recognize the seriousness of his disorder and to refer him to a treatment center.

SEX DIFFERENCES IN THE ADJUSTMENT OF CHILDREN

There are definite sex differences in the adjustment, behavior, and mental health of boys and girls. Boys, it seems, have more trouble getting along with society, their psychological problems are more pronounced, and they have considerable more difficulty in school than do girls. These conclusions have been confirmed by numerous studies and bear important implications for the guidance of children.

Delinquency and Maladjustment

Evidence that delinquency is a problem which involves boys more frequently than girls is quite conclusive. Juvenile court statistics show that boys are in trouble with the law five times more often than girls (76). This same ratio holds true for the number of boys and girls confined to juvenile detention homes (52).

Studies of the adjustment and mental health of children also reveal boys to be in an unfavorable position as compared with girls. Rogers (56) found three times as many serious mental hygiene problems among boys than girls in his study of 1524 elementary school children. Snyder (61) reported a ratio of four maladjusted boys to each girl among elementary school children. Similar data were secured by Mangus and Seeley (45) in their inventory of adjustment among third and sixth graders.

Other investigations (46, 81), while showing some variance in the proportion of maladjusted boys to girls, report consistent findings of a higher incidence of disturbed behavior among male children. This relationship pertains also among children confined to mental hospitals. The California Department of Mental Hygiene (11, 12) reported the boys' wards in state mental hospitals generally are full and have a waiting list, while girls' wards have available beds. Admissions to California State Mental Hygiene Clinics likewise showed a greater ratio of boys to girls. In 1957, two-thirds of all admissions under the age of 17 were boys.[1]

All told, this evidence indicates that almost from the beginning, boys have a more difficult time of adjusting to life than do girls. Data on delinquency, truancy, maladjustment, and psychosis show that in each of these categories boys predominate.

Sex Differences in School Achievement

The commonly held belief that girls do better than boys in school is amply substantiated by the facts. There is a higher percentage of failure among boys in every grade and every subject (2); boys comprise the bulk of early school-leavers (72); they dislike school more than girls do (67); and on standardized achievement tests, boys score from six months to a year-and-a-half below girls in elementary and high schools (53).

Pauly (53) has suggested that the differences in achievement reported between boys and girls are probably not sex differences but ma-

[1] California Department of Mental Hygiene, Statistical Research Bureau, *Preliminary Statistical Report California State Mental Hygiene Clinics,* Fiscal Year ending June 30, 1957, Sacramento, 1957, Table 1.

turity differences. He advocates that a six months' differential in legal school-entering ages be established to reduce the handicap caused by the slower growth rate of boys. However, differences in maturity may not be the only factor contributing to the scholastic disadvantage of boys. Day (16), for instance, made an extensive analysis of elementary and high school pupils and found that despite equal intelligence, a girl is one and one-third times as likely as a boy to receive high grades in school. Similarly, St. John (62) could find no significant difference in intelligence or scholastic aptitude among the boys and girls studied in a Boston suburb, yet over a four-year period, boys were noted to fare, on the average, 7 percent worse than girls in grade progress.

Interpretations of Sex Differences in Adjustment

Many of the adjustment differences of boys and girls may be due to cultural influences. From early childhood, boys and girls are expected to act, look, and feel in different ways. By the time a youngster reaches the teens, there has been a long piling up of differences in treatment and expectations. The girl is more protected, has less freedom than the boy, must conform more closely to parental requirements, and must develop the characteristics of a little lady (77). Boys are permitted much more freedom in their behavior and in the expression of their emotions. Consequently, they develop more outward aggression, more gang associations, and are less subject to the close supervision usually imposed on girls.

These differences in cultural impositions may account for the distinguishing emotional behavior of boys and girls. Boys learn to turn their drives outward, to act out their feelings, and to release their tensions through overt expression. As a result, they are more likely to become involved in delinquent or antisocial acts, and to get into trouble by rebelling against adult authority. Because boys bring their problems forcibly to the attention of adults, the chances are four to one that when teachers are asked to pick out a maladjusted child, they will select a boy (74, 5).

Girls are culturally conditioned to release their tensions through psychological escape mechanisms, while displaying outward compliance and passivity (74). Their conflicts are internal, rather than interpersonal. They are more inclined to be timid, depressed, reflective, and meditative (28, 36). Their anxiety and hostility are more likely to be hidden behind a façade of politeness and obedience, and they learn to be prudent and circumspect in reacting to frustrations (*34*). It is, therefore, quite possible that the findings with regard to the number of boys who lead troubled lives, as compared with girls, may not necessarily prove that girls are better adjusted than boys. It may mean that observers, noting only what is on the surface, make this judgment because they do not interpret correctly the subjective way in which girls experience their difficulties.

Some justification for this viewpoint is found in data on patients admitted to mental hospitals. As shown in Table 9, more women than men

TABLE 9.   First Admissions to State Hospitals for Mental Disease in 1953, by Sex, for Four Types of Psychoses[a]

Disorder	Number of Male Admissions	Number of Female Admissions
Involutional Psychotic Reaction	1,344	3,243
Manic-Depressive Reaction	1,478	2,073
Psychotic-Depressive Reaction	345	410
Schizophrenic Reactions	11,772	13,592
All Psychoses	15,706	19,904

[a] Adapted from U.S. Department of Health, Education and Welfare, Public Health Service, National Institutes of Health, *Patients in Mental Institutions 1953*, Part II, "Public Hospitals for The Mentally Ill," Public Health Service Publication No. 495, 1956, Table 8, p. 26.

are hospitalized for disorders which usually are associated with escapist behavior, withdrawal, or repression. Also, more women than men are committed to hospitals for psychoneurotic reactions. This may indicate that the problems of girls escape attention because their troubles are submerged, permitting them to intensify and reach serious proportions before evidence of maladjustment is manifested.

Differences in the school achievement of boys and girls seem to be influenced also by the way in which teachers react to the general behavior and conduct of children. While girls appear to have better study habits than boys, and are more willing to undergo the discipline required to obtain high marks, this factor alone does not entirely explain differences in achievement. As early as 1929, Hartshorne, May, and Maller (*31*) noted that when pupils are rated by teachers, girls were consistently higher than boys. "The difference between the sexes in reputation . . . ," they observed, "is so much greater than it is found to be on the tests that one is inclined to believe that a sex prejudice may be at work which rates the boys lower than they really are and the girls higher than they really are."

Recent studies (62) affirm this observation. There appears to be a halo effect at work in the awarding of grades to children. Quiet, docile, obedient behavior is rewarded with high marks, while the aggressive, resistant behavior, commonly displayed by boys, is more likely to antagonize teachers and result in low marks in conduct and effort, and consequent devaluation of academic accomplishment. Furthermore, since boys do not adapt so well to quiet, orderly classroom routine, they experience considerable thwarting in school. This results in emotional reactions which influence test performance and results in lower achievement scores.

There is some indication that the predominance of women teachers in the public schools may also work to the detriment of boys. Tschechtelin (73) found that women teachers significantly prefer girls in their ratings of personality characteristics of children. Since most elementary school teachers are women, boys receive a much greater volume of adverse appraisals than do girls. Douglass and Olson (20) conducted a similar investigation into the marks given to students by men and women teachers in high schools. They found that in groups of boys and girls equated on intelligence, no significant difference existed in the marks given to boys and girls by men teachers, but women significantly favored the girls.

While it would be premature to conclude that the sex of the teacher is responsible for the academic difficulties of boys, this factor does appear to have some significance. Evidence seems to indicate that teachers are not adjusting themselves or their school procedures to the needs of boys as well as they do to the needs of girls. As a result, boys experience much more frustration in school, and their interest in achievement is lower than that of girls (40).

ADJUSTMENT PROBLEMS OF CHILDREN WITH PHYSICAL OR MENTAL LIMITATIONS

There are several million school children in this country who, because of physical or mental limitations, are faced with particularly difficult adjustment problems. According to the United States Children's Bureau (15), this group includes approximately

> 75,000 with cleft palate and lip
> 275,000 with epilepsy

285,000 with cerebral palsy
675,000 with rheumatic fever heart disease
866,000 with serious visual defects
1,000,000 with orthopedic defects
1,700,000 with severe speech disorders

In addition, about 1½ million youngsters are classified as mentally retarded (*41*), and an undetermined number have a variety of other ailments, such as nephritis, diabetes, asthma, allergies, hearing, and orthodontic defects.

All told, there are over 5 million children of school age who have physical or mental afflictions that set them apart from ordinary youngsters. These handicapped, or exceptional, children live under greater emotional stress than do normal children. They require much understanding and careful handling in the school. Some school systems employ visiting teachers, psychologists, speech and hearing therapists, physiotherapists, or special education teachers who are trained to work with handicapped children. However, services of this type are not sufficiently widespread to provide adequate care for all children with disabilities. In fact, the United States Office of Education found that in 1952 only 497,-216 exceptional children were enrolled in special programs (*75*). This means that the great majority of children who need special assistance are either not in school, or are in classrooms where they receive only the help that a regular teacher can give them.

Sources of Adjustment Difficulties

Children with physical or mental limitations are subject to all the adjustment problems that normal children have, but these problems are itensified by three factors: First, the reactions and behavior of parents toward their handicapped child influences profoundly his emotional behavior. Secondly, the problem of establishing interpersonal relations among persons from whom he differs physically or mentally presents a serious obstacle to the achievement of group acceptance. Third, many physical and mental disabilities are accompanied by psychological or behavioral reactions which the child cannot control and which influence his personal adjustment and social acceptance. These three factors have been discovered to be significantly associated with the feeling of isolation which forms the basis for many of the behavior problems displayed by these youngsters.

PARENTAL INFLUENCES. Many parents love their handicapped children fully and wisely. They accept them for what they are, encourage them to develop their potentialities, and do not try to make them over. For many other parents, the birth of a physically or mentally defective child is a difficult burden to bear. They may feel guilty over the child's handicap and in various ways punish themselves for his affliction; they may feel injured by fate, or may even refuse to acknowledge that their child is different until his disability becomes grossly apparent.

In response to these feelings, parents may reject their children overtly, or in disguised ways. This rejection may be expressed in the rigidity with which they hold a youngster to a prescribed diet or medical schedule, or in the excessive and unrealistic demands made of him. Parents who blame themselves for their child's handicap may overprotect the youngster to the extent that he is never given an opportunity to utilize the abilities he has. They prolong his infancy, his childhood is protracted, and he may be kept emotionally dependent, or indulged, throughout life (*24, 57*).

The psychological correlates of these parental attitudes are reflected in the child's behavior. The indulged child may become the family tyrant who uses his handicap as a big stick to satisfy a never ending series of claims and demands. The youngster who has been rejected, criticized, coerced, or punished will shrink from others and anticipate nothing but hurt. As with other rejected children, he harbors much hostility which is expressed physically, or psychologically, through striking out at the more fortunate world. These youngsters have a conspicuous tendency toward destructiveness and aggression.

Other children have an excessive need for affection, care, and attention. It is difficult for them to make an independent move without sustained assistance and encouragement. They refuse to embark on exploratory ventures, holding on to their habits, routines, and familiar environment as sources of psychological support.

Because of overprotection, rejection, or lack of social experience, the handicapped child often comes to school an unhappy, asocial individual who feels isolated from others. His lack of contact with children or adults outside the family may leave him functioning at a very immature level of interpersonal and group behavior. This immaturity accentuates his feeling of isolation, and makes it increasingly difficult for him to find companionship or emotional satisfaction (*42*).

INTERPERSONAL RELATIONS. The attitude of normal children toward a malformed body or defective mind quite often intensifies the emotional problems of handicapped children. Many youngsters, and adults too, are uneasy in the presence of a person who has a defect. They may feel pity or curiosity and be self-conscious or uncertain as to how to behave without seeming oversolicitous or unnatural. Nor is it uncommon to feel revulsion toward a disabled child and react to these feelings by expressing hostility or superiority, or by trying to ignore him altogether.

Sometimes the behavior or appearance of a defective child may actually instill fear in children. For instance, the epileptic child who has a grand mal seizure in the classroom may present a shocking sight to youngsters. The muscle spasms, foaming at the mouth, tongue chewing, urinary and fecal incontinence, excessive salivation, and post-convulsive depressed and confused state which accompanies these seizures is a spectacle few children can overlook or forget (70).

School experiences such as these tend to isolate the handicapped child still further. Moreover, youngsters are notoriously prone to pick on the weakness of others and taunt them with names such as "dummy," "limpy," "four eyes," or "fits," to mention only a few. To an already sensitive child who knows he is different from others, such taunts can be sheer torture.

PSYCHOBIOLOGICAL SOURCES OF MALADJUSTMENT. In addition to the difficulties mentioned above, the physical nature of a child's handicap, and its characteristic behavior concomitants, may have a direct bearing on his emotional reactions. A few of these are mentioned below to illustrate this problem:

Effects of brain damage. Youngsters who have sustained severe brain damage, either from trauma or disease, tend to be extremely fidgety and impulsive. These reactions are considered to be epileptic equivalents of motor discharges and not easily subject to voluntary control (38). Such children have difficulty integrating feeling and action, and are prone to emotional outbursts and hyperactive behavior. Brain-damaged children are likely to lack judgment, to be defiant and hostile, and to vacillate in their emotional responses (47). Their attention span is very brief and their concepts of time, space, and distance immature (29).

The allergic or asthmatic child. These children react to emotional situations with an outbreak of physiological symptoms. They have a touchy disposition, are emotionally insecure, prone to anxiety, and resistant to any change in routine or environment. Their constitutional sensitivity makes them more easily subject to emotional upsets than normal children. They are likely to be dependent, hypersensitive, irritable, and have a low frustration tolerance (*24, 25*).

Epileptics. The behavior of epileptics will vary with the nature of their disorder and the extent to which it is controlled by medication. Three primary types of epileptic attacks have been recognized: *Grand mal* seizures, previously described, can result in intellectual deterioration, organic brain disease, and psychoses. *Petit mal* attacks induce a transient loss of consciousness not accompanied by convulsion. These attacks, lasting from 5 to 30 seconds, may involve staring or dizzy spells, twitching, eye rolling, or drooling, but usually have no after-effects. *Psychomotor* epileptic attacks, while the least frequent of the three types, often effect a change in personality. During these attacks the child may become destructive, aggressive, or extremely active. When the attack ceases, there is no recollection of this disturbed behavior (*70*).

Bradley (*6*) has discovered five traits which are associated so frequently with the behavior of epileptic children as to be considered characteristic of this disorder. These are: (1) erratic variability in mood or behavior, (2) hypermotility, (3) irritability, (4) short and vaccillating attention span, and (5) a rather selective difficulty in mathematics as a school subject. These behavior characteristics appear to be as important as the physical ailment in creating adjustment problems for epileptic children.

The mentally retarded. The mentally retarded youngster not only grows at a slower pace than the average child, but his total growth ends earlier. His retardation is general and progressive, and becomes more pronounced as the child ages. His immaturity often leads to social misbehavior and nonacceptance of personal and social responsibility. Inability to hold his own in the competitive surroundings of a classroom may lead him into antisocial behavior in order to attract attention (*57*).

Physical deviations. Children who have orthopedic handicaps, cleft palates, or other types of physical disabilities are subject to adjustment problems which center around ego development. The body image is known to be a vital part of ego formation. Therefore, if a child rejects his body, or conceives it to be inadequate, his ego formation may be impaired.

Often, children with physical deformities have basic feelings of anxiety and apprehension which stem from self-pity, or from the belief that their handicap represents a form of divine punishment. These feelings may lead to introversion, withdrawal, or neurotic manifestations, or through the action of compensating mechanisms, may result in incorrigibility or delinquency. In either case, the physically handicapped child is susceptible to feelings of being an outcast, and has difficulty forming close associations with others (*24, 43*).

These are but a few of the organic, psychological, and social bases for the adjustment problems of children with mental or physical limitations. They help explain why these youngsters so often are immature, antisocial, fearful, hostile, withdrawn, or aggressive, and they point to some of the areas with which these children will need help if they are to develop adequate personalities and learn to share in the lives of normal individuals.

The Handicapped Child in the Classroom

Despite the fact that handicapped children tend to be academically retarded and have more than their share of emotional problems, with proper help and training they are capable of becoming happy and useful persons. Studies have shown that a handicap will not prohibit a youngster from achieving vocational success and social acceptance, provided he develops the appropriate skills and the ability to work harmoniously with others (*33, 41*). This suggests that schools can best serve the handicapped child by helping him gain social acceptance, by promoting his feelings of personal adequacy, and by encouraging him to develop his individual potentialities as fully as possible.

PERSONAL ADEQUACY. Children who receive much attention and care during early childhood may develop so strong a feeling of dependency that later, when this care should no longer be needed, they experience feelings of helplessness or panic if it is withdrawn. In school such children need to be treated with a combination of realism and sympathy. They must not be given too much assistance; nor should they be forced to relinquish their dependency patterns too rapidly. Under careful guidance they can learn to make their own decisions and assume increasing responsibility for their own welfare. If they are taught self-sufficiency gradually and they are socially accepted, handicapped children can be helped to overcome their feelings of inadequacy and develop a sense of self-esteem.

SOCIAL ACCEPTANCE. Handicapped children in a regular classroom often are the most isolated and rejected children in the group. In most cases it has been found that the rejection of these youngsters is due to their social inadequacies rather than to their handicaps or inability to keep up with other children (*18, 35*). This fact is highly significant in view of the handicapped child's almost pathetic need for social acceptance. This need is so intense that the teacher who can help these youngsters develop the characteristics conducive to social acceptance, or who can maneuver a group of children into making a handicapped child feel needed and wanted, may do more for him than can be accomplished by professional therapists.

DEVELOPMENT OF INDIVIDUAL ABILITIES. All children need the feeling of accomplishment derived from doing things for themselves. This need is particularly acute for handicapped children because there are so few things they can do on their own. They need help in discovering their abilities, and praise for hard-won achievement. Accomplishments that seem so small as to be hardly worth mentioning may represent real effort to these youngsters. Their smallest successes must be acknowledged so that they may develop the courage to attempt more difficult tasks.

To help a handicapped child make the best use of his powers, the teacher must be aware of his reactions to failure. Failure is critical to these youngsters and they have a tendency to retreat from a task at which they have failed. Too much pressure on a handicapped child can set back his emotional development and make an invalid of a child who with reassurance and warm understanding might have a reasonably satisfactory life (*44, 78*). To illustrate how this may occur, Kanner (*38*) describes the case of a child whose failure and humiliation in school, rather than his basic handicap (mental retardation), led to a disturbed condition which required therapeutic help:

> Recently a mother brought her five and one-half year old boy to our clinic because the school recommended that he be retained in kindergarten for another year. The teacher complained that Kenneth was immature, cried much in the classroom, became frustrated when he was unable to keep within the lines while crayoning, and generally had poor motor coordination . . . he talked at random and out of turn, interfered with instruction and was not tolerated. His work even at kindergarten level was inadequate, and he was forever deprived of the praise which the other children received. His pathetic helplessness, his clumsiness, the observation that his drawings were never put up on the wall for everybody to see, and the occasional taunts which came from some of his classmates, resulted in a diffuse, painful feeling of being different,

of falling short, of the futility of every effort on his part to do as well as the rest of the children. Was it, then, Kenneth's low intelligence quotient which caused him to cry, to be restless, to wonder if his classmates liked him?

Obviously, this teacher did not understand the emotional struggles which Kenneth was undergoing, and instead of relieving his frustrations, accentuated them by holding him to the standards of normal, better endowed children. All of this was too much for a child who was already living in the shadows of rejection and isolation.

Thus, teachers who encounter children with mental or physical disabilities need to be sensitive to the special needs and problems of these youngsters. They must neither reject nor overprotect them; neither push them too hard nor permit them to do less than they are capable of doing, but try to assess their abilities and limitations and make realistic provisions for their psychological, social, and academic development. These, it will be noted, are the same principles which apply to the education of all children whose mental health is valued by the school.

Adjustment Problems of the Gifted Child

Although the gifted children are commonly included in the category of "exceptional" children, their adjustment problems are quite different and merit special consideration. Investigators have found that gifted children, generally, are superior in mental health as well as mental ability. They tend to be more stable emotionally, more independent, and more self-assured than average children. Their insanity [2] rates are slightly lower than the expectancy rates for the general population, and the rate of nervous disorders also is low (66, 69).

This does not mean that gifted children have no adjustment problems. It has been found that 20 to 25 percent of this group display minor personality problems and that almost one in 20 presents serious maladjustment problems (80). Moreover, the more superior the child is intellectually, the more difficulty he has adapting himself to the ordinary world. Terman (68) has observed that the adjustment problems of very superior children are so intense that the child with an IQ of 180 has one of the most difficult jobs of social adjustment that any human being is ever called upon to meet.

---

[2] The term "insanity" is used here in its legal rather than psychological sense, and refers to officially recognized mental abnormalities.

While superior children represent only a small proportion of the total child population, educators have become seriously concerned with the wastage of talent among them. The Educational Policies Commission (22) discloses that in many states only half of the gifted youth who are graduated from secondary schools go on to college. Personal and social maladjustment has been found to be one of the most significant factors associated with this curtailment of education among superior students. There is reason to believe that if educators became more concerned with the mental health of these youngsters, rather than devoting their attentions exclusively to the intellectual development of superior children, many of our potential leaders would not drop out of school and become unhappy, frustrated, unproductive individuals.

SOCIAL ACCEPTANCE PROBLEMS OF THE GIFTED CHILD. The superior child often finds himself cut off from communication with other children. The interests, activities, conversation, and play of his chronological equals may appear immature to him. His own intellectual interests are so far beyond the comprehension of average children that they find no common ground for establishing social relationships. This estrangement may cause the bright child to seek comfort in solitary play, sedentary activities, and intellectual pursuits. The higher the child's mental ability, the greater is the tendency toward isolation from normal group activity. Children with IQ's of 160 and above, for instance, commonly are excluded, or exclude themselves, from play with other children. They are likely either to stand on the sidelines and watch, play by themselves, or spend their time with books (82).

Social isolation may cause a gifted child to become cynical and intolerant of others with normal ability. In the elementary and high school they may be lonely individuals who attempt to dominate their contemporaries and are antagonistic toward authority. Not until they reach college, where their intellectual abilities may help them achieve social recognition, do they learn to mingle with people as equals. By this time, they may have developed personality quirks which label them as "queer geniuses" and further accentuate their difference from others.

Many times teachers intensify the social difficulties of a gifted child by giving him so much special attention that other children resent him. This process was observed in a sixth grade class where Bruce, with an IQ of 150, was the teacher's pride, always ready with the right answer and with involved explanations which the other children could not understand. The children called him "the Professor," and treated him as something of a freak. When Bruce began to sense his isolation, he brought his problem to the teacher. Together they decided that it might be better for Bruce not to dominate the class discussion and permit other children more opportunity to express themselves. He did this, and before long the youngsters began to warm up to him.

It is not uncommon for gifted children to so crave social approval that they deliberately suppress their intellectual superiority. This is not a healthy means of adjustment, for by suppressing his abilities, the superior child may fail to develop his full potentialities and thus expose himself to further frustration.

EFFECTS OF OVEREMPHASIS ON INTELLECTUAL DEVELOPMENT. Parents and teachers may unknowingly contribute to the adjustment difficulties of a gifted youngster by exploiting his cleverness, pushing, or overstimulating him. The school may do the same thing through acceleration or enrichment programs which provide for the intellectual development of the superior child, while isolating him further from the social activities of the classroom. The extra attention received by the superior child in a regular classroom, together with the special privileges and freedom from group regimentation which he may enjoy, are not calculated to improve his acceptability to less privileged children of ordinary talents.

The superior child who is accelerated in his school progress is likely to find himself among youngsters of similar mental age but more advanced social maturity. These conditions cause the superior child to feel insecure and inadequate, exclude him from extracurricular activities, and make it more difficult for him to achieve group acceptance (82).

These are some of the circumstances which force the superior child to rely upon intellectual activities as a source of psychological satisfaction. This leads to an unbalanced personality and to emotional problems which may dissipate his energies to the point where his talents are not utilized efficiently.

PSYCHOLOGICAL NEEDS OF THE GIFTED CHILD. The implication of these findings is that whatever plan is used to encourage the intellectual development of superior children, provisions must be made for helping them achieve satisfying personal and social adjustment. The gifted child who does not learn to understand people is likely to be less successful than one who has average talents, but greater social skill (69). To realize their full potential, superior children need to face their giftedness with realism and modesty, and learn how to use it in social relationships with others.

Much of this learning must take place in the early years of school, before their tendencies toward solitary activities become fixed. Special attention must be given to the development of opportunities through which the gifted child can obtain satisfaction from recreation, social activities, manual work, and other interests which will help form a bond between him and his playmates. Parents and teachers must realize that the superior child is still a child who, for the sake of his mental health, must be encouraged to derive satisfaction from nonintellectual, as well as intellectual, interests and to use his giftedness in a way which will lead to a more harmonious adjustment of his whole personality (*22*).

SUMMARY

Youngsters who are chronically maladjusted, prepsychotic, handicapped, or exceptional will make serious demands on the teacher's time and energies because their problems are so complex and their need for assistance so imperative. Ideally, specialists would be secured to work with these children so that the regular classroom teacher can concentrate on the needs of normal or average children. However, many practical considerations interfere with the realization of these ideal circumstances, and the teacher is left with the problem of what to do with youngsters whose lives may be permanently distorted unless help in some form is secured.

This chapter has sought to outline some of the basic factors which will help a teacher understand the nature and origins of the adjustment problems of deviate youngsters. Through wise guidance and intelligent manipulation of classroom influences, many of these youngsters can be provided with experiences which will help prevent further deterioration of their behavior. If this is not possible, as in instances where a child's problems are so severe that the teacher cannot cope with them, the ability to recognize symptoms of chronic maladjustment and to differentiate them from the temporary upsets experienced by normal children will enable the teacher to refer disturbed children for treatment before their disorders reach a critical point.

PROBLEMS AND PROJECTS

1. Illustrate through case descriptions the effects of teaching exceptional children in special classes as compared to keeping them in the regular classroom with their age-mates.
2. Describe some techniques which may be used to help a child avoid em-

barrassment over his appearance or physical defects. What can the teacher do to prevent children from teasing a child with physical defects?

3. Have several men and women teachers evaluate the personality of boys and girls in their classes. Contrast these evaluations with IQ or achievement test scores. Do you find any evidence of sex discrimination?

4. It has been suggested that boys should enter school six months later than girls. Do you agree? What are your observations of the behavior of average boys in a classroom?

5. Should an epileptic child under medication be permitted in a regular classroom? Describe the behavior of epileptics you have observed.

6. Cite an illustration of symptomatic behavior which disguised the real adjustment problems of a child.

7. What are some conditions in school which tend to aggravate the adjustment problems of children? Illustrate.

8. What special or unique adjustment problems do each of the following groups represent in a regular classroom situation: the hard of hearing, the visually handicapped, the speech disordered, the crippled, the low vitality child?

9. Evaluate the techniques of acceleration, homogeneous grouping in special classes or schools, dismissed time, elective courses, and enrichment within the classroom, in terms of their implications for the adjustment of superior children.

10. Describe some circumstances where inexpert treatment of a child's behavior symptoms actually intensified his basic problems.

SELECTED REFERENCES

1. Barber, L. K., "Immature Ego Development as a Factor in Retarded Ability to Read," in *Research Relating to Children,* Bulletin II, U.S. Children's Bureau, 1953, p. 139.

2. Beechy, A., "Pupil Failure in the Elementary Schools," *Educational Research Bulletin,* Ohio State University (May, 1943), 22:123–125.

3. Birren, J. E., "Psychological Examinations of Children Who Later Became Psychotic," *Journal of Abnormal and Social Psychology* (January, 1944), 39:84–96.

4. Bolton, A., "A Prophylactic Approach to Child Psychiatry," *Journal of Mental Science* (July, 1955), 101:696–703.

5. Bower, E. M., "A Process for Identifying Disturbed Children," *Children* (July–August, 1957), 4:143–147.

6. Bradley, C., "Behavior Disturbances in Epileptic Children," *Journal of the American Medical Association* (June, 1951), 146:436–441.

7. Bradley, C., "Benzedrine and Dexedrine in the Treatment of Children's Behavior Disorders," *Pediatrics* (January, 1950), 5:24.

8. Bradley, C., "Early Evidence of Psychoses in Children," *Journal of Pediatrics* (May, 1947), 30:529–540.

9. Bradley, C., and Bowen, M., "Amphetamine (Benzedrine) Therapy of Children's Behavior Disorders," *American Journal of Orthopsychiatry* (January, 1941), 11:92.

10. Bradley, C., and Bowen, M., "Behavior Characteristics of Schizophrenic Children," *Psychiatric Quarterly* (April, 1941), 15:296–315.

11. California Department of Mental Hygiene, *Biennial Report for 1950–52* (Sacramento), 1953.

12. California Department of Mental Hygiene, *Statistical Report* (Sacramento), 1956.

13. Campbell, J. D., "Manic-Depressive Disease in Children," *Journal of the American Medical Association* (May, 1955), 158:154–157.

14. Coleman, J. C., and McCalley, J. E., "Nail Biting and Mental Health," *Mental Hygiene* (July, 1948), 32:428–454.

15. Davens, E., "Services to Crippled Children 1935–55," *Children* (July–August, 1955), 2:139–144.

16. Day, L. C., "Boys and Girls and Honor Ranks," *School Review* (April, 1938), 46:288–299.

17. Demerath, N. J., "Adolescent Status Demands and the Student Experiences of Twenty Schizophrenics," *American Sociological Review* (1943), 8:513–518.

18. De Prospo, C. J., "Opportunities for the Exceptional Child," in *The Adolescent Exceptional Child,* The Woods Schools (Langhorne, Pennsylvania), 1954, pp. 19–30.

19. Despert, J. L., "Psychosomatic Study of Fifty Stuttering Children," *American Journal of Orthopsychiatry* (January, 1946), 16:100–113.

20. Douglass, H. R., and Olson, N. E., "The Relation of High School Marks to Sex in Four Minnesota Senior High Schools," *School Review* (April, 1937), 45:283–288.

21. Drum, W., "Recognizing Behavior Problems in Children," *The Coordinator,* Bulletin of the Oregon Coordinating Council on Social Hygiene and Family Life (February, 1954), 2:3–6.

22. Educational Policies Commission, *Education of the Gifted,* National Education Association, 1950.

23. Federal Security Agency, Public Health Service, *Patients in Mental Institutions 1949,* Public Health Service Publication No. 233, 1952.

24. Federal Security Agency, Social Security Administration, Children's Bureau, *Emotional Problems Associated with Handicapping Conditions in Children,* Children's Bureau Publication No. 336, 1952.

25. Fine, R., *The Personality of the Asthmatic Child,* Unpublished Doctoral Dissertation, University of Southern California (Los Angeles), 1948.

26. Friedlander, D., "Personality Development of 27 Children Who Later Became Psychotic," *Journal of Abnormal and Social Psychology* (July, 1945), 40:330–335.

27. Gesell, A., and Ilg, F. L., *Infant and Child in the Culture of Today,* Harper & Brothers, 1943.

28. Guilford, J. P., and Martin, H., "Age Differences and Sex Differences in Some Introvertive and Emotional Traits," *Journal of General Psychology* (October, 1944), 31:219–229.

29. Harmer, R. M., "A New Life for Brain-Injured Children," *California Teachers Association Journal* (May, 1954), 50:24–25.

30. Harris, A. J., "What Is a 'Normal' Child?" *Journal of Teacher Education* (1952), 3:58–61.

31. Hartshorne, H., May, M. A., and Maller, J. B., *Studies in the Nature of Character,* vol. II, The Macmillan Company, 1929, p. 156.

32. Hayes, M. L., *A Study of Classroom Disturbances of Eighth-Grade Boys and Girls,* Columbia University Press, 1943.

33. Hill, A. S., *The Forward Look: The Severely Retarded Child Goes to School,* U.S. Department of Health, Education and Welfare, Office of Education, Bulletin 1952, no. 11, 1952.

34. Jersild, A. T., *Child Psychology,* Prentice-Hall, Inc., 1954.

35. Johnson, G. O., "A Study of the Social Position of Mentally Handicapped Children in the Grades," *American Journal of Mental Deficiency* (July, 1950), 55:60–89.

36. Johnson, W. B., and Terman, L. M., "Some Highlights in the Literature of Psychological Sex Differences Published Since 1920," *Journal of Psychology* (January, 1940), 9:327–336.

37. Kanner, L., "Early Behavior Problems as Signposts to Later Maladjustment," *American Journal of Psychiatry* (May, 1941), 97:1261–1271.

38. Kanner, L., "The Emotional Quandries of Exceptional Children," in *Helping Parents Understand the Exceptional Child,* The Woods Schools (Langhorne, Pennsylvania), May, 1952, pp. 21–28.

39. Kaplan, L., "Annoyances of Elementary School Teachers," *Journal of Educational Research* (May, 1952), 45:649–665.

40. Kaplan, L., *The Status and Function of Men Teachers in Urban Elementary Schools,* Unpublished Doctoral Dissertation, University of Southern California (Los Angeles), 1947.

41. Kelman, H. R., "A Program for Mentally Retarded Children," *Children* (January–February, 1955), 2:10–14.

42. Landis, C., and Bolles, M. M., *Personality and Sexuality of the Physically Handicapped Woman,* Paul B. Hoeber, Inc., 1942.

43. Lurie, L. A., "Endocrinology and the Understanding and Treatment of the Exceptional Child," *Journal of the American Medical Association* (May, 1938), *110*:1531–1536.

44. Mahler, M. S., "Play as a Learning Process," in *The Exceptional Child in Infancy and Early Childhood,* The Woods Schools (Langhorne, Pennsylvania), May, 1950, pp. 28–32.

45. Mangus, A. R., and Seeley, J. R., *Mental Health Needs in a Rural and Semi-Rural Area of Ohio,* Ohio State Division of Mental Hygiene, 1950.

46. Mangus, A. R., and Woodward, R. H., *An Analysis of the Mental Health of Elementary School Children,* Ohio State Division of Mental Hygiene, 1949.

47. Marcus, I. M., "The Problem of Evaluation," in *The Adolescent Exceptional Child,* The Woods Schools (Langhorne, Pennsylvania), 1954, pp. 10–19.

48. Minneapolis Public Schools, *Resource Guide: Mental Health, Personality Growth, and Adjustment,* 1954, pp. 16–17.

49. Mitchell, J. C., "A Study of Teachers' and Mental Hygienists' Ratings of Certain Behavior Problems of Children," *Journal of Educational Research* (1943), *36*:292–307.

50. Morris, D. P., Soroker, E., and Burruss, G., "Follow-Up Studies of Shy, Withdrawn Children: 1. Evaluation of Later Adjustment," *American Journal of Orthopsychiatry* (October, 1954), *24*:743–754.

51. Norman, E., "Reality Relationships of Schizophrenic Children," *British Journal of Medical Psychology* (1954), *27*:126–141.

52. Norman, S., and Allen, D. F., *California Children in Detention and Shelter Care,* California Committee on Temporary Child Care (Sacramento), 1954.

53. Pauly, F. R., *Further Research on Sex Differences, Legal School Entrance Age and Related Problems,* Paper presented at 119th Annual Meeting of the American Association for Advancement of Science (St. Louis, Missouri), December 29, 1952.

54. Pilzer, E., "Disturbed Children Who Make a Good School Adjustment," *Smith College Studies in Social Work* (1952), *22*:193–210.

55. Prout, C. T., and White, M. A., "The Schizophrenic's Sibling," *Ciba Reports,* May 23, 1955.

56. Rogers, C. R., "Mental Health Findings in 3 Elementary Schools," *Educational Research Bulletin* (March, 1942), *21*:69–79.

57. Roselle, E. N., "Changing Attitudes Toward the Mentally Handicapped," in *The Exceptional Child Faces Adulthood,* The Woods Schools (Langhorne, Pennsylvania), 1955, pp. 44–60.

58. Rosenfeld, G. B., and Bradley, C., "Childhood Behavior Sequelae of

Asphyxia in Infancy—With Special Reference to Pertussis and Asphyxia Neonatorum," *Pediatrics* (July, 1948), *3*:74–84.

59. Schrupp, M. H., and Gjerde, C. M., "Teacher Growth in Attitudes Toward Behavior Problems of Children," *Journal of Educational Psychology* (1953), *44*:203–214.

60. Silver, A. A., "Diagnosis of the Various Syndromes Encountered in the Retarded Pre-Adolescent Child," in *The Pre-Adolescent Exceptional Child,* The Woods Schools (Langhorne, Pennsylvania), 1953, pp. 10–19.

61. Snyder, L. M., "The Problem Child in the Jersey City Elementary Schools," *Journal of Educational Sociology* (February, 1934), *6*:343–352.

62. St. John, C. W., "The Maladjustment of Boys in Certain Elementary School Grades," *Educational Administration and Supervision* (December, 1932), *18*:659–672.

63. Stewart, N., "Teachers' Concepts of Behavior Problems," *Growing Points in Educational Research,* Official Report, American Educational Research Association, 1949, pp. 302–310.

64. Stone, S. A., Castendyck, E., and Hanson, H. B., *Children in the Community,* U.S. Children's Bureau Publication No. 317, 1946.

65. Stouffer, G. E. W., Jr., "Behavior Problems of Children as Viewed by Teachers and Mental Hygienists, a Study of Present Attitudes as Compared with Those Reported by E. K. Wickman," *Mental Hygiene* (1952), *36*:271–285.

66. Strang, R., "Mental Hygiene of Gifted Children," in P. Witty (ed.), *The Gifted Child,* D. C. Heath and Co., 1951, pp. 131–162.

67. Tenenbaum, S., "Uncontrolled Expressions of Children's Attitudes Toward School," *Elementary School Journal* (1940), *40*:670–678.

68. Terman, L. M., and Oden, M. H., *The Gifted Child Grows Up,* Stanford University Press, 1947.

69. Terman, L. M., and Oden, M. H., "The Stanford Studies of the Gifted," in P. Witty (ed.) *The Gifted Child,* D. C. Heath and Co., 1951, pp. 20–46.

70. "The Epilepsy Problem," *Therapeutic Notes* (October, 1953), *60*:241–245.

71. Thompson, C., "The Attitudes of Various Groups Toward Behavior Problems of Children," *Journal of Abnormal and Social Psychology* (1940), *35*:120–125.

72. Tompkins, A., "Where Are the Boys?" *School and Society* (July, 1949), *70*:8–10.

73. Tschechtelin, M. A., "An Investigation of Some Elements of Teachers and Pupils Personalities," in H. H. Remmers (ed.), *Further Studies*

in Attitudes, Series VI, Purdue University, Division of Educational Reference, 1943, p. 68.

74. Ullmann, C. A., "Identification of Maladjusted School Children," Federal Security Agency, Public Health Service, *Public Health Monograph No. 7,* Public Health Service Publication No. 211, 1952.

75. U.S. Department of Health, Education and Welfare, Office of Education, *Biennial Survey of Education in the United States, 1952–54,* 1954, chap. 5.

76. U.S. Department of Health, Education and Welfare, Social Security Administration, Children's Bureau, *Juvenile Court Statistics, 1956,* Children's Bureau Statistical Series No. 47, 1958.

77. U.S. Department of Health, Education and Welfare, Social Security Administration, Children's Bureau, *The Adolescent In Your Family,* Children's Bureau Publication No. 347, 1954.

78. Waring, E. B., "Exceptional Children," in *The Exceptional Child in Infancy and Early Childhood,* The Woods Schools (Langhorne, Pennsylvania), May, 1950, pp. 17–27.

79. Wickman, E. K., *Children's Behavior and Teachers' Attitudes,* Commonwealth Fund, 1928.

80. Witty, P. (ed.), *The Gifted Child,* D. C. Heath and Co., 1951.

81. Woodward, R. H., and Mangus, A. R., *Nervous Traits Among First Grade Children in Butler County Schools,* Ohio State Division of Mental Hygiene, 1949.

82. Zorbaugh, H., Boardman, R. K., and Sheldon, P., "Some Observations of Highly Gifted Children," in P. Witty (ed.), *The Gifted Child,* D. C. Heath and Co., 1951, pp. 86–105.

PART IV

HUMAN RELATIONS IN THE CLASSROOM

As children go through school they learn the traditions and customs of our culture and acquire skills which will enable them to become self-sustaining members of society. These are important functions of the school. Equally important are the influences exerted upon the personality formation of children. If schools are to equip children for living, they must help them become well-adjusted, adequate persons who can make the most of their potentialities, live with themselves comfortably, and get along well with others.

In the three chapters which follow, the contributions which classroom living can make to the personality development of children is discussed. These chapters describe the principles and techniques which should prevail in classrooms where the mental health of children is considered to be a primary objective of education.

CHAPTER 12

Mental Hygiene Functions
of the Teacher

THE MENTAL hygiene viewpoint has given rise to many school practices which contribute to the personality development of children. However, our schools, by and large, are still emphasizing education for literacy rather than education for living. Although there is much verbal support for mental hygiene services, school practice shows that there is relatively little implementation of this objective.

Two recent surveys of the mental hygiene services provided by the public schools indicate how far we have to go before it can be said that schools are seriously concerned with the mental health of children. One study of 611 elementary schools in 19 states found that only 46 percent employed a visiting teacher, 35 percent had school counselors, 33 percent had school psychologists, and 45 percent used teachers of special education (24). The fact that over one-third of our schools are employing persons who have specialized training in mental hygiene represents a gain over the conditions which existed a generation ago when only a handful of school systems felt it necessary to use the services of these persons. But another study made by the Department of Psychiatry of Columbia University shows how inadequate are the mental hygiene services available to children. This study, involving 350 school systems over the nation, disclosed that (1) about 80 percent had no classroom discussion of mental hygiene problems, (2) in 85 percent of the schools where such problems were discussed there were no staff personnel trained in mental hygiene, and (3) in 17 percent of the schools there were no mental hygiene services of any kind.[1]

[1] *The New York Times,* February 22, 1954.

This neglect of the mental health of school children is thought to be an essential factor in problems of maladjustment and delinquency. A poignant summary of how children are affected by the lack of mental health services in our schools was made by a psychiatrist who had studied the work experiences of several thousand young people on their first job in the business world. Dr. V. V. Anderson states:

. . . I was struck with the enormous amount of turnover in these junior jobs amongst youngsters who were supposedly carefully selected, with the aid of the school system, as being potentially good employees. In fact, the separation among employees in this group proved to be thirteen times the frequency expected from the personnel as a whole.

In seeking information as to the reasons given for discharge, we found statements like the following—"dissatisfied with every job given him"; "doesn't know how to work"; "poor production"; "too much of a day-dreamer"; "bad work habits"; "resentment of authority"; "antagonistic atti-tude towards the head of the department"; "dawdling and fooling in the departments"; "lack of interest"; "attendance problems"; "always late and fre-quently absent for half a day"; "leaving department and wandering around over the store"; "always running to the hospital for some complaints"; etc., etc.

The above were typical explanations made by the department heads as to reasons for laying off these youngsters. We did not find anywhere such statements as poor intelligence, lack of education, bad health, insufficient skill to do the work, etc. As a matter of fact, we were struck with the good health, high intelligence, and apparent general ability of these youngsters. Our own studies of the individuals themselves, however, brought out the immaturity of their emotional life, the lack of integration of their personali-ties, faulty attitudes, poor insight into themselves and their job relations, apparent indifference to the organizations' standards, inadequate sense of reality as to the meaning of work, lack of feeling of responsibility for adapt-ing themselves to the conditions of the job itself, and its environment, emo-tional conflicts over home problems, love affairs, personal relations at work, and the like.

Hordes of boys and girls are turned out into industry each year whose work habits and mental attitudes toward reality, whose ways of meeting important life situations and whose personalities are so immature and in-fantile as to invite shipwreck when later faced with the job and work dif-ficulties of everyday life. The common job failures and job misfits, the lay-offs, the discharges and resignations that we daily come in touch with among these young people, just starting on their work careers, are not traceable to a lack of instruction in geography, arithmetic, English, etc., nor to some temporary situation arising in connection with their work, as often as they are the outcome of deep-seated personality faults that should have been recognized and intelligently dealt with, in all justice to the individual, much earlier in the game, and at a time when preventive work gives promise of successful achievement. There is no reason for feeling that business men or health authorities will assume this responsibility. The fullest development of the individual's capacities, his normal growth and fitness for citizenship becomes the job of our school system. (2)

It is clear that the mental health of children must be given much greater emphasis in our school programs if education is to make a significant contribution to the prevention of personal and social disorders. In this chapter we consider the functions of the teacher in this process and how he may influence classroom climate and the mental health of children. Subsequent chapters will deal with mental hygiene practices which may be used in the school and classroom to aid the personality development of children.

THE TEACHER'S ROLE IN THE CLASSROOM

Important as curriculum, physical facilities, methods, materials, finances, and administrative organization may be, the classroom is the key unit in the school system, and the teacher is the agency through which mental hygiene influences are brought to bear upon children. How well the school succeeds in promoting the mental health of children depends upon what teachers do to, and for, children in the course of their daily classroom life.

Teachers play a great many different roles in the lives of children. These may be classified roughly into professional roles and personal roles. As a professional person, the teacher must have a scientific, objective knowledge of children, be skillful in teaching methods, and competent in the technical aspects of the educational process so that he can act as a judge, referee, counselor, inspector, source of knowledge, group leader, and representative of society.

Equally important is the personal role of the teacher in the classroom. By the very nature of his position, the teacher is a parent-figure, an object of identification, a target for confidences, aggression, and displaced hostility, and a source of emotional support. Teaching is one of the few occupations where the practitioner's professional success is so closely related to his personal qualities. Teachers retain their effectiveness as professional persons only so long as they remain warmly human, sensitive to the personal needs of children, and skillful in establishing effective relationships with them (9, 27).

Observations of Teacher Personality and Child Behavior

Reference has been made earlier to the damage wrought in schoolrooms where the teacher is immature, poorly balanced, maladjusted, or inadequately equipped to deal with children. The presence of such personalities in the classroom can provide a serious barrier to the healthy development of children.

On the other hand, there is evidence that a well-adjusted, mature teacher who is professionally competent and can establish rapport with children may have a positive influence on their mental health. Observations of the classroom behavior of teachers and pupils confirm this viewpoint. For instance, Laycock's study (30) of the personality of teachers and their effects on child behavior show the direct nature of this relationship. A few of his observations are listed to illustrate how children reflect the tensions, anxieties, happiness, or unhappiness of their teachers:

CASE 1:
Teacher was unimaginative, repressed, and of a heavy type of personality. No motivation present. No evidence of vigor or enthusiasm. *Result:* Atmosphere of classroom was dead. Pupils worked quietly and listlessly and without enthusiasm. Teacher's attitude that school tasks were "something to get done" had communicated itself to the pupils.

CASE 3:
A man who is an elderly veteran. He is dirty and untidy, nervous, jittery and dashes about. He berates children who don't know the answers. His teaching is didactic and authoritarian. No development of class as a cooperative group. *Result:* Pupils appear fearful, timid, insecure, and repressed.

CASE 5:
Teacher is young and attractive. Pupils participated and enjoyed activity. Pupils gathered around piano and sang. Teacher appeared to be aware of the pupils' emotional, social, physical, and intellectual development. She created the "we" feeling. She seemed to like her children and seemed secure and well adjusted. *Result:* Classroom gives the impression of being a busy, happy workshop.

CASE 11:
Teacher is young, pleasant, and poised but she doesn't thrill pupils or lift them enough. Appears well adjusted and emotionally stable, but she

is not of the warm, out-going type. She really doesn't love her job or her pupils. A deadly calm persists in the room, rather than tension. *Result:* Pupils are listless and work in a routine manner.

CASE 13:

Middle-aged and unmarried teacher. She is dithery and flits from one thing to another. Appears quite fastidious. Religious texts are written at the top of the blackboard. *Result:* Pupils think she's a "fuss-pot." They are rude, tense, and intolerant.

Similar studies by Baxter (4) and Cunningham (11) confirm the existence of a direct relationship between teacher behavior and child behavior. These observations are supported by Perkins (35) whose research indicates that when the teacher is domineering or reproving, the classroom atmosphere is cold, the group is more emotional, and the teacher less able to understand and accept the child's viewpoint. But if the teacher is warm and friendly, respects children, and fosters group participation, more learning takes place and child development is encouraged.

Qualities Children Desire in Teachers

Studies of pupil evaluations of their teachers show that youngsters are quite aware of the personal and professional competencies required of teachers. This is true at every level of the educational ladder. One of the most extensive of these studies was conducted by Witty (49) through a radio contest in which children in grades one through twelve were asked to write on the subject, "The Teacher Who Helped Me Most." Based on letters from some 33,000 pupils, the qualities mentioned most frequently as characteristic of the best-liked teachers were:

1. Coöperative, democratic attitude.
2. Kindliness and consideration for the individual.
3. Patience.
4. Wide interest.
5. Good personal appearance and pleasing manner.
6. Fairness and impartiality.
7. Sense of humor.
8. Good disposition and consistent behavior.
9. Interest in pupils' problems.
10. Flexibility.
11. Use of recognition and praise.
12. Unusual proficiency in teaching.

In another study, high school freshmen were asked to offer suggestions regarding desirable teacher-pupil relationships. Analysis of these suggestions revealed a yearning to be understood and to have friendly relationships with the teachers. They rated the ideal teacher as one who is understanding, sympathetic, and friendly; one who could discuss a student's personal problems and offer helpful suggestions, who would assist pupils in planning for the future, and help them win group approval (48).

At the college level, students are more concerned with the instructor's teaching ability, but they, too, place a high value on personal qualities which tend to foster good instructor-student relationships. This was shown in studies by Bousfield (7) and Haggard (22) who asked college students to list the qualities considered desirable in college instructors. The qualities mentioned, in order of frequency, are listed here:

Bousfield	*Haggard*
Interest in students.	Ability or skill in teaching.
Fairness.	Personality to put the course across.
Pleasing personality.	Sense of humor.
Humor.	Ability to get along with students.
Mastery of subject.	Broadmindedness.
Good voice.	Knowledge of subject matter.
Tolerance.	Patience and helpfulness.
Clearness.	Consideration in giving assignments.
Effective Teaching.	
Poise.	

In these studies, students from the first grade through college are saying in different ways that what they want is a square deal from a teacher who is humane, friendly, understanding, patient, and capable. They are aware of the importance of an instructor's mastery of subject matter and teaching skills, but make it clear that they consider equally important his qualities as a human being.

Rapport and Professional Relationships

Teachers must be able to establish rapport with children without developing personal entanglements which may compromise their professional relationships. A teacher's personal relations with a child are not the same as the relationship between the child and his parents. Parent-child relationships are based on feelings of intimacy which the teacher must not attempt to imitate. The teacher's relationship with children should be based on friendliness, but must retain an essential quality of objectivity. Affectional ties with pupils may prevent a teacher from using his insight into child behavior and from exercising the intelligent guidance expected of him.

To illustrate how some teachers have managed to establish rapport with children without overstepping the bounds of professional propriety, let us examine some cases in which these functions are demonstrated. The first is a situation representative of the heart-tugging emotions experienced by many parents and children at the beginning of each school year:

> Don would be 5 in September and eligible for kindergarten. For weeks he had been talking bravely about going to school. On Monday morning, the first day of school, Don was cheerful and obviously happy—until breakfast was over and his mother was ready to take him out. Then Don became subdued. It was a mild day and he wore a sweater, but Don said, "Mommy, I'm cold." As they approached the school, Don was quiet. His big brown eyes had a brilliance that promised tears. They came to the kindergarten room and were met at the door by the teacher. Then Don began to cry, "Mommy, don't leave me, Mommy!"
>
> The kindergarten teacher had a policy of requesting parents to leave the child and depart immediately—no drawn-out farewells, no weaning, no bribes, promises, or assurances. This situation can be a shock to a child, but Don's teacher knew he needed support, so she held his hand when mother left and continued to keep him close by until Don calmed down and began to take an interest in the other children. Before long he was among them, timid, quiet, looking, rather than participating, but well on the way toward weathering the first great emotional crisis in his life.

What might have happened to Don if the teacher had tried to replace his mother's love by substituting her own love? What might have happened if the teacher had been hard, uncompromising, or dictatorial? What feelings might this little fellow have developed toward the school, toward adults, toward his parents, if the teacher had not known how to provide emotional support without making the child dependent? These are, of course, rhetorical questions, but their answers are reflected in the case histories of children for whom entering school is one of the most traumatic experiences in their lives.

Here is another instance where a teacher's personal influence enabled him to fill an emotional void in a child's life and modify his behavior.

This account is by a young man teacher who understood how to function as a father-figure without becoming a substitute father:

> Delchi is an 8-year-old boy who lives with his mother and 18-year-old brother in a rickety house near the railroad tracks. The neighborhood is in a large industrialized area of a major city. Delchi's father is dead. His mother works part-time in a factory and is not in good health. The family is supported by the older son, also a factory worker. There is no one at home when Delchi is dismissed from school, so he loiters around the school building, or plays in the nearby city dump, or around the railroad tracks.
>
> As might be expected, Delchi is a problem at school. He lies without hesitation and has a sneery, shifty, not-to-be-trusted air. Once he removed some money from a teacher's purse and was apprehended. He is continually disrupting the class by irritating other children, fighting, kicking, pulling hair, wriggling his chair, or shuffling his feet. The children have remarked, "We work better when Delchi isn't here."
>
> Delchi's favorite sport was to go into the lavatory, soak paper toweling in water, and throw it against the walls. This activity was curtailed by restricting his lavatory privileges to the recess time when a monitor could accompany him.
>
> As the only male teacher in the school, I took a special interest in Delchi when he was assigned to my room. I made an effort to be honest and fair with the boy and to reward his achievements. He was given extra kindness and attention. Several times I went out with him to explore the interesting things he had discovered in the fields surrounding the school. Delchi thrived under this treatment. Perhaps it was the first time any one respected him as a person and took an interest in his problem. Perhaps, also, I became the father surrogate which he had unconsciously been seeking. One day Delchi took my hand and with a genuine smile said, "I like you, Mr. Smith."
>
> Delchi stopped being so aggressive and began to be accepted by the children. His bullying has almost ceased, he is much less surly and belligerent in class, and has even acquired a girl friend. In coöperative group activities, Delchi is often chosen the leader. He tries very hard to be fair, follows directions, coöperates well, and shares his responsibilities with the other children. He has frequent lapses into misconduct, but expresses his regret when spoken to and seldom needs more than a gentle reminder to set him back onto the right track. In general, Delchi is becoming a normal, coöperative, accepted, and accepting child.

It is quite possible that Delchi was diverted from a career of delinquency by this teacher who saw the child's need for a personal relationship with a male authority figure and for social acceptance. Fortunately, this relationship was not carried to the point of dependency, as is the case where a child will behave while with one teacher but not with others.

These cases illustrate the kind of personal relationships which should exist among teachers and children. Unfortunately, there are many teachers who, because of their personal make-up, attitude toward teaching, or assignments, have neither the time nor the inclination to establish rapport with children. Here, for example, are some statements derived from interviews with 100 sophomores who withdrew from eight high schools in California (32). These youngsters were asked, "How many of your teachers seem really to care about you as a person who needs individual understanding and attention?" "Few," "none," or "one" were the typical answers of these drops-out. Apparently most of them had looked in vain for a warm friendship with their teachers.

Many of these boys and girls wanted help badly from their teachers. As one said, "They could have helped me in lots of ways. I used to have trouble, and if they could only have put me straight." These students identified two critical problems in establishing friendly relationships with teachers. One was the fear of asking for help. "The teacher should ask the students as the students are afraid to ask the teachers," was the way they put it. The other problem was their inability to get near the teacher outside of class hours. "Everybody is too busy!" said one youngster. "They have so many meetings and committees and stuff that they don't have time to just talk to you."

These are expressions of hurt and disappointment which school people should note carefully. Too many children encounter "efficient" teachers rather than "responsive" teachers during their school years. This is reflected not only in the expressions quoted above, but in more extensive studies such as those of Smitter (42) and Grant (19), where the reactions of junior and senior high school students to their teachers were analyzed. Smitter, studying the role which teachers played as advisers in junior high school, asked the youngsters to name the person to whom they would turn with their personal problems. Only 11 percent mentioned a teacher, and very few looked upon teachers as models or sources of inspiration. Similar results were secured by Grant in a study of high school seniors. Only 21 percent of the students indicated that they would approach a teacher or principal for advice on personal or social matters.

If our conception of education is to turn out adjusted as well as informed youngsters, then the establishment of personal relations with children must not be something that is done after all other obligations are met. The evidence shows that good human relations in the classroom lead to good academic learning as well as social and emotional growth (9). This implies that in order to achieve its goals at all, the school must select teachers who are professionally competent and who have the personal capacity for establishing wholesome relations with children, and must then give them the time and opportunity to function effectively in both areas.

Relationships with Socially or Academically Inferior Children

There appears to be a natural tendency for teachers to prefer the most popular children and to pay less attention to the isolates or unpopular children. This conclusion is derived from sociometric research, such as conducted by Gronlund (20), and from studies of how teachers distribute approval and disapproval among children. DeGroat and Thompson (13) studied pupil opinions of how teachers evaluated their behavior and found children felt that those who received the most teacher approval were those who were most intelligent, showed the highest academic achievement, and scored highest in adjustment as measured by a personality inventory. In another study of sixth graders, Thompson (44) similarly demonstrated that children who received the most teacher approval were the best scholars, were better adjusted, and enjoyed the highest social acceptance in the group. This problem of teacher discrimination among pupils exists in the high school also. About one in five high school students say that teachers play favorites (37).

Such findings should lead teachers to be cautious about letting their personal feelings interfere with child relationships. The teacher's support and acceptance is especially important for those children who have already come to think of the world as hostile and critical. If left alone these youngsters acquire unfortunate attitudes early in life, and their apprehension, fearfulness, or defiance become intensified as they encounter teachers who do nothing to relieve their frustration.

CLASSROOM CLIMATE AND MENTAL HEALTH

The feeling tone which exists in the classroom has much to do with the mental health of children. The most effective learning takes place when children are in a warm, friendly environment where they enjoy full, busy, gratifying days. Moreover, a supportive classroom climate may provide an antidote to the unpleasant experiences many children have outside of school. To a great many boys and girls, school is the only place where they can find friendship, acceptance, and recognition —factors which make it possible for them to resist the pull of negative forces in the home and neighborhood. One of the teacher's primary functions, then, is to create a classroom atmosphere in which children are happy, and where their needs for recognition and belonging are satisfied.

Classroom Climate in the Elementary School

Elementary schools have placed more emphasis on classroom climate than have secondary schools because it is generally recognized that young children, for the most part, operate on the basis of feeling rather than thought or intellect. Some of the procedures commonly followed in establishing a pleasant feeling tone in the elementary school classroom are these:

1. *The room is made as pleasant as possible.* The room is made warm with color, rugs, lamps, children's furniture, and curtains. If these facilities are not available, bright, attractive pictures, bulletin boards, interesting displays, and exhibits are used to give the room a human atmosphere.
2. *The teacher is friendly and encourages friendliness among children.* A record is kept of birthdays so that they may be recognized in some simple way. Concern is shown over children's absences. The teacher chats with children after school and during play periods about something that has personal meaning for them. Interest is shown in their vacations, special trips, and out-of-school activities. Notice is taken of children's appearance, and comments made on a new haircut, dress, or pair of shoes. The teacher is pleasant with children, smiles, sits down beside them once in a while, pats them on the back, and lets them know he is human.
3. *Children are helped to feel personally significant.* The teacher searches for ways in which each child can learn some special skill or achievement well enough to rate with his classmates, even if it is only how to spin a top. Children are encouraged to do as many jobs around the room as they can. A system of rotating offices is established so that each child has something to do. Confidence in children is shown and they are given responsibilities that will demonstrate this confidence.
4. *The teacher is sensitive to children's feelings.* He listens to the talkative child, draws out the quiet one, welcomes newcomers to the class, and accepts a child's flowers, cards, bugs, leaves, and other offerings

graciously. He finds ways in which children can serve others so that they may experience the satisfaction of giving something of themselves. He does not harp or nag, or constantly pick up every mistake children make. If it is necessary to criticize children, the teacher lets them know that they are still accepted even when their behavior is out of bounds. (*25, 36, 41*)

These are but a few of the many techniques used in the classroom to make young children feel comfortable and emotionally secure so that they can put their minds to the learning tasks which confront them.

Classroom Climate in Secondary Schools and Colleges

The need for recognition and belonging is as important in the secondary school and college classroom as it is in the elementary classroom. The general procedures used in the elementary school apply at higher levels of education, although the techniques used will, of course, be varied in terms of the increased maturity of students.

As shown earlier, high school youngsters, like elementary school children, desire recognition as individuals and prefer teachers who help them develop a feeling of personal worth. In addition, they want their teachers to help them become better acquainted with their peers. They would like to learn how to look nice and dress right, how to use good manners, how to act before others, how to be at ease in a group, and how to take part in a conversation (*48*).

Perhaps the greatest improvement in classroom climate is needed at the college and university level. Here students get relatively little personal attention while the subject matter taught is given primary emphasis. College students do not minimize the importance of teaching subject matter in the classroom, but feel that it can be done with more recognition for students as individuals, and in an atmosphere of improved classroom relationships. They offer the following specific recommendations to college instructors:

1. Become more aware of student reactions.
2. Talk to students informally before and after class.
3. Learn the names of students so that you can greet them by name when you meet them outside of class.
4. Recognize good work with a few words of praise, or with notes in the margins of papers.

5. Have the student feel free to offer suggestions or express grievances without endangering relationships with the instructor. *(33)*

Group Activity and Classroom Climate

The group behavior of children is another important element of classroom climate. Research in business and industry, as well as in education, shows that acceptance by one's peers promotes the ego development of individuals in the group, improves their morale, and gives them a sense of self-worth, security, and belonging *(6, 39, 47)*. These will be recognized as feelings which have an important bearing on whether a student is emotionally free to concentrate on academic learning.

Since children are deeply affected by the attitudes of their companions in the classroom, teachers must make an effort to promote socialization. This will require the development of situations which bring children together in working groups. Committee work, group projects, dramatization, team play, student government, teacher-pupil planning, and the friendship grouping of children are some of the means through which socialization can be promoted.

Teachers, generally, go along with the idea that children should be with their friends when social activities or social learning is under way. They are more hesitant about using such groups for academic work, fearing that when children are with their friends, more play than work results. However, there is some evidence that if children are permitted to work with their friends, instead of being grouped as "bluebirds," "blackbirds," or "buzzards," according to their ability, they learn more and produce more work. Klugman's experiment *(29)* with arithmetic problems provides some support for this view. This study consisted of comparing one group of elementary school children working in pairs with another group where children worked individually. It was found that the pairs did more problems correctly, although they were noisier and took more time than the children who worked independently. Other investigators have taught academic subjects using friendship groups and have found that in these groups there is much mutual assistance, discussion, rejection and acceptance of information, and exchange of experiences. These are noisy processes which may lead one to suspect that not much learning is taking place, but children do learn effectively and pleasantly when they work with youngsters whom they like *(10)*.

Studies at the high school and college level show even more clearly that group work can promote social interaction without jeopardizing academic accomplishment. They indicate that students who work in groups learn just as much as those who work independently and derive greater mental health benefits through the feelings of mutual assistance and obligation and the acceptance and recognition which group interaction provides (*12, 50*). The teacher who requires children to work independently all of the time, and keeps friends apart in an effort to reduce socialization, may have a quiet classroom, but there is serious doubt that this is the type of classroom climate most conducive to efficient learning and personality development.

STUDYING CHILDREN IN THE CLASSROOM

Too many teachers touch only the superficial lives of children because they do not know nearly as much about boys and girls as they do about subject matter and teaching methods. It is generally assumed that a few formal college classes in psychology, or an occasional in-service study program, will prepare a teacher to work with children. Research and experience shows that training activities of this type merely provide a background for the study of children and that to really understand them, teachers must continually study the youngsters with whom they work.

Child study need not be so technical and complicated that it requires special training of the teacher or makes undue demands on his time. If teachers had sufficient time and were trained in clinical and social work techniques, they could visit homes, study the social, psychological, and economic structure of the community, administer a variety of personality tests, inventories and projective devices, and conduct case study investigations which would provide real insight into the motivation of child behavior. However, there is little likelihood that either the time or training will be provided to enable teachers to conduct such extensive studies. What teachers need are some practical child-study techniques that can be used in the everyday course of their duties, and which will help them understand how children feel and act.

In the following pages are described some techniques and devices which have proved useful for understanding children, and which most teachers can use within the limits of their time and training. Teachers who have the skill, facilities, and background for engaging in more extensive investigations will find more comprehensive child-study guides in the references listed at the close of this chapter.

Studying Reactions to the Out-of-School Environment

Since only a small part of a child's time is spent in school, the teacher needs to know something about his out-of-school life in order to interpret his behavior in the classroom. Without this knowledge, demands may be made of children which they are unable to fulfill, or teaching may contradict a child's conditions of living to the extent that classroom life becomes an unpleasant experience. Here, for example, is a case where a teacher's lack of understanding created an intolerable situation for a child:

> In one school the son of a bartender became a problem child. His teacher was an ardent champion of temperance. One day, when the class was engaged in discussing the effect of alcohol on the human body, one of the children mentioned that Billy's father was a bartender downtown. Billy soon grew unruly and disobedient. A clever principal inquiring into the matter was able to establish rapport with Billy and find out the reason for his behavior. Billy believed that he had lost caste with other students because they agreed with the teacher in not respecting his father's occupation. He knew that the teacher regarded his father as a person who was engaged in an evil activity. The problem regarding Billy was not resolved easily. Fortunately, his difficulties were diagnosed early, and he was placed with a different teacher and a different group. No one can tell what permanent marks such difficulties may leave. The teacher must be alert that they do not arise in the first place, for they may be productive of permanent harm. (5:112)

If a teacher knows something about the social-class influences on a child, his home relationships, his peer associations, and his recreation and leisure-time activities, he may find ways of relieving some of the troublesome problems affecting him. At least he will be more patient, sympathetic, and tolerant toward the child and will avoid intensifying his difficulties.

A general impression of the social and cultural environments from which children come can be gained by observing the neighborhood, type of housing, and the recreational and play facilities available to them. Further information on a child's background and history, parents' occupations, and the like may be derived from data recorded on cumulative records, and from talks with other teachers, children, and parents.

This type of cursory study is helpful, but it cannot be relied upon implicitly because children do not always react to their environment in the way adults expect them to. Social workers frequently are chagrined when they try to remove children from seemingly sordid surroundings where they are badly treated and place them in a better environment, only to find that children would rather be with parents who abuse them than in clean, attractive homes with foster parents. This indicates that children's reactions to their environment is sometimes more significant than the environment as perceived by others. Therefore, it is necessary to observe the behavior of children in their unorganized and informal activities, and to encourage spontaneous expressions to find a clue to how they feel about themselves, their environment, and other people.

Observations of Children in Informal Settings

An impression of children's inner feelings can be gained by observing their activities on the playground, in club or recreational groups, or wherever they are away from an organized academic setting. In these informal, unguided activities, children show their spontaneous impulses, and a keen observer can learn much about the way they think and feel. For example, the conversation of children in these free settings is often very revealing. Not only do they express their own thoughts, fears, aspirations, and emotions, but they reflect also their interpretations of the teachers and parents—sometimes so faithfully that even the tone of voice and favorite expressions can be recognized.

Observation of children at play may be particularly rewarding, since children impose their individuality upon play materials and thus communicate their feelings with or without verbalization. If a child avoids the sandbox or clay pail, if he dislikes games involving physical contact, prefers solitary play or play with children of the opposite sex, smashes things, disrupts games, will not take turns, or cries easily, he is expressing himself almost as well as if he could verbalize the feelings which make him act that way.

Spontaneous play is so valuable a diagnostic tool that it is used rather extensively in child-study clinics. Through play with miniature housekeeping toys and small-size human figures, the child often will reveal inner feelings that are deeply buried, and demonstrate reactions toward himself and his family which he could not articulate (28). One child who was observed in a kindergarten where such toys were provided was noted to put the mother doll in the toy oven, close the door, take it out, and replace it, repeating this act over and over during intervals between other play activities. It wasn't difficult to surmise that this child had certain feelings toward her mother which were being expressed in this play sequence.

Interpreting children's play requires sensitivity, sympathetic insight, and much patience. Hasty judgments on the basis of a few observations are of little value. Children must be observed over a long period of time before any valid interpretations can be made of their play activities. By patiently and intelligently reading the language of play, the teacher can get a glimpse into the inner personality dynamics of children (17). Observation techniques are effective with older children, too, but are more difficult to use because of the increased complexity of personality structure. However, much can be learned about boys and girls through observing their extracurricular activities, club, and social activities—and the nature of their participation in these enterprises.

These observation techniques do not yield precise data, but they do furnish a starting point for further study that may help provide a balanced view of a child's many-sided behavior.

Self-Expression as a Diagnostic Aid

Another way of uncovering the inner thoughts, feelings, and attitudes of children is through encouraging their response to statements, questions, problems, or issues which have emotional implications. Creative writing, unfinished stories, "open questions," and art expression are some of the techniques which the classroom teacher can use to encourage the self-expression of children.

CREATIVE WRITING. Teachers commonly require children to write themes or compositions as part of their work in language arts. This procedure can be used to study children's feelings as well as their writing. Instead of assigning an emotionally neutral subject, children are asked to write about topics such as: "How it feels to be scolded," "What I don't like about my home," "The time I was left out," "Things that make me mad and what I do about it," "Three wishes for myself or my family," and other subjects having emotional implications. This may sound like a negative approach, but children need avenues through which to express their gripes and frustrations. By writing them out, they not only release tension, but tell the teacher things he would otherwise be unable to learn.

As an illustration of how this works, here is a bit of writing by a seventh grade boy that tells a great deal about his feelings toward life at home:

> I think practicing is worth while to a certain extent, but when it comes to slave labor that's the limit. Siberia is nothing compared to an hour and a half of working your fingers and lips to the point where you think they are going to fall off. I come home for lunch, practicing . . . after dinner, practicing! I go to bed at night. What do I dream about? Practicing! Books are black and white. What do they remind me of? Practicing! I go to orchestra. What do we get there? Practicing. There's a trumpet at the bottom of every glass of milk I drink. I could be playing football and get everything knocked off. But no, I'm practicing and getting my fingers knocked off. (3)

In another instance, an eighth grade boy wrote about things which made him feel inferior. He listed them as follows:

1. I think that nobody in the room likes me, in fact I know it.
2. I know that I'm unwanted, but it makes me no difference.
3. I know that I am unwanted because I'm never invited over to anybody's house, or to any parties, while everybody else goes.
4. I know that my parents don't like me because I can't live with them.
5. But all of this makes no difference. (21)

This technique taps a child's experiences and his feelings about them. It is easy to use, takes little time, serves the same purpose as other exercises in grammar, punctuation, and writing, and tells the teacher a great deal more about children.

UNFINISHED STORIES.   Attitudes about particular problem situations can be revealed by asking children to write a conclusion to a short story that is purposely arranged to have no ending. Here are two examples of unfinished stories:

1. Jim is a nice kid. Almost everybody likes him. One day he was sitting in a booth at the drug store having a friendly soda with some guys and gals when his favorite teacher came in. What do you think he did?
2. Elsie is one of those people that everyone knows he should be nice to, but somehow she doesn't belong. She wears funny clothes, maybe, or maybe she doesn't seem to know what fun is. One day a gang of boys and girls who know each other and have fun together were headed for "the joint" to have cokes. Elsie happened to be on the sidewalk almost to the joint. As the group came up, she said, "Hello, where are you going?" Obviously she wanted to go too. What did Jim say to her? What would you have said if you had been there? (31)

The endings which students provide may help the teacher gain insight into their values and attitudes. This technique can be adapted for use at almost any school level, and for any situation which the teacher considers worthy of investigation. As will be shown later, the problems and the answers provided make good material for use in group discussions.

THE OPEN-QUESTION TECHNIQUE. This device makes use of a series of statements which youngsters are asked to complete. In doing so, they reveal their feelings about the issues involved. Here are two such exercises reported by Shaftel (40). In each case, the child inserted the words enclosed in parentheses:

CASE 1:

I wish . . . (Mother would not die).
The thing that bothers me most . . . (is my brother).
The trouble with some homes is . . . (they fight).
I used to be afraid . . . (of the dark).
If I could only . . . (sleep in).
When praised . . . (I feel good).
My father wants me . . . (to be anything I want to be).
I cannot understand . . . (what makes me mad).
A brother . . . (likes to tease).
One must never . . . (fight).
Most of all . . . (I want to be happy).
It is wrong . . . (to make people feel bad).
I boil up when . . . (my brother teases me).
I despise . . . (people who criticize).
Sometimes I dislike . . . (my brother because he teases me).
When the teacher says . . . (you can't do it, I feel that I can).
I need . . . (friends).
I can work best . . . (when my teacher is in the room).
Sometimes I hate . . . (my father because he suggests things to do I don't want to do them).

Evidently, this child is indicating that she may be lonely, insecure, unhappy, made miserable by a brother whom she feels to be more loved by her parents.

CASE 2:

I get angriest when . . . (somebody says I'm a Nigger).
The trouble with home is . . . (I have none).
I don't like parties . . . (because of people).
I used to be afraid . . . (I was to be called a Negro).

Father . . . (I have none father).
When praised . . . (I am none).
Because of Dad . . . (I not have fun).
When I think . . . (I have a lot to think).
My mother . . . (wants me to be a good boy).
I cannot understand . . . (what makes me silly).
A brother . . . (is a lot of fun).

I wish . . . (I was grown up).
When the teacher says . . . (be still I am).
One must never . . . (be afraid).

The sources of this boy's insecurity and inferiority are obvious. The school can't change his color or bring his father back to him. The school can, however, work to have this boy's classmates accept him more fully and help him to participate more in school life.

Where the observations and general impressions of a teacher lead him to suspect the nature of a child's problems, a series of questions similar in form to those described above can be used to test these impressions and elicit further information regarding the child's feelings.

ART EXPRESSION. Children's free art work may provide valuable material for personality studies, if properly interpreted. Various investigators who have done extensive work with the analysis of children's paintings claim that colors, techniques, and themes used in painting are projections of inner feelings (*1, 8, 18*). Brick (*8*), for example, makes these observations regarding color:

Muddy, dark colors. In states of anxiety and depression, children were observed to choose dark and muddy colors only.

Black. Children obliged to repress emotions use either black or pencils only.

Water consistency of colors. It has been observed that children always use very watery colors when they are afraid and resistant to revealing their emotions.

Dominant yellow and red dominant. Use of yellow and red was significant as expression of hostility and aggression in acute emotional conflicts.

Cover mechanism—regression. The sudden smearing over of well-started or even finished pictures give evidence of acute emotional conflicts.

These observations were based on a study of 200 children, ages 9 to 15, in a regular school setting where they had free choice of subject and art medium. It represents the kinds of interpretations which have been made from children's paintings.

Another indication of what might be learned from children's art work is derived from an investigation in which 600 children were asked to draw pictures of themselves and their families. It was found that the social isolates omitted themselves from the drawing or made themselves completely different from other members of the family (16).

Art expression has yielded these, and many other interpretations of personality, intelligence, attitudes, and feelings. However, teachers must not be too hasty in drawing inferences from children's art work. In conjunction with other diagnostic techniques, paintings and drawings may provide some additional clues to children's feelings and reactions. But much more research is needed before it can be said positively that a child's art expressions are a reliable indication of his inner feelings.

DISCUSSION TECHNIQUES. Children who hesitate to talk about their troubles often can be encouraged to do so in a group situation where free expression stimulates discussion and releases inhibitions. In one sixth grade classroom (23) this was done by setting up a "Personal Problems Box" into which children dropped problems they would like to discuss with the class. Some of the problems suggested for discussion were:

Whenever I go to the store, I have to take my little brother along, which I don't like . . . What can I do?

There is someone in our room who is always saying unkind things about other people and I don't like it. How can I get her to stop this bad habit?

I am not very popular and I don't know why. I am a boy. Can you tell me some things to do to make people like me better?

Once a week the children were divided into panels of six to discuss the problems presented. This gave the children a chance to get some of their troubles out into the open so that solutions could be found for them. It also helped the teacher discover what was bothering them.

Studying the Social Relationships of Children

Since the acceptance or rejection felt by a child in his classroom group has an important bearing on mental health, the teacher needs a technique for finding out which children "belong" in the group and which do not. It might be thought this could be ascertained readily by a teacher after a few weeks of association with a particular group of children. However, it has been found that teachers tend to overestimate the popularity of children who adjust well to adults, and underestimate the acceptance of youngsters who are low in academic standing. They are prone to misjudge the position of a noisy child who is in a number of groups but not accepted by any of them, and the degree of isolation experienced by the quiet child who is tolerated by others but not really accepted (45:150).

THE SOCIOMETRIC DEVICE.   To provide more reliable information about how children feel toward each other, a sociometric device has been developed. This is described in detail by Jennings (26) and Northway (34). Essentially, the sociometric analysis consists of securing written or oral expressions of friendship through a series of questions which explore different aspects of social interaction. Some of the questions which have been used are these:

If your mother said you could invite one friend for dinner, who would it be? _____

If this child couldn't come, whom would you ask? _____

Suppose the second person couldn't come, who would be your next choice? _____

Suppose you needed help with your reading or arithmetic and the teachers told you to ask a friend for help, whom would you ask? _____

We are going to rearrange our seats. Name the three persons with whom you would like to sit _____ _____ _____

When children have made their choices, the results are tabulated in chart form. In this way it can be determined which children are most popular, which choices are reciprocated, and which youngsters are not wanted by the others.

GUESS-WHO TESTS.   After the patterns of social acceptance in the classroom are distinguished by means of a sociometric test, the teacher may wish to find out why certain children are more popular than others. The "Guess-Who" test, game, or questionnaire is one way of doing this (38). The technique consists of eliciting from children the names of youngsters who fit a given pattern of behavior. A series of behavior descriptions are formulated and the children are asked to supply the name of a child who fits each description. The behavior descriptions are prepared on the basis of observations or tentative hypotheses regarding the acceptance or rejection of certain children. For instance, if it is suspected that a child is being rejected because he is immature, questions such as these may be asked:

Who is so quiet in class that you would not know he was there? _____.
Who always wants to have his own way? _____
Who never likes to play rough games? _____
Who is always crying about something? _____

Children's responses to such questions will either confirm the teacher's suspicions, or suggest other avenues for study.

Another way of using this technique is to build the questions around specific school situations which have meaning for students. For example, if a cast is to be selected for a class play, each child can be given a number and asked to complete the following questionnaire (*14*):

Suppose your class was going to produce some plays for which 12 characters are needed. Twelve kinds of people are described below. Next to the description of each character, write the number of one classmate you think best suited for each part because he (or she) is just that way naturally. You may choose the same classmate for more than one part if you wish.

1. Someone who is always in good humor; who smiles or laughs a good deal; who makes others happy.

   1. _____

2. Someone who is very shy about meeting people; who prefers to work alone rather than with others.

   2. _____

3. Someone who is snobbish and conceited; who feels superior to others in the class; who likes to order others around.

   3. _____

4. Someone who is always willing to coöperate; who is always ready to help others do a job.

   4. _____

5. Someone who is a "sore loser"; who can't take it when things go wrong; who grumbles or finds excuses easily.

   5. _____

6. Someone who is a "bookworm"; who prefers reading books to almost any other activity.

   6. _____

7. Someone who is usually a leader whenever something is started; who frequently suggests new things to do; who is respected by others.

   7. _____

8. Someone who always seems unhappy; who rarely smiles and never seems to have fun.

   8. _____

9. Someone who is always dependable and careful; who always completes a task when others want to drop it.

9. _____

10. Someone who is very friendly; who likes people and is well liked by others.

10. _____

11. Someone who likes to "show off" knowledge at every opportunity; who makes others feel they know less.

11. _____

12. Someone who is always outstanding in everything; to whom all things come easily and naturally.

12. _____

Which parts do you think you could play?

Write the number of the character or characters here _____

Similar questionnaires can be devised for selecting members of a committee, choosing class officers, or for any other activity which involves social choices. This not only helps to select children for a project or activity, but it also gives the teacher some valuable information about the personality characteristics of children.

Studying Social Relationships in the Secondary School

Sociometric techniques have had greatest acceptance and use in the elementary school, but in modified form they can be used to evaluate the social relationships of high school students.

Ullmann (46) has devised a combination "Guess-Who" and sociometric test which can be used to determine how older children rate each other in terms of social acceptability. The instructions and questions he used are reproduced here because they represent a technique which can be fitted into various units of instruction so that youngsters feel that they are doing another class exercise, rather than taking a test.

SOCIOMETRIC TEST FOR HIGH SCHOOL STUDENTS
Adapted from Ullmann (46)

Sooner or later, even though they may first go to college or into one of the armed forces, all boys and girls will apply for a job. Success is getting and holding a job depends not only on what you may have learned, but also on the kind of personality you have developed during school days—right now.

If you were a newspaper circulation manager and were hiring young men to be route managers or were hiring young women to be in charge of the complaint department, you would look for persons who as boys and girls in high school had shown that they could plan and run a school activity or program. They would be the ones who had shown good ideas, who had worked hard and stuck to the job until it was finished.

They were known as *Dependable.*

If you were a hotel manager and were employing young men to be desk clerks or young women to be hostesses, you would want to fill the jobs with persons who liked to meet and deal with people. These would be persons who as boys and girls in high school always liked other children. They were the ones who were usually glad to have others join in their clubs and games.

They were known as *Friendly.*

If you were a store manager and were employing cashiers, you would want people who always told the truth, whose promises could be counted on, who returned things they found.

They were known as *Honest.*

If you were the head of a police force and were choosing young men for training as detectives or young women for plain-clothes police women, you would look for persons who as boys and girls in high school always could be depended upon to do what was right no matter what other people thought. They were not afraid to be unpopular. They looked out for the rights of other children. They would stick up for the right even if their friends were against them.

They were known as *Reliable.*

Some jobs need people who can work most of the time by themselves rather than with other people. This would include such jobs as forest ranger, laboratory technician, bookkeeper. If you were hiring people for these jobs you would want to know whether as boys and girls in high school they were ones who stayed out of groups, spent their time by themselves, away from the crowd.

They seemed to want to be *Alone.*

We are going to look for signs of dependability, friendliness, honesty, reliability, and aloneness by observing these qualities among the students in the class. First, on the sheet of paper with the names of all the members in your class, mark off your own name with a *wavy line.* Then with *straight lines,* cross out the names of any students whom you do not know very well.

Now, if you were the newspaper circulation manager and were hiring people for their *dependability,* which three boys or girls would you hire? Put a "D" in front of their names.

If you were the hotel manager and were hiring people who were *friendly,* which three boys or girls from your class would you hire? Put an "F" in front of their names. (Do not choose the same three that you hired for dependability!)

If you were the store manager and were hiring people for their *honesty,* which three boys or girls would you pick from those who have not already been picked? Mark these names with an "H."

If you were the head of the police force and were looking for people who were *reliable,* which three boys or girls would you pick? Put an "R" in front of three names you have not already picked.

If you were hiring for jobs where people had to work *alone* much of the time and wanted people who did not care to mix with the group, which three boys or girls would you pick? Mark these names with an "A."

Which three boys or girls are likely to have a hard time getting a job and will probably need the most advice or help from the guidance counselor, the school, or an employment office? Mark these names with an "S."

If you need to, look back at the descriptions of people who were dependable, friendly, honest, reliable, or alone for help in making up your mind. You may erase or change your marks if you wish. When you finish, you should have 1 mark beside each of 18 names—3 D's, 3 F's, 3 H's, 3 R's, 3 A's, and 3 S's.

The teacher may revise this technique to suit his particular group and purposes by adding additional traits to be rated, by omitting the limitation to three different children for each trait, or by rephrasing the entire test so that negative, rather than positive characteristics are rated.

SUMMARY

The school's influence on the mental health of children depends largely upon the emotional relationships established between teachers and children in the classroom. The teacher can be a positive force for the development of mental health if he is himself a well-adjusted, mature person who can relate to children, understands the forces influencing them, and is skillful in manipulating the classroom environment to meet the needs of boys and girls.

Not only do children seek such qualities in their teachers, research shows that as teachers learn to maintain warm, human relationships with children, they establish an atmosphere in which children feel secure, relaxed, and ready for new learning experiences. This results in a wholesome and productive climate for intellectual and emotional development. For many youngsters, the classroom becomes the only place where they can find some relief from the unpleasant experiences encountered in home and community, and where they can gain the courage and strength that will make life outside of school more tolerable.

To accomplish these ends, teachers need to know a great deal more about children than can be gained from formal college courses. They must make the study of children a continuing process, using the simple techniques described in this chapter and advancing to the use of more scientific instruments just as soon as they are qualified to do so by training and experience. As teachers gain a basic understanding of the forces and circumstances which affect the growth of boys and girls, they will be better prepared to make use of the mental hygiene techniques described in the next chapter.

PROBLEMS AND PROJECTS

1. Many writers urge teachers to record their observations of children in the form of "anecdotal records." Describe these and discuss their practical utility.
2. Working in groups of three, select a child and carry out the following procedures:
   (a) Secure responses to "open-end questions."
   (b) Study the child's art work.
   (c) Observe the child in informal play situations.
   Pool your findings. How much have you learned about the child? Check the composite picture you have developed with what the teacher knows about the child.
3. Place children in friendship groups for a period of one week and observe their academic work and general behavior. To what extent do you feel this is a practical technique? What precautions should be observed in using it?
4. Ask a teacher to select the leaders, isolates, cliques, and hangers-on among a group of children. Administer a sociometric test and compare your findings with the teacher's observations.
5. Develop some unfinished stories which deal with prejudice toward minority groups. Have children complete these. Interpret your findings.
6. Do children differ in their need for teacher approval and group approval? Give some examples and try to explain the differences.

7. Review some of the books on child study listed in the references. Suggest some practical child-study techniques which a teacher can use and which have not been mentioned in this chapter.
8. Discuss some of the dangers involved in interpreting personality or intelligence on the basis of children's art work.
9. What evidence is there that light, color, or physical surroundings have an influence on the morale and well-being of children?
10. Cite some additional evidence on the relative merits of individual vs. group learning.

SELECTED REFERENCES

1. Alschuler, R. H., and Hattwick, L. W., *Painting and Personality: A Study of Young Children,* University of Chicago Press, 1947.
2. Anderson, V. V., "The Integration of Psychiatry with Education," New York Society of Clinical Psychiatry, *Society Proceedings,* Annual Meeting, January 13, 1938, pp. 337–355.
3. Applegate, M., "As Useful as a Toothbrush," *A Monograph for Elementary Teachers,* no. 75, Row, Peterson and Co., 1955.
4. Baxter, B., *Teacher-Pupil Relationships,* The Macmillan Company, 1941.
5. Beck, R. H., Cook, W. W., and Kearney, N. C., *Curriculum in the Modern Elementary School,* Prentice-Hall, Inc., 1953.
6. Bettelheim, B., and Sylvester, E., "Therapeutic Influence of the Group on the Individual," *American Journal of Orthopsychiatry* (1947), *17*:684–692.
7. Bousfield, W. A., "Students' Ratings of Qualities Considered Desirable in College Professors," *School and Society* (February, 1940), *51*:253–256.
8. Brick, M., "Mental Hygiene Value of Children's Art Work," *American Journal of Orthopsychiatry* (January, 1944), *14*:136–147.
9. Bush, R. N., *The Teacher-Pupil Relationship,* Prentice-Hall, Inc., 1954.
10. Buswell, M., *The Relationship between the Social Structure of the Classroom and the Academic Success of the Pupils,* Unpublished Doctoral Thesis, University of Minnesota, 1950.
11. Cunningham, R., *et al., Understanding Group Behavior of Boys and Girls,* Bureau of Publications, Teachers College, Columbia University, 1951.
12. Deutsch, M., "Social Relations in the Classroom and Grading Procedures," *Journal of Educational Research* (1951), *45*:145–152.
13. DeGroat, A. F., and Thompson, G. G., "A Study of the Distribution of Teacher Approval and Disapproval Among Sixth-Grade Children," *Journal of Experimental Education* (1949), *18*:57–75.

14. Division of Tests and Measurements, Bureau of Educational Research, Board of Education of the City of New York, *Casting Characters for Class Plays,* Mimeographed, 1948.
15. Driscoll, G., *How to Study Children,* Bureau of Publications, Teachers College, Columbia University, 1941.
16. Flemming, E. L., "Feelings of Isolation as Reflected in Children's Drawings of Their Families," in *Research Relating to Children,* Bulletin II, Supplement 4, U.S. Department of Health, Education and Welfare, Social Security Administration, Children's Bureau, 1956, pp. 23–24.
17. Frank, L. K., and Frank, M. H., "Play Is Serious Business," *National Education Association Journal* (January, 1954), 43:29–31.
18. Goodenough, F. L., and Harris, D. B., "Studies in the Psychology of Children's Drawings," *Psychological Bulletin* (September, 1950), 47:369–433.
19. Grant, C. W., "How Students Perceive the Counselor's Role," *The Personnel and Guidance Journal* (March, 1954), 32:386–388.
20. Gronlund, N. E., "Relationship between the Sociometric Status of Pupils and Teachers' Preferences for and against Having Them in Class," *Sociometry* (May, 1953), 16:142–150.
21. Hackett, C. G., "How a Guidance Center Serves the Schools," *Studies in Higher Education,* Division of Educational Reference, Purdue University, Bulletin No. 79, September, 1951.
22. Haggard, W. W., "Some Freshmen Describe the Desirable College Teacher," *School and Society* (September, 1943), 58:238–240.
23. Harrison, J., "Our 'Solving Six' Panel," *Health Notes,* Scott, Foresman Service Bulletin, vol. 7, no. 2, Spring, 1955.
24. Hulslander, S. C., "Assisting Youth Adjustment in Elementary Schools," *The Personnel and Guidance Journal* (March, 1954), 32:392–394.
25. Hymes, J. L., Jr., *A Pound of Prevention,* Teachers' Service Committee on the Emotional Needs of Children, Caroline Zachry Institute, 1947.
26. Jennings, H. H., *Leadership and Isolation,* Longmans, Green and Co., 1950.
27. Jewett, A., *Influence of the Teacher's Information about Pupils on Pupil-Teacher Relationships,* Unpublished Doctoral Dissertation, Stanford University, 1951.
28. Klein, M., "The Psychoanalytic Play Technique," *American Journal of Orthopsychiatry* (April, 1955), 25:223–237.
29. Klugman, S., "Cooperative vs. Individual Efficiency in Problem Solving," *Journal of Educational Psychology* (January, 1944), 35:91–100.
30. Laycock, S. R., "Effect of Teacher's Personality on the Behavior of Children," *Understanding the Child* (April, 1950), 19:50–55.
31. Magnuson, H. W., Gipe, M. W., and Shellhammer, T. A., "Evaluating

Pupil Progress," *Bulletin of the California State Department of Education,* vol. XIX, no. 14 (Sacramento), December, 1960.

32. McCreary, W. H., and Kitch, D. E., "Now Hear Youth," *Bulletin of the California State Department of Education,* vol. XXII, no. 9 (Sacramento), October, 1953.

33. Nelson, A. G., "Better Teacher-Student Relations," *Phi Delta Kappan* (May, 1955), 36:295–302.

34. Northway, M. L., *A Primer of Sociometry,* University of Toronto Press, 1952.

35. Perkins, H. V., "Climate Influences Group Learning," *Journal of Educational Research* (1951), 44:115–119.

36. Raths, L. E., and Burrell, A. P., *Do's and Don'ts of the Needs Theory,* Modern Education Service, 1950.

37. Remmers, H. H., and Shimberg, B., *Examiner Manual for the SRA Youth Inventory,* Science Research Associates, 1949.

38. Rogers, C. R., *Measuring Personality Adjustment in Children Nine to Thirteen Years of Age,* Bureau of Publications, Teachers College, Columbia University, 1931.

39. Schacter, S., *et al.,* "An Experimental Study of Cohesiveness and Productivity," in D. Cartwright, and A. Zander (eds.), *Group Dynamics,* Row, Peterson and Co., 1953.

40. Shaftel, G., "Education for Human Relations," *California Journal of Elementary Education* (November, 1953), 22:112–119.

41. Shane, H. G., "Sense of Security," *National Education Association Journal* (October, 1949), 39:497–498.

42. Smitter, F., "Experiences, Interests and Needs of Eighth Grade Farm Children in California," *Bulletin of the California State Department of Education,* vol. 20, no. 5 (Sacramento), July, 1951.

43. Spector, S. I., "Climate and Social Acceptability," *Journal of Educational Sociology* (November, 1953), 27:108–114.

44. Thompson, G. G., *Child Psychology,* Houghton Mifflin Co., 1952, p. 550.

45. Torgerson, T. L., and Adams, G. S., *Measurement and Evaluation,* Dryden Press, 1954.

46. Ullmann, C. A., *Identification of Maladjusted School Children,* Public Health Monograph No. 7, Federal Security Agency, Public Health Service, Publication No. 211, 1952.

47. Watson, G. B., "The Surprising Discovery of Morale," *Progressive Education* (January, 1942), 19:33–34.

48. Williams, C. C., Jr., "When Pupils Rate the Teacher," *Phi Delta Kappan* (April, 1954), 35:283–284.

49. Witty, P. A., "Evaluation of Studies of the Characteristics of the Effective Teacher," *Improving Educational Research,* American Educational Research Association, 1948, pp. 198–204.

50. Zelany, L. D., "Experimental Appraisal of a Group Learning Plan," *Journal of Educational Research* (September, 1940), 34:37–42.

CHAPTER 13

Mental Hygiene in Teaching

OVER the past several decades a number of mental hygiene techniques have been developed for classroom use. Experience has shown that if teachers use these techniques skillfully and consistently, the school will approach its full potential as an agency for mental health.

In this chapter we examine some of the mental hygiene practices which have been used successfully in the classroom. These practices fall in two categories: (1) those which are used to help children express, clarify, and modify their emotions and emotional reactions; and (2) techniques which have been found useful in helping children understand human relations and individual behavior.

THE EXPRESSION AND CLARIFICATION OF FEELINGS

One of the most difficult learning processes for children is that of recognizing, accepting, and managing their feelings—particularly those which arise from frustration or social restriction. The teacher can facilitate this learning by accepting the fact that all children have disturbing feelings, and by making provisions for their expression and clarification. As these feelings are brought into the open, youngsters can be helped to understand them and to modify the behavior which they induce. Some of the techniques which may be used in the classroom to provide for the expression and clarification of feelings are described in the following paragraphs.

Emotional Expression Through Physical Activity

Most schools recognize the necessity for scheduling recess and recreation periods so that children have an opportunity to run around and work off some of their accumulated energies.

In addition to these usual programs of physical education and recreation, children need activities to which they can turn when emotional pressures require immediate expression. Adults know how important it is to keep busy when under emotional strain or anxiety. Commonly, we work, walk, dig in the garden, play golf, rake leaves, wash dishes, or do something active to reduce our anxiety. Similar outlets need to be provided for children. They need to hammer, pound, shred newspapers, sing, paint, draw, beat a drum, punch a bag, or bat a ball when emotional pressure becomes intense. Not all children will do these things at all times, but facilities should be available so that a teacher can give an upset youngster something to do before his emotions reach a point where he takes them out on others.

It is important to consider physical activity as a therapeutic measure, not a privilege which may be withdrawn as a disciplinary device. Disciplining a youngster by keeping him in during a play period when he should be out throwing a ball is a questionable practice. Instead of enabling him to get some of his bad feelings out, he is made to bottle them up, on the assumption that depriving him of play will teach him to control his behavior. The fact is, his behavior will be modified more readily if he is given enough physical activity to drain off his emotional energy so that he is not forced to react blindly to feelings which he cannot control.

Interviews and Discussion

Verbal expression of feelings is a psychotherapeutic technique based on the principle that as people talk about their troubles the emotional charge accompanying them is released, even though the basic problems remain unsolved. The homely advice, "When in trouble, talk it out with someone," is well substantiated by clinical experience. For instance, Dr. Martin Gumpert, a well-known geriatrician, is quoted as saying: "The number of patients a geriatrician can see is limited. . . . They need to talk about their troubles. And when I say talk, I mean talk. I often hear a patient repeat the same thing eight or ten times. This is a waste of time neither for the patient nor for the physician. It is important. I have seen arthritis, stomach pains, migraine, and other discomforts vanish before my eyes as the patient went on talking."[1]

Children, too, need a sympathetic and willing listener who has the time and patience to hear them out. By talking about their problems, some of the anxiety associated with them is released.

Small children, normally, are communicative and seldom need more than a sympathetic ear and a little encouragement to talk about the things that trouble them. As they grow older, children learn to disguise their feelings and are much more sensitive about them. It then becomes necessary for the teacher to evoke expression of these feelings without seeming to pry, and without violating a youngster's sense of privacy.

The nondirective interview technique has been recommended as an effective way to encourage discussion of personal problems. Essentially, this consists of reflecting verbally the child's feelings or behavior in order to start him talking. Once he begins to express himself, the teacher should not moralize, lead him on, or offer advice, but merely indicate that he understands how the child feels. It is the child who must do the talking, for he is the one who has emotional problems to express. This technique is described more fully in the references by Rogers (*40*), Axline (*5*), and Conn (*10*) which are listed at the end of this chapter.

When children will not respond to a personal interview, group discussion techniques may sometimes provide a medium through which they will express their feelings. This technique has been mentioned in the preceding chapter as a means through which teachers can study children. It is also a useful therapeutic medium, for as children express their feelings in a group situation, and as they learn that their feelings are accepted and shared by others, they feel more comfortable about them (*14*).

These group conferences cannot always be conducted on the basis of frank, personal discussions. With older children it is often necessary to use an indirect or impersonal approach. High school students, for instance, like to talk about personality and the problems associated with it, but to save face they pretend to talk about someone else, or some mythical person, although their comments frequently can be identified as having personal application. In such instances, discussion can be used

---

[1] *The New Yorker,* June 17, 1950, p. 34.

in conjunction with some of the other expressive techniques described below.

Expression Through Writing

Sometimes intense emotions in children can be reduced by having them describe in writing how they feel and why. For instance, a fourth grade teacher encountered two excited youngsters who came running to her, each shouting his side of the story. She had them take a sheet of paper and write down what had happened, telling them not to bother about spelling or punctuation. The outcome, as she described it, was this: "At first they write fast, pressing down as hard as they can on their pencils. But gradually, they cool off. By the time they have finished, they are almost back to normal. I then read their stories, we talk them over, and things work out pretty well" (28).

Another teacher, confronted by a group of middle grade boys who were highly agitated by what they considered the unfairness of a teacher who had umpired their ball game, used this same technique to quiet them down. The boys came into the room with indignant voices, flushed faces, and flashing eyes. Obviously, something had to be done. Their teacher handled the situation this way:

I told them that I knew that they felt angry and mad, and suggested that they write me a "secret" letter, telling just what had happened, how they would have settled it, and how they felt about it. I explained that since the letters were to be anonymous and seen only by members of this group, they could say anything they wished.

Given free rein, they wrote some blistering comments including such descriptive adjectives as "stinky," "dumb," "unfair," and "skunky." Some letters were even decorated with drawings of Mr. Green. As each boy gave me his letter, I folded it without reading it. When all had been collected, I shuffled them and redistributed them to the boys at random for reading aloud to the group. It was interesting to note that they began to make favorable statements about Mr. Green. After all the letters were read, they were destroyed and the boys were reminded not to talk to anyone about the matter. . . .

The effect of writing about what had happened and what they would have done about it gave the boys emotional release and helped them to see the situation objectively. (59)

It is important that the discharge of emotion through writing be followed by a talk with the teacher, or a group discussion of the problem.

This helps children view their problems more clearly and enables them to consider the emotion-producing situation objectively. Writing is not a technique which can be used with all children; however, it is another medium for the expression and clarification of feelings and, as such, should have a place in the classroom.

Art and Music

Much has been writen about the therapeutic values of art and music. It has been said that art can provide relief from shock or other trauma, that it gives deep satisfaction of a creative nature, helps strengthen the ego, provides expression for unconscious fears and anxieties, and contributes to the resolving of strong inhibitions (7).

While there is little scientific evidence to justify all of these claims (15), art probably does provide one of the richest forms of expression available to children. At a very early age, boys and girls derive great satisfaction from drawing, painting, building, and modeling. They become absorbed in their work with art materials and secure much pleasure and relaxation from the motor activity and from the creative and aesthetic experiences involved. Occupational therapy, a technique used extensively with emotionally disturbed persons, is an illustration of the practical application of art for therapeutic purposes.

With young children, art materials often provide a ready outlet for intense emotions which might otherwise be discharged through aggression. The following anecdote told by an observer in a kindergarten class shows how a youngster's angry feelings were dissipated through the use of water paints:

One of the boys became so angry with another child that he attempted to strike him with a hammer. The teacher prevented him from doing this, and suggested that he make a "mad picture" of just how he felt. A large sheet of paper was brought out and the child agreed to paint. He spent about five minutes at the easel and after finishing the picture he painted the paint rack where his paint had dripped. After this was done he seemed noticeably relieved. He laughed and said, "I sure painted a mad picture, didn't I?" He then began to stuff it in the waste paper basket. The teacher asked him if he didn't want to keep it. He laughed and said, "No." He obviously realized that this picture was not the same kind he usually painted and kept. His "mad feelings" having been spent, he cleaned up his easel and paints and went over to the reading table and looked at books with a group of other children.

The next day in a "mad" spell, the teacher again stopped the boy from doing another child physical harm and said, "Let's paint it as you did yesterday." The boy remarked, "I sure did get it all over didn't I?" and again painted out his feelings. It was noted that these two paintings in no way resembled any of the other paintings that have been made in the kindergarten this year.

Of course, this technique does not always work, particularly with older children. It is, however, an avenue of expression which permits a child to get rid of his strong feelings without taking them out on other children.

Art may contribute to human relationships by providing children with a means for communicating their problems and feelings to others. Youngsters who are not sufficiently skilled in writing or spelling to express themselves well may be enabled to do so through a technique called "picture writing." This technique consists of having children fold a large sheet of paper into as many frames as are needed to tell a story through a sequence of pictures. The paper is then spread out, and with pencil or crayon a series of sketches is made in comic-strip form. The stories are shared with the group by reading from the picture writing. In this way children not only express their feelings and experiences, but do so in a way that can be understood by the group (31).

The effect of music on the emotions and activities of men has been proclaimed for centuries. There is some experimental evidence that music will stimulate or relax a person depending upon the type of music that is heard. This has been demonstrated by Alexander (1) who had groups of college students draw as they listened to stimulating then relaxing music. He found that stimulating music produces increased motor energy and an overall disturbance of the neuromuscular, respiratory, and circulatory systems, while soothing music had a reverse effect.

While considerably more research is required to determine the specific effects of music on personality development, those who work with children have had many occasions to note how tension may be relieved through listening to music, singing, playing, or rhythmic body movements (9). Teachers have observed how quiet music relaxes tired muscles and soothes high-strung emotions, while action music excites children and stimulates them to activity (37).

The playing of a musical instrument may in some cases provide a child with a medium through which he can gain social acceptance and develop self-confidence and assurance. Many a child who was not too well accepted by his classmates has opened the door to group acceptance through his skill with a musical instrument or his place in a band or orchestra.

Thus, it appears that music and art have immediate value as means through which tensions may be relieved, and long-term value in aesthetic appreciation, creative expression, and the achievement of security. If they are used as adjuncts to therapeutic techniques, rather than taught as subjects to be learned, music and art can make a contribution to mental health (*61*).

Role Playing and Dramatics

The tendency for children to engage in dramatic play appears to be almost universal. They assume the roles of real or fictitious figures and derive great pleasure from spontaneously enacting these roles in various forms of dramatic play, ranging from tea parties to space conquest.

Building upon this tendency to act out experiences, psychologists have developed techniques which may be used to explore feelings and human relationships. These techniques have been named *psychodrama*, in which individuals participate in situations which involve interpersonal relations, and *sociodrama*, which deals with intergroup relations. The purpose of these devices is to enable children to release and clarify their feelings through dramatization, and to develop skills in human relations through experimenting with real life situations (*26*).

If children are to learn from such experiences, the problems selected must be ones which are vital and meaningful to them. The teacher's function is to help children define the situation and to encourage their participation. He accepts their interpretations without passing judgment so that children can explore their problems and receive the full impact of the emotions brought out.

In enacting role-playing situations, the following techniques have been found useful:

1. Select a situation or problem which involves personalities or issues arising out of conflicting desires, beliefs, or aspirations. These problems may be derived from something the children have read, or from actual experiences. Review the situation or incident, and with the help of the class, describe each of the roles to be taken.
2. Choose participants, selecting children who are well informed on the issues or directly involved in them. After youngsters have had experience

with role playing, they may be permitted to volunteer for the parts to be taken.

3. Send the participants out of the room for two or three minutes to discuss the roles they are to play. Keep this planning period short because the players should portray spontaneously the way the characters feel and act, not recite rehearsed lines.

4. Prepare the audience by directing their observations to the action which is to ensue and asking them to analyze whether this is the way real people would feel and act.

5. Have the players present the situation. Here the teacher offers encouragement when needed and reminds the children when they step out of a role, but otherwise allows the action to follow its own pattern. When a dead end is reached, the play is cut off. As a rule, few role-playing situations will last more than five to fifteen minutes.

6. Follow-up: Role playing is a learning device; therefore the group should be encouraged to discuss how the people felt and acted, the patterns of behavior illustrated, and how the problem could be handled in better ways. Children may wish to reënact the conflicts portrayed to demonstrate better ways of solving the problem. (6, 22)

To illustrate how role playing may be used to express and clarify feelings and modify behavior, the following description of a situation which occurred in a sixth grade class is cited:

Last semester it was necessary for me to have a substitute teacher more frequently than usual. When I returned to class, a sixth grade group, the children were making remarks such as, "That old substitute," "I hate substitutes." When even the better adjusted children became upset, it was evident that something had to be done. Knowing that in a day or two I would again be absent, I decided to try role playing instead of discussion as a means of helping them acquire a better understanding of what had become a difficult situation.

So I said, "How would you like to act out just what happened yesterday with the substitute teacher instead of telling me about it?" They thought it would be fun. "When we act out something we need a cast. We all will have different parts. From what you tell me there will have to be a substitute teacher, some children who tried to cause her trouble, and some who did not. Now someone will have to be the substitute teacher and the rest of you can assume your parts as we start to act it out. Ruth volunteered to be the substitute. I asked the children to remember that she had left home in a hurry to come to a class she did not know; that she even had to inquire in the office where the room was; and that everything was new and strange to her.

In order to help the group get the most out of the experience, I asked different children to watch for certain things. Some were to notice how Ruth seemed to feel about being their teacher; others were to notice how she showed emotion. Some pupils were instructed to act just as they felt like doing when the substitute teacher came into the room.

Ruth entered the room with all the airs of a grown-up who was about to take over a strange class and who wanted them to be on her side. "Good Morning, children," she said sweetly. "I just know you are going to be good children today." Then she started to call the roll. The children giggled at mispronounced names, wiggled, answered "presiden" and were soon out of order. Although flustered and upset, Ruth tried very hard to get them with her. By that time her face was flushed and she was really angry at them . . .

At this point our discussion began. I asked Ruth how she felt when she was up there playing the part of the substitute. "It made me mad," she replied. "If it was my business to teach that class, then I wanted to do it. I felt just like walking out that door and going home when they would not help me." She looked as if she meant it too. Then Ruth went on, "I feel all jumbled up inside as if I were going to cry. I'm just so mad."

Some children commented on how they felt while all of this was going on. They made such comments as: "We took advantage of her," "I feel that we were unfair to her," "I felt just like we were having a substitute teacher," "We didn't remember our manners," and, "I felt ashamed of us." Others mentioned how red in the face Ruth was and that she looked unhappy and mad.

A couple of days later they again had a substitute. That evening she called me and said, "I've had the most wonderful day. This was the loveliest class I ever had. When I went home, I wasn't even tired." She was a substitute teacher they had given a rough time earlier in the year. (59:32–33)

By studying the activities of children and observing the conflicts in which they are involved, the teacher can discover similar problems which may be explored through dramatic techniques. Those who have used this approach feel that the spontaneity of discussion, the outpouring of complaints, inhibitions, insights, and aspirations has a major influence on shaping attitudes and values (24, 60). Dramatics give children an opportunity to verbalize their feelings and develop an understanding of the effects of certain attitudes and behavior on others. They see how their own behavior appears in the eyes of their classmates, and accept from them suggestions and controls which would be rejected if they came from teachers or parents. Out of these experiences comes a freedom of expression not found in formal types of group learning, and a capacity to meet more effectively the human relationship problems encountered in daily life.

READING AND MENTAL HEALTH

Books and stories can make a vital contribution to the mental health of children. They provide a medium through which boys and girls may be encouraged to discuss their personal problems; they make available a means through which youngsters can escape, temporarily, from their tensions and frustrations; and they furnish vicarious experiences which enable children to gain deeper insight into their own behavior by experiencing the life problems of others.

Reading Encourages Discussion

By selecting reading materials which deal with personal problems common to a given age group, the teacher can encourage children to bring their own problems out into the open. Stories lend authority and objectivity to the feelings and behavior involved, and provide an impersonal basis around which to begin a discussion.

Problems which are a source of concern to a particular child or group of children may be opened to discussion in this same manner. By selecting books or stories which deal with these special concerns, youngsters can be led to view them objectively and without the emotional defences that are thrown up when these matters are approached on a direct and personal basis.

An illustration of how this process works in the classroom is provided by an eighth grade English teacher (29). This teacher became aware that many children in the school lived in homes where friction ran high. She invited children to bring to school fiction which portrayed family life situations, and supplemented this by bringing several pertinent books of her own selection to the classroom. The class set out to learn something about family life by reading these books and reporting to the class. The teacher encouraged them to discuss the feelings of the people involved, rather than merely relate the action or plot.

At first, the class members listened to the reports. Then they gradually entered into a discussion of the opinions expressed regarding the appropriateness of the behavior depicted by characters in the story. These discussions were supplemented with book panels, sociodrama, and oral and written reactions to open-end questions. The teacher noted that as children began to understand the problems portrayed, they applied these understandings to their personal situations and became more sensitive to the causal factors underlying the friction within their own homes.

Reading for Psychological Escape

There are times when all people, young and old, need to get away from the anxiety, boredom, or frustrations of daily life. As discussed earlier, this is an acceptable form of adaptation if it enables the individual to relax for a while so that he can later face his problems emotionally refreshed.

The devouring of comic books is probably a manifestation of this need for escape. Many parents and teachers fear that children may be stimulated to acts of violence or destruction through comic books, but psychologists are not agreed on this point. Symonds (49), for instance, states: "Instead of fearing the reading of comic books, parents should realize that these books reduce the probability of such behavior because the need which might produce the behavior is drained off."

Thorndike (54) and Arbuthnot (2) also offer assurance that comics, rather than being harmful, provide vicarious release from tensions and aggressions, and stimulate children's reading. On the other hand, several psychiatrists have expressed the viewpoint that comics, especially those which depict violent action, expose children to a viciously distorted and unreal world which they are not emotionally prepared to evaluate (58).

While this discussion must await further research before a scientifically valid conclusion can be reached, it is a matter of record that children, particularly preadolescents, are tremendously interested in comics, especially those which deal with mystery, romance, excitement, and fighting, and in characters which are strong, beautiful, brave, and have superhuman capacities (25). It has been said that they pour their feelings into these stories and drain off their aggression and hostility with a minimum of danger to their psychological and social balance (38:86). This interest appears to be self-limited in that after the age of 14, interest in comic books tapers off sharply. Only about one-fourth of the youngsters in this age group read them at all, and this reading is slight and occasional. There is almost no reading of comic books after the age of 15, although over 80 percent of the adult population follow the comic strips in newspapers (21, 47).

Reading for escape should be recognized as a normal mode of adjustment which has a place in the classroom. Children should be provided with fairy tales, modern fantasies, mystery and adventure stories, and other reading materials which will give them moments of peace when they need it. How this escape type of reading may help a child during a difficult period of adjustment is illustrated in Arbuthnot's description of a little girl who began to consume fairy tales one after another:

> She was running away from unhappy competition with a brighter, prettier, older sister. She escaped to a world of fantasy where the youngest daughter, the cinder girl, always comes into her own and triumphs. Mooning over her fairy tales, the child left her room in disorder, dodged study periods, and allowed herself to become more and more untidy. She was using books, good enough in themselves, as a screen between herself and the problems she would not face. She needed help rather than censure. When that help was forthcoming and when through a series of small successes and increasing acceptance by her school group she began to find her place in the world, she turned away from her fairy tales, and *Heidi* replaced "Cinderella." Stories about girls who achieved in spite of difficulties helped her in her own struggle to achieve and to belong. (27)

So long as reading for escape does not give children false ideas of life, or encourage them to run away from their problems and responsibilities, fantasy stories have considerable therapeutic value. They alleviate hostility by providing an outlet for aggression, and furnish a safe inner world into which the individual can escape for a while when he needs a change.

Reading as a Form of Therapy

Books have helped many individuals surmount difficult problems of adjustment by providing characters and situations which can be emulated, or which stimulate insight into emotional problems and the determination to overcome them. Behavior can be altered so significantly through reading that this process has been recognized as a sound therapeutic technique and termed *bibliotherapy*.

The classroom provides an excellent opportunity to use bibliotherapy with children. It has been found that when youngsters are presented with a variety of books suited to their reading levels, interests, and emotional concerns, they will select reading materials which pertain to their personality problems. The following description of the use of this technique with a group of 150 delinquent boys, ages 8 to 18, illustrates this process:

Most of them want to read about aggressive characters. Psychiatrists tell us that this is because the boys feel so much underlying aggression and because they can identify themselves with these characters and thus gain relief from their own feelings.

They like to read about danger. Their volcanoes must be erupting; their animals fighting. . . . We find that stories about poor boys who made good are popular. Maybe our boys see a ray of hope for themselves in these successes.

Certain boys want stories so far removed from any life they know that they cannot possibly identify themselves with the characters. Some of the most disturbed boys feel this way. They don't want to read about present-day characters; instead, they devote themselves to stories of the Middle Ages, "when knights were bold." However, some of the boys who like this kind of story have other reasons. One youngster, telling us about one of these stories, said of a character named Philip: "I like to read about Philip because he was a toughie before he became a knight." Then he added, "I wish it had told more about him when he was a toughie." (*13*)

It was noted later that as reading became an accepted and pleasurable activity, boys often sought stories about someone whose problems were similar to theirs and who was able to work out a solution. Jimmy, a colored youngster, sought out stories about little colored boys. George, who was worried about being too fat discovered the story of a boy who could never do anything really well because he was fat and clumsy. The story of how the boy in the book faced his problems and "came through" helped George by showing him that his problems were not unique, and by giving him a new slant on his own life (*42*).

To use bibliotherapy effectively, the teacher must understand the usual problems of the age group with which he works, and the specific problems of individual children. With this knowledge he can select books which will have therapeutic value. The range of mental hygiene materials available in modern books is so extensive that there is hardly a problem of emotional growth for which suitable reading materials cannot be found. To show the manner in which writers have woven mental hygiene and human relations themes into children's books, the following brief, annotated bibliography is provided:

SELECTED READINGS HAVING MENTAL HYGIENE AND HUMAN
RELATIONS THEMES, ARRANGED BY GRADE LEVELS

GRADES 1–3
Bell, Thelma H., *Mountain Boy*, Viking, 1947.

A mountain boy saw no need for reading or counting, until his mother tells him a story.

Dudley, Nancy, *Linda Goes to the Hospital,* Coward-McCann, 1953.
Going to the hospital for an operation can be a difficult experience for a child.

Fielder, Jean, *Big Brother Danny,* Holiday House, 1953.
Danny's snug little world is shattered by the arrival of a baby, but he works out an adjustment.

Hogan, Inez, *We Are A Family,* Dutton, 1952.
Stories about animals and their families help children to become aware of the security that comes from belonging to a family.

Macdonald, Golden, *Little Frightened Tiger,* Doubleday, 1953.
A timid tiger grows brave when he discovers that everybody is afraid of something.

Marino, Dorothy, *Little Angela and Her Puppy,* Lippincott, 1954.
Little Angela is lonely in the big city. She has no one to play with until she gets a pet.

Newberry, Clare T., *Ice Cream for Two,* Harper, 1953.
Mother-son relationships. Bruce, alone in an apartment while mother was looking for work, made friends and acquired a kitten.

Zim, Herbert S., *What's Inside of Me?* Morrow, 1952.
A picture book that helps children to understand their bodies.

GRADES 4–6

Bard, Mary, *Best Friends,* Lippincott, 1955.
An unhappy sixth grader brings happiness to a little French girl.

Caffrey, Nancy, *Mig O' The Moor,* Dutton, 1953.
For children who are afraid of animals or feel shame because they cannot live up to too-ambitious goals set for them.

Coleman, Earl S., *Winners Losers,* Longmans, Green, 1953.
A shy girl interests herself in others and finds friends.

Girvan, Helen, *Patty and the Spoonbill,* Funk and Wagnalls, 1953.
Difficulties over the disappearance of a picture brings Patty new insight into human relations.

Lenski, Lois, *Mama Hattie's Girl,* Lippincott, 1953.
Story of a Negro family and how Lulu Bell learns about getting along with others.

Rounds, Ruth, *It Happened to Hannah,* Dutton, 1954.
Hannah's warmth of feeling and appreciation of others wins her the friendship of children who are of other faiths and racial backgrounds.

Slobodkin, Louis, *The Amiable Giant,* Macmillan, 1955.
A modern fairy tale which conveys a lesson in brotherhood.

Stuart, Jesse, *The Beatinest Boy,* Whittlesey House, 1953.
> An account of a boy's struggles to earn money for his grandmother's Christmas present.

GRADES 7–9

Armstrong, Richard, *Sea Change,* Robert Bentley, 1953.
> A young boy matures and learns the true value and meaning of hard work.

Hall, Marjory, *Star Island,* Funk and Wagnalls, 1953.
> Accepting responsibility as head counselor helps Carolyn to overcome her own shyness and awkwardness.

Jacobs, Emma A., *A Chance to Belong,* Holt, 1953.
> Jan, a Czech DP, slowly begins to understand his father's problems and is helped to find his place among other high school seniors.

Jones, Lloyd, and Jones, Juanita, *Bring on the Band,* Westminster Press, 1953.
> Jeff learns the importance of team work by winning a place in the school band.

Leonard, Burgess, *One-Man Backfield,* Lippincott, 1953.
> A football story through which a group of boys mature into men.

Reynolds, Barbara L., *Emily San,* Scribners, 1955.
> How American children make friends with the Japanese.

Robinson, Gertrude, *Spindleshanks,* Oxford University Press, 1954.
> The conquest of fear and physical handicap.

Yates, Elizabeth, *A Place for Peter,* Coward-McCann, 1952.
> A 13-year-old boy wins the right to a place of his own in the world.

GRADES 10–12

Carr, Harriet H., *Borghild of Brooklyn,* Farrar, Straus and Cudahy, 1955.
> A story of a 15-year-old Norwegian girl growing up in America.

Hall, Marjory, *Greetings from Glenna,* Funk and Wagnalls, 1953.
> Glenna had to go to work while her friends went to college. She discovers how to make a new world for herself.

Lotz, Philip H., *Unused Alibis,* Association Press, 1951.
> Biographical sketches of courageous men and women who overcame social or physical handicaps instead of using them as alibis.

Marriott, Alice, *Greener Fields,* Crowell, 1953.
> Vignettes of American Indian life with hints on how to make friends with people of a different culture.

Means, Florence C., *Alicia,* Houghton Mifflin, 1953.
> A Spanish-American girl's struggle to overcome her feelings of inadequacy.

Stolz, Mary, *In a Mirror*, Harper, 1953.

> An overweight college girl matures and realizes that her overeating is a defense to cover other shortcomings.

Stolz, Mary, *Ready or Not*, Harper, 1953.

> Novel of a young girl who had to run her motherless family and grow up at the same time.

Stone, Monica, *Nisei Daughter*, Little, Brown, 1953.

> The story of a Japanese family and their life in a detention camp.

Thomas, Will, *The Seeking*, Wyn, 1953.

> Autobiography of a Negro journalist who moves his family to Vermont to escape racial prejudice.

This is merely a partial list of the materials available. By consulting standard booklists and reviews, the teacher can select reading matter which has direct reference to the problems of his children. The reference by Heaton and Lewis (23), and publications of the American Council on Education (46), are also useful sources of information regarding books which may have therapeutic application in the classroom.

THE TEACHING OF MENTAL HYGIENE

Knowledge of growth and an understanding of human interaction becomes more and more important to a child as he grows older and faces to an increasingly greater extent the problem of guiding his own development. Mental hygienists feel that such learning is too important to be left to chance. They recommend that definite provisions be made in the school curriculum to provide instruction in mental hygiene.

The problem of how to make knowledge of mental health available to children in school has been approached in three ways. One approach is the organization of separate courses in mental hygiene; another is informal, or incidental instruction arising out of the needs and interests of children; and a third technique is the use of mental hygiene units in established courses. Each of these methods has its merits and weaknesses.

Mental Hygiene Courses

The Bullis Project, described in Chapter 4, is an example of a separate course in mental hygiene. Such courses have the advantage of presenting an organized body of materials in a planned, scheduled program. However, neither psychiatrists nor educators are entirely satisfied with this form of instruction. In evaluating the Bullis Project, the Committee on Preventive Psychiatry made this observation: "The teacher asked the questions and the children vigorously waved their hands. They competed for the teacher's attention so that they would be called upon to give answers. Some of the answers were regarded by the teacher as right or wrong, and the student got to know whether he had done well or not" (*35*).

Such didactic, moralistic teaching, noted the Committee, is not calculated to develop in children the attitudes and understanding they will need to work out their human relations problems. If the mental hygiene course is presented as so much subject matter to be mastered, then, asks the Committee, are not the contents likely to be pigeonholed and forgotten soon after the course is completed?

This is the fundamental criticism of mental hygiene instruction which is too tightly organized and taught in a formal manner. The purpose of these courses is not to teach students to distinguish between right and wrong answers, but to help them clarify their problems and resolve them in accordance with their needs and abilities. This cannot be done if children are required to accumulate information which is tested and graded. Therefore, it has been suggested that mental hygiene not be taught as a separate course, but that it be woven into the fabric of existing courses so that it pervades the school program.

Informal Instruction in Mental Hygiene

The chief value of informal instruction in mental hygiene is that it occurs at a time when problems are real and immediate, and motivation is high. Learning activity which arises out of conflicts on the playground or in the classroom, or which are stimulated by stories or real experiences, have the advantage of high interest and timeliness. The teacher does not wait for these activities to arise spontaneously, but selects reading materials, encourages discussion, and uses critical incidents to stimulate a study of personal and social relationships.

The study of issues developing from the needs and interests of children is a fairly common practice in the elementary school. Teachers frequently capitalize upon situations which occur in the classroom and turn them into learning experiences. We have noted earlier, in our discussion of the expressive techniques which may be used in the classroom, how the teacher observes the development of problem situations and uses these experiences to help children clarify and release their emotions. This same technique may be used to teach mental hygiene principles. For example, in a sixth grade classroom the boys were causing difficulty by refusing to accept girl partners in games, and they even made a fuss about sitting or standing near girls. The teacher discussed this problem with the children and found they were interested to learn that all children go through various phases in their attitudes toward the opposite sex, and that at this particular age indifference and sometimes dislike of the other sex was common. This led to a study of social relationships at various ages, and culminated with an agreement by the boys to be good sports and accept the girls during mixed social activities.

Although such informal teaching of mental hygiene has many merits, it is subject to two weaknesses—the ability and attitude of the teacher, and the interests of children. Unless the teacher is sensitive to the problems of children, inventive, trained or experienced in child psychology and mental hygiene, and interested in the mental health of youngsters, impromptu instruction may be haphazard and superficial. Also, young people, especially adolescents, while much concerned about their own emotional and social development, are so sensitive that they may not readily participate in discussions of personal problems. These factors may lead to a lack of continuity in mental hygiene instruction. Growth problems receive sporadic attention, fluctuating with the whims of children and the teacher's ability and interests.

Units in Mental Hygiene

The use of mental hygiene units which are set up as definite segments of existing courses has been recommended as a compromise between informal instruction in mental hygiene and the establishment of separate courses. This plan has the advantage of integrating mental hygiene with other courses so that it does not become a discipline in itself, and, at the same time, providing for the consistent and planned consideration of mental hygiene problems at various levels of maturity.

In the elementary school these units may be built around problems and situations which commonly confront children and which fit naturally into the instructional program. These units will vary with social and psychological conditions existing among the children, the particular course with which the instruction is integrated, and the specific problems existing in the classroom. Some illustrations of the types of units which have been developed by elementary school teachers follow (4):

A first grade teacher developed a unit entitled "The Kinds of Homes in Which People Live." Children found or made illustrations of family work and play. They selected from magazines, or drew, pictures which showed what various members of the family do to help each other. These pictures were mounted on the bulletin board under captions: "Father Helps," "Mother Helps," "We Help." Each child made a "Helping at Home" scrapbook in which he drew pictures or pasted snapshots and pictures cut from magazines to show the various ways in which boys and girls help at home.

A third grade teacher worked out a unit on human relations as part of the health period. This unit dealt with the function, responsibility, and values of the family, and the need for tolerance and understanding.

In the fourth grade, the study of pioneer life lent itself to the development of a unit dealing with how the pioneers lived and worked together as contrasted with how people live and work together today. This developed an appreciation of the values of human coöperation.

A sixth grade teacher used a puppet show in the girls' health class as the stimulus to a unit on parent-child relations. The children wrote a skit dramatizing their most pressing human relations problems, most of which were centered around family life. They made and dressed finger puppets, constructed a stage and invited the parents to see the presentation. This project enabled the children to project their own emotions and attitudes, encouraged their study of family relations and the behavior of parents and children, and also portrayed to the parents how their rules and behavior were interpreted by the children.

These units are quite flexible, and vary considerably in their content and the experiences provided for children. The teacher plans the units in the sense of providing time for them, assembling materials, and thinking through the purpose behind them. The actual direction the units take is determined largely through teacher-pupil planning.

Beginning with the seventh grade, or at the junior high school level, a more formal and systematic organization of units in mental hygiene is recommended (35). The Minneapolis Public Schools have prepared such a series of units for use in health, physical education, social studies, and homeroom classes. The following overview of these units illustrates the scope of the program (39):

GRADE 7: LOOKING AT ONESELF
  Identifying and learning to resolve personal problems.
  Making an adjustment to junior high school.
  Developing leisure-time activities.

Developing effective study habits.

Making an effective use of time.

Understanding the physical growth changes of adolescence.

GRADE 8: LOOKING AT OTHERS

Identifying the social needs of human beings.

Developing the concept of the personality.

Understanding the basis of effective human relationships in family, school, and social living.

Understanding human reproduction.

Developing age-group values and standards.

Uncovering prejudices and intolerance.

GRADE 9: LOOKING TOWARD ADULTHOOD

Understanding the necessary adjustments and personality requirements for various vocational areas.

Analyzing propaganda and human relationships involved in group, mob, and public action.

Working out effective boy-girl relationships.

Making an adjustment to a new social world.

Understanding maturity.

Identifying the values and standards of this society.

GRADE 11: UNDERSTANDING SELF AND OTHERS

Knowing the meaning of personality.

Knowing one's own self.

Accepting oneself and others.

Understanding what is meant by a well-adjusted personality.

Learning ways of using self-knowledge for personality growth.

Understanding and accepting the differences among individuals.

Understanding the satisfactions necessary for a happy life.

Learning ways of achieving satisfactions for oneself and others in social relationships.

Accepting responsibility of citizenship as a participating member of groups.

Perceiving other philosophies and developing one's own.

These are not subject matter units taught by the teacher, but areas of study and experience. Children make investigations, read, put on skits, plays and shows, keep records, maintain a question box, invite speakers to the classroom, conduct surveys, write papers on ideas and problems for presentation to the class, and generally take an active part in carrying out these units.

Another organization of mental hygiene units is reported by Ojemann

(35). The emphasis here is upon teaching children to look at human behavior in an analytical way. This is done through development of the following units in ninth grade social science classes:

UNIT I: HOW IT HELPS US TO KNOW WHY PEOPLE ACT AS THEY DO
This unit outlined the analytical approach to human behavior.

UNIT II: WHERE DO PEOPLE GET THEIR DIFFERENT WAYS OF ACTING?
Why are some people aggressive?
Why are some people shy?
Why do some people rely on emotional outbursts to gain their satisfactions?
Why do people alibi or daydream?
How do physical differences in individuals affect their behavior?

UNIT III: SOME PRACTICE IN LOOKING AT SOCIAL PROBLEMS IN TERMS OF PEOPLE'S BEHAVIOR
Causes, treatment, and prevention of delinquency.
The effect of autocratic and democratic forms of government.
The attitudes of people in defeated countries.
The effect of opportunities for gaining security and status on law observance.

UNIT IV: SOME PRACTICE IN THINKING ABOUT YOUR PLANS FOR YOUR OWN DEVELOPMENT
In this unit the student was helped to appreciate that such activities as studying, taking part in class discussions, working or playing with others, and enjoying leisure-time activities are forms of behavior. He was then asked to examine his current behavior both in class and out of class to estimate what motives are satisfied by them. On the basis of this analysis, he was encouraged to work out plans for the next year or two for guiding his own development.

It will be noted that there is little similarity among the units described. Some have a personal orientation; others at the same grade level are aimed at social living problems. Some involve the students actively; others are largely teacher-centered. This lack of consistency implies that not enough planning on the part of curriculum workers has gone into the development of mental hygiene units. Or it may mean that mental hygiene units must be developed with particular reference to the problems and life situations of a given group of children, and hence cannot be standardized.

It is probable that both of these observations have some foundation. That is, mental hygiene instruction will be improved as curriculum directors, teachers, administrators, and mental hygiene specialists work together to develop effective instruction. But the nature of this instruction will be dependent upon circumstances which pertain in a given school and classroom. It can hardly be expected that the problems of living affecting children in a slum area school will be the same as those which concern children of business or professional groups. Therefore, more than in any other area of instruction, human relations experiences must be evolved from the real life experiences of children.

RESOURCE MATERIALS FOR MENTAL HYGIENE INSTRUCTION

A number of teaching aids are available for conducting instruction in mental hygiene. Included among these are books and pamphlets for children, films, film strips, plays, tape recordings, and records. A brief description of these materials is included here to illustrate the types available and where they may be used.

Books for Children

Some publishers have developed series of readers which deal with human relations problems commonly encountered by children at various levels of development. Perhaps the most comprehensive series is published by Scott, Foresman and Company under the title, "Health and Personal Development Series." These are graded readers beginning with grade one and extending through high school. The titles and some of the mental hygiene concepts dealt with are as follows:

GRADE 1: *Happy Days with Our Friends,* and *Good Times with Our Friends*
Assuming responsibility, helping in the family, coöperating with others, taking turns, being responsible for small children, nightmares and fears, accepting the physically handicapped, coöperation with parents, adjusting to frustration, care of possessions, solving problems.

GRADE 2: *Three Friends*
Dreams and fears, sharing, taking turns, sense of humor, taking advice from older brothers and sisters, dishonesty, responsibility for belongings, adjusting to illness, family relationships, perseverance, understanding the faults of ourselves and others.

GRADE 3: *Five in the Family*
Friendliness and social relationships, accepting new children, responsibility, promptness, courtesy, initiative, ingenuity, adapting to desires of group, doing things for others, jealousy.

GRADE 4: *The Girl Next Door*
Hobbies, amusing oneself, discussing feelings, showing off, accepting

criticism, friendliness, accepting children who are handicapped or different, accepting personal difficulties, seeking independence.

GRADE 5: *You*

Individual differences, common feelings and emotions, accident proneness, effects of emotions on the body, how to get rid of unhappy feelings, psychological evasion of problems, body changes.

GRADE 6: *You and Others*

Basic differences in people, behavior toward opposite sex, being a good sport, emotional causes of behavior, how emotions effect body functioning, social behavior, self-consciousness, understanding one's feelings, growth patterns of boys and girls.

GRADE 7: *You're Growing Up*

Everyone has problems, uneven body growth, psychological adaptation to body changes, psychological and social needs, family relations problems, friendship changes, self-consciousness, handling strong feelings and emotions, making friends, learning to work in groups, overeating.

GRADE 8: *Into Your Teens*

Lazy spells, appetites, awkwardness, friendliness, need for acceptance, affection and achievement, substitute behavior, common worries, self-appraisal, boy-girl relations, popularity, causes of physical changes, friction in the family, responsibilities in home and school, preparing for future home and vocational life, work habits.

HIGH SCHOOL: *Teen-Agers*

What personality really means, growing up socially, understanding your body, being a good family member, looking toward the future.

These books have teacher's editions which discuss the social and psychological principles upon which the stories are based, provide lesson plans for the units in the text, and offer suggestions for working with parents on problems common to the age group concerned.

At the junior and senior high school levels there are many types of reading materials which have to do with the problems of growing youngsters. Science Research Associates (57 West Grand Avenue, Chicago) publishes an extensive series of inexpensive booklets which includes over 125 titles relating to the life adjustment problems of children. One series of booklets is written at the fifth and sixth grade levels and contains such titles as "How You Grow," "Getting Along in School," "Clubs Are Fun." Another series for high school students includes booklets entitled "You and Your Mental Abilities," "How to Live with Parents," "Increasing Your Self-Confidence," "Understanding Yourself," "Understanding Sex," "Your Personality and Your Job," "Dating Days," "Growing Up Socially," "What You Should Know About Parenthood."

These booklets lend themselves to use in homerooms, orientation, family living, or problems classes, and also may be used for mental hygiene or human relations in English, social studies, science, home economics, business education, and health classes. This agency provides filmstrips, guides, and suggestions for the use of these materials.

National Forum Incorporated, Chicago, is another publisher of printed materials for use in mental hygiene instruction. This organization issues the National Forum Guidance Series which consists of a number of books written for teen-agers. Among them are "About Growing Up," "Being Teen-Agers," "Discovering Myself," "High School Life," and "Planning My Future."

Another type of teaching aid, developed by the New York State Department of Mental Hygiene, is in the form of a "Blondie" comic book. This book consists of four cartoon stories adapted for use in grades six through nine. Each story deals with mental health principles in a way which has appeal for children. The stories and the mental hygiene concepts dealt with are the following:

Scapegoat: The need to release pent-up feelings, emotional control, how to meet disappointments, the displacement of feelings.

Love Conquers All: Patterns of behavior which contribute to harmony in the home.

Let's Face It: Assuming responsibility, facing difficult situations, overcoming obstacles, family coöperation.

On Your Own: Developing individual interests while maintaining family harmony.

To help teachers use this comic book, the Ohio Division of Mental Hygiene has prepared a teaching guide which lists supplementary films for each of the units and recommends teaching procedures (47).

These are a few sources of publications in mental hygiene written for children. There are many other publishers and agencies which issue such materials. Many book publishers have one or more books in this field, although they are not always classified as mental hygiene or human relations readings. There are also a number of Public Affairs Pamphlets in this area, and a variety of publications available from the United States Office of Education, the United States Children's Bureau, and the United States Government Printing Office.

Plays and Skits

The National Association for Mental Health and various state and local mental health agencies issue series of plays and dramatic sketches based on mental hygiene themes. Among those which can be used with older children are these:

The Ins and Outs: A play for teen-agers about an incident in the lives of five high school students.

The Case of the Missing Handshake: This deals with the problem of good manners for pre-teen-agers.

Tomorrow is a Day: A play about a 15-year-old girl's lack of self-confidence.

Random Target: This deals with an 11-year-old boy's bullying behavior, and demonstrates the need for youngsters to express their hostility without hurting others.

And You Never Know: Events arising from a 12-year-old girl's jealousy of her younger sister. (*30*)

These plays are half-hour presentations which require no scenery and very few props. A discussion guide is provided with each to help the teacher lead children toward the development of insight into the principles demonstrated.

Films on Mental Hygiene

In recent years many films have been made to illustrate mental hygiene concepts and help children understand their social and emotional development. It is quite impossible to describe all of these films, since it would take a good-sized volume to merely list them. Selected below are a few samples of 16-millimeter sound motion pictures which may be used in conjunction with some major mental hygiene topics:

FILMS DEALING WITH SOCIAL INTERACTION

"Everyday Courtesy": Behavior patterns of high school students (Coronet).

"Let's Play Fair": The need to share, take turns, and observe rules (Coronet).

"Telephone Courtesy": Shows value of good telephone manners (American Telephone and Telegraph).

"Dating: Do's and Don't's": Shows progress of a date from selection of companion to last goodnight (Coronet).

"The Other Fellow's Feeling": Typical problems of young adolescents; emphasizes effects of teasing and ridicule (Young America).

FILMS ON FAMILY LIFE

"Appreciating Our Parents": A guide for children in developing attitudes of respect for father and mother (Coronet).

"Family Teamwork": How children and parents help each other (Frith Films).

"Patty Garman, Little Helper": How the family lives together and how children help in the family (Frith Films).

"You and Your Family": Problems of teen-agers and parents (Association Films).

"Head of the House": The emotional problems of a young boy rebelling against his father's overly repressive discipline (United World Films).

FILMS WHICH HELP CHILDREN UNDERSTAND THEMSELVES

"Act Your Age": Deals with emotional immaturity (Coronet).

"The Bully": Story of a junior high school boy who is too aggressive (Young America).

"Self-Conscious Guy": How a boy finds help for this problem (Coronet).

"Don't Be Afraid": Fear of the dark; understanding causes of fears (Encyclopaedia Britannica Films).

"Facing Reality": An adolescent boy uses defence mechanisms to cover up feelings of failure and frustration (McGraw-Hill).

FILMS WHICH HELP DEVELOP AN UNDERSTANDING OF HUMAN GROWTH

"Baby Meets His Parents": Points out how heredity, human relationships, and environment affect personality (Encyclopaedia Britannica Films).

"Human Growth": Reproduction and sex differences for grades six to nine (E. C. Brown Trust).

"Physical Aspects of Puberty": Describes changes in physical maturation and social implications of development (McGraw-Hill).

"Age of Turmoil": Shows emotional behavior of 13- to 15-year-olds (McGraw-Hill).

"Human Beginnings": The origins of human life told for primary grade children (Eddie Albert Productions).

Teachers and curriculum workers who wish a more complete listing of motion pictures on mental hygiene and human relations should contact the audio-visual centers of school districts, universities or public libraries. The following agencies distribute films or publish lists of available films in this field:

Coronet Films, 69 East South Water Street, Chicago.

International Film Bureau, 57 East Jackson Blvd., Chicago.

Association Films Inc., 35 West 45th Street, New York.

Encyclopaedia Britannica Films, 1150 Wilmette Ave., Wilmette, Ill.

McGraw-Hill Book Company, 330 W. 42nd Street, New York.

Young America Films Inc., 18 East 41st Street, New York.

Mental Health Materials Center, Room 713, 1790 Broadway, New York.

Mental Health Film Board, 166 East 38th Street, New York.

U.S. Office of Education, Visual Services, Washington, D.C.

U.S. Children's Bureau, Washington, D.C.

U.S. Department of Health, Education and Welfare, Public Health Service. *Mental Health Motion Pictures*, 1952, and *Supplement*, 1956.

Records and Tapes

The National Institute of Mental Health, Bethesda 14, Maryland, has sponsored the development of half-hour records for use on radio programs. Each record presents in dramatic form the story of an individual with emotional problems. Several of these are suitable for classroom use. Among these are: "The Hidden Scar," a record dealing with the emotional problems of a young girl whose birth mark serves as an alibi for her adjustment problems, and, "First Flight," which describes the emotional cross-currents of adolescence. Further information on the availability of mental hygiene recordings may be secured from the Institute.

More adaptable for classroom use are the instructional tapes which have been designed to help boys and girls understand their behavior. The Department of Audio-Visual Instruction, Kent State University, Kent, Ohio, provides a duplicating service which transfers programs from master tapes to those sent in by the user. Some of the subjects and titles available are

Growing Up Is Serious Business	What Is Normal Growth?
It's Human to Get Frightened	What's on Your Mind?
An Introduction to You	How About a Date?
Growing into Maturity	Let's Look at Jobs

Most of these tapes are about 15 minutes in length and are designed to encourage discussion and further study. Once the tapes are returned to the user, they may be retained, thus providing a convenient way of building a file of instructional aids.

SOME EFFECTS OF MENTAL HYGIENE EDUCATION

Although mental hygiene education is still in its early stages, sufficient evidence has accumulated to portray, in general terms, the results which might be expected if it becomes a more intrinsic and pervasive part of the school program.

It can be said with considerable certainty that the mental hygiene understandings derived by children in school have a definite influence on their basic attitudes and behavior—an influence which may be even stronger than other personality-molding forces in the environment. One indication of this comes from the Philadelphia Early Childhood Project (56) where teachers were trained to play two contrasting roles with young children to determine whether classroom experiences can affect children's attitudes toward minority groups. In one role, they permitted children to believe that the prejudicial attitudes toward minority groups existing among their families and friends was a normal and expected part of life. The alternate role involved teaching children to appreciate the diversity and differences among various races and religions in American life. The teachers succeeded in changing children's views and attitudes in accordance with the role they assumed.

Many other studies have shown that as children are taught to understand their own behavior and the behavior of others, they improve their individual adjustment, mental health, and social relationships. Ojemann's experiments (34, 35) offer some interesting evidence on this point. He used equated groups of tenth graders, teaching one group principles of development and how motivating forces influence behavior. The control group followed the regular academic program. A significant reduction in social conflicts occurred in the experimental group. Also, the attitudes and behavior of the youngsters improved measurably (33).

Rosenthal (41) carried on a somewhat similar experiment with a fifth grade in a low economic area in New York City. He established a coöperative, democratic, permissive atmosphere in the classroom, encouraged group activities, and held 13 half-hour lessons on mental hygiene patterned after the Bullis Technique. Although this study was conducted for a very short period of time, it was found that children who were originally disliked by the group improved their social status. Also, an improved quality of human relations among the children was evidenced. Personality tests showed major improvement in the areas of sense of personal freedom, social standards, social skills, and school or occupational relations. These improvements were not matched by an equated class conducted over the same period using standard teaching techniques.

Other studies, such as those of Flory (18), Taba (50, 51, 52, 53), and the Staff of Intergroup Education in Cooperating Schools (44, 45), show that when mental hygiene instruction is included in the school program, social relationships improve, deviate behavior diminishes, more desirable personality adjustments are achieved, and better personal habits are formed.

How deeply this type of education influences children was shown by Fleming's experiment (*17*) with youngsters having psychosomatic symptoms. He selected 26 children in nine elementary classrooms who were identified by a physician as having psychosomatic disturbances. These youngsters were compared with 12 other children with psychosomatic symptoms found in three other classrooms. The experimental group of 26 was taught by teachers who emphasized warm, friendly, helpful, relaxed relationships. The teachers in the comparison group continued to emphasize the fulfillment of subject matter requirements and made no special effort to meet the emotional needs of children. At the close of this experiment, a marked reduction in frequency of psychosomatic symptoms was found in the experimental group, and there was a significant improvement in school attendance. The control group, on the other hand, showed no improvement in the frequency or intensity of psychosomatic symptoms, and attendance became worse during this period.

While these studies are not sufficiently comprehensive or conclusive to justify extensive claims regarding the results to be expected from education for mental health, many workers in this field feel that they are sufficiently indicative to warrant the attention of educators. Some believe that planned education for mental health is the most urgent need of our schools. Lawrence K. Frank (*19*) goes so far as to say: "We could wisely sacrifice much of our academic achievement for better personality integration and social adjustment. . . ."

Fortunately, there is no need for such sacrifice. Data provided by Fleming (*17*), Burrell (*8*), Feyereisen (*16*), and other investigators show that where emphasis is placed on meeting the emotional needs of children and improving human relations, there are significant gains in learning, work habits are bettered, interest in school work is increased, and truancy is reduced. These studies indicate that as teachers emphasize the emotional adjustment of children there is no loss in academic achievement, but an overall improvement in all aspects of child growth.

SUMMARY

This chapter has described two aspects of classroom instruction in mental hygiene. One relates to the experiences which should be provided to help children release their feelings and learn to manage their emotions. This may be done through individual and group discussions, writing, art, music, dramatics, physical activity, books, and stories.

The second aspect of education for mental health is instruction in the principles of growth and human behavior which must be understood in order to establish good human relationships. This may be done informally with young children through experiences which arise naturally out of their interests and activities. With older youngsters, a more systematic approach is recommended through the development of mental hygiene units which will enable children to explore more thoroughly the problems of human relations common to their age and circumstances.

To aid the teacher in providing mental hygiene learning experiences, a variety of resource materials are available for classroom use. These include books developed around mental hygiene and human relations concepts, plays, films, audio-tapes, records, filmstrips, and an assortment of inexpensive pamphlets and booklets which provide background information for the teacher's own use. Some of the sources of these materials have been listed.

Although it may appear that inclusion of mental hygiene instruction in an already crowded curriculum imposes an additional burden on the teacher, many of the techniques described here may be used as part of existing programs and require no great expenditure of time. Academic achievement is not compromised by the introduction of mental hygiene instruction in the school curriculum. On the contrary, evidence shows that by emphasizing human relations and mental health, learning is improved and better personal and social integration results.

PROBLEMS AND PROJECTS

1. Cite an example from your own experience of an instance where the reading of a book or story contributed to the solution of a personal problem.
2. Discuss the psychological effects of a mental hygiene program in the school and a drab environment in home or community. To what extent may resentments or frustrations be produced by this contrast?
3. Develop a unit of instruction in mental hygiene which would fit into your particular grade or subject curriculum.
4. Present a psychodrama in class which illustrates the conflict of a child and his teacher. Discuss the process in terms of the feelings experienced.
5. Suggest some problems suitable for psychodrama or sociodrama at various age levels.
6. Apply one or more of the release techniques with a group of children and report on its effectiveness.
7. Some mental hygienists have cautioned that the use of mental hygiene

techniques by teachers may stir up anxieties in children, rather than relieve them. Discuss this in terms of your observations and experiences.

8. Select a problem in behavior or human relations common among children of a particular age group and prepare an annotated list of books which focus on this problem.

9. Review the *Case Studies in Instruction* prepared by the Staff of Intergroup Education in Cooperating Schools (*44, 45*), What practical techniques are suggested for teachers at various grade levels who seek assistance with mental hygiene instruction?

10. Review the *Human Relations Study of an Eighth Grade* reported by Taba (*51*). Discuss how the findings and techniques apply at other grade levels.

SELECTED REFERENCES

1. Alexander, H., "An Investigation on the Effects of Music on Personality by Way of Figure Drawings," *American Journal of Psychotherapy* (October, 1954), 8:687–702.

2. Arbuthnot, M. H., "Children and the Comics," *Elementary English* (March, 1947), 24:171–183.

3. Arbuthnot, M. H., "The Child and His Books," *The Supervisor's Notebook,* vol. 12, no. 1, Scott, Foresman Service Bulletin, February–March, 1948.

4. Avery, C. E., and Kirkendall, L. A., *A Progress Report on the Oregon Developmental Center Project in Family Life Education,* E. C. Brown Trust (Portland, Oregon), August, 1952.

5. Axline, V. M., *Play Therapy,* Houghton Mifflin Co., 1947.

6. Bernard, H. W., *Mental Hygiene for Classroom Teachers,* McGraw-Hill Book Company, 1952.

7. Brick, M., "Mental Hygiene Value of Children's Art Work," *American Journal of Orthopsychiatry* (January, 1944), 14:136–147.

8. Burrell, A. P., "Facilitating Learning Through Emphasis on Meeting Children's Basic Emotional Needs: An In-Service Training Program," *The Journal of Educational Sociology* (March, 1951), 24:381–393.

9. Cole, F. E., "Music Serves the Exceptional Child," *California Journal of Elementary Education* (May, 1956), 24:233–234.

10. Conn, J. H., "The Play Interview as an Investigative and Therapeutic Procedure," *Nervous Child* (1948), 7:257–286.

11. Cook, L. A., "What We Face in Family Living," in H. H. Cummings (ed.), *Improving Human Relations,* National Council for the Social Studies, National Education Association, Bulletin No. 25, November, 1949, pp. 100–104.

12. Cook, R. W., "Helping Teachers to Help Themselves in Music," *California Journal of Elementary Education* (May, 1956), 24:239–242.

13. Craig, L. P., "Boys and Books Get Together," *The Child*, vol. 16, no. 7, March, 1952.

14. Detjen, E. W., and Detjen, M. F., *Elementary School Guidance*, McGraw-Hill Book Company, 1952.

15. Dewdney, S. H., Metcalfe, E. V., and Burd, F. W., "Art Therapy at Westminster Hospital," *Canadian Psychiatric Association Journal* (January, 1956), 1:24–34.

16. Feyereisen, K., *Improving Learning Through an Emphasis on Human Relations*, Unpublished Doctoral Dissertation, Ohio State University, 1947.

17. Fleming, R. S., "The Effects of an In-Service Education Program on Children with Symptoms of Psychosomatic Illness," *The Journal of Educational Sociology* (March, 1951), 24:394–405.

18. Flory, C. D., Alden, E., and Simmons, M., "Classroom Teachers Improve the Personality Adjustment of Their Pupils," *Journal of Educational Research* (September, 1944), 38:1–8.

19. Frank, L. K., "The Reorganization of Education to the Promotion of Mental Hygiene," *Mental Hygiene* (October, 1939), 23:529–543.

20. Garry, R., "Sociodrama in a High-School Adjustment Class," *School Review* (1953), 61:151–157.

21. Gesell, A., Ilg, F. L., and Ames, L. B., *Youth: The Years from Ten to Sixteen*, Harper & Brothers, 1956.

22. Grambs, J. D., and Kinney, L. B., "Sociodrama in High School Classes," in H. H. Cummings (ed.), *Improving Human Relations*, National Council for the Social Studies, National Education Association, Bulletin No. 25, November, 1949, pp. 95–100.

23. Heaton, M., and Lewis, H. B., *Reading Ladders for Human Relations*, American Council on Education, 1955.

24. Hendry, C. E., "Role Practice Brings the Community into the Classroom," *Sociometry* (1944), 7:196–204.

25. Hill, G. E., and Trent, M. E., "Children's Interests in Comic Strips," *Journal of Educational Research* (1940), 34:30–36.

26. Hollister, W. G., and Husband, G. W., "Sociodrama: A Way of Teaching Mental Health Skills," *Public Health Nursing*, September, 1951.

27. Jersild, A. T., *Child Psychology*, Prentice-Hall, Inc., 1954.

28. Johnson, K. C., "How Is Health Being Taught Today?" *Health Notes*, vol. 6, no. 2, Scott, Foresman Service Bulletin, Spring, 1954, pp. 1–4.

29. Lewis, G. M., *Educating Children in Grades Seven and Eight*, U.S. Department of Health, Education and Welfare, Office of Education, Bulletin 1954, No. 10, 1954.

30. *List of Mental Health Publications and Audio-Visual Aids,* The National Association for Mental Health, January, 1956.
31. Oftedal, L., "Picture Writing: A New Tool in Creative Expression," *The Elementary School Journal* (September, 1948), 49:37–46.
32. Ohlendorf, F., "Instrumental Music in the Long Beach Elementary Schools," *California Journal of Elementary Education* (May, 1956), 24:227–229.
33. Ojemann, R. H., "Changing Attitudes in the Classroom," *Children* (July–August, 1956), 3:130–134.
34. Ojemann, R. H., *Personality Adjustment of Individual Children,* Department of Classroom Teachers, American Educational Research Association of the NEA, 1954.
35. Ojemann, R. H., Nugent, A., and Corry, M., "Study of Human Behavior in the Social Science Program," in H. H. Cummings (ed.), *Improving Human Relations,* National Council for the Social Studies, National Education Association, Bulletin No. 25, November, 1949, pp. 70–77.
36. *Promotion of Mental Health in the Primary and Secondary Schools: An Evaluation of Four Projects,* Committee on Preventive Psychiatry, Report No. 18 (Topeka, Kansas), Group for the Advancement of Psychiatry, 1951.
37. Pugh, S., "Music as Part of the School Day," *California Journal of Elementary Education* (May, 1956), 24:249–252.
38. Redl, F., and Wattenberg, W. W., *Mental Hygiene in Teaching,* Harcourt, Brace and Co., 1951.
39. *Resource Guide: Mental Health, Personality Growth and Adjustment,* Minneapolis Public Schools, 1954.
40. Rogers, C. R., *Counseling and Psychotherapy: Newer Concepts in Practice,* Houghton Mifflin Co., 1942.
41. Rosenthal, S., "A Fifth Grade Classroom Experiment in Fostering Mental Health," *The Journal of Child Psychiatry* (1952), 2:302–329.
42. Russell, D. H., "Identification Through Literature," *Childhood Education* (May, 1949), 25:397–401.
43. Shaftel, G., and Shaftel, F. R., *Role Playing the Problem Story,* National Conference of Christians and Jews, 1952.
44. Staff of Intergroup Education in Cooperating Schools, *Curriculum in Intergroup Relations,* American Council on Education, 1949.
45. Staff of Intergroup Education in Cooperating Schools, *Elementary Curriculum in Intergroup Relations,* American Council on Education, 1950.
46. Staff of Intergroup Education in Cooperating Schools, *Literature For Human Understanding,* American Council on Education, 1950.
47. State Planning Committee for School and Community Health Educa-

tion, *The Blondie Comic Book: A Teaching Aid in Mental Health,* (Columbus, Ohio), Mimeographed, September, 1953.

48. Stephens, J. M., *Educational Psychology,* Henry Holt and Co., 1951.
49. Symonds, P. M., "Implications of Fantasy for Education," *Elementary School Journal* (January, 1949), 49:273–277.
50. Taba, H., *School Culture: Studies of Participation and Leadership,* American Council on Education, 1955.
51. Taba, H., *With Perspective on Human Relations,* American Council on Education, 1955.
52. Taba, H., Brady, E. H., and Robinson, J. T., *Intergroup Education in Public Schools,* American Council on Education, 1952.
53. Taba, H., and Elkins, D., *With Focus on Human Relations,* American Council on Education, 1950.
54. Thorndike, R. L., "Words and the Comics," *Journal of Experimental Education* (1941), 10:110–113.
55. Thorpe, L. P., *The Psychology of Mental Health,* Ronald Press, 1950.
56. Trager, H. G., and Yarrow, M. R., *They Learn What They Live,* Harper & Brothers, 1952.
57. Wagner, J., "An Eighth Grade Studies Racial Intolerance," in H. H. Cummings (ed.), *Improving Human Relations,* National Council for the Social Studies, National Education Association, Bulletin No. 25, November, 1949, pp. 65–70.
58. Wertham, F., *Seduction of the Innocent,* Rinehart and Co., 1954.
59. Wittker, E. M., "Practices in Group Guidance," *Good Guidance Practices in the Elementary School,* Bulletin of the California State Department of Education (August, 1955), 24:29–44.
60. Zander, A., and Lippitt, R., "Reality Practice as Educational Method," *Sociometry* (1944), 7:129–151.
61. Zanker, A., and Glott, M. M., "Individual Reactions of Alcoholic and Neurotic Patients to Music," *Journal of Nervous and Mental Disease* (April, 1956), 123:395–402.

CHAPTER 14

The Control and Management of Children

HOW to manage children in the classroom has always been, and remains today, one of the foremost problems of teachers. The success or failure of an instructional program depends upon the teacher's ability to control a group of 30 or 40 young, active, growing individualists. Control techniques, or discipline, is also a matter of vital importance to children. How well they learn, their attitudes toward school and toward each other, are influenced greatly by the disciplinary tactics employed by the teacher. Parents, too, show considerable concern over the matter of school discipline—often advocating a return to the firm hand which allegedly instilled in children the standards of hard work and respect for authority, said to be lacking among the youth of this generation (51).

Classroom discipline is so critical a problem, and so close to the emotions of teachers, children, and parents, that a comprehensive understanding of its mental hygiene implications is vital for the intelligent management of children.

MENTAL HYGIENE AND DISCIPLINE

Mental hygienists view discipline as a learning process. The ultimate purpose of discipline is the emergence of a mature adult who is capable of functioning with a minimum of external control, and who has the qualities of self-reliance, and social sensitivity that are characteristic of mature persons. This state of development emerges gradually through a long-time process of education.

Objectives of Control Techniques

Discipline as a form of external force must be imposed upon a child for his own protection while he is learning the lessons of self-control. As he progresses toward maturity, external restraint should give way progressively to self-direction in accordance with the child's capacities. At each stage of growth he must have such freedom from external restraint as he can use wisely. To continue external direction after the child is capable of self-control will damage his personality much like prohibiting a child from walking when he is able to do so. On the other hand, to give a child more freedom than he can manage is to impose upon him conditions beyond his capacity.

Discipline, then, from a mental hygiene viewpoint, involves a process of gradually reducing restraints on a child as he develops inner controls so that he may learn to become a just, kind, understanding, mature person. These are qualities which do not emerge fully developed when the individual enters adulthood, but which are built up over a long period of time (38).

Classroom Implications

Many teachers desire a quiet, orderly classroom where children respond promptly to directions. This type of atmosphere is much more tolerable than the noise and bustle which occurs when youngsters are permitted to experiment with self-management. However, if they are kept constantly under the thumb of the teacher, children cannot learn to function autonomously. They must have opportunities to practice coöperation, make self-initiated choices, participate constructively in testing their behavior, and develop a feeling of responsibility toward others through personal interaction. Children who are controlled too closely by adults are denied these experiences and may not learn to internalize controls or make them a part of their basic behavior patterns.

These principles must not be construed to mean that children do not need teacher control and direction. Most boys and girls seek security in adult authority. If that authority is consistent, reasonable, and directed toward helping children accept the authority of the group, the task, or personal and social responsibilities, it is entirely possible to regulate the behavior of youngsters without destroying their capacity for self-direction.

In summary, classroom discipline cannot be limited to maintaining order so that learning may proceed effectively. This is a vital aspect of the management of children, but even more important are the behavior patterns being created—whether children develop the inner controls that will keep them from acting in asocial ways when they are not under adult supervision. From the standpoint of mental health, the important consideration is that experience with discipline teaches the child to see that authority is beneficial, and encourages him to internalize this authority, rather than reject it as something foreign to his pattern of living (35).

These theoretical considerations have been presented in order to clarify the issues involved in making choices regarding the types of control and management techniques to use in the classroom. We can now look at the problems of discipline with these values in mind, and with some perspective regarding their implication for child development.

CONDITIONS WHICH INFLUENCE THE CLASSROOM BEHAVIOR OF CHILDREN

Contrary to some opinion, our schools are not populated with knife-wielding rowdies who defy or attack their teachers. The consensus of 10,000 teachers in a national study indicates that fewer than 1 percent of the children in school are real trouble-makers (36:104). Unfortunately, this small minority, through acts of aggression, vandalism, and general lack of concern for the welfare of others, forces itself upon the attention of the community and leaves the impression that school discipline is ineffective.

The great majority of school children cause little serious trouble in the classroom. However, the wise management of 30 or 40 normal, active youngsters has never been an easy task. If the teacher is to take a more basic approach to discipline than merely maintaining order in the classroom, he must learn a great deal about the personal, social, and environmental factors which influence the behavior of children. These factors are described in the succeeding pages under five categories: (1) situational or environmental factors, (2) teacher-induced conditions, (3) learning tasks and educational standards, (4) personality characteristics, and, (5) group influences.

Situational and Environmental Factors

Social-class conflicts, irresponsible or inadequate parents, and poor family conditions have been discussed earlier as factors that give rise to emotional problems which may be reflected as misbehavior in the class-

room Other environmental conditions which predispose children to behavior may create discipline problems. These include class size and grade
level, the size of the school system, the availability of community
services, and administrative policies. Misbehavior arising out of unfavorable conditions in these areas often has origins which lie beyond
the teacher's sphere of influence. These factors are mentioned here
primarily because the solution to the problems they create may require
the attention of school officials and community agencies.

SIZE OF SCHOOL AND SCHOOL SYSTEM.   Discipline problems are
more frequent and acute in large urban school systems than they are in
small school systems. The National Education Association reports that
the typical teacher in a large school system has more than twice as many
trouble-makers, and is three times more likely to have been subjected
to physical violence by a pupil than is a teacher in a small school
system (36:66).

Why teachers in large cities and large schools have more trouble
with children than do teachers in small cities is not clearly understood.
It is possible that the heterogeneity of population in large cities, the
anonymity of individuals which comes with increased size, the diffusion
of family influences, weakened community cohesiveness, and the concentration of minority and lower social-class groups in large urban centers
are factors which affect this situation. At the present time these are
merely speculations which await scientific testing. No doubt the real
causes will be found rooted deeply in the complex economic, sociological,
and psychological problems associated with urbanization.

CLASS SIZE AND GRADE LEVEL.   Teachers in the junior high school
can expect to have more trouble with discipline than elementary or high
school teachers. The percent of teachers who classify their pupils as mis-
behaving frequently and being difficult to handle is 8.3 for the junior
high school, 5.3 for the elementary school, and 4.9 for the senior high
school (36:67). The characteristics of children at various ages, and the
differing philosophies and techniques of education which prevail at these
school levels, may account for these findings.

Evidence on the relationship of class size to pupil behavior shows
quite clearly that as the size of the class increases, discipline problems
multiply. In the elementary school, teachers who have 45 or more pupils
in their class have more than twice the number of behavior problems
than do teachers who have 25 to 29 pupils. In the secondary school, a
similar pattern exists; 44.6 percent of the teachers report that their

largest groups are the most difficult to manage, while less than 1 percent say this of their smallest groups (36:68). Thus, by increasing class size, certain economies may be effected in the school program, but this is done at the expense of making the class more difficult to manage, and, consequently, jeopardizing the value and quality of instruction.

COMMUNITY CONDITIONS. The impact of social-class influences on the development of children was described in Chapter 8. Teachers who work in schools situated in neighborhoods that are predominantly business or industrial are three times more likely to be subjected to physical violence by pupils than teachers in residential neighborhoods. Pupil behavior is worse in dying or deteriorating neighborhoods than it is in stable areas; worse in areas where there are two or more different races than where people are all of the same race; worse where the general living conditions of the residents are low, than where they are very good; worse where community recreation facilities are poor, where the quality of guidance programs offered by churches, civic groups, or youth organizations are inferior, and where parents do not coöperate with the school (36).

All of these factors have a marked influence on misbehavior of children in school. Together they impose a very serious burden on teachers, a burden made more onerous by the fact that there is little a teacher can do to alter these conditions or effect a change in the socioeconomic environment which produces them. There are strong indications that such conditions force teachers to use arbitrary or psychologically unsound techniques for controlling children.

ADMINISTRATIVE POLICY. Many teachers would like to adopt positive classroom management procedures but are prevented from doing so by the administrative conditions imposed upon them. If school officials and parents believe in authoritarian control in the classroom, if they place great emphasis upon order, system, and quiet, and rate teachers in terms of how well these objectives are achieved, it becomes difficult for teachers to avoid the use of repressive measures. Few teachers are sufficiently secure and confident to challenge such policies, particularly when they are reinforced by uninformed public sentiment (46).

Another aspect of administrative policy which has much to do with discipline in the classroom is the expectation that a teacher can attend to the needs of maladjusted children along with a large group of relatively normal youngsters. A maladjusted child can create problems of discipline which are beyond the teacher's ability to cope with. Even one such youngster in a classroom greatly increases a teacher's discipline difficulties with all children. This conclusion is borne out by teacher opinion (*36*), and studies such as that of Carter (*13*) which showed that 4 percent of the pupils may cause 40 percent of the disciplinary trouble in a classroom.

Further verification is found in a follow-up study made by the Pennsylvania Hospital (*31*) where 66 children of normal intelligence who had been admitted to the psychiatric division of the hospital for repeated truancy, stealing, purposeful lying, disobedience or defiance of authority, and similar behavior problems, were followed to the age of 18 or over. Of the group, only about 21 percent eventually made an adequate social adjustment. If such results are secured with youngsters who have psychiatric care, it can hardly be expected that the ordinary disciplinary methods used in school would be adequate to cope with these children. When school officials fail to recognize the burden placed on teachers by maladjusted children, a general deterioration of classroom discipline can result.

Teacher Attitudes Toward Classroom Discipline

Underlying many problems of classroom management are teacher attitudes toward discipline, the standards of behavior set for children, and the techniques used to attain these standards.

Whether or not a teacher has discipline problems depends upon his interpretation of what constitutes acceptable behavior. Many teachers actually create a climate for misbehavior by establishing rules which violate the conditions of growth. They may insist upon quiet orderliness, complete subservience to authority, long periods of enforced concentration, and other patterns of behavior which are incompatible with the natural exuberance and energy of children. When such requirements exceed the limits of a youngster's tolerance, they may precipitate reactions which are more a rebellion against unreasonable restrictions than a form of asocial behavior.

A teacher's ability to tolerate or accept the immature behavior of children appears to be affected by a number of personal factors. It has been found that teachers whose health is exceptionally good seem to be more tolerant of youngsters than those who are in poor health. Also, age and experience are associated with ability to manage children. Teachers under 25 and over 65 years of age seem to have the most difficulty with discipline problems. As teachers advance in maturity and experience, they apparently have fewer discipline problems until a point of diminishing returns is reached around the age of 50 or 60. Thereafter they appear to be less tolerant of pupil misbehavior and their discipline problems increase (36:74).

TEACHER PERSONALITY.   Misbehavior in the classroom may be a product, also, of the teacher's personality and values. Previous chapters have described a number of teacher characteristics which children dislike or which may actually arouse resentment and hostility. One personality trait which creates more disciplinary problems than it solves is worthy of additional mention. This is the attitude that teachers must maintain their dignity at all costs in order to maintain their authority. Based on the assumption that children will lose their respect for an adult who displays human feelings, some teachers remain aloof, cold, and remote. They admit to no failings, never take children into their confidence, and set up an impenetrable psychological barrier just as soon as they enter the classroom. Cold, hard rules administered by an unemotional unresponsive teacher can hardly be expected to reach the inner personality of youngsters.

Another factor which causes difficulty is the frustration which teachers may experience when they cannot achieve success with all their children. Many teachers set high standards of behavior for children and feel defeated if all youngsters do not reach them. Here, again, we touch upon the need for teachers to admit they are human. No one is omnipotent, not even the teacher. Educators would spare themselves much anxiety if they openly acknowledge that many of the problems which children bring to school have been so long developing that they are not amenable to modification by the teacher. This is not an admission of failure, but simply a statement of fact which is well known to clinicians and others who have therapeutic relationships with children.

CONTROL TECHNIQUES.   The need for preserving order or for molding children into a quiet, obedient class has led teachers to adopt coercive techniques which depend upon fear and force for their effect. This form of control is a poor substitute for good child management, yet teachers ask for more authority to use coercion in the classroom. The NEA report previously cited (36) found that 77 percent of the elementary teachers, 62.5 percent of the junior high school teachers, and 37.4 percent of the senior high school teachers would like to be allowed to administer corporal punishment to children. Although many of these teachers stated that corporal punishment would be used only as a last resort, it might be asked, if this is an effective way to manage children, why not use it in the first place?

The answer has been made clear in our earlier discussion. Punishment has been forbidden in most schools because it aggravates behavior problems and is an ineffective method of controlling children. Coercion is appealing as a disciplinary technique because it brings quick results. It is ineffective in the long run because it does not teach children how to behave when they are no longer subject to authority (*43*).

These conclusions are supported by a number of research studies. Long and Farley (*26*) showed that where schools use corporal punishment, children tend to dislike their teachers and have feelings of fear and insecurity. Anderson and his associates (*2, 3, 4*) found that domination by the teacher produces resistant, insecure, suspicious children who pay less attention to their work and who frequently are in conflict with each other. Studies of school drop-outs reveal that the frustration induced by restrictive discipline is largely responsible for the dissatisfaction which influences these youngsters to leave school early (*28*).

It is fair to say that dominated, overrestricted children are not well-behaved youngsters. This is evidenced by their quarreling, rudeness toward each other, careless work and handling of materials, and the general disorder which occurs when they are not under supervision (*18:98*). Teachers who try to maintain order by sheer force may succeed in achieving a semblance of discipline, but it usually exhausts the teacher and increases the internal tension of children. This applies to psychological coercion as well as physical coercion. A nagging, negativistic attitude on the part of the teacher is as likely as actual physical punishment to bring out negative responses in children. Threatening, scolding, sarcasm, and other forms of psychological punishment may be fully as painful and distressing as physical punishment.

Learning Tasks and Educational Standards

Many discipline problems may be traced to an academic curriculum which imposes upon children learning tasks that are unchallenging, unstimulating, and unrelated to their needs. When coupled with an educational organization which forces youngsters to achieve artificial standards without consideration for their psychological growth requirements, a fertile field for the development of discipline problems is established.

EFFECTS OF ACADEMIC EMPHASIS IN THE CURRICULUM. Prominent among the influences which contribute to the academic frustration of children are meaningless tasks which have little to do with their real problems of living. How such school programs may affect American youth was shown in a study conducted by the California State Department of Education (*28*). A survey of some 13,000 young people who had gone through the high school program in California was conducted to determine how well these youngsters had been prepared to meet the problems of life. Some of the significant findings of this study are shown in Figure 8. These will be summarized in the next few paragraphs.

If the objective of our schools is to make youngsters literate, they are

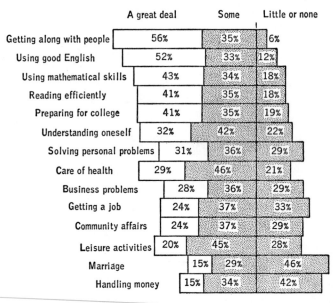

FIGURE 8. Preparation for Life Activities. (Adapted from W. H. Mc-Creary and D. E. Kitch, "Now Hear Youth," *Bulletin of the California State Department of Education,* vol. 22, no. 9, October, 1953, p. 21. By permission of the California State Department of Education.)

succeeding. Less than one in five of the graduates was dissatisfied with the help received in using English or mathematics, in learning to read, or preparing for college. However, if it is the goal of the school to teach the application of fundamental skills to the solution of life problems, the picture is quite different. Graduates felt the schools were derelict in teaching them the skills and knowledge needed for use of leisure time, participation in community and civic affairs, preparation for marriage, getting a job, and handling money—areas related directly to the life activities which confronted them.

In the eyes of many youth, schools are not concentrating on things which are important to them. One girl, speaking for the 75 percent of high school graduates who felt they had insufficient help in preparation for marriage, said:

> The majority of girls eventually marry—regardless of how much they prepare for a career. The most important career any woman has is raising her children and how much education does any mother receive before parenthood? The best the majority of us can do is buy Spock and hope for the best. That puts our first few children in the guinea pig class. They deserve much more than that. Classes in clothing, good budgets, personal hygiene, child care, and child psychology should be required of *every* girl graduate and those courses that pertain to child raising required of all boys. (28:12)

An important conclusion derived from this study was that teachers can alleviate the dissatisfaction of high school youth, and reduce the tendency to leave school early by making subject matter more meaningful through calling attention to the connection between what is studied in school and its application to economic, social, or personal life (28:43).

This does not mean that all education must be practical, vocationally oriented, or devoid of instruction which will provide youngsters with a broad understanding of our culture. Rather, it suggests that the school curriculum is already heavily weighted in the academic area, and weak in its adaptation to the needs and problems of youth. As a result, many youngsters are dissatisfied with school and want to leave as soon as possible.

Compulsory school laws which keep youngsters in the classroom many years after they have reached the limit of their academic educability have created some major problems for teachers. These boys and girls pass an unhappy, frustrated existence during the dragging years of school, and either mark time until they are old enough to leave, or find compensating diversions in some form of misbehavior or escape. Without judging the merits of compulsory attendance laws, it is evident that educators need to acknowledge the futility of trying to cram additional academic learning into such children, and instead seek ways to teach them skills which will contribute to their usefulness as citizens in our society.

These comments are not intended to imply that all teachers should be indicted for uninspired teaching, or that all schools are insensitive to the needs of children. There are many children who look upon learning as a real challenge and who pursue the school curriculum with eagerness and enthusiasm. And there are many teachers who through skill, imagination, and personal inspiration challenge and stimulate their pupils. Yet, it cannot be denied that large numbers of children experience feelings of repeated frustration and failure which generalize into negative attitudes toward the school and lead to misbehavior in the classroom.

SCHOOL ORGANIZATION AND DISCIPLINE. Sometimes the organizational procedures associated with mass education compound the difficulties created by an unsatisfactory curriculum. The graded subject basis upon which most schools are founded assumes that each year children with marked individual differences and a variety of backgrounds will advance regularly in their intellectual maturity so that their achievement matches the learning requirements of the grade. Although the fallacy of this assumption has been demonstrated, it still underlies much school practice.

Because this graded structure is psychologically unsound, it requires a pressure system dependent upon extrinsic forces to make it work. Children lack self-motivation; therefore teachers must use a variety of artificial motivating devices to make learning more palatable and to move children toward established standards. The rewards, punishments, report cards, failure, and threat of failure which accompanies this program are themselves responsible for many problems of control and management (6:17). Worry over grades, compulsiveness about assignments, aggression, hostility, listlessness, casualness toward learning, psychological and physical truancy, feelings of inadequacy, and attitudes of evasion or "just getting by" are some of the outcomes which may be expected when educational standards and school practices are not synchronized with the growth and learning processes of children (32:296).

Individual Development and Discipline

Even when the curriculum is reasonable, the teacher skillful, and the administrative organization satisfactory, there will still be problems of discipline in the classroom because of certain personality and growth characteristics of children. We know, for example, that the physical condition of a youngster may be responsible for his misbehavior in school.

Lack of sleep, malnutrition, overstimulation at home, or an incipient illness may make a child irritable, unable to concentrate, fidgety, or difficult to manage in the classroom (48).

Anxieties carried over from home to school is another source of behavior difficulty. These may stem from a major crisis in the home, a chronic condition of unsatisfactory family relations, or an accumulation of small irritations resulting from nagging, reproof, and scolding. Teachers place a large share of the blame for school discipline problems on such factors (36:99).

The intelligence of children also seems to affect the control and management problems of teachers. Contrary to popular belief, a room full of bright youngsters is not harder to handle than a group of dull or below average boys and girls. There are four and one-half times as many teachers of bright children who report their youngsters to be exceptionally well behaved as do teachers of children who are below average in intelligence (36:83).

MISBEHAVIOR AS A CONSEQUENCE OF NORMAL GROWTH. In addition to these factors there are several aspects of normal behavior which, if not understood, can lead to problems of control and management. One is the inclination of teachers to modify or discourage forms of behavior which are characteristic of a certain age. For example, Gesell, Ilg, and Ames describe the typical behavior of an 11-year-old as follows:

Eleven is an active developmental transition. . . . There is a restless, seething, and somewhat explosive quality about his schoolroom behavior. He wriggles in his seat. He has bursts and flurries of activity with intervals of pronounced fatigue. He fluctuates from a bad mood to vivid exuberance.

. . . . .

He is in a phase of growth which makes trouble for himself and teacher, but it is not a true state of belligerency. He can be very fond and even affectionate toward a teacher. His school mates are important to him too, and for the same reason: he has much to learn from them. He does it by contact, by nudging, poking, chasing, teasing. He joins a transient cluster of his pals and enters into their intrigues. He is highly competitive. His games call for supervision. (20:451)

Teachers may feel the urge to suppress children who act this way, and at times may have to do so. On the other hand, youngsters who are full of buoyant energy and whose muscles and feelings urge them to be off on some physical or manipulative activity cannot be expected to sit still and study without protest.

This conflict between the natural growth tendencies of children and the school's requirement for order and self-restraint results in tensions which may be considered a normal state of affairs. Teachers should learn to temper control with flexibility, and remember that many acts of misbehavior are not willful, but merely symptoms of growing individuality. They must be tolerant of a certain amount of misbehavior, for too much interference and restraint may prolong a phase of growth, or make it more difficult for a youngster to pass through this phase into a higher level of maturity (*11*:138).

Group Influences on Classroom Behavior

Individual behavior is influenced by the complex, shifting network of interpersonal relations existing within the classroom group. Group forces may make a child a bully or a scapegoat; a leader or an isolate. The group may reward rebellious or unruly behavior, or deny status to those who violate accepted standards (*29, 32*). Lack of acquaintance with group dynamics may seriously interfere with a teacher's ability to control children. The effects of group climate and the psychological forces operating within a group are matters which have particular implications for the management of child behavior.

GROUP CLIMATE AND BEHAVIOR. The now classical experiments of Lewin, Lippitt, and White (*25*) with groups of 10-year-old boys have shown how group atmosphere influences individual behavior. Observations were made of the reactions of boys to an authoritarian, a democratic, and a laissez-faire group climate. It was found that in an authoritarian atmosphere the boys showed aggressive domination toward one another, or they became submissive and apathetic. They had little interest in their work, and displayed 40 times more overt hostility toward one another than did the boys in the democratic group.

In the democratic groups there was a moderate amount of aggression, but most of it was friendly. The boys made constructive suggestions to one another, had satisfying social relations, a high interest in their work, assumed individual responsibility, and were able to work in the absence of the leader.

The laissez-faire groups, where complete freedom was allowed, caused the boys literally to run wild. Little work was accomplished, there was much aggression, play, and silliness, and a great deal of confusion and insecurity.

While it is unwise to make sweeping generalizations from these experiments, a few conclusions are warranted. One is that authoritarian discipline will reduce misbehavior in the classroom at the cost of reducing interest in achievement and increasing latent or active aggression. Another implication is that a democratic classroom atmosphere may be more noisy than an authoritarian classroom, but there will be more constructive group activity, more coöperation among the children, and greater potential for the development of self-control by individuals.

These conclusions are widely accepted by teachers. Yet fear that children will get out of hand if not dealt with strictly has resulted in a limited application of democratic procedures in classroom practice. Dalton (*17*), for instance, found only a slight relationship between what teachers said they believed about democracy in the classroom and what they actually practiced. There appears to be a general tendency for teachers to espouse democratic principles while actually practicing a modified form of authoritarianism with their children.

PSYCHOLOGICAL FORCES WITHIN THE GROUP. It is common knowledge that a troublesome youngster when placed among a group of well-behaved children may modify his behavior rather dramatically, while in another group he may be more troublesome than ever. This is a characteristic of group influence over individuals. A group develops distinctive attitudes and patterns of behavior which make its members act in accordance with a collective force. This force is so strong that individuals tend to bend in the direction of majority opinion, even when the majority is wrong (*7, 22*). Attitudes adopted by the group have been found to be more binding than attitudes reached on an individual basis. As children grow older, expectations of the group and its demands on individuals become better defined and less forgiving toward those who do not abide by group expectations (*16*).

Group contagion, or the spread of behavior through a group, also has important implications for classroom discipline. The behavior of normally restrained individuals at a football game or out-of-town convention is an illustration of how group contagion can sweep individuals into patterns of behavior which they do not exhibit individually. Redl (*39, 40*) refers to this phenomenon as a form of "group psychological intoxication." It can cause children to lose their sense of proportion, move them to enthusiasm or hostility, spread restlessness or irritation through the group, or weld them into solid support for a joint purpose.

These findings emphasize the importance of understanding group dynamics and group management. The way in which the teacher organizes the class and the subgroups within it may determine the climate of behavior which will prevail. Teachers who prevent children from developing a group feeling by keeping friends separated, forcing children to report on each other's misbehavior, or emphasizing individual attainment intensify their discipline problems because they do not harness the force of the group for the control of behavior (*43*).

PREVENTIVE DISCIPLINE

Many teachers would like to be provided with a series of procedures which may be applied to specific types of misbehavior. The management of children is a complex problem of human relationships which cannot be reduced to such simple techniques. There are no practices which apply uniformly to any given type of misconduct. Each incident and each situation is somewhat unique, involving a variety of personal, social, and environmental factors which must be taken into consideration.

For these reasons, we shall not attempt to discuss the techniques or devices for managing children which have been handed down as pedagogical folkways. As teachers develop an understanding of child behavior, and learn to analyze a situation in terms of its emotional implications, routine control measures will evolve. More important are the preventive measures which can be taken to eliminate or minimize the factors contributing to the misconduct of children. This is a long-range approach which, while it may not have immediate appeal to many teachers, holds greater promise for decreasing the frequency and intensity of discipline problems.

Preventive Discipline and School Administration

Many problems of school discipline will not be solved until school officials reëxamine their values and reappraise what they are requiring of teachers. As has been mentioned, if teachers are assigned large classes containing children who have emotional difficulties which stem from parental neglect, mistreatment, poor living conditions, or demoralized neighborhoods, child management problems are inescapable. Moreover, if these teachers are rated as incompetent when they do not maintain quiet and order, or keep academic achievement up to standard, tension and anxiety are built into classroom life. Under these circumstances, teachers may deliberately disregard what they have learned about child development and resort to control techniques which they know to be psychologically unsound.

Those who are responsible for the formation of school policy and the administration of school affairs must take a more forceful role in the establishment of conditions favorable to good child management. The types of administrative support which teachers desire are shown in the following list of recommendations which emerged from a national survey of teacher opinion on school discipline:

1. Do not assign very young or old teachers to groups of children which are difficult to manage.
2. Avoid imposing work on teachers to the point that they get insufficient rest and relaxation. Good physical and mental health are related to the ability to manage children. Tired teachers do not have the patience or flexibility for tolerating the behavior of children, and are prone to react emotionally to situations which in a relaxed state they could accept with ease.
3. Encourage the organization of community recreation programs and youth activities which will keep children wholesomely occupied. Out-of-school recreation and guidance have a direct bearing on children's behavior within school.
4. Provide leadership and assistance in securing parent coöperation. Unsatisfactory home relations and home influences are at the core of many disciplinary problems.
5. Give teachers a voice in determining policies regarding discipline. In many instances these policies are instituted without consulting teachers and without a clear understanding of the effects of these policies on teachers and children.
6. Teachers require help with severely handicapped and maladjusted children. Special classes for deviate children, or at least counselors and psychologists who have time to devote to these youngsters, are forms of assistance which teachers need badly.
7. Small classes and a flexible curriculum are conditions which enable a teacher to institute good child management practices. (36)

These points will be amplified in the succeeding chapter. The important thing to note here is that classroom discipline is a coöperative affair which must involve school officials and the community, and cannot be left to the teacher alone.

Teacher Attitudes and Practices

Despite the popular admonition that teachers should start out being "tough" with children and ease up when they have become properly responsive to authority, research shows that this is not the formula for successful discipline. Competent teachers are more likely to use positive, rather than negative measures for the control of children (*12, 14, 45*). They have regard for the ego development of boys and girls, and accept the idea that children have a long way to go before self-direction is possible. In general, observations of successful teachers indicate that they anticipate potential sources of trouble in the classroom, maintain close interpersonal relations with children, and use nonpunitive techniques which redirect behavior without undermining self-esteem (*33, 46*).

ANTICIPATING BEHAVIOR PROBLEMS. The alert teacher can foresee circumstances which might give rise to misconduct. For example, children who arrive at school early can get off to a bad start unless early morning routines and rules are established. The handling of work materials, rainy-day activities, after recess or after lunch procedures, changing from job to job, or room to room, what to do when work is finished—all of these must be planned so that children know what to do and carry on with a minimum of supervision.

The routines of the room can be planned with children so that there is no question of what to do or when. It will take practice and patience to establish these routines, and there is danger of overorganizing a classroom. However, careful attention to these matters will result in a well-managed group of youngsters who know what they are doing and feel comfortable and secure in their classroom.

NONPUNITIVE PREVENTIVE TECHNIQUES. There are a number of nonpunitive measures which may be used to short-circuit many tendencies toward misbehavior. These include various uses of verbal appeals, such as calling a child by name when he is out of order, verbal reminders, simple inquiries, requests for cessation of an activity, the defining of limits, verbal rewards and encouragement, repeating directions, or reasoning with a child.

Some attention has been devoted to methods of improving the effectiveness of verbal appeals. Johnson (*23*), for example, has provided some helpful suggestions for the use of language in controlling the behavior of children. It appears that verbal controls are most effective when they are positive, constructive, simple, and concise. Blanket statements, complicated requests, and negative admonishments are confusing to children (*47*).

By making his physical presence felt in a pleasant way the teacher can regulate behavior without severity or harshness. Redl and Wattenberg (*41*) refer to such techniques as "signal interference" or "proximity control." This may be done through a meaningful smile, a questioning look, a nod of the head, a gesture, a gentle hand on a child's arm or shoulder, or by merely standing or sitting next to a youngster who is about to lose his self-control. Many times misconduct can be averted by letting the child alone and modifying his environment. This has been described as "situational assistance" (*41*). It might call for the rearranging of seating, creating appropriate activities for a child, promoting group acceptance, or providing a rich supply of books, instructional materials, play equipment, and various other types of teaching materials.

The deliberate acceptance of misbehavior is sometimes the best technique for handling a situation. The teacher who tries to stop every little wrongdoing in the classroom will wear himself out and the children as well. Crisis situations can often be avoided by simply accepting certain behavior rather than reacting to it. Although the ideal of many teachers is an orderly classroom, it has never been proven that effective learning requires the high degree of order and restraint which some teachers insist upon (*46*).

Finally, teachers must not expect to be successful with all their pupils. The expectation that one teacher can relate to an entire group of children in such a way that misbehavior will be eliminated completely is unreasonable. In many cases, misconduct is an expression of complex forces which happen to reach a crisis in the classroom. Also, some children simply are not capable of responding to positive forms of management, and there is nothing the teacher can do about the conditions which make this so. The wise teacher will accept this situation, do all he can to aid the personality development of children, and not permit himself to be drawn into conflicts which can only lead to hostility (*46*).

Preventive Discipline Through Instruction

The academic program of the school can be a deterrent to misbehavior if it is oriented realistically to the learning activities which are important to children, and if it offers opportunities to satisfy the need for achievement. Youngsters whose interests and energies are absorbed in meaningful experiences have little inclination toward misconduct. The learning situation itself becomes a source of discipline which is accepted as necessary because it makes possible the attainment of desired goals.

THE CURRICULUM. Children learn not with their minds alone but with their entire beings. The curriculum must be designed to nurture the total growth of children, rather than their intellectual development alone. This calls for the organization of learning experiences adapted to the psychological and social requirements of growing boys and girls.

The fear that children will not learn the "essentials" in such a school program has been proved groundless (1). The views of mental hygienists on this issue were summarized some years ago by a committee of educators and physicians in the following words:

> It would be well for those teachers who have some control over content and method to ask, "What difference does it make whether the child learns this or not?" If it is vital material that he likes, he will attack it with a vim. If it is uninteresting or unsuited to his needs and abilities, the possibility of developing poor mental health habits is present. He may become mischievous and get into difficulties with his teacher. He may develop poor work habits. He may seek satisfaction in daydreaming. In fact, the potentiality of good or poor mental health is inherent in the curriculum . . . The curriculum should be so selected, organized and administered that the children will be given worthwhile activities of interest to them, adapted to their abilities and fitted to their needs. (30)

While this is not the place to analyze the details of such a curriculum, two general points related directly to the problem of pupil management are worth emphasizing. First, it is important to encourage the study of real life problems and to provide children with the skills for doing so. Unless knowledge and skill are applied to the solution of matters which concern children, classroom work becomes artificial and unrelated to life outside of school.

Secondly, learning experiences must be planned with pupils if the curriculum is to be adjusted to their needs and interests. When youngsters are permitted to formulate learning experiences in terms of their varied abilities and concerns, they enter into learning earnestly and eagerly. Matters which are current in their thinking, and which affect them in significant ways become a stimulus to learning and a guide to behavior.

If these conditions are established, misbehavior will be replaced by a desire to work together and abide by the requirements of the learning situation. This type of teaching requires greater skill than is demanded by a formal curriculum, but it provides a setting for learning which makes problems of discipline and control secondary issues.

ACADEMIC ACHIEVEMENT.   The sense of achievement is a basic psychological need which can be satisfied through academic accomplishment. Most normal children enjoy learning. They are curious and eager for new knowledge and experience real emotional satisfaction when they master a skill or acquire new information. Any school which does not help children expand their intellectual horizons denies them this source of satisfaction.

To satisfy the need for achievement, each child must be permitted to seek academic success in terms of his own abilities and personality, and not be judged by comparison with others. Some teachers feel that this is compromising educational standards. The choice must be made of either denying that diversity exists among children and making them all attain established grade or subject standards, or adopting flexible standards which will give each child some success and make academic learning a stimulating experience. It is difficult to provide the differentiation of subject matter and teaching methods which the latter course of action requires. Yet this is the only way to avoid the discouragement and compensatory behavior which occurs when children encounter frustration and failure in their learning activities.

Encouraging Self-Management

There are many behavior problems which children will work out themselves if given an opportunity to do so. What they require is a sympathetic teacher who is able to accept the instability which accompanies various periods of growth, and a form of classroom organization which allows them to experience the process of self-management.

ACCEPTING THE PROBLEMS OF GROWTH. There are times when youngsters have difficult growing experiences which may be reflected as an inability to sit still, lack of attention, irritability, or other reactions which annoy teachers. Very often, time, patience, and a minimum of pressure will help a child regain control over his behavior. This may mean easing up on academic requirements for a while, permitting activities which are best liked, or just carrying the child along for a period without expecting much of him until equilibrium is restored. The solution to problems created by growth is not to be found through an attack upon behavior, but through a better understanding of what a child is undergoing.

PROVIDING OPPORTUNITIES FOR SELF-MANAGEMENT. Children tend to abide by rules and regulations which they set themselves in order to achieve a goal or objective. A form of classroom organization which utilizes the intrinsic motivation of attaining rewards through the consequences of one's own efforts, rather than through a teacher's generosity, will provide an atmosphere which encourages the self-regulation of behavior (50:280). Through self-managed activities, children work out their individual problems of relationship with one another and learn to live within certain restrictions which they recognize as necessary in order to provide everyone with equality of opportunity.

In the early grades this may be done through rotating periods as class officers, so arranged that youngsters have experience with responsibility and the making of decisions. At a later age, class government becomes more formally organized with officers, committees, elections, self-determined rules, and other activities which give children a real stake in the function of the class or school. These are important experiences for children. Through them they learn to act like responsible beings and gain experience in governing themselves effectively and independently.

Using Group Influences in the Control and Management of Children

Research in group dynamics has shown that individual behavior is influenced strongly by the group to which a person belongs. The force of the group has been used to change the behavior of people when individual instruction failed to do so. Dietary practices (24, 27), weight reduction (44), and the learning of motor skills (15, 53) are some forms of behavior which have yielded to group influences.

The persuasiveness of group decisions and the reassurance and support which youngsters derive from a group can be important factors in child management. To use group processes effectively the teacher must be able to share his authority with the group, encourage group cohesiveness, and create a social atmosphere for group action.

SHARING AUTHORITY. The teacher who shares authority with the class does not weaken his position, but gains the power of group force. It has been found that when children participate in the making of decisions, violation of these decisions becomes an offense against the group instead of an offense against the authority of the teacher. Children are inclined to be severe with such offenders, and it sometimes becomes necessary for the teacher to protect the transgressors, rather than impose discipline upon them (34).

Eagerness to plan their own affairs may cause children to undertake responsibilities beyond their capacity. The teacher must guide children without squelching their initiative and enthusiasm. He must be dis-

3. The behavior of a group of children changes as different teachers are encountered. What explanation for this is suggested by the experiments of Lewin and his associates?

4. From your observation and experience, how would you explain the increase in discipline problems occurring in large schools and large cities? Select a particular situation and analyze the factors involved.

5. To what extent do the child management principles discussed here apply to: (a) schools located in slum areas? (b) schools where there are organized conflicts among minority groups? Discuss any adaptations which would be needed in these situations.

6. Discuss "level of aspiration" in terms of its implications for child management (see *42*).

7. The typical behavior of normal 11-year-olds has been described. Describe normal forms of behavior of children at other ages which might be interpreted by the teacher as misconduct.

8. Evaluate the following procedures as disciplinary techniques: (a) isolation from the group; (b) penalizing a class until the offender admits his guilt; (c) encouraging the group to isolate a child because he did something which penalized the entire class; (d) discussing a child's behavior with the class.

9. Why do you think a large proportion of teachers would like more authority to administer corporal punishment? Are there situations where corporal punishment is necessary?

10. What effects have you observed of requiring high school age youngsters to remain in school after they have ceased to benefit from academic instruction? What are some plans that have been developed to meet the needs of these youth?

11. Describe situations where the following factors led to discipline problems: (a) the physical environment in the school; (b) teacher management procedures; (c) administrative practices.

SELECTED REFERENCES

1. Aiken, W. M., *The Story of the Eight-Year Study,* McGraw-Hill Book Company, 1942.

2. Anderson, H. H., and Anderson, G. L., "Social Development," in L. Carmichael (ed.), *Manual of Child Psychology,* John Wiley and Sons, 1954.

3. Anderson, H. H., and Brewer, J. E., "Studies of Teachers' Classroom Personalities. II. Effects of Teachers' Dominative and Integrative Contacts on Children's Classroom Behavior," *Applied Psychology Monographs* (1946), no. 8.

4. Anderson, H. H., Brewer, J. E., and Reed, M. F., "Studies of Teachers' Classroom Personalities. III. Follow-up Studies of the Effects of Dominative and Integrative Contacts on Children's Behavior." *Applied Psychology Monographs* (1946), no. 11.

5. *As You See It,* San Diego Unified School District, Board of Education (San Diego, California), January, 1957.

6. Averill, L. A., *The Psychology of the Elementary School Child,* Longmans, Green and Co., 1949.

7. Berenda, R. W., *The Influence of the Group on the Judgments of Children,* Bureau of Publications, Teachers College, Columbia University, 1950.

8. Birch, J. W., and Stullken, E. H., *Solving Problems of Problem Children,* Public School Publishing Co. (Bloomington, Illinois), 1956.

9. Bovard, E. W., "Psychology of Classroom Interaction," *Journal of Educational Research* (1951), 45:215–224.

10. Bradford, L. P., "The Pupil and the Group," *NEA Journal* (February, 1957), 46:103–105.

11. Bush, R. N., *The Teacher-Pupil Relationship,* Prentice-Hall, Inc., 1954.

12. Campbell, N. C., *The Elementary School Teacher's Treatment of Classroom Behavior,* Bureau of Publications, Teachers College, Columbia University, Contributions to Education No. 668, 1935.

13. Carter, G. W., *A Study of Disciplinary Behavior in Its Socio-Economic Setting,* Unpublished Doctoral Dissertation, University of California (Berkeley), 1941.

14. Celler, S. L., "Practices Associated with Effective Discipline: A Descriptive Statistical Study of Discipline," *Journal of Experimental Education* (June, 1951), 19:333–58.

15. Coch, L., and French, J. R. P., Jr., "Overcoming Resistance to Change," *Journal of Human Relations* (1948), 1:4.

16. Cunningham, R., *et al., Understanding Group Behavior of Boys and Girls,* Bureau of Publications, Teachers College, Columbia University, 1951.

17. Dalton, M. B., *Classroom Democracy Functionally Defined and Measured,* Unpublished Doctoral Dissertation, Washington University (St. Louis, Missouri), 1949.

18. English, H. B., *Child Psychology,* Henry Holt and Co., 1951.

19. Festinger, L., and others, *Theory and Experiment in Social Communication,* Research Center for Group Dynamics, University of Michigan, 1950.

20. Gesell, A., Ilg, F. L., and Ames, L. B., *Youth: The Years from Ten to Sixteen,* Harper & Brothers, 1956.

21. Goodykoontz, B., *Helping Children Get Along in School,* Science Research Associates, 1955.
22. Jahoda, M., and Cook, S. W., "Are Your Opinions Your Own?" *NEA Journal* (September, 1955), 44:357–358.
23. Johnson, M. W., *Verbal Influences on Children's Behavior,* University of Michigan Press, Education Monographs No. 1, 1939.
24. Lewin, K., "The Dynamics of Group Action," *Educational Leadership* (January, 1944), *1*:195–200.
25. Lewin, K., Lippit, R., and White, R. K., "Patterns of Aggressive Behavior in Experimentally Created Social Climates," *Journal of Social Psychology* (1939), *10*:271–299.
26. Long, H. B., and Farley, L. E., *Teacher Behavior Most Disliked By Students,* Unpublished Doctoral Dissertation, Stanford University, 1948.
27. Maier, N. R. F., *Psychology in Industry.* Houghton Mifflin Co., 1955.
28. McCreary, W. H., and Kitch, D. E., "Now Hear Youth," *Bulletin of the California State Department of Education,* vol. 22, no. 9, October, 1953.
29. McKeachie, W. J., "Individual Conformity to Attitudes of Classroom Groups," *Journal of Abnormal and Social Psychology* (1954), 49:282–289.
30. *Mental Hygiene in the Classroom,* Report of the Joint Committee on Health Problems in Education of the National Education Association and the American Medical Association, American Medical Association, 1949.
31. Morris, H. H., Escoll, P. J. and Wexler, R., "Aggressive Behavior Disorders of Childhood: A Follow-Up Study," *American Journal of Psychiatry* (June, 1956), *112*:991–997.
32. Morse, W. C., and Wingo, G. M., *Psychology and Teaching,* Scott, Foresman and Co., 1955.
33. Moustakas, C. E., *The Teacher and the Child,* McGraw-Hill Book Company, 1956.
34. Mowrer, O. H., "Authoritarianism vs. 'Self-Government' in the Management of Children's Aggressive (Anti-Social) Reactions as a Preparation for Citizenship in a Democracy," *Journal of Social Psychology* (1939), *10*:121–126.
35. Mowrer, O. H., "Discipline and Mental Health," *The Harvard Educational Review* (1947), *17*:284–296.
36. National Education Association, Research Division, "Teacher Opinion on Pupil Behavior, 1955–56," *NEA Research Bulletin* (April, 1956), vol. 34, no. 2.
37. Passow, A. H., and MacKenzie, G. N., "Research in Group Behavior," *The Nation's Schools* (April, 1952), 49:71–73.

38. Pullias, E. V., "Discipline and Mental Hygiene," *Education* (May, 1946), 66:569–572.

39. Redl, F., "Child Study in a New Setting," *Children* (January–February, 1954), *1*:15–20.

40. Redl, F., "The Phenomenon of Contagion and 'Shock Effect' in Group Therapy," in K. R. Eissler, *et al.* (eds.), *Searchlights on Delinquency,* International Universities Press, Inc., 1949, pp. 315–328.

41. Redl, F., and Wattenberg, W. W., *Mental Hygiene in Teaching,* Harcourt, Brace and Co., 1951.

42. Sears, P. S., "Levels of Aspiration in Academically Successful and Unsuccessful Children," *Journal of Abnormal and Social Psychology* (1940), *35*:498–536.

43. Sheviakov, G. V., and Redl, F. (Revised by S. K. Richardson), *Discipline for Today's Children and Youth,* Association for Supervision and Curriculum Development, National Education Association, 1956.

44. Simmons, W. D., "Weight Reduction in Groups," *California's Health* (July, 1954), *12*:1–5.

45. Slobetz, F. B., "How Elementary Teachers Meet Selected School Situations," *Journal of Educational Psychology* (October, 1951), *42*:339–356.

46. Symonds, P. M., "Classroom Discipline," *Teachers College Record* (1949), *51*:147–158.

47. Symonds, P. M., "What Education Has to Learn from Psychology," *Teachers College Record* (April, 1956), 57:449–462.

48. Trow, W. C., "When Are Children Ready to Learn?" *NEA Journal* (February, 1955), *44*:78–79.

49. Trow, W. C., Zander, A. E., and others, "Psychology of Group Behavior: The Class as a Group," *Journal of Educational Psychology* (1950), *41*:322–338.

50. Tuttle, H. S., *Dynamic Psychology and Conduct,* Harper & Brothers, 1949.

51. *What Should Our Schools Accomplish?* National Citizens Commission for the Public Schools, October, 1955.

52. Wiles, K., *Teaching for Better Schools,* Prentice-Hall, Inc., 1952.

53. Zander, A., "Resistence to Change—Its Analysis and Prevention," *Advanced Management* (January, 1950), *15*:9–12.

CHAPTER 15 ⎯⎯⎯⎯⎯⎯⎯⎯⎯⎯⎯⎯⎯⎯⎯

Human Relations in School Administration

PREVIOUS chapters in this text have described the influence which parents and teachers exert on the mental health of children. This influence finds its optimum application in a school where the administrative atmosphere encourages good human relations.

In this chapter, we examine the personal and interpersonal problems of teachers and parents, and how they are affected by administrative policies and practices. An understanding of these factors should enable the administrator to establish conditions which will minimize tensions, antagonisms, and frustrations so that the home and the school may work together effectively for the welfare of children.

MENTAL HEALTH HAZARDS IN TEACHING

Teachers are ordinary human beings performing a difficult and demanding job. Exposed to constant public scrutiny, and to the strain of living with children for long periods of time, teachers often need the support of administrators who understand their problems. Among the various factors which may have an adverse effect upon teacher morale and mental health, three appear to be of major importance. These are: (1) professional pressures, (2) community expectations, and (3) relations with school authorities.

Emotional Pressures on Teachers

While workers in business and industry have obtained a 40-hour work week, and are contemplating even a further reduction in working hours, teachers spend from 45 to 52 hours per week on their jobs or in job-related activities (52, 54). The myth that teaching is a 9:00 A.M. to 3:00 P.M. job, with long summer vacations, dies hard, but the facts show that this is a demanding occupation. As one teacher put it ". . . I find that after working with a roomful of lively children for six hours, I face four to six more hours of school work each day, and almost every week end is taken up with school work. This situation has recently been getting worse instead of better. I have given up hobbies and recreational, church, and community activities" (53:73).

Not only do teachers work longer hours than most wage earners, they are under constant emotional pressure. Classes are large, and there is hardly a moment in the day when a teacher is free from children. Nor is there escape from children after school, for with lessons to plan, papers to grade, and various behavior problems to ponder, the teacher lives in a child's world most of his waking day (52, 53). When the teacher's time and energies are further taxed by being required to participate in scout activities, youth centers, Sunday schools, and similar functions, he has little time to lead a normal life.

Curriculum Problems

Expanded concepts of the functions of education have introduced another source of tension for teachers. In recent years, legal requirements and educational policy have pyramided teaching responsibilities to a point where it is impossible for teachers to do everything demanded of them and do it well. Teachers are required to disseminate information on the effects of alcohol, tobacco, and narcotics; they must know how to recognize symptoms of disease in children, teach sex education, deal with behavior problems, administer a variety of tests, teach about religion, inculcate moral and spiritual values, transmit the culture, and perform many other special services—all without jeopardizing instruction in the fundamental skills. The few short years which a teacher spends in college cannot possibly equip him to perform all these duties. There is need for considerably more realism regarding the teacher's job and the functions he should perform (54).

Pressure for Professional Improvement

For purposes of professional advancement, certification, or salary improvement, teachers often are caught up in a whirl of meetings, courses, and other activities commonly termed "in-service education." The personal and professional improvement of the teacher, which usually is the justification for these activities, may be submerged in a scramble after "service points," or in the multiplicity of meetings, workshops, institutes, and conferences sponsored by various special interest groups in the school system. How such activities drain the energies of teachers is illustrated by the statement of this tired teacher: "We have in-service teacher meetings, such as art workshops, general curriculum workshops; grade level meetings, building meetings, district meetings, county institutes, P.T.A. meetings, child-study meetings, and book review meetings. I counted the hours I spent in these meetings and the extra time devoted to clerical work, and found that during the school year it amounted to six weeks to two months of overtime counted on the basis of 8-hour days" (53:73).

Even when teachers succeed in meeting the requirements for professional improvement set up by the school system, they find few ladders to climb. For most teachers there is no possibility of further vertical movement in a school system. The best they can do is move horizontally—to better schools in better neighborhoods, or to schools where the principal is more advanced in his thinking, or where working conditions are more challenging (4).

Vertical advancement usually means moving into administration or supervision. Many teachers do not wish such positions, or are not qualified for them. Those who do wish to go into administration or supervision find the channels clogged by an oversupply of candidates, or by organizational obstacles in the school system (63).

Relations with School Officials

The increased size and complexity of school systems has created a professional hierarchy which imposes barriers between teachers and administrators. These barriers are reinforced through economic rewards, social distinctions, and the distribution of powers. At the lower levels of this hierarchy, teachers and their immediate supervisors and principals commonly maintain friendly, coöperative relations. Relations become more strained as the higher rungs of administration are approached, reaching a state of isolation at the level of the "downtown office" (8).

The top echelons of administration are so far removed from the classroom that there is a common belief among teachers that these administrators identify themselves with the more powerful community elements rather than with teacher (7). Few teachers are personally acquainted with the superintendent, and they are not encouraged to be friendly with members of the school board. In some large school systems the lack of personal interest in teachers by the administration reaches a point where teachers feel little kinship with their nonteaching colleagues. After studying teacher-administration relationships in a large city school system, Gould remarked:

Beyond an initial interest in the physical health of teachers, administrators seem to have taken no account of this phase of personnel management until a teacher becomes too ill to do her work, or so unbalanced socially, mentally or emotionally that her eccentricities direct unfavorable attention to her. Rarely, if ever, has a school system, large or small, taken so much account of teachers as human beings that definite efforts have been made administratively to retain and build up their physical efficiency and their emotional and social balance. (23)

This lack of communication between teachers and the higher echelons of administration can create hostility and antagonism which interfere with the teacher's efficiency and emotional health.

Community Pressures

Although communities do not restrict the personal lives of teachers as much as they did in the past, they still impose upon them conditions of behavior which make it difficult to achieve complete identification with the people among whom they work and live.

There is an implicit understanding among people that teachers must represent to children a model of adult perfection. Teachers are forced to conceal their human weaknesses, and suppress natural inclinations to live and act like other adults (51, 54). The community treats them with polite courtesy, but rarely invites them to join groups which form the basis for community identification. People seem to fear that the presence of teachers will destroy the informal fellowship of such groups. This lack of identification with the community leads to a tendency for teachers to socialize within their own professional group, rather than with other groups in the community. Such relationships bar the teacher from participating in community life to the extent that they achieve a feeling of belonging (7).

Problems of Men Teachers

In addition to the mental health hazards common to all teachers, men have some special problems by virtue of their status as a minority group in the profession. These problems have not been entirely appreciated by communities and school officials. This may account for the fact that teaching, which was once a profession for men alone, is now predominantly a woman's field.

Three factors have been identified as critical mental health hazards for men teachers. These are: (1) financial insecurity, (2) lack of professional status, and (3) social isolation (46, 58).

FINANCIAL INSECURITY. The National Education Association summarized the financial problems of the man teacher in this cryptic statement: "The financial plight of the married men, many with one or two children, is one of the greatest tragedies of this prosperous age in which we live" (51).

Men teachers, most of whom are married, have financial difficulties from the very beginning of their careers. At the end of the first year of teaching, the average man teacher is without money, and almost 18 percent are left with a debt of at least $750. Financial insecurity forces the man teacher to work during the summer and in off hours. In 1955, almost 40 percent of the men teachers earned extra income during the school year, and two-thirds of them worked during the summer (54). With an average teaching salary in 1956 of $3887 for elementary teachers and $4594 for secondary teachers, the married man with a family to support is understandably frustrated. His inability to maintain a standard of living equivalent to that of other men of similar training and experience who did not go into teaching, leaves him feeling financially and psychologically inadequate.

LACK OF PROFESSIONAL STATUS. It is difficult for a man teacher to maintain status among men in other occupations when his position is stigmatized as the work of a woman. This problem is particularly acute in the elementary school where the man teacher is likely to be the only male in the building, with the exception of the custodian or engineer.

The man teacher feels the need for assignments and responsibilities which will distinguish his work from that of women teachers and enable him to maintain a masculine role. Too often, no consideration is given to the needs and aspirations of men teachers. Their work is not distinguished by salary, function, or opportunity for professional advancement. Indeed, there is evidence that the man teacher is exploited by assigning to him duties which are not desired by women. A college professor, who was once an elementary teacher, put it this way: "The man teacher in the elementary school is expected to sweep up the educational rubbish and damage that is created by self-centered lady teachers. Boys who set off firecrackers in school, who smash drinking fountains, or who cannot contain their urine, are collected in a madhouse and placed in charge of a man teacher" (*38*). No doubt this statement is rather extreme. However, it emphasizes the feelings which many men teachers have toward their work.

SOCIAL ISOLATION. The man teacher often feels like an intruder in the feminine atmosphere of the school. In the elementary school he receives so little recognition that seldom does one find a rest room or lounge set aside for men teachers, although women teachers, and even the custodian, have such facilities.

Men maintain friendly professional relations with their feminine colleagues, but do not form close associations with them. They are left out of the cliques and friendship groups, and tend to be more friendly with the school custodian or engineer than with the women teachers. Men are particularly sensitive about working under the direction of women administrators. Schools that are built for women and run by women may not provide an atmosphere in which a man can maintain his self-respect and feel comfortable and socially accepted. This is an important factor in influencing men to seek administrative positions, secondary school assignments, where the ratio of men to women is more evenly balanced, or to leave the profession for other occupations (*38, 50*).

ADMINISTRATIVE LEADERSHIP AND TEACHER MORALE

The preceding discussion was not meant to leave the impression that all teachers are disgruntled or unhappy. On the contrary, most teachers are relatively happy in their work and derive much satisfaction from performing functions which use their training, interests, and capacities (*51, 54, 63*).

The fact remains, however, that there is a great need in our schools for personnel policies which focus on human relations. Business management has discovered that personnel policies founded on mental hygiene principles will increase production, reduce absenteeism, and diminish spoilage and accidents (*42*). Similar improvement in teacher morale and efficiency can be expected if school administrators become more concerned with the human aspects of education.

What Teachers Ask of Administrators

Various surveys of the job-related annoyances of teachers have disclosed a number of persistent irritations which might be relieved by administrative action. The following requests and recommendations, while not a complete list, indicate the administrative procedures which teachers feel would alleviate some of their more troublesome problems (9, 37, 45, 51, 52).

CLERICAL ASSISTANCE. Teachers feel that the time required for completing official records and reports, keeping registers and roll books, handling money, and other tasks of a nonprofessional nature could be better spent preparing class work. This is a common source of irritation to teachers which could be removed by providing more secretarial or clerical assistance.

CURRICULUM. Teachers want freedom to plan learning experiences for children and to arrange the learning environment of the classroom. They would like administrators and supervisors to provide stimulating and helpful assistance in these areas, without circumscribing this freedom. Specifically, they request help in understanding and using courses of study and curriculum guides and in making effective use of community resources.

HELP WITH CHILDREN. The management of children is a major concern of teachers. Assistance is needed in handling discipline problems and in working with exceptional children. Teachers recommend three types of administrative aid: First, add personnel, rooms, and facilities to provide for services of a specialized nature. Secondly, provide monitors who would take over supervision of lunchrooms, hallways, playgrounds, buses, and other duties of a housekeeping nature which burden the professional staff. Third, they want principals who understand the behavior problems of children and who are willing to help with troublesome cases.

PERSONAL ASSISTANCE. Teachers would like to have their administrators accessible so that they can talk with them without going through channels. In this way, grievances can be corrected before they grow into major problems.

Administrators are expected to encourage social activities among the staff, recognize and appreciate good work, and provide each individual with a sense of professional status, responsibility, and freedom.

ADMINISTRATIVE MANAGEMENT. Teachers want to participate more fully in administrative affairs, particularly in the formulation of policies regarding the management of children, teacher salaries and welfare, and the curriculum. Time for such participation could be found, they say, if there were fewer programs, meetings, money-raising projects, and other special events. More administrative concern over classroom interruptions, a more equitable system of dividing duties among teachers, efficient procurement and distribution of textbooks and supplies, and the provision of at least one free period during the day, are additional administrative practices which teachers advocate.

Some of these requests may appear contradictory or utopian. However, they represent matters which trouble teachers and which should concern administrators. The percentage of enthusiastic teachers in a school system rises and staff morale increases as these sources of irritation are removed.

Interpersonal Relations of Teachers and Administrators

We have mentioned but a few of the mental health problems of teachers and the administrative adjustments required to resolve them. There is so much variability in the specific conditions which might pertain in any given school or school district that no useful purpose would be served by analyzing further the detailed problems of teachers and what administrators could do about them. More important is an understanding of the general pattern of relationship which has been found to underlie an administrative atmosphere that nurtures mental health and wholesome interpersonal relations. Open channels of communication, provisions for recognizing the work of each individual and accepting him as an important person, and the sharing of responsibility are means through which successful administrators manage to get people to work *with* them, rather than *for* them.

MAINTAINING OPEN CHANNELS OF COMMUNICATION.   Industrial concerns faced with the problem of lowered production have found that channels of communication which permit a two-way flow of ideas, criticisms, and suggestions stimulate morale and efficiency. A worker who is troubled by personal problems or anxieties related to his job is not at his best. He needs a person in authority with whom he can talk.

This need is greater in education than in industry, for the teacher works with human beings rather than materials (56, 67). The school administrator must make himself available to teachers and be a willing, sincere listener. He should encourage not only verbal communication, but also the communication of feelings which often are more important than the words expressed (11). He must have the patience and insight to refrain from offering hasty solutions, and encourage people to reach their own decisions.

These are difficult and time-consuming responsibilities for a busy administrator. They cannot be done with one eye on the clock, or by showing concern over being kept from other important tasks. It takes time to talk over one's problems, and routine work may have to be set aside, or made up in evening hours. Yet, if better human relations are to be built, teachers must have a share of the administrator's time (*35*).

PROVIDING RECOGNITION AND ACCEPTANCE.   Administrators must be alert to ways in which they can enhance the self-respect and professional confidence of teachers. Teachers, like others, have a need for recognition which must be satisfied over and over again so that they have a continuing sense of achievement. This may be done through informal talks, through the judicious use of public praise, or through more formal procedures such as bulletins, newsletters, school board action, or newspapers. Designating outstanding teachers as supervisors of cadets, consulting with them regarding developments in their teaching specialty, or encouraging them to experiment with new techniques are other ways to acknowledge professional ability.

Teachers also need the security of knowing that they have the support of their administrators. This support must be genuine and should demonstrate the administrator's sincere concern for each individual on his staff. The shallow, superficial friendliness of the "glad-hander" or back-slapper does not satisfy this requirement. Teachers need to feel that their leaders are persons of integrity and professional competence with whom they can establish bonds of trust and confidence. Such administrative support builds feelings of self-reliance and self-respect (*1*).

SHARING RESPONSIBILITY.   Business and industry have found it profitable to encourage the collaborative thinking of employees toward the solution of administrative problems. The sharing of administrative responsibilities not only reduces costs and improves operational efficiency, but fosters a feeling of cohesiveness which makes for better human relations among the staff (*12, 31, 40*).

Educators have yet to try this technique on a broad scale, but there is evidence that it will work as well in the schools as it does in industry. To exercise the type of leadership required in democratic administration, an executive must have sufficient faith in his staff to delegate responsibilities and decisions which he could manage himself perfectly well. He must be receptive to ideas, willing to see others make mistakes as they learn, and content to exercise broad control over administration in order to gain the benefits which result from improved staff morale (*12*).

These procedures do not relinquish to teachers the administration of schools. They make the administrator the chief coördinator of a professional team instead of the sole source of authority. Although there are many problems associated with the decentralization of administration, this approach to personnel management has been found to make the most effective use of human resources (1).

PROBLEMS ENCOUNTERED IN DEMOCRATIC ADMINISTRATION. Certain problems may be expected to arise when democratic procedures are introduced in school administration. One is the confusion of roles which may result. By broadening the base of administration, teachers may assume functions which traditionally have belonged to administrators. It is possible, also, that a few teachers who are dynamic and aggressive may exert a dominating influence in the school, and perhaps not see clearly their responsibilities to other teachers and to the community. These difficulties can be avoided by clarifying the role of each person involved in an activity, establishing the policies by which decision-making groups must abide, outlining the work to be done, and defining the framework within which teachers may act on administrative matters (12).

Another type of problem encountered is the resistance which teachers themselves offer to democratic administrative practices. Many teachers have been conditioned to having administrators make their decisions, handle their problems, and smooth out their conflicts. They resent having to serve on committees, and have little patience with the compromise, delay, and evasion which may result from a form of administration which lacks a dominating personality (8). It is true, also, that unpleasant experience with administrators who invite teachers to work on committees, then act upon preconceived decisions, instill a sense of futility in teacher groups.

Teachers may also resist assuming responsibility for administration because they fear to challenge the existing order of things. The authority roles established in an educational organization make changes in personal relations difficult. However enlightened an administrator may be, if he has the power to make promotions, to rate teachers, and to determine their assignments and salaries, teachers will not feel free to participate openly in a reconstruction of working relations (8, 34). They tend to protect themselves by verbalizing responsibilities but not following through with appropriate action, or by avoiding open criticisms of people who work close at hand, and instead generalizing problems and placing the blame on sources beyond the reach of the immediate group. Appeals to the influence of the "system," the "philosophy," "educational authorities," or other impersonal agencies may be used to avoid coming to grips with issues which involve personalities.

Such factors introduce real and serious obstacles to the sharing of administrative responsibility. They do not make the task impossible, but call for expert leadership on the part of administrators. Hughes has decribed the nature of this leadership in these words:

> This means that the leader must be skilled at creating a climate which is conducive to initiative. He must know how to draw from each all that each has to give. He will encourage in each a feeling of responsibility. He will also challenge each to contribute maximum creative powers to the group project. He will not suppress deviators among the staff in an effort to create uniformity. He will be liberal in his attitude toward constructive criticism. The leader will need to discriminate among varying contributions, to subordinate some to others, and to see what they all may mean together. His ability to minimize his own influence and power in the interests of encouraging maximum contributions from the group is highly important in advancing group unity and personal satisfactions, and usually, in addition, is more successful in a practical sense in terms of group purposes. (*34:366*)

Thus conceived, it may be seen that sharing responsibility does not reduce the requirement for administrative leadership, but increases it. The administrator has more need for skill in group processes, for understanding the basic motives of human behavior, and for a comprehensive knowledge of conditions which hamper or stimulate good human relations (*1*).

ROLE OF THE ADMINISTRATOR IN HOME-SCHOOL RELATIONS

The home and the school cannot operate in two separate worlds without affecting children adversely. It would be unnecessary to stress this point were it not for the fact that it is so frequently ignored. The school program has become so complex and professionalized, and modern parents are so occupied with home, economic, and social activities that communication between the home and the school may break down despite the sincere interests of both groups in the welfare of children.

The school principal is in a position to bring about constructive relationships between the home and the school by developing a climate of understanding in which parents and teachers can work harmoniously. To do this he must be aware of the factors that impede coöperation among parents and teachers, and develop skill in the use of techniques which influence human relations.

Human Relations Problems of Parents and Teachers

While teachers and parents are vitally concerned with the growth of children, their different responsibilities, backgrounds, and interests may lead to strained relationships. Among the many factors which may produce friction between teachers and parents, those described below appear to be most critical and persistent.

RELATIONSHIP TO CHILDREN. The different roles which teachers and parents play in the lives of children may give rise to misunderstandings and conflict. Parents see the child as an individual in whom they have a great emotional investment. They have difficulty being objective or analytical about their own youngster and tend to judge the school in terms of how he progresses.

Teachers have a relatively temporary relation with children and are inclined to see them as members of a group. Their perceptions of youngsters are more objective because they are less involved with them emotionally. Also, their success is not measured by the progress of an individual, but by the accomplishment of the group.

Because of these different orientations toward children, parents and teachers may have difficulty communicating with each other. Procedures which appear reasonable, as viewed by a parent concerned with his own child, may be unreasonable when judged in terms of the influence on others. In seeking to balance the interests of individual parents against the welfare of the group the teacher may unintentionally raise barriers between the home and the school.

PERSONAL-PROFESSIONAL DIFFERENCES. Teachers who have devoted years of study to educational processes sometimes find it difficult to work with parents whose concepts of education were formulated during their own school days. Being unfamiliar with changes in learning theory, educational values, and teaching methods, parents may be suspicious of innovations. These suspicions may lead to criticism of the school or to efforts to remedy the situation through home instruction.

Differences arising from this source might be avoided if teachers could explain the educational program to parents. However, it is no simple matter to interpret, in layman's language, a vast body of information which has taken years to acquire. Not only do teachers lack time for this, but many have a strong feeling that their professional training and experience have qualified them to make decisions regarding educational matters, and that these decisions should not be questioned by laymen (5). Obviously, such attitudes do not encourage coöperation among parents and teachers.

COUNSELING PROBLEMS. Teachers may be disconcerted by parents who seem unable to accept advice on how to manage their children. Parent counseling is a skill that requires much tact and insight. The advice offered, while scientifically sound and well intended, may so disturb established patterns of relationship in the home that to accept it would mean giving up a whole way of life. Parents cannot be expected to make such adjustments readily. Their resistance to change, while frustrating to teachers, is a natural form of self-protection.

Another factor which makes parent counseling difficult is the difference in family life experience which separates many teachers and parents. The unmarried or childless teacher is in a particularly vulnerable position when it comes to advising parents on how to raise children. No amount of formal education will convince some parents that the teacher has learned so much from books that he can understand the complex problems with which the home is struggling (44).

When advice and counsel fail, there is an inclination to blame parents for the behavior of their children. This is unfortunate because in many cases parents are doing all they can to cope with handicaps such as poor housing, bad working hours, economic insecurity, personal problems, or unmanageable behavior characteristics which the child may have inherited. Little has been accomplished by the antiparent laws enacted by some communities. Punishing parents has no demonstrable effect on curbing the misbehavior of children, and often succeeds in intensifying the despair which parents feel over their inability to manage their children (70). Criticizing parents only increases their feelings of guilt and incompetence, and emphasizes their failure.

OTHER SOURCES OF TENSION. There are many other personal and professional factors which tend to erect barriers between teachers and parents. Parents who resent having teachers inquire into family affairs when the purpose is to understand the child's problems, who extend their authority into the school by stipulating what may or may not be done with their children, who are themselves maladjusted, or who will not respond to efforts by the school to work out common problems tax the patience and energies of teachers.

It is equally true that inadequate teachers who use ridicule and sarcasm, who fill a child with fears and tensions, who make unwarranted demands on parents, or who otherwise reveal a lack of tact, courtesy, professional competency, or understanding are guilty of widening the breach between home and school.

Administrative Influences on Parent-Teacher Relationships

A number of administrative decisions reach into the home and affect the relationships of teachers and parents. The admission, classification, and promotion of pupils, reporting procedures, and visits of parents to the school are common sources of stress.

ADMISSION POLICIES. Most school governing boards set arbitrary age standards for school entrance which make little allowance for individual variations in readiness. As a result, some children who are chronologically eligible, but mentally, socially, or emotionally unprepared for school are admitted, while youngsters who fall short of the chronological age minimum by a few weeks or months, but who otherwise are quite ready for school, are denied admission. Such inflexible policies create anxiety in the home, and present teachers with many problems which could be avoided by school entrance procedures which assess more adequately the readiness of children for school experience (*18, 29, 30*).

CLASSIFICATION AND PROMOTION. The classification and promotion of children in the regular school program is another source of irritation to teachers and parents. Although ungraded (*19, 71*) and multigraded (*57*) classes in the elementary school have been found to improve academic achievement and social adjustment, most schools still use the criteria of academic achievement and chronological age to organize instructional groups. This leads to periodic emotional crises, and does not produce the homogeneous groups desired.

Promotion and retention policies are also matters of concern to parents and teachers. Research shows beyond question that the average repeater of a grade or subject learns no more the next year, and may even do poorer work (*14, 15, 49*). Not only is failure an ineffective way of improving learning, it has an adverse effect on pupil adjustment and attitudes toward school (*47, 48, 60*). Children do better work, learn more effectively, and achieve better personal and social adjustment if they continue with their age group instead of being forced to repeat a class or subject (*27*).

Efforts to overcome the inadequacy of nonpromotion policies through "continuous progress" plans, have met with limited success. Where these plans have been tried, children are found to be appreciably more relaxed than they are under the graded system and make better progress in their studies (*21, 22, 68*). There are, however, many teachers and parents who object to passing a child on when he has not mastered a grade or subject. They argue that the basic skills are cumulative and if a child falls behind, his difficulties are compounded as he moves through school. Objections are voiced also by secondary schools, colleges, and employers who fear that automatic promotions will reduce the high school diploma to the status of an attendance certificate and weaken educational standards (*28*).

These are problems which must be worked out with parents and the professional staff. The facts of child growth and learning are known, but the organizational adaptations required of the school are still in the experimental stages. Progress in these areas must come slowly, for if people are pushed too fast into programs they do not fully comprehend, they may be frightened into retaining the traditional programs with which they feel secure.

REPORTING PROCEDURES. There are few areas of school life which produce more tears, discontent, jealousy, and misunderstanding than the traditional report card. Because of their different backgrounds and motives, parents and teachers may develop conflicts over what the report card is and what it should do. Teachers are inclined to look upon the report as a documentary statement of the school's goals and programs, and an evaluation of the individual in terms of his total growth. Parents may have little sympathy with such broad goals. They want to know how their child is doing in comparison with others and how closely he approaches a standard of achievement set for all.

These problems are difficult to reconcile and require much coöperative thinking, planning, and administrative leadership. The elementary school has moved toward the resolution of conflict over report cards by introducing parent-teacher conferences. This is a promising practice which has met with much success. Teachers and parents who have tried conferences like them and consider them superior to older reporting practices (*13, 32, 43, 66*).

The secondary school has made less progress toward the solution of reporting problems. Departmentalization not only makes it difficult for a teacher to know enough about children to discuss their progress with parents, but assigns so many children to each teacher that it becomes a formidable effort to schedule conferences with all the parents of all the children, or to expect parents to find time to talk with all the teachers of their children. Moreover, the subject matter emphasis in the high school, college entrance standards, and graduation requirements make quantitative measurement difficult to avoid.

HOMEWORK.   The school principal may be called upon to mediate disputes over the matter of homework. This is a problem which has plagued teachers, parents, and students for many years. Parents often feel that homework is a necessary part of education, and its completion is made a prerequisite to the granting of various privileges. The notion that the road to success is paved with completed homework assignments may lead to nagging, punishment, and various forms of pressure which create strife in the home and antagonism toward the school.

There is reason to question whether the conflicts which homework creates are worth the results produced. Fine (16) assembled evidence. on both the elementary and secondary level which indicates that a child's marks and his progress in school are affected very little by whether or not he is assigned homework. Furthermore, for some children homework assignments become an excessive addition to the school day which crowds out needed social and recreational activities. It has been shown that when homework is carefully limited, there is less strain and tension in children and their attitude toward the work which must be done is improved (33, 66).

IMPROVING HOME-SCHOOL RELATIONS

The great concern which parents have for the school can be turned into a constructive force for education if teachers and administrators are willing to grant parents the role of participants in the educational enterprise. Too many schools keep parents at a distance. They are invited to special events, entertainments, festivals, open house, and similar "show" occasions, but they are not allowed to get their hands on the actual work of education. Invitations to visit the classroom are often hedged with restrictions which make parents feel they are not really wanted. Here, for instance, is the content of a mimeographed notice sent home by one principal:

Parents are invited to visit the school at any time. However, classroom visits must be limited to twenty minutes, and prior arrangements must be made with the principal's office at least two weeks before the desired visitation day.

Perhaps from the point of view of administrative convenience such formal arrangements are necessary. However, few parents would regard this notice as a sincere invitation to participate in school activities. School officials are inclined to underestimate the interest of parents in education and the power they can wield when they become involved in the work of the school.

Working with Individual Parents

Some schools have recognized the great contribution parents can make to the education of their children and have formed a real partnership with the home. In such schools, parents are in and out of the building all the time, not by invitation, but actually participating in the educational program. They are called upon to contribute their skill and information to children. Parents may serve as assistants in the kindergarten, as leaders in special programs and projects; they may plan menus and supervise the lunchroom, conduct special classes in crafts, chemistry, or electronics, or handle the school publicity. All of these things, and many more, have been done by parents. Their efforts not only enrich the instructional program, but provide children with a greater sense of security because of the unity between home and school (*17, 20, 41*).

It takes time and much organizational ability to integrate the services of parents in a school program. However, schools that have tried this partnership find that parents become such enthusiastic supporters of the school that the results more than make up for the energy expended.

Working with Parents in Groups

Many schools have found that working with organized groups of parents is an effective way to build an understanding of the school program. Groups representing the parents in a particular classroom, parent committees, and parent-teacher associations are the most common types of organizations working with the school.

CLASSROOM GROUPS. Teachers have found it profitable to meet with the parents of their children in order to become acquainted, and to explain the program of education. Often such meetings are preceded by an observation of classroom activities and a discussion of what was done and why. Some teachers go even farther than merely explaining the program to parents. They organize parent study groups which work on various aspects of the curriculum and plan instructional experiences with the teacher. The extra time it takes to work with parent groups returns worth-while dividends in improved home-school relations, more profitable parent-teacher conferences, and better instructional procedures (*25, 26*).

PARENT COMMITTEES.   The accomplishments of parent committees show that parents can contribute more to the school than merely conducting paper drives or carnivals. Committees of parents have done some notable work in curriculum improvement. In one instance, a committee working with the schools and with business firms in the community developed a work-experience program and facilitated the training and placement of business education students (*41*). Parents have developed instructional guides in arithmetic, devised reporting systems, participated in textbook selection, planned courses for superior students, and even published pamphlets on modern school procedures. Not only do parents contribute to the school program in these ways, but they provide a bulwark of support for them and accomplish results which the school staff could not achieve alone (*10, 17, 25, 41*).

PARENT-TEACHER ASSOCIATIONS.   Parent-teacher associations enroll persons who have a basic interest in the school and a general feeling of good will toward education. It is unfortunate that the attitude of some educators keep the PTA from realizing its full potentialities for the service of children and for betterment of the school. In many instances, school officials skillfully confine the PTA to innocuous programs concerned primarily with money-raising activities. Or, these organizations become so busy with their own structure, or with state and national programs, that they have little opportunity to discuss the problems of their own schools (*65*).

Educators may hesitate to take too dominant a role in the PTA, thinking this to be an organization of parents which should be run by parents. Lacking close coöperation with educators, parents, because of their friendliness toward teachers, may avoid the discussion of critical issues which might imply dissatisfaction with the school program. They confine themselves instead to nonsensitive activities which do not tap the great potential of their organization for service to schools.

When educators encourage the PTA to deal with crucial school matters, parents respond with enthusiasm, attendance at meetings increases considerably, teachers and parents become more sympathetic toward each other's functions, and there is a heightened interest in the schools (*2*).

PARENTS WHO CANNOT BE REACHED.   Despite all efforts to bring parents into a harmonious working relation with the school, there will be some who cannot be reached. These people do not keep appointments, they are inarticulate, they seem to have no anxiety about their children, and they do not identify with the school. When they are approached by teachers, they may be either actively or passively resistant and impossible to bring into any kind of satisfying relationship with the school (69).

Unfortunately such parents cannot be left entirely alone because their children often are disturbing influences in the school. To reach these people, administrators may have to call upon resource agencies in the community. This makes it necessary to maintain a file of local, regional, and state resources with essential information regarding the type of service offered, eligibility requirements, referral procedures, and personnel. With exact knowledge of how and where to secure assistance, the principal may be able to reach into the homes of resistant parents and achieve results which the teacher could not accomplish unaided (24).

SUMMARY

Throughout this text emphasis has been placed on the teacher's role in influencing the mental health of children. Teachers cannot fulfill this responsibility without the assistance of school administrators and parents. This chapter has directed attention to the personal and professional pressures which affect teachers and the administrative procedures which might be used to reduce the mental health hazards to which teachers are exposed.

In addition to alleviating the specific pressures which trouble teachers, it is the obligation of school officials to establish an administrative atmosphere which will nurture mental health and wholesome interpersonal relations. The maintenance of open channels of communication, consideration for the teacher's need for recognition and acceptance, and the sharing of administrative responsibility have been described as fundamental components of an atmosphere which contributes to a high level of staff security, satisfaction, and morale.

A further responsibility of the administrator is to understand the factors which may cause friction among teachers and parents. These may arise from teacher attitudes and behavior, from administrative practices, or from the action of parents. As ways are found to remove the tensions which impair the harmonious relations of teachers and parents, the home and the school are brought into an effective working relationship, staff morale is improved, children feel more secure, and parents become enthusiastic supporters of the school program.

PROBLEMS AND PROJECTS

1. Analyze the emotional pressures on teachers in your school in terms of (a) time utilized on special days, weeks, drives, etc.; (b) time devoted to educational and civic activities such as meetings, institutes, courses, workshops, and community services.
2. Analyze community influences on teachers in your school in terms of (a) friendship patterns, (b) membership in selective community organizations, and (c) expectations of the community.
3. How can the professional status of men elementary school teachers be improved without antagonizing the women teachers?
4. Some schools have experimented with the use of nonprofessional assistants who perform housekeeping duties and duties of a routine nature. Summarize the findings of these experiments and discuss the value of this technique as a means of relieving pressures on teachers.
5. How are teacher-principal relations affected by (a) merit ratings, (b) classroom visitations, (c) educational philosophy? Suggest techniques for overcoming any interpersonal tensions involved.
6. List some administrative practices which irritate or annoy teachers. How may these be overcome without the expenditure of money?
7. What formal training do administrators receive in human relations? What is the current thinking regarding the type of training needed?
8. Describe the interpersonal relations of successful administrators with whom you have worked. What techniques contribute most effectively to the improvement of staff morale?
9. How adequately are teachers trained to make home visits? What training do social workers and public health nurses receive in this area? Suggest procedures which teachers should follow in making home visits.
10. Describe techniques which schools have used to improve relationships with people in the community who have no children in school.
11. Evaluate the effectiveness of all-school programs (carnivals, plays, festivals, etc.) as means of improving home-school relations.
12. How may the school testing program affect teacher-parent relations? Should parents be informed of the results of intelligence and achievement tests? Why or why not?

SELECTED REFERENCES

1. American Association of School Administrators, "The Superintendent as Instructional Leader," *Thirty-Fifth Yearbook,* National Education Association, 1957.

2. Avery, C. E., and Kirkendall, L. A., *A Progress Report on the Oregon Developmental Center Project in Family Life Education*, E. C. Brown Trust (Portland, Oregon), August, 1952.
3. Balser, B. H., "Further Report on Experimental Evaluation of Mental Hygiene Techniques in School and Community," *American Journal of Psychiatry* (February, 1957), *113*:733–739.
4. Becker, H. S., "The Career of the Chicago Public Schoolteacher," *American Journal of Sociology* (March, 1952), *57*:470–477.
5. Becker, H. S., "The Teacher in the Authority System of the Public School," *Journal of Educational Sociology* (November, 1953), *27*: 128–141.
6. Bettelheim, B., "Mental Health and Current Mores," *American Journal of Orthopsychiatry* (January, 1952), *22*:76–88.
7. Brookover, W. B., *A Sociology of Education*, American Book Company, 1955.
8. Bush, R. N., *The Teacher-Pupil Relationship*, Prentice-Hall, Inc., 1954.
9. Chase, F. S., "Factors for Satisfaction in Teaching," *Phi Delta Kappan* (November, 1951), *33*:127–132.
10. Committee on Mental Health in Education, *Report of the Conference on Mental Health in Schools and Teacher Education Institutions*, Federal Security Agency, Office of Education and Public Health Service, 1949.
11. Cornell, F. G., "Socially Perceptive Administration," *Phi Delta Kappan* (March, 1955), *36*:219–223.
12. Corson, J. J., "How to Delegate Responsibility," *Nation's Business*, May, 1956.
13. D'Evelyn, K. E., "Individual Parent-Teacher Conferences," Bureau of Publications, Teachers College, Columbia University, *Practical Suggestions For Teaching*, no. 9, 1945.
14. Elsbree, W. S., "Why Teachers Fail Pupils," in *Pupil Progress in the Elementary School*, Bureau of Publications, Teachers College, Columbia University, 1943, pp. 12–22.
15. Farley, E., and others, "Factors Related to the Grade Progress of Pupils," *Elementary School Journal* (November, 1933), *34*:186–193.
16. Fine, B., "No More Homework?" *New York Times Magazine*, January 13, 1952, p. 16.
17. Fitzwater, G. H., "Co-operation Helps Individual Classrooms," in *Citizen Cooperation for Better Public Schools, The Fifty-third Yearbook of the NSSE, Part I*, University of Chicago Press, 1954, pp. 75–107.
18. Forester, J. J., "At What Age Should a Child Start School?" *School Executive* (1954), *74*:80–81.
19. Fries, H. C., "A Continuous Progress School," *American School Board Journal* (July, 1949), *119*:52.
20. Gabbard, H. F., *Working with Parents*, Federal Security Agency, Office

of Education Bulletin 1948, no. 7, Superintendent of Documents, 1949.

21. Golden, L., "Shall Elementary Pupils Be Retained?" *Monthly Bulletin,* Office of the County Superintendent of Schools, Los Angeles County, (January, 1955), *13*:8–9.

22. Gordon, J. B., "Mental Hygiene Aspects of Social Promotion," *Mental Hygiene* (January, 1950), *34*:34–44.

23. Gould, A., *The Mental and Physical Health of Teachers With Special Reference to Los Angeles,* Unpublished Doctoral Dissertation, University of Southern California (Los Angeles), 1940.

24. Hansen, M. M., "Parent and Community Co-operation and the Use of Available Resources," in *Good Guidance Practices in the Elementary School,* Bulletin of the California State Department of Education, vol. XXIV, no. 6 (Sacramento), August, 1955, pp. 59–72.

25. Hass, C. G., "It's All to the Good," *NEA Journal* (February, 1955), *44*:108–109.

26. Heffernan, H., and Marshall, L. E., "Reporting Pupil Progress in California Cities," *California Journal of Elementary Education* (November, 1955), *24*:67–77.

27. Heine, M. K., *Survey of No Failure Program,* Unpublished Masters Project, University of Southern California (Los Angeles), July, 1949.

28. *Helping Teachers Understand Children,* Commission on Teacher Education, American Council on Education, 1945.

29. Hobson, J. R., "High School Success of Underage Children," *Research Relating to Children,* U.S. Department of Health, Education and Welfare, Social Security Administration, Children's Bureau, Bulletin No. 4, 1956, p. 83.

30. Hobson, J. R., "Mental Age as a Criterion for School Admission," *Research Relating to Children,* U.S. Department of Health, Education and Welfare, Social Security Administration, Children's Bureau, Bulletin No. 4, 1956, p. 83.

31. Hollister, W. G., "Bettering Human Relations in the Job Setting," *American Journal of Nursing* (May, 1954), vol. 54.

32. Holsinger, E. A., *Parent-Teacher Conferences,* Unpublished Masters Project, University of Southern California (Los Angeles), 1952.

33. "Homework," *NEA Journal* (September, 1957), *46*:366–374.

34. Hughes, J. M., *Human Relations in Educational Organization,* Harper & Brothers, 1957.

35. *Industrial Applications of Medicine and Psychiatry,* American Management Association, Personnel Series No. 130, 1949.

36. Kaplan, L., "Tensions in Parent-Teacher Relationships," *Elementary School Journal* (December, 1950), *51*:190–195.

37. Kaplan, L., "The Annoyances of Elementary School Teachers," *Journal of Educational Research* (May, 1952), *45*:649–665.

38. Kaplan, L., *The Status and Function of Men Teachers in Urban Elementary Schools,* Unpublished Doctoral Dissertation, University of Southern California (Los Angeles), 1947.

39. Kaplan, L., and O'Dea, J. D., "Mental Health Hazards in School," *Educational Leadership* (March, 1953), *10*:351–354.

40. Katz, D., *et al., Productivity, Supervision and Morale in an Office Situation,* Institute of Social Research (Ann Arbor, Michigan), 1950.

41. Kindred, L. W., and Allen, W. P., "Co-operation Improves Individual Schools," *Citizen Cooperation for Better Public Schools, The Fifty-third Yearbook of the NSSE, Part I,* University of Chicago Press, 1954, pp. 108–147.

42. Lagemann, J. K., "Job Enlargement Boosts Production," *Nation's Business* (December, 1954), *42*:34–37.

43. Laycock, S. R., "Individual Teacher-Parent Conferences: How They Can Be Improved," *Understanding the Child* (January, 1952), *21*:8–11.

44. Lonsdale, B. J., "Parent-Teacher Conferences—An Experience in Human Relations," *California Journal of Elementary Education* (November, 1955), *24*:78–90.

45. Lonsdale, B. J., and Marshall, L., "In-Service Education Programs in Selected California Districts," *California Journal of Elementary Education* (August, 1956), *25*:30–51.

46. Lott, P. D., *A Study of the Characteristics, Background and Activities of Men Elementary Teachers and Some Factors Affecting Their Adjustment and Morale,* Unpublished Doctoral Dissertation, University of Michigan, 1953.

47. Mangus, A. R., and Seeley, J. R., *Mental Health Needs in a Rural and Semi-Rural Area of Ohio,* Division of Mental Hygiene of the Ohio State Department of Public Welfare, Ohio State University, Ohio Agricultural Experiment Station, February, 1950.

48. Mangus, A. R., and Woodward, R. H., *An Analysis of the Mental Health of Elementary School Children,* Division of Mental Hygiene of the Ohio State Department of Public Welfare, Ohio State University, Ohio Agricultural Experiment Station in Cooperation with the Butler County Mental Hygiene Association (Hamilton, Ohio), July, 1949.

49. Meeusen, E. J., "Effect of Retardation on Students," *Research Relating to Children,* Bulletin II, Supplement 1, U.S. Children's Bureau, 1954, p. 53.

50. Miller, V. R., "Man Around the School House," *New York State Education* (1953), *40*:336, 382.

51. National Education Association, Research Division, "First-Year Teachers in 1954–55," *NEA Research Bulletin* (February, 1956), vol. XXXIV, no. 1.

52. National Education Association, Research Division, "Teaching Load in 1950," *NEA Research Bulletin* (February, 1951) vol. XXIX, no. 1.
53. National Education Association, Research Division, "Teacher Opinion on Pupil Behavior, 1955–56," *NEA Research Bulletin* (April, 1956), vol. XXXIV, no. 2.
54. National Education Association, Research Division, "The Status of the American Public School Teacher," *NEA Research Bulletin* (February, 1957), vol. XXXV, no. 1.
55. Parle, G., "Group Therapy for Problem Parents," *NEA Journal* (May, 1954), 43:269–272.
56. Rankin, P. T., "Fostering Teacher Growth," *Mental Health in Modern Education, The Fifty-fourth Yearbook of the NSSE, Part II,* University of Chicago Press, 1955, pp. 354–374.
57. Rehwoldt, W., and Hamilton, W. W., *An Analysis of Some of the Effects of Interage and Intergrade Grouping in an Elementary School,* Unpublished Doctoral Dissertation, University of Southern California (Los Angeles), December, 1956.
58. Rogers, D., "Study of the Reactions of Forty Men to Teaching in the Elementary School," *Journal of Educational Sociology* (1953), 27:24–35.
59. Ruth, A. B., *A Study of Human Relations Techniques for the Elementary School Principal,* Unpublished Masters Project, University of Southern California (Los Angeles), 1952.
60. Sandin, A. G., "Social and Emotional Adjustment of Regularly Promoted and Non-Promoted Pupils," *Child Development Monographs,* No. 32, Society for Research in Child Development, National Research Council, 1944.
61. Smith, J. A., "Occupational Stress and Emotional Illness," *Journal of the American Medical Association* (July, 1956), 161:1038–1040.
62. Smith, W., *Administrative Policies and Practices and Their Relation to Teaching Efficiency,* Unpublished Doctoral Dissertation, University of Southern California (Los Angeles), 1954.
63. Spencer, L. M., Gehlmann, F., and Maris, E. F., *What Los Angeles Educators Think of Their School System,* Los Angeles City Board of Education, 1953.
64. Stevens, L., "What Has Raymond Done Now?" *Phi Delta Kappan* (May, 1957), 38:320–323.
65. Stolz, H. R., "Cooperation with Parents," *Understanding the Child* (January, 1938), 6:14–18.
66. Strang, R., "Guided Study and Homework," *NEA Journal* (October, 1955), 44:399–400.
67. Sutherland, R. L., "Mental Health in Industrial Relations," *Mental Hygiene* (April, 1950), 34:192–195.

68. Tucker, M. B., "The Shoe Didn't Fit," *NEA Journal* (March, 1956), 45:159–161.
69. Whelan, R. W., "Changed Approaches to the Unreached," *Children* (July–August, 1954), 1:131–137.
70. Witmer, H. L., "Parents and Delinquency," *Children* (July–August, 1954), 1:131–137.
71. Wrightstone, J. W., "What Research Says About Class Organization for Instruction," *NEA Journal* (April, 1957), 46:254–255.

APPENDIX: AUDIO-VISUAL AIDS FOR INSTRUCTORS

The teaching aids listed on the following pages have been selected for their special relevance to the problems discussed in the chapters to which they pertain. This list is fairly extensive because one teaching aid may focus upon a particular subject, and many subjects are included in each chapter. It is not suggested that instructors use all the audio-visual aids described here, but that they select those which apply to the course being taught, the nature of the student group, and the points which are to be emphasized. Some instructors have students preview these materials and present them to the class. This procedure not only relieves the instructor of a time-consuming chore, but increases the effectiveness of teaching by encouraging student participation.

Most of the teaching aids mentioned below may be secured from the audio-visual centers of large universities, or from public libraries, state departments of mental hygiene, and local mental hygiene associations. Other sources of supply are the Film Library of the National Association for Mental Health, 13 East 37th Street, New York 16, New York, or the Mental Health Materials Center, 1790 Broadway, New York 19, New York. If the teaching device is not available from these agencies, special note is made of its source of supply in the annotation which accompanies each audio-visual aid.

CHAPTER 1. NATURE OF PSYCHOLOGICAL DISORDERS

Films

City of the Sick—20 minutes, sound.
A documentary film about life in a state mental hospital.
Breakdown—41 minutes, sound.
Story of a schizophrenic breakdown and the treatment provided in a modern mental hospital.
Mental Hospital—20 minutes, sound.
Describes a patient's experiences in a mental hospital.
Out of True—41 minutes, sound.
Describes psychiatric treatment of mental illness in a mental hospital.
Shades of Gray—66 minutes, sound.
Portrays various mental disorders experienced by soldiers during training and combat.
Mental Development Series
No. 1. Schizophrenia: Simple Type Deteriorated—11 minutes.
No. 2. Schizophrenia: Catatonic Type—12 minutes.
No. 3. Schizophrenia: Hebephrenic Type—13 minutes.
No. 4. Paranoid Condition—13 minutes.
No. 5. Organic Reaction Type, Senile—10 minutes.
No. 6. Depressive States, I—12 minutes.
No. 7. Depressive States, II—11 minutes.
No. 8. Manic State—15 minutes.
In each film a psychiatrist describes the type of mental disorder illustrated. Interviews with patients bring out typical symptoms of the disease.
Activity for Schizophrenia—30 minutes, sound.
Follows a schizophrenic patient from his entry into a veteran's administration hospital through the various phases of his recovery.
The Atascadero Story—26 minutes, sound.
Describes the sex psychopath and his treatment in a mental hospital. Available from California Department of Mental Hygiene.

Tapes and Records

Weathering the Storms—filmstrip with 33⅓ RPM record.
Describes psychoneuroses and explains how they can be prevented.
Psychoneurosis, Anxiety Type—33⅓ RPM record.

Dr. O. Spurgeon English presents the genesis of the neuroses with suggestions for treatment.

The Big Headache—30 minute tape recording.

Discussion of frustration and its relationship to psychosomatic illness.

CHAPTER 2. PREVALENCE OF PSYCHOLOGICAL DISORDERS IN THE UNITED STATES

Films

Mental Health: Keeping Mentally Fit—30 minutes, sound.

Describes good mental health and its importance to the individual and to society. Illustrates symptoms of emotional disturbance.

Search for Happiness—17 minutes, sound.

Shows how people turn to futile measures to escape anxiety and tension. Emphasizes need for sound mental health.

What's on Your Mind?—10 minutes, sound.

Contrasts scientific approach to treatment of mental illness with efforts of people to find their own remedies.

Back to Life—30 minutes, sound.

Story of a man who enters a mental hospital and his rehabilitation.

To Serve the Mind—25 minutes, sound.

A report on methods of treating mental illness and the various services needed in a community.

Search for Sanity—30 minutes, Kinescope.

Tour of a state mental hospital showing typical scenes and describing various therapies.

We, the Mentally Ill—30 minutes, Kinescope.

Depicts the treatment of mental illnesses and how shortages of facilities and personnel affect the lives of patients.

Mental Illness—67 minutes, sound.

Shows the work being done at Tulane University on mental illness. The treatment of mental illness is illustrated.

Out of Darkness—60 minutes, sound.

Story of a girl's two and one-half month stay in a mental hospital. Shows operation of a mental hospital and illustrates psychotherapeutic processes.

Report on Mental Illness—26 minutes, sound.

Shows how a woman suffering from a deep depressive psychosis is treated and rehabilitated. Discussion of how and why people break down and what can be done to help them. Available from California Department of Mental Hygiene.

The Nation's Mental Health—19 minutes, sound.

> States the basic problems of mental illness, shows techniques of treatment, and describes the work of the National Association for Mental Health.

Working and Playing to Health—35 minutes, sound.

> Illustrates recreational, occupational, and industrial therapies in a modern mental hospital.

The Mental Hospital Volunteer: Someone Who Cares—22 minutes, sound.

> Points out extent of mental illness in our country, shows some of the conditions which exist in mental hospitals, and describes activities of volunteers in hospital work.

This Charming Couple—17 minutes, sound.

> Discusses problems of marriage and divorce.

Tapes and Records

Meet Your Mind—10 filmstrip frames with recording, 20 minutes.

> Dr. William C. Menninger discusses the national problem of mental health.

Out of Sight, Out of Mind—33⅓ RPM record (in *The Tenth Man Series*), 15 minutes.

> How personnel shortages, lack of finances, and public apathy influence the work of a state mental hospital.

Recall to Life—30 minute tape recording.

> Concerns rehabilitation of the mentally ill in a hospital.

CHAPTER 3. MALADJUSTMENT IN THE SCHOOLS

Films

Crossroads of Life—33 minutes, sound.

> Describes treatment of juvenile delinquents in an institution, and emphasizes need for better methods of prevention and treatment.

Juvenile Delinquency—25 minutes, sound.

> Deals with activities of the Youth Bureau of the Detroit Police Department. Pays particular attention to the kinds of boys who become involved with the police.

Face of Youth—28 minutes, sound.

> Shows how two boys are helped to overcome their problems through the efforts of parents, nurse, teacher, and guidance center.

Stuttering—25 minutes, sound.

> Presents clinical proof that stuttering is without organic basis.

Why Vandalism—17 minutes, sound.

This film probes the causes which lead three boys of varying backgrounds to destroy a classroom.

Drug Addiction—22 minutes, sound.

How a teen-ager gets started on drugs and his consequent degradation.

Who's Delinquent?—16 minutes, sound.

A community studies its juvenile delinquency problems and makes efforts to find solutions.

Boy in Court—12 minutes, sound.

Shows the workings of the juvenile court. Based on the story of young delinquents involved in a car theft.

A Criminal Is Born—20 minutes, sound.

Dramatization of boys turning to crime because of parental neglect.

Kid Gangs—26 minutes, sound.

Depicts juvenile gangs in action. Explains the role of social agencies and the police in combating the gang problem.

Am I Guilty?—15 minutes, sound.

Presents problem of juvenile delinquency and suggests solutions.

The Camarillo Story—26 minutes, sound.

Describes a hospital for maladjusted children as seen through the eyes of an 8-year-old prepsychotic girl. Available from California Department of Mental Hygiene.

Children Behind the Wall—35 minutes, sound.

A survey of what is being done and what needs to be done for emotionally disturbed children.

Children in Trouble—10 minutes, sound.

Discusses the cost, causes, and prevention of juvenile delinquency.

Know Your Children—20 minutes, sound.

Describes causes of juvenile delinquency and responsibility of parents and the community for its prevention and cure. An Australian film.

Psychoneurosis with Compulsive Trends in the Making: Life History of Mary from Birth to Seven Years—60 minutes, silent.

Follows the ego development of a child and shows how a neurosis is developed.

To Be Again—26 minutes, sound.

A presentation of emotional disturbances in children and the program of therapy used in a state hospital. Story is based on the care and treatment of a 9-year-old girl.

What About Juvenile Delinquency?—11 minutes, sound.

Dramatizes a gang's brutal attack on an innocent adult. Designed to provoke discussion of juvenile delinquency.

Tapes and Records

Juvenile Delinquency—33⅓ RPM record, 14 minutes.
   Case story of a juvenile delinquent.
Drug Addict—33⅓ RPM record, 14 minutes.
   Story of an orphaned boy who at the age of 14 took up drugs and crime.
Mental Health and the Treatment of Delinquents—60 minutes, tape recording.
   How schools and other community agencies can coöperate in the prevention of juvenile delinquency. Available from the Audio-Visual Center, Kent State University, Kent, Ohio.

CHAPTER 4. MENTAL HYGIENE PROGRAMS IN SCHOOLS AND COMMUNITIES

Films

A Friend at the Door—28 minutes, sound.
   The story of how social workers help people solve personal problems.
Boy with a Knife—19 minutes, sound.
   Shows how a group worker reaches a gang of boys who are headed for delinquency. A case story from the files of the Los Angeles Youth Service Agency.
Hard Brought Up—40 minutes, sound.
   Deals with two boys caught in an act of delinquency. Describes the activities of child-welfare services.
Problem Drinkers—19 minutes, sound.
   Story of an alcoholic's downfall and subsequent rehabilitation.
Three Steps to Start—26 minutes, sound.
   How a town launched a program to cope with its youth problems.
Step by Step—22 minutes, sound.
   How neighborhood tension was reduced by neutralizing juvenile delinquency in a city.
They Grow Up So Fast—27 minutes, sound.
   How a community develops a physical education program for children.
Chance to Play—20 minutes, sound.
   Shows the need for playgrounds and recreation centers.
Make Way for Youth—22 minutes, sound.
   How a typical American town organizes a youth program after being startled into action by a tragedy.

Investment in Youth—22 minutes, sound.

Develops the theme that youth is a nation's most valuable resource.

Lambertville Story—20 minutes, sound.

The story of a community's efforts to establish a teen-age recreation center.

Lessons in Living—22 minutes, sound.

Shows how a school project revitalized a community by giving the children a part in community life.

No Place to Go—20 minutes, sound.

Describes the establishment of an organization in Seattle to fight juvenile delinquency.

Camping Education—35 minutes, sound.

Describes a camping program which is integrated with the public schools.

The Centre—22 minutes, sound.

Tells about the activities of the Pioneer Health Center (London) and how it serves the entire family.

Through Play Children Grow—25 minutes, sound.

Shows the operation of an extended school service program maintained by the Greensboro, North Carolina, public schools.

When All the People Play—27 minutes, sound.

Tells how a rural district came alive under the stimulus of a community recreation program.

Citizens of Tomorrow—14 minutes, sound.

Shows how citizens can form a boys' club in a community, and typical activities of the club.

Who Is My Neighbor?—23 minutes, sound.

Illustrates the practical assistance offered by welfare agencies in the community by showing how the problems of one family were solved.

Children on Trial—62 minutes, sound.

Shows steps taken by official welfare departments in England to rehabilitate delinquent youngsters.

Tapes and Records

As the Kids Go—15 minutes, record. Narration by Eddie Albert.

Demonstrates that a recreation center can be an antidote to juvenile delinquency.

Everybody Gets into the Act—15 minutes, record. Narrated by Eddie Albert.

Describes ways in which parents can take part in the organization of a recreation center.

The People Around Us—33⅓ RPM record, 30 minutes.
> Concerns various people in the community who can help others in times of emotional crises.

Out of the Shadow—33⅓ RPM record (in *The Tenth Man Series*), 15 minutes.
> Demonstrates the value of social service departments in helping ex-patients readjust to the world.

The Lady and the Lawmakers—33⅓ RPM record (in *The Tenth Man Series*), 15 minutes.
> Dramatizes political aspects of mental health problems and the role of citizens in the community.

Hi, Neighbor!—recording of a series of 10 plays.
> Dramatizations of the mental health aspects of family living showing how emotional problems can be solved through the use of community resources.

Cecily Comes Home—30 minutes, record.
> Deals with community attitude toward mental illness.

CHAPTER 5. PSYCHOLOGICAL FORCES IN THE HOME

Films

Lonely Night—62 minutes, sound.
> Family experiences and child-care practices which lead to the development of good mental health. Deals with psychiatric treatment of a young woman in an attempt to overcome her fear of loneliness.

Palmour Street—27 minutes, sound.
> Emphasis on how parents affect the mental health of their children.

Sibling Relations and Personality—22 minutes, sound; and *Sibling Rivalries and Parents*—11 minutes, sound.
> These films analyze the development of normal children as influenced by family forces.

The Development of Individual Differences—13 minutes, sound.
> Compares the environmental factors that influence the behavior of children in two families. Deals with sibling relations, social expectancies, behavior patterns and attitudes of parents, and the physical surroundings of the home.

Grief—45 minutes, silent.
> Shows the effects upon infants of prolonged absence of the mother. Dr. Spitz's study of infantile autism.

Problem Child—20 minutes, sound.
> Story of a mother who believes she has a problem child. Emphasizes importance of a baby being loved and wanted.

Baby Meets His Parents—11 minutes, sound.

Shows how human relationships and environmental factors experienced during first year of life can affect personality.

Somatic Consequences of Emotional Starvation in Infants—30 minutes, silent.

Shows the difference between children raised in families and in foundling homes.

Some Basic Differences in Newborn Infants During the Lying-in Period—23 minutes, silent.

Emphasizes the importance of the mother's emotional adjustment to her newborn infant.

Tapes and Records

A Child's Guide to a Parent's Mind—3 cartoon filmstrips with record narration.

Designed to stimulate discussion of how parents speak and act without realizing the effect on their children.

The Inquiring Parent, Series III—records.

Sixteen programs suggesting ways of dealing with children in the family and in the community.

The Family in the Changing World—33⅓ RPM record.

An address by Dr. William C. Menninger.

CHAPTER 6. PATTERNS OF PARENT-CHILD INTERACTION

Films

Meeting Emotional Needs in Childhood—30 minutes, sound.

Describes behavior of 7- to 10-year-olds at home and at school, with emphasis on how to satisfy the need for security.

Preface to a Life—29 minutes, sound.

Longitudinal study of personality development along three possible patterns as influenced by the actions and expectations of parents.

Roots of Happiness—24 minutes, sound.

Elements that make for happy family living, with emphasis on the role of the father.

Your Children and You—29 minutes, sound.

Shows common problems encountered by parents in bringing up children.

The Family—20 minutes, sound.

Depicts the interpersonal relationships and problems of a working-class family.

Parents Are People Too—15 minutes, sound.

Informal discussion of parent-teen-age relationships conducted by a class of teen-agers and their teacher.

A Family Affair—31 minutes, sound.
> The defiance of an adolescent son severely strains family ties and brings to the surface smoldering resentments.

In Time of Trouble—14 minutes, sound.
> Suggests that some unhappy homes could be made happier if father took a greater share in the family activities.

Families First—17 minutes, sound.
> Shows how two contrasting patterns of family life mold the characters of children.

Tapes and Records

The Silver Cord—33⅓ RPM record.
> Dr. E. A. Strecker discusses "Momism."

Family Life—A series of tape recordings designed for parents and teachers. Tapes available from Audio-Visual Center, Kent State University, Kent, Ohio. Series includes following selected titles:

Family Recreation—9 minutes.
> Some of the whys and hows of doing things together as a family group.

Growing Up Is Serious Business—10 minutes.
> Some of the ways in which adolescents and their parents can see the other's point of view.

Age of Adventure—11 minutes.
> How to understand preadolescent children.

Children Need Freedom of Activity—9 minutes.
> How parents can provide opportunities for children to work off their excess energy.

Helping Your Child Act His Age—11 minutes.
> Stresses the fact that children must grow at their own speed and not be molded into miniature adults.

The Overprotective Mother—15 minutes, tape recording.
> Shows how overcompensation may hurt those we most desire to aid. Available from Audio-Visual Center, Kent State University, Kent, Ohio.

That's My Old Man—15 minutes, record. Narration by Eddie Albert.
> How fathers try to be "pals" with their preadolescent sons, and the problems encountered.

CHAPTER 7. DISCIPLINARY PRACTICES IN THE FAMILY

Films

Fears of Children—29 minutes, sound.
> Demonstration of how parental influence led a 5-year-old boy to develop certain fears.

Shyness—23 minutes, sound.

A study of three children showing how the demands of parents can destroy confidence and predispose children to shyness.

Discipline—20 minutes, filmstrip, silent.

Deals with discipline in the home.

Life with Junior—18 minutes, sound.

A typical day in the life of a 10-year-old boy. Stresses need for realization that obedience in itself is not as important as helping a child achieve self-discipline.

Head of the House—40 minutes, sound.

A dramatic portrayal of the emotional problems of a young boy rebelling against his father's overly repressive discipline.

Tapes and Records

A Place to Grow—11 minutes, tape recording.

Some of the ways in which parents can help their children achieve self-discipline. Available from Audio-Visual Center, Kent State University, Kent, Ohio.

Discipline—15 minutes, tape recording.

Discussion of discipline from the viewpoint of parents. Available from Audio-Visual Center, Kent State University, Kent, Ohio.

CHAPTER 8. SOCIAL-CLASS INFLUENCES ON MENTAL HEALTH

Films

High Wall—30 minutes, sound.

Presents a case study of race prejudice and describes its roots in home life.

The Toymaker—15 minutes, sound.

Puppets play together happily until they discover differences in their appearance. Describes basis for conflicts in human relations.

Neighborhood Story—20 minutes, sound.

How tension and hostility is produced in a substandard home, and how a settlement house influences a 10-year-old boy and his family.

Children of China—11 minutes, sound.

Shows different types of family relationships and the influence of Chinese tradition on contemporary life.

English Children—11 minutes, sound.

Family life of a railway engineer in Yorkshire.

French Children—11 minutes, sound.

Typical events in the life of a Breton farm family.

India's Children—16 minutes, sound.
   Portrays the children of India and the village life into which they are born.

Irish Children—10 minutes, sound.
   Farm life and household activities of an Irish brother and sister.

Italian Children—11 minutes, sound.
   A visit to an Italian family near Assisi.

Mexican Children—11 minutes, sound.
   Home life of Mexican family.

South Pacific Island Children—11 minutes, sound.
   Family life in the Fiji Islands.

Migrant Laborers and Their Children—18 minutes, sound.
   Describes the New York State program for migrant families. Available from New York State Department of Health.

Again—Pioneers!—68 minutes, sound.
   Deals with attitudes of communities toward migrant families.

And So They Live—25 minutes, sound.
   Shows life in a poverty-stricken rural community in the South, and the need for better adaptation of the school program to community problems.

To Live Together—30 minutes, sound.
   Deals with lessons taught by harmonious living in an interracial camp.

Personality and Emotions—13 minutes, sound.
   Stresses the desirability of recognizing emotions for what they are and using them to build happier and richer personalities.

Tapes and Records

Racial Tension and Delinquency—45 minutes, tape recording.
   Available from Audio-Visual Center, Kent State University, Kent, Ohio.

CHAPTER 9. DYNAMIC FORCES IN HUMAN BEHAVIOR

Films

Children's Emotions—21 minutes, sound.
   The development and handling of children's emotions up to age 11. Emphasis on fear and anger.

Emotional Health—20 minutes, sound.
   Shows how disturbed emotions may be reflected in physical symptoms.

Facing Reality—12 minutes, sound.
   Explains defense mechanisms. Shows how a teacher helps an adolescent boy to handle his fears.

Frustration Play Techniques—4 reels, sound.

Illustrates the use of projective techniques for studying ego development in young children.

Your Children's Sleep—22 minutes, sound.

Explains the psychological background of anxiety and fear.

Balloons: Aggression and Destruction Games—18 minutes, sound.

Shows how 4- and 5-year-olds reveal their aggressive and destructive impulses through responding to opportunities to break balloons.

Anger at Work—21 minutes, sound.

Explains some of the techniques people use to handle feelings of anger, resentment, and frustration.

Children's Fantasies—27 minutes, sound.

Explores the reasons for a child's fantasies and explains how fantasies develop.

Attitudes and Health—10 minutes, sound.

How emotional problems may affect physical health.

Don't Get Angry—12 minutes, sound.

Explains anger as a natural emotion which cannot be avoided but which can be managed in a mature way.

Understanding Your Emotions—16 minutes, sound.

How emotions affect voluntary and involuntary behavior. Uses three teen-agers to illustrate effects of emotions on behavior.

Control Your Emotions—13 minutes, sound.

Presents the basic principles of psychology which apply to the control and direction of emotions.

Unconscious Motivation—40 minutes, sound.

Guilt feelings are induced in two students under hypnosis. A psychologist helps them discover the cause of their feelings. Shows how repressed conflicts can influence behavior.

Tapes and Records

Backsliding to Babyhood—10 minutes, tape recording.

Why a child may regress to earlier patterns of behavior. Available from Audio-Visual Center, Kent State University, Kent, Ohio.

Its Human to Get Frightened—9 minutes, tape recording.

Discusses how fears affect our lives. Available from Audio-Visual Center, Kent State University, Kent, Ohio.

CHAPTER 10. DEVELOPMENTAL CHARACTERISTICS OF NORMAL CHILDREN

Films

Twins Are Individuals—16 minutes, sound.

Behavior studies of twins in infancy, childhood, and adolescence. Shows relative influences of heredity and environment.

Children Growing Up with Other People—23 minutes, sound.
> Social development from infancy through adolescence.

Social Development—16 minutes, sound.
> Describes social behavior at various age levels.

He Acts His Age—15 minutes, sound.
> How a child's emotional development normally keeps pace with his physical growth. Illustrates typical behavior at various ages.

From Sociable Six to Noisy Nine—22 minutes, sound.

From Ten to Twelve—26 minutes, sound.
> These films describe the physical and emotional development of children from 6 to 12. Behavior which may normally be expected during this period is illustrated.

The Meaning of Adolescence—16 minutes, sound.
> Overview of the changes occurring in the adolescent years. Emphasizes the unsure status of the adolescent.

Age of Turmoil—20 minutes, sound.
> Deals with ages 13 to 15. Illustrates behavior which reflects the emotional turmoil of young adolescents.

Farewell to Childhood—20 minutes, sound.
> Story of the rebellion and mistrust of a normal teen-ager, and her parents' efforts to understand her.

Social-Sex Attitudes in Adolescence—22 minutes, sound.
> Shows how teen-agers can be helped to adjust to the opposite sex.

The Teens—26 minutes, sound.
> Shows normal behavior of three teen-agers. Illustrates positive parent-child relationships.

Developmental Characteristics of Preadolescents—18 minutes, sound.
> Shows successive stages of development among 8- and 9-year-old boys and girls.

What Are Your Problems—filmstrip, 55 frames.
> Brings out the problems of teen-agers and approaches to their solution.

Tapes and Records

The Middle-Aged Child—6 records, 12 faces.
> Recordings of an address by Dr. Benjamin Spock. Describes behavior of the child from 6 to puberty.

Problems of Adolescence—15 minutes, tape recording.
> Discusses the pattern of adolescent growth, why emancipation is necessary, and how adolescents can be encouraged to take responsibility. Available from Audio-Visual Center, Kent State University, Kent, Ohio.

First Flight—30 minutes, record.

Emotional cross-currents of adolescence are described by a high school teacher.

CHAPTER 11. BEHAVIOR DEVIATIONS IN CHILDREN

Films

The Quiet One—70 minutes, sound.

Deals with the life of a neglected child and his treatment in an institution for boys.

Angry Boy—32 minutes, sound.

Story of a boy caught stealing at school and his successful treatment in a guidance clinic.

The Feeling of Hostility—32 minutes, sound.

Life story of a girl who developed hostility and resentment toward others, and how she was affected by experiences in home and school.

The Feeling of Rejection—20 minutes, sound.

Case study of a girl with psychosomatic complaints. Shows how her problems originated from childhood experiences.

Pay Attention: Problems of Hard-of-Hearing Children—29 minutes, sound.

Describes some of the adjustment problems and ways in which teachers and parents can help the hard-of-hearing child.

Report on Donald: The Story of a Stutterer—20 minutes, sound.

Describes early experiences with teachers and classmates, and influence of a speech clinic.

Teacher As Observer and Guide—22 minutes, sound.

Demonstrates methods of working with slow learners and how to aid their personality development.

Activity Group Therapy—50 minutes, sound.

Shows how a group of emotionally disturbed boys age 10–11 act out their problems in a group situation.

Children Limited—30 minutes, sound.

Describes the problems, conditions, and treatment of mentally deficient and retarded children.

A Day at Washington Boulevard School—21 minutes, sound.

Shows the educational program and therapeutic techniques used in a Los Angeles School for handicapped children.

Search—26 minutes, sound.

Depicts attitudes and aspirations of a handicapped child.

For Those Who Are Exceptional—43 minutes, sound.

Shows six different programs in special education, including programs for the mentally retarded, physically handicapped, deaf, speech defectives, hard of hearing, and emotionally disturbed.

Focuses on the importance of interpersonal relationships. Uses the public health nurse to demonstrate.

The Inner Man Steps Out—27 minutes, sound.
Story of a supervisor who has trouble handling people.

The Child in the Middle—18 minutes, sound.
A film to help parents and teachers understand their respective roles in helping the child in school. Dramatizes the parent-teacher conference.

World in a Schoolroom—17 minutes, sound.
Shows how one community arranged for resource people to lend their particular talents to the school program.

Guidance Problem for School and Home—17 minutes, sound.
Presents problem of a 7-year-old who lacks interest in school.

The Supervisor as a Leader—Part I, 14 minutes, sound; Part II, 14 minutes, sound.
Illustrates good and poor supervisory practices. Available from U.S. Office of Education.

The School and the Community—14 minutes, sound.
Shows how schools and community working together can produce an educational program geared to students' needs.

Tapes and Records

Production 5118—30 minutes, color, sound.
Dramatic presentation of a study in interpersonal communication. Stresses importance of communication failures.

Parents Have Homework, Too—9 minutes, tape recording.
Some of the things parents can do to further good home-school relationships. Available from Audio-Visual Center, Kent State University, Kent, Ohio.

How the School Can Educate for Mental Health—33⅓ RPM record, 40–44 minutes.
Dr. Ojemann discusses role of educators in improving the mental health of children. Available from Educational Recording Services, 5922 Abernathy Drive, Los Angeles 45, California.

The Other Parent—25–30 minutes, tape recording.
A new teacher learns there are good and bad sides to teaching. Available from state departments of education.

The Line is Busy—33⅓ RPM record, 13½ minutes.
Story of how fund raising, class pageants, and other duties outside the classroom result in an overworked teacher. Available from NEA.

Big Little Things—filmstrip with recording.
Points out that workers must have someone who will listen to their complaints. Shows how conferences should be handled.

INDEXES

INDEX OF NAMES

INDEX OF SUBJECTS

Behavior disorders, 4, 14
in normal people, 4
nonpsychotic, 5, 14–18
Behavior patterns, preverbal, 116
Behavior symptoms, interpretation of, 230
Bestiality, 17
Bibliotherapy, 357
Body image, 299
Books for mental hygiene instruction, 367–369
Brain damage, 298
Bronx Three Schools Project, 93
Bullis Project, 96, 97, 361, 362

California Department of Mental Hygiene, 21, 31, 39, 45
Catalepsy, 8
Chemotherapy, 40
Child-rearing within social classes, 198–201
Child-study techniques, 329–340
art expression, 334, 335
creative writing, 331, 332
discussion techniques, 335, 336
"Guess-Who" tests, 336–338
observation, 329–331
open-question technique, 333, 334
sociometric devices, 336, 338–340
unfinished stories, 332
Childhood, 257–263
adjustment to authority, 259, 260
ethical and moral development in, 262
intellectual development in, 262, 263
physical growth in, 257, 258
sexual interests in, 261
social behavior in, 258, 259
Children, acceptance by teachers, 324
adjustment in school, 213–219
admission to school, 420
affected by death in family, 107
affected by divorce, 107
allergic and asthmatic, 298, 299
Arapesh Indian, 115
brain-damaged, 298
behavior of, 185–187, 201–204, 281–305, 327, 328
classification and promotion of, 420, 421
crimes committed by, 48–50

Children—(*Continued*)
developmental characteristics of, 254–276
discipline of, 167–188, 203–204, 210, 217, 218, 380–402
dominated, 150–153
elementary school, 257–263
emotional dependence of, 109
epileptic, 298, 299
ethical and moral development of, 262
exceptional, 295–304
expression and clarification of feelings in, 346–355
family status and, 122
first-born, 123–125
gifted, 90, 209, 302–305
home influences on, 105–131, 156–162
in-between, 125–127
in low-income families, 111, 112
in mental hospitals, 292
in orphanage, 118–121
in urban and rural areas, 106
inner feelings of, 330, 331
interpretation of play activities of, 330, 331
intolerant, 172
maladjustment of, 57, 58
manic-depressive, 290, 291
mental health, neglect of, 316, 317
mental health, surveys of, 54–57
mental hygiene programs for, 96–99
mentally retarded, 296, 299
needs of, 229–232
neglected, 119
normal, development of, 254–276
of alcoholic and psychotic parents, 138
of lower-class parents, 200, 201
of maladjusted parents, 136–140
of middle-class parents, 199–200
of migrant families, 112, 113, 203
of schizophrenic parents, 137
of unresponsive parents, 121, 122
of upper-class parents, 199
of working mothers, 109
only, 130, 131
ordinal position in family, 122–136
overindulged, 153–155
overprotected, 145–148
play interests of, 203